Modelling Cognition

Modelling Cognition

Edited by

PETER MORRIS
University of Lancaster

JOHN WILEY & SONS
Chichester · New York · Brisbane · Toronto · Singapore

Library of Congress Cataloging-in-Publication Data:

Modelling cognition.

  Based on the International Workshop on Modelling
Cognition at Lancaster University in July 1985.
  Includes index.
  1. Cognition—Mathematical models—Congresses.
2. Cognition—Data processing—Congresses.
3. Artificial intelligence—Congresses. I. Morris,
P. E. (Peter Edwin), 1947– . II. International
Workshop on Modelling Cognition (1985: Lancaster
University) [DNLM: 1. Cognition—congresses.
2. Models, Psychological—congresses.
BF 311 M6888 1985]
BF311.M565 1987   153′.0724   86-28229

ISBN 0 471 91432 0

British Library Cataloguing in Publication Data:

Modelling cognition.
  Cognition—Data processing   2. Artificial
  intelligence—Data processing
  I. Morris, Peter, *1947–*
  006.3   BF311

ISBN 0 471 91432 0

Typeset by Acorn Bookwork, Salisbury, Wiltshire
Printed in Great Britain by St Edmundsbury Press

List of Contributors

JOHN ANDERSON

Department of Psychology, Carnegie-Mellor University, Shenley Park, Pittsburgh, Pennsylvania 15213-3890, USA

GORDON BOWER

Department of Psychology, Stanford University, Stanford, California, USA

C. FRANKLIN BOYLE

Department of Psychology, Carnegie-Mellor University, Shenley Park, Pittsburgh, Pennsylvania 15213-3890, USA

WILLIAM BREWER

Department of Psychology, University of Illinois at Urbana-Champaign, 602 E. Daniel Street, Champaign, Illinois 61820, USA

DONALD BROADBENT

Department of Experimental Psychology, University of Oxford, South Parks Road, Oxford OX1 3UD

DAVIDA CHARNEY

Department of Psychology, Carnegie-Mellor University, Shenley Park, Pittsburgh, Pennsylvania 15213-3890, USA

ANDREW ELLIS

Department of Psychology, University of Lancaster, Fylde College, Bailrigg, Lancaster LA1 4YF

ROBERT FARRELL

Department of Psychology, Carnegie-Mellor University, Shenley Park, Pittsburgh, Pennsylvania 15213-3890, USA

JOHN FOX

Imperial Cancer Research Fund Laboratories, PO Box No 123, Lincoln's Inn Fields, London WC2A 3PX

DENNIS HAY
Department of Psychology, University of Lancaster, Fylde College, Bailrigg, Lancaster LA1 4YF

DOUGLAS L. HINZMAN
Psychology Department, University of Oregon, Eugene, Oregon 97403, USA

GEORGE HOUGHTON
Laboratory of Experimental Psychology, School of Biological Sciences, University of Sussex, Falmer, Brighton BN1 9QG

STEPHEN ISARD
Laboratory of Experimental Psychology, School of Biological Sciences, University of Sussex, Falmer, Brighton BN1 9QG

PHILIP LEVY
Department of Psychology, University of Lancaster, Fylde College, Bailrigg, Lancaster LA1 4YF

PETER MORRIS
Department of Psychology, University of Lancaster, Fylde College, Bailrigg, Lancaster LA1 4YF

LYNNE REDER
Department of Psychology, Carnegie-Mellor University, Shenley Park, Pittsburgh, Pennsylvania 15213-3890, USA

BRIAN J. REISER
Department of Psychology, Carnegie-Mellor University, Shenley Park, Pittsburgh, Pennsylvania 15213-3890, USA

ROGER C. SCHANK
Department of Computer Science, Yale University, 10 Hillhouse Avenue, PO Box 2158, Yale Station, New Haven, Connecticut 06520 USA

NOEL SHARKEY
Centre for Cognitive Science, University of Essex, Wivenhoe Park, Colchester, Essex

ROBERT J. STERNBERG
Department of Psychology, Yale University, Box 11A, Yale Station, New Haven, Connecticut 06520 USA

ANDREW YOUNG
Department of Psychology, University of Lancaster, Fylde College, Bailrigg, Lancaster LA1 4YF

Contents

Preface ix
Introduction xi

Part I: Going beyond the representation

1 Modelling cognition: some current issues
  Philip Levy 3
2 Questions and thought
  Roger C. Schank 21
3 Coping with novelty and human intelligence
  Robert J. Sternberg 57
4 Cognitive principles in the design of computer tutors
  John R. Anderson, C. Franklin Boyle, Robert Farrell and Brian J. Reiser 93
5 Initial skill learning: an analysis of how elaborations facilitate the three components
  Davida H. Charney and Lynne M. Reder 135

Part 2: Theoretical issues

6 Simple models for experimentable situations
  Donald Broadbent 169
7 Schemas versus mental models in human memory
  William F. Brewer 187
8 Making decisions under the influence of knowledge
  John Fox 199

Part 3: Some cognitive models

9 Recognition and recall in MINERVA 2: analysis of the 'Recognition Failure' paradigm
  Douglas L. Hintzman 215

10   A model of memory organization for interacting goals
     Noel E. Sharkey and Gordon H. Bower 231
11   Why to speak, what to say and how to say it: modelling language
     production in discourse
     George Houghton and Stephen Isard 249
12   Modelling the recognition of faces and words
     Andrew W. Ellis, Andrew W. Young and Dennis C. Hay 269

Author Index 299
Subject Index 303

Preface

In July, 1985, I organized for the Cognitive Psychology Section of the British Psychological Society the International Workshop on Modelling Cognition. The chapters published in this volume arose out of that meeting, the contributors being selected for the special contributions that they made to the Workshop.

In recent years there has been an enormous growth in cognitive science and cognitive psychology. The International Workshop on Modelling Cognition drew together many of the leading workers in these growth areas and the chapters in this volume reflect the key issues that they raised.

The book has been organized into three sections reflecting the main themes of each chapter. The first section is entitled 'Going Beyond the Representation. It highlights, through the many contributions in this section from the internationally eminent authors, one of the main themes of the workshop. This is the need to consider how knowledge stored in the cognitive system is used if adequate models are to be developed. The second section is called 'Theoretical Issues' and represents a sample of the issues in our conceptualizing of the appropriate approaches to modelling cognition that were raised at the Workshop. The final section titled 'Some Cognitive Models' describes four important attempts to model aspects of cognition.

The volume presents an exciting sample of the best work in cognitive science. It reveals both the strengths of this vigorous new science and also some of the key questions that the very success of attempts to model cognition have raised. It will, I hope, provide stimulating reading to anyone interested in cognitive psychology, artificial intelligence and intelligent, knowledge-based systems, and any of the disciplines related to cognitive science.

Peter Morris
4th March 1987

Introduction

PETER MORRIS

The chapters in this book represent extensions of papers given at the International Workshop on Modelling Cognition at Lancaster University in July 1985. From the 28 papers that were given the 12 that form the chapters of this book were selected for the special contributions that they made.

In recent years there has been an enormous growth in cognitive science and cognitive psychology. In part, this represents a desire to apply the newly available power and flexibility of modern computers to the modelling of human cognitive abilities. The reader will quickly appreciate the importance of computer models and computational approaches to the understanding of human cognition from even a brief glance through the contents of this volume. However, the development of models of human cognition has not been solely through computer modelling. The value of a cognitive model which is not yet simulated upon a computer is well illustrated by Chapter 12 with its rich insights into the processes by which we recognize and remember faces.

One major theme of the workshop was the recognition that when we come to try to model human cognition we need to take into account in our models many processes that go beyond a simple representation of a large collection of knowledge. This theme of going beyond the data base and asking how the stored knowledge is actually used occurs in several of the chapters in this book. It is particularly obvious in Part 1 which I have called 'Going Beyond the Representation'. It is, nevertheless, an important theme in Chapter 8 and also Chapter 10. Part 2 of the book has been titled 'Theoretical Issues'. It represents a sample of the issues in our conceptualizing of the appropriate approaches to modelling cognition that were raised in the workshop. Part 3 has been called 'Some Cognitive Models'. In it four examples of interesting attempts to model cognition are described.

The book begins with a chapter by Philip Levy on some current issues in modelling cognition. Having been chairman of the committee of the Economic and Social Research Council which deals with cognitive psychology and having been involved in British attempts to fund research on information technology, Professor Levy is extremely well equipped to survey the current state of attempts to model cognition. The chapter provides stimulating challenges to many of the confident assumptions that have been made by cognitive scientists attempting to simulate human cognition. Professor Levy points out that there are many psychological questions still requiring answers before good cognitive models can be developed. It is not that the old questions about thinking and decision-making have been superseded by the new approach but rather that the new power of cognitive modelling may help us to unravel what have always proved difficult problems. Professor Levy concludes that our immediate task is to review all the *old* issues from the newer computational perspective.

In the second chapter Professor Roger Schank asks what would be involved in programming a computer to be creative and to think on its own. He argues that creativity means asking questions. To be creative the computer must be aroused by what it perceives and must wonder about its world. Professor Schank argues that there is an intimate relationship between understanding and asking questions. The chapter well illustrates one theme of Part I: that adequate attempts to simulate human cognition will require more than the storage of vast amounts of knowledge. The human thinker is continually being presented with novel information in his or her environment and also responding in novel ways. A major problem for cognitive science is to explain the way that people cope with novelty and use their available knowledge in creative and individual ways.

The issue of coping with novelty arises from another perspective in the third chapter by Robert Sternberg. As Professor Sternberg comments, 'Nothing is so certain in life as the existence of uncertainty.' He argues that the ability to cope with novelty is an important source of continuity in intellectual development. He presents some cognitive models of coping with novelty and discusses how this ability to cope relates to intelligence.

In their chapter, Anderson, Boyle, Farrell and Reiser apply Anderson's ACT* theory to develop a set of principles for computer tutoring. They set out to base their model upon how successful students solve problems and how such students are taught by individual tutors. In doing so they identify eight principles for intelligent tutoring. When applied to teaching LISP and geometry these principles lead to a marked improvement in learning. The chapter indicates how cognitive modelling is reaching the stage where the models can be used to raise important questions about the way we acquire new information and it illustrates the possibilities of valuable applications of models such as Anderson's.

In Chapter 5 Charney and Reder continue the question of the way that new information acquisition can be improved. They identify three basic components in learning a skill. The first is learning the kinds of procedures that are available and the objects upon which they operate. The second is learning how to execute the procedures, and the third is to learn when the procedures should be applied. The authors consider the type of examples that can and should be used when teaching the application of rules. As in the preceding chapters it becomes clear that we should not think of cognition as merely involving the formation of a large knowledge base. For that knowledge to be useful and applied appropriately the conditions surrounding its use must be learned. Successful and rapid learning requires some form of elaboration and examples. However, the selection of appropriate examples raises considerable problems in the possible misinterpretation of the information.

In Chapter 6 Donald Broadbent illustrates the power of even the smallest microcomputer to aid the thinking of psychology theorists. He illustrates with a series of examples how several widely known theories that have been previously presented in verbal terms turn out, when modelled on a microcomputer, to lead to different conclusions to those drawn by their proposers. Dr Broadbent argues that the availability of microcomputers makes it easy for anyone to explore the implications of their psychological models, and, in so doing, to avoid misinterpretation and woolly thinking.

In Chapter 7 Professor William Brewer discusses the concepts of schemas and mental models. He draws a distinction between underlying knowledge structures and particular, episodic representations that are formed from these underlying structures. He also distinguishes between representations that are derived from old, generic knowledge and representations which are constructed at the time of use. He argues that these distinctions help to clarify some of the confusions in the recent experimental literature and to suggest directions for future research.

In Chapter 8 Dr John Fox points out that decision-making is central to cognition. He argues for a change in direction from traditional views of decision-making towards a knowledge-based view of decision-making so that the mathematical traditions of studying the topic can be linked with our growing understanding of the computational basis of knowledge-based skills. He criticizes the traditional accounts of uncertainty and human approaches to probability. He argues that skilled decision-takers can exploit quantitative information and can often use general knowledge to cope with uncertainty.

In the remaining chapters of the book the authors introduce accounts of their models for particular components of the cognitive system. In the first chapter (Chapter 9) of Part 3 Professor Douglas Hintzman discusses his MINERVA 2 model of human memory. The model was developed with the aim of explaining memory for specific experiences and for the acquisition of abstract concepts. Professor Hintzman concentrates upon the application of the model to the 'recognition failure' paradigm. He concludes that the model provides a reasonable account of the relationship between recall and recognition even though it was developed with other experimental tasks in mind. In the process of his attempts to assess his model his simulations highlight several factors that will affect rates of recognition and recall that have not, normally, been noticed.

In Chapter 10 Dr Noel Sharkey and Professor Gordon Bower discuss four experiments investigating their Goal Integration Network (GIN) model. Sharkey and Power emphasize the importance of understanding the goals and plans of other individuals when interpreting their actions. The model assumes that goals and plans are stored in memory as an associative structure. Whenever a goal is retrieved from memory the plans associated with fulfilling that goal become more available to other memory processes. Sharkey and Bower report four experiments which support and develop this model. They argue that people have prewired structures in memory corresponding to goals and plans and that much of the storage of information about a character is done so in this framework.

In Chapter 11 Drs George Houghton and Stephen Isard describe a computational model of language production in which two individuals in a simple world can converse with each other to achieve simple practical goals within that world. To make such a dialogue possible Houghton and Isard have to consider a wide range of issues involving interaction frames, grammars and lexicons. The complexities to be faced by any attempt to model real-world cognition are well illustrated by the problems that have had to be resolved by Drs Houghton and Isard to computationally model even the simple world and dialogue that they have tackled.

In Chapter 12 Drs Andrew Ellis, Andrew Young and Dennis Hay describe their model of face recognition and compare it to models that are currently popular for the recognition of words. Unlike most other chapters in the book the authors do not base their model on computational procedures, although, no doubt, a computational model could be developed. The chapter illustrates that there is considerable potential for understanding human cognition without tackling the complexities of a computationally based model.

The reader of this volume will soon become aware of the range and power of recent attempts to model human cognition. Aspects of cognition are being confidently tackled which a few years ago were hardly even recognized as existing. Our understanding of the processes of cognition have developed enormously in recent years and the chapters in this book contribute to that understanding. Against such a background of confident and successful activity it is, perhaps, unfair to point out one or two weaknesses in current efforts to model cognition. It is, in any case, not the fault of current modellers of the cognitive processes that the processes which they are attempting to model are so inadequately described in the psychological literature. It is, however, strange that the development of the models usually precedes the collection of any detailed data on the phenomena being modelled. One would have expected factual knowledge about the world to be driving the development of the models, at least in the early stages. The lack of good empirical data means that there are few constraints upon the models that are produced. It is, perhaps, ironic but salutary to recognize that good model construction depends upon good data collection and description. Secondly, and perhaps relatedly, there seems to be little consensus about the important aspects of cognition that require modelling, and the types of models that are needed. Finally, there seems to be little connection, with a few notable exceptions, between the development of the models and any application and use of them. In other words, the choice and development of models of human cognition seems to depend very much upon the personal interests of the modellers and very little upon the empirical and practical demands of the world. There is nothing wrong with this, except that it may prove progressively harder to justify the activities of cognitive modelling to those outside the excitement of the discipline. That is, however, for the future. For the present the reader is invited to enjoy the examples of excellent attempts to model cognition that are represented in the following chapters.

Part 1: Going beyond the representation

Modelling Cognition
Edited by P. Morris
©1987 John Wiley & Sons Ltd.

1

Modelling cognition: some current issues

PHILIP LEVY
University of Lancaster

INTRODUCTION

Addressing cognitive psychologists, I propose to offer a broad sketch of the current funded research scene in Britain in relation to computer-oriented modelling of aspects of human intelligence, to point up some limitations of several models used for cognition and to draw attention to areas where 'more research is needed'. I base my observations, in part, upon having seen several hundred proposals to a research council over the past three years, and, in the other part, upon a close reading of newsletters, reviews and workshop reports distributed through the Alvey Directorate, the British Government's agency for information technology (IT), over a similar period. Anticipating my conclusions, the 'current issues' referred to in the title have been around for a long time.

The economic importance of developments in the information technologies has led governmental and other agencies to pour sizeable funds into IT-related research and development projects. As is natural to governments, and to the industrial and commercial interests they hope to advance, a rather short-term perspective tends to be adopted, at least in those areas of cognition with which I am concerned here, despite ambitions to the contrary. The focus tends to be on the knowably achievable rather than upon the possibly, desirably and imaginably achievable. Development of the knowably achievable is not to be disdained; rather it is a matter of the balance to be struck between seeking fundamental advances and ensuring satisfactory exploitation of what is known. Real-world testing of research ideas and economic urgencies have always had a role in science at large, sometimes spurring and sometimes misdirecting basic research.

One consequence, however unwitting, of the press towards immediacy of solution is to increase the gap between what might be characterized as the never-mind-the-process-feel-the-result approach and the represent-the-process approach. The distinction between making a machine do the job as best it can and attempting a closer representation of human process and human intelligence is, of course, a long-standing one. The boundary is fuzzy, but there are clear examples at either extreme. The still essential role of the human sorter operator in the British Post Office, who scans the envelope and punches in the postcode, shows the machine not to have significantly greater intelligence for 'reading' than the early card-sorting machines; but it is a solution of sorts and at least provides some relief for human arms and legs. It still requires very expensive hardware to read even mechanically printed and accurately positioned character sets, let alone to confront human cleverness in reading a variety of casually drawn handwritten symbols placed in a somewhat uncertain position on an envelope. The research challenge continues, and whether or not the pursuit of something closer to human intelligence, in performance or in process, is worth the chase is another, and perhaps again economic, matter.

Meanwhile, there are some obvious dangers of the gap between this caricature of the 'artificial intelligence' approach and what I will refer to as the 'cognitive intelligence' approach for those areas of greatest challenge and of lowest historical levels of research in cognition. I am referring to the arena of the 'higher cognitive processes'—thinking, reasoning, planning, decision-making and problem-solving—which, while never truly to be separated from such topics as perception, memory, action and language, remains an under-populated area. When Neisser's (1967) book marked the stylistic turn from 'experimental' psychology to 'cognitive' psychology, topics like thinking occupied one final chapter, a form of postscript to areas regarded as more securely researched. The Wundtian prejudice against 'higher psychical processes' is currently reflected in the financial weight of governmental and Research Council funding in IT. Among topics of psychological interest, such things as vision, robotics, speech, syntactical linguistics and 'interfaces' of various kinds, achieve massive priority, perhaps because they seem both to have eminently 'objective' goals and to be most nearly 'do-able'. The higher mental processes, while not altogether ignored, are most heavily represented in funding terms by studies of various forms of logic programming ('inference engines'), most of these studies being largely uninformed by, if not indifferent to, studies of knowledge structures and inference mechanisms in humans.

The obvious dangers to which I refer resemble those of designing a vehicle of some power, but leaving undefined such things as the terrain and whether it can reverse appropriately away from a position facing a wall. While one trend in cognitive psychology has been to recognize the limits of processing approaches which do not pay sufficient regard to the specific contents being processed, IT developments have snatched at the available structures and 'shells' for cognition. Further, the massive cash flow has generated an uncertain dynamic among the needs of the three areas of training, development and research. The severe shortage of trained manpower and the dual press of the intellectual and economic challenge has pulled large numbers of cognitive psychologists at least part way towards the IT research market-place. The questions are: What has cognitive psychology to say about the 'shells' and can it manufacture any 'eggs'? Are cognitive psychologists well prepared for the challenge?

NEW SUNS FOR OLD LAMPS

It is obvious that the increasing availability of computers, whether of a conventional or a novel architecture, has given cognitive psychologists access to a range of new and remarkable general structures for the expression of complex models. These, combined with a variety of high-level programming languages, and especially those oriented by artificial intelligence (AI), provide building blocks for ever more powerful formal analogies than we have been accustomed to. Overall, we have many new modes of embodying theories and of testing speculations. We should, however, recall Johnson-Laird and Wason's general warning (1977, p. 10) that our theories are usually richer than those bits that can readily be implemented in the explicit form required for a computable model. But the cognitive science 'community' has been set the challenge, *inter alia*, of developing expert systems. This is clearly a test—and a rather severe one—of how well we understand and hence can model the higher mental processes; or, it is a challenge to improve upon human abilities.

Now, I have heard the view expressed by one or two eminent cognitive psychologists that the development of expert systems is a 'dull problem', that an expert system is merely a set of propositions or a set of rules, some data or knowledge and some inference mechanisms, perhaps with some probabilities strewn around. I suppose that this is true of many available implementations. Current expert systems are typically conceived of as some assembly of 'knowledge base', 'inference engine' and 'user interface' (e.g. CCTA, 1985). The knowledge base is, perforce, to be formatted in 'oven-ready' style for inferencing, which undoubtedly begs questions about the nature of human knowledge and human inferencing. The notion of a user interface as an add-on device also begs questions about the separability of explanation devices from knowledge structures.

Many existing expert systems are not very impressive when compared to the best human expertise; or, if impressive, they are acutely tailored in that they deal with a very narrow area of discourse and they have taken some of the best talents in the AI business several person-years to develop. It is obvious that *some* of their features provide an advance on human expertise. The management and accessing of data bases by computers can be more efficient and reliable. Their ruthless logic can be advantageous (and sometimes not!). Their perseverance in search tasks is to be admired. Their memory is beyond that of a herd of elephants. And so on. But a number of elements are lacking and these deserve attention from cognitive psychologists. What are these 'elements' and what might cognitive psychologists contribute? To what extent can better sightings of cognitive intelligence illuminate the rather structural artificial intelligence approaches?

Two kinds of things claim to illuminate the scene in my observation. These are what I will call 'old lamps' and 'moonbeams'. The first—old lamps—are the models we have typically brought to bear upon the study of human thinking and reasoning. The second—moonbeams—are the source of much hand-waving in the near darkness about psychology's readiness to attack some rapidly emerging problems of simulating expertise. I consider these in turn.

Old lamps

Cognitive science is said to be an interdisciplinary enterprise—linguistics, psychology, computing, anthropology, philosophy, and so on—and that the computational representation of models is its common test-bed. However, I see in the relation of psychology to this interdisciplinarity some analogy with remarks made by American humorist, Mort Sahl, about US–Soviet relations during the early Cold War period. About the capture of spies in both countries, he noted that first the Russians would put an American in gaol, and then—in retaliation—the Americans would put an American in gaol. This did not quite meet the need, he observed. The analogy is that linguists spend a lot of time on linguistic models, that computer scientists spend a lot of time on computational models, that philosophers spend a lot of time on logical models and that psychologists spend a lot of time on linguistic, computing, logical and, generally, other people's models. This has meant psychologists taking on the disciplinary limitations of other people's formalisms and other people's issues. We have a long history of doing this one way or another. Consider the list given in Table 1.

Table 1   Some formalisms adopted by psychologists

Logic—classical
Probability theories—classical, Bayesian
Decisions—expected utility theory
Linguistic theories—e.g. Chomsky
Philosophies of science—e.g. Popper

I have no doubt that we learn a great deal from other people's models; each of them represents a considerable intellectual exercise of potentially general value; and we would properly be deemed ignorant not to be aware of them. But each is adjacent to, rather than self-evidently central to, cognitive psychology's questions and issues.

Logic

Take 'logic' for example. For more than 50 years psychologists have explored classical forms of logic. By 'classical' I am referring to the Aristotelian syllogisms, employing the quantifiers *all*, *no*, *some* and *not*, and to the so-called 'connectives' *if/then*, *and*, *or* and *not* used in relatively natural linguistic forms. Psychologists have been remarkably single-minded in the attention given to classical logic in spite of the lip-service that is paid from time to time to the several other logics (e.g. modal, multi-valued, non-monotonic, deontic, temporal). Much research has shown that at least some of the time and under some circumstances even highly intelligent subjects are not very good at classical logic problems.

Johnson-Laird's (1983) review of this line of research probably exposes more clearly than any other how limited is the *psychological* interest to be found in a vast experimental literature. Recall that he (and Bara) asked subjects (Ss) to construct conclusions in their heads for pairs of premises of the Aristotelian type. Their errors—their declaration of some invalid conclusions and their failure to find some valid ones—can be related, in Johnson-Laird's terms, to the difficulties of constructing integrated mental models of the premises and of testing all possible models for lack of contradiction of a supposed conclusion. Limitations of mental space and, relatedly, of the ability to construct the alternative mental models are key factors which are provoked in various degrees by manipulable features of the task (e.g. figure, mood). Thus Johnson-Laird most clearly reduces the role of logic *qua* logic to that of a task variable, and removes it from its long-standing role as a putative process account, even for the narrow area of reasoning about logical problems. In this sense all the evidence about Ss performing on logical problems has no greater status in the study of reasoning than that about their performance on cryptarithmetic problems or on 'cannibals and missionaries' problems.

Why does this matter in the present context? There are several bundles of reasons. First, the psychological or cognitive intelligence interest lies in the continuity of comprehension and inference processes in the construction and manipulation of mental models, whether those in Johnson-Laird's account of language and logic or those in Gentner and Stevens's (1983) accounts of reasoning about the physical world. The most extreme artificial intelligence approach has been to start with items of knowledge so tidied and polished that inference is reduced to logic, or to *mere logic* as we humans ought to say. Of course, there is a sense in which all inferences are, in principle, reducible to strict deductive or logical inferences. Where knowledge is made sufficiently explicit, inference becomes a mere technical ('logical') problem and one well on the way to solution with the development of special software systems like PROLOG and POPLOG. Even without these facilities, however, and given sufficiently explicit knowledge, we can envisage a rather unsophisticated and tedious 'search-for-all-connections-test-and-try' program that would serve: that is what machines are good at. What they are not good at—or, strictly, what is largely missing from expert systems of the AI mould—is the cognitive intelligence of a more general human inferencing power. This, I suspect, resides in the continuity of processing from perception and retrieval to comprehension, comprehension to construal of possibilities, and construal to inference, and storage, and back again.

Secondly, the study of reasoning has for too long dwelt upon that narrow formalism of classical logic, which has been used—rather as nonsense syllables were used for verbal learning—as paradigmatic for all reasoning. I will give some quick pointers to my unease with our devotion to classical logic. First, unlike professional philosophers of logic, psychologists have tended to ignore the many doubts about the breadth of relevance and appropriateness of classical logic. Of course, logic is a much broader subject for philosophers than psychological experimentation has typically allowed. Next, whereas our culture embodies other formalisms (e.g. algebra) in the education system, it seems to have made the judgement that classical logic, or indeed any logic, is not worth such an investment. Some may deplore this: No logic in our schools? Its absence or neglect may say something about the weakness of the philosophers' trade union relative to that of mathematicians; or it may represent a true judgement on the bounded value of formal logics in human affairs.

In general, however, we allow ourselves to be lulled by the beauty of some formalisms into regarding the mapping of a problem as a one-step process. This is true if we are doing our mathematics homework. In life, people exhibit several skills beyond any formalism that they may employ. They *recognize* that a problem exists (and they do or do not have the motivation to solve it). By some recognition or matching process, automatic or otherwise, they *select* some thinking tool, perhaps a formalism. They *in-map* the problem to mental symbols to give it some manageable shape. They *manipulate* the representation so produced, perhaps using paper and pencil or some other external aids, to help them hold and manipulate the symbols of the representation. They *out-map* to see what the solution might mean in real-world terms (e.g. language of communication, actions). They may not like, or may not believe, the 'solution' and they may return to the original expression of the problem for a rethink. The automaticity provided by the use of some formalism represents but one of the five clevernesses required of a successful human problem-solver. The problem is that while Frege's historic distancing of logic from language—the development of a symbolic logic and formal procedures—was good for logic, and ultimately for machine kinds of inference, it necessarily ignores the comprehension of language, the in- and out-mapping from and to the world, the selection of possible mappings, and formalisms for non-linguistic knowledge.[1] It is in this light that machine (deductive) inference can be regarded as a relatively trivial operation, in the sense that it has no psychological content whatsoever once the mapping to a formalism has been performed. Indeed, psychologists could be regarded as having used logic as a source of language-disguised puzzles—somewhat in the way that word-algebra problems have been used—rather than as the study of language-expressed reasoning.

Incidentally, I recently engaged two young people (a motor mechanic and a welder), not educated beyond O-level, in Project Aristotle, an attempt to see whether persons untrained in logic could rediscover all the valid forms of the Aristotelian syllogisms. They were presented with the task in the form of a problem to be solved, roughly as follows: 'Here are four kinds of sentence: *All As are Bs*, *No As are Bs*, *Some As are Bs*, *Some As are not Bs*. Combine them in pairs, using the letters *A*, *B* and *C*, where *A* and *C* can be used once each but not in the same sentence and *B* must appear in both sentences. For which pairs of such sentences are there valid conclusions and what are they?' This might be characterized as a study of natural reasoning about an unnatural problem. Over the next several hours, they tripped across a whole gamut of findings in the experimental literature. They rediscovered the 'atmosphere' effects, which, we should recall, have some validity as expressed in the eight classical rules for the syllogism (e.g. Jevons, 1870, pp. 127–8). They had doubts about conversion ('Does "All As are Bs" mean that "All Bs are As?'); they had doubts about the definition of 'Some' ('at least one and possibly all'); and about the distinction between 'true' and 'valid' (cp. Braine, 1979, p. 35). They recognized that there were special difficulties with one of the figures;[2] and that some particular instantiations led to dangerous confusions of real-world truth and logical validity.

The more interesting findings in relation to human problem-solving are the following. It took them some time to systematize their attack on the problem

---

[1] Andy Ellis has drawn my attention to a paper by Sommers (1978) in which an attempt is made to reverse Frege's revolution; a form of logic is offered which takes greater note of the linguistic origins of propositions

[2] Strictly, the study explores the figures defined by later logicians, because Aristotle did not explore what we would now call the 'complete problem space'. He regarded one of the four figures—patterns of positioning of A, B and C—as 'so imperfect and unnatural in form' that he never allowed the existence of the figure at all. Jevons (1870, pp. 147–8) remarked: 'It is to be regretted that so needless an addition was made to the somewhat complicated forms of the syllogism.'

by laying out the 64 possible sentence pairs for all distinct configurations of A, B and C and the quantifiers. They continued to be seduced by 'possibility' rather than 'necessity' as a characteristic of a conclusion. They persisted in the belief that a 'pattern' of valid conclusions would emerge on their, by then, systematic spatial display, on one side of a piece of paper, of all possible syllogisms.

The overall outcome was that they found all valid conclusions except for the complete set of those which have the form 'Some As are not Bs'. These they regarded as 'useless' conclusions and reported 'no conclusion' in preference. I excused them from their labours at this point! Other observations, which probably have greater relevance to natural reasoning, are as follows:

(a) Whereas, in other tasks I have used, Ss often show great reluctance to use the paper and pencil most pointedly provided, Project Aristotle was clearly a big enough task to demand such tools. At the limits of mental space with lesser tasks we may not judge well enough whether or not we are coping 'in our heads'.

(b) The Ss failed in about eight hours of work (with breaks) to develop any clear external representation of the task. Sentences were sometimes written down, but neither Euler circles nor Venn diagrams were invented; nor was anything like Johnson-Laird's 'tokens' representation in (external) evidence. When the task was near complete, I personally found the 'tokens' representation both convenient and persuasive in discussion with them to illuminate their small number of failures, and they wished that they had known about the method earlier; but there was no recognition that they had used any such method, nor any method but speaking sentences over to themselves and to each other.

We might next look at the sort of problem, shown in Table 2, that some people—presumably also not trained in logic—do for pleasure (at least they *pay* to buy puzzle books full of these). When I pay Ss who are not trained in logic to tackle such problems, a common stumbling-block is not their ignorance of the logical operators but their failure to acknowledge the limitations of mental space and the need to shed inhibitions about using paper and pencil, perhaps to make exploratory scribbles and perhaps to invent codes for themselves. Given a *big enough* problem, like Project Aristotle or the one in Table 2, Ss usually overcome these inhibitions. Their struggles are then in the area that Mary Smyth and I have tended to label as *s*-logical, for 'strategic–logical', rather than *c*-logical for 'classical–logical'. The *s* also stands for systematizing, selecting, sorting, searching, supposing, symbolizing, signifying, schematizing, specifying, sucking-and-seeing and other strategic components of thinking. Perhaps these are the 'logical' skills that deserve a place in the school curriculum rather than the formal logics?

Overall, psychologists have been obsessed with a limited range of logical

Table 2   Food for thought (from *Logical Challenge*, No. 6, Foxgate, London, 1985)

1. Lemon sponge followed spinach only if Stuart ate steak, otherwise sponge followed sweet corn and Stuart ate salmon.
2. If Simon ate sultana roll then salad was served with sausages, otherwise Simon chose sorbet and salad accompanied spaghetti.
3. If Sheila had sole she also had salsify; otherwise she had salmon and sweet corn. She did not have sorbet.
4. Strawberries followed spaghetti only if Stuart had salmon, otherwise strawberries followed steak and Stuart had sausages.
5. Soufflé followed spinach only if Susie had sole, otherwise Susie had spaghetti and soufflé followed sprouts.
6. Sarah had steak only if a man had salmon, otherwise Sarah had sausages. She did not have sprouts.

What did each person have—main dish, vegetable and sweet?

models, regarded as normative, which are applicable to a very limited range of human reasoning. Presumably there is no quarrel with the view that while human expertise may be wholly *reducible* to logic, it is not often immediately expressed in a form which is readily amenable to such a reduction. This is an issue about cognitive intelligence in the first instance. As Newell (1981, p. 16) wrote of the role of logic, it is 'a tool for the analysis of knowledge, not for reasoning by intelligent agents'.

Uncertainty and decision

Much the same thing has happened with probability theories and with the expected utility models in relation to risk and decisions. Decades of experimentation show that not even professional gamblers, or financial managers, or even some economists one suspects, are particularly good at following the prescriptions of these models, let alone the armies of university students that have engaged in gambling and decision studies as experimental subjects. People are not naturally very good at some problems derived from these formalisms. There are several reasons for this. None of the reasons are offered in the spirit of claiming that we are wholly rational if only various defects in the problem statements or in our processing were corrected or allowed for. I offer them to give some perspective on the issues.

First, logics and probability theories have taken centuries to emerge and to develop. If these formalisms represent natural, untutored skills, such as we seem to expect our Ss to possess, why did they take so long to emerge in our history and why are they so difficult to teach! (Actually, as I pointed out earlier, logic, unlike mathematics and statistics, is not widely taught.) Secondly, each of the formalisms was developed, not as an externalization of something necessarily natural even to the best human thinkers, but for some well-specified purposes, some limited range of abstractions. The popular combination of 'deductive logic plus statistical theory' in some expert systems surely misrepresents the nature of expertise. In practice, expert systems which are based upon this formula require that all the probabilities, for every combination of conditions—say those for symptoms and diseases in a medical expert system—are observable or are otherwise specifiable. Where data bases are inadequate for this purpose, the alternative is to extract judged probability or uncertainty values from the experts; but research over the decades has shown that such numerical judgements are doubtfully scaled, subject to various misperceptions and biases, and are probably incoherent or inconsistent as a collection. Experts in substantive fields are not notably less prone to errors in probability judgements than the rest of us.

Statistical arguments and expected utility theory provide quite beautiful forms of rationality for decision-making when participants feel secure in the numbers to be inserted in the equations. But there's the rub: there is little point in characterizing a reasoning or decision process as rational in these terms if the essential numbers are doubtfully obtained (cp. Simon, 1983).

Thirdly, the underlying issue for cognitive intelligence is not immediately that of finding the right numbers to represent uncertainty but of analysing the different kinds of uncertainty in reasoning and in decision-making. Thus, for a start, Kahneman and Tversky (1982) distinguish two major kinds of attribution: the external uncertainty of a spinning coin or other such mechanism; and the internal uncertainties of ignorance or insufficient knowledge. Johnson-Laird (1983, p. 198) offers a third kind: an inability to decide an issue because it is outside the 'rules' of the system (e.g. How large can the goalkeeper's gloves be?). Mamdani, Efstathiou and Pang (1985) distinguish the seven kinds of uncertainty shown in Table 3, only some of which fit the purposes for which the current formalisms were designed.

Fox (1984a) returns us to the way in which we use language to express uncertainty. He begins by noting the different kinds of uncertainty indicated by the *confidence* in a rule, the *reliability* of a fact and the *likelihood* of a

Table 3   Uncertainties (from Mamdani, Efstathiou and Pang, 1985)

—one's belief in a given proposition
—the likelihood of a simple, compound or conditional event
—the extent of a proposition concerning a continuous variable
—the imprecision about any information
—any exception to a general rule
—the mandate for performing some action
—the relevance of one piece of information to another

---

hypothesis; and he continues by exploring the hierarchy of relations among terms expressing security of belief like *perhaps*, *possible*, *likely*, *improbable*, *doubted*, *assumed* and *implausible*. In general, Fox (1980, 1984b) is persuasive that we should postpone use of the more formal and abstract representations of knowledge until we have made sufficiently explicit the qualitative bases for decision-making.

The apparent generality of common probability theory may cause us to forget that there are in fact different theories, or different developments of the same theory, for different kinds of uncertainty in nature. That is why scholars have devised a variety of representations for random processes in science (e.g. Bose–Einstein, Fermi–Dirac and Maxwell–Boltzmann statistics). The choices to be made between classical statistical inference, the several variations on Bayesian themes, likelihood arguments and decision–theoretic positions remain highly controversial. Problems with the in-mappings from our questions and the out-mappings to our answers are the sources of these controversies, and not whether the central mathematical manipulations are correct. Uncertainties in Nature and Life may also provide motivation for other representations, such as those found in religions, laws, management philosophies and political regimes. It is facile to assume that a single form of probability theory could capture the texture of all uncertainties.

Linguistic models

Turning now to linguistic models, rightly or wrongly, I took Johnson-Laird's *Mental Models* (1983) to be a graveyard of some linguistic models (as with logic) from a psychologist's point of view. This is a pity because, if we are honest, we have lived off linguistic theories as a source of experiments in cognitive intelligence for two decades now. It is good that linguistic theory has been strong, even brazen, when cognitive theorizing has been struggling towards the higher processes. It is also helpful to us that linguistics has begun the return journey from sentences and syntax through semantics to pragmatics. Perhaps soon both disciplines will be dealing with at least pairs of sentences, two speakers, issues of social contexts, shared assumptions, types of inferences and so on. Sperber and Wilson (1986) offer a most thoughtful and extended account of these matters. Here is the greatest hope of interdisciplinarity, but—and perhaps this is a good sign—the theories seem less well developed as formalisms in this area.

But there are also several worrying points. First, linguistics has offered some more immediately tractable, or at least try-able, forms of theory for IT and some good cognitive psychologists are being seduced by this new form of reductionism. Secondly, IT funds seem to flow on the notion that linguistics can provide some kinds of 'interfaces'. Certainly, linguistics can make a good start on such problems; it is, for example, worth pushing language-oriented syntactical approaches to the limit. In that limit, however, the cognitive intelligence approach must be that language is not a mere 'interface' to our intelligence. Language is too important, central one might say, to be regarded as stopping a centimetre or two inside our ears in some syntactically oriented, sentence-decoding device; yet that, crudely, is the sort of 'model' the funders seem to favour. I must confess to being a strong admirer of the work of Winograd and Schank who, although in my experience they often rouse strong and passionate criticisms from some psychologists and linguists, tackle inference, language and uncertainties in ways which are rather unlike those typically seen in expert systems. In particular they offer some view of how the 'yolk' and 'white' of knowledge might fill the 'shells' of logic to enrich the syntactical systems on offer. In particular, Schank's 'syntaxes' of action, intention and implication are somehow more psychologically appealing, no matter that they may be said to be excessively tailored to particular areas of world knowledge.

Philosophy of science

I list philosophy of science as a formalism because Popper seems to be taken as a normative model, not so much for how we should conduct research, but for how people should test their hypotheses in reasoning and decision-making. It is true that attempts to falsify hypotheses provide crucial boundary tests for hypotheses alongside confirmatory data. What is neglected in Popper's prescriptions and by those who worry about our bias towards affirming or confirming hypotheses are two essentially human properties, which serve as the engines of science and much else. (Recall that Popper passionately scorns psychology along with sociology and astrology.) The first is our facility for generating and modifying hypotheses, an activity for which prescriptions are hard to come by. The second is our propensity to believe in something (e.g. a hypothesis), and belief is one feature which sustains us, for good or evil, in face of uncertainty.

But then we must remember that there are other philosophies of science, and my theme has been that we should not take other disciplines, nor any single formalism, *too* seriously. A reading of Kuhn and Lakatos would suggest the addition of several social psychological and sociological factors; for example, that refutation is more likely to arise from another group of scientists rather than from within the group creating the conjecture, or from the collapse of a theory under the weight of its protective belt of modifications. It may be that expert systems would better imitate human intelligence by adopting the model of a collection of experts, each of whom has a strong belief in a different theory, and they are to fight it out. In fact, the blackboard model for expert systems is designed to take on this style, but one which is rather beyond the current 'shells' for reasoning. In general, the questions are: Must we repeat the whole history of philosophy of science in the arena of expert systems? Must we rediscover that some kinds of 'facts' rest on, or only arise within, particular theoretical positions and that experts are notable (and especially interesting) for their disagreements in the most challenging areas of their subject?

Popper, of course, side-stepped the classical issue of induction. This you will recall was treated for centuries as the accumulation of evidence for a possible generalization and as a somewhat awkward problem in probability theory. A study by Thagard and Nisbett (1982) nicely illustrates human ability to risk generalizations on limited data and to evalute them. Philosophers, psychologists and students alike were given the three sets of observations, shown in Table 4, which purported to arise from a visit to a newly discovered island. They were asked to say how confident they were in the three generalizations offered. All groups had greatest confidence in the generalization about the new metal fluoridium, next highest for that about the colour of shreebles, and lowest for the universality of their nesting materials. Subjects' justifications often made reference to background knowledge about the typical *variability in kinds of things*.

In contrast, many of our laboratory studies in concept formation and rule induction have been positively Baconian in their philosophy of science. Induction rules devised for expert systems are currently repeating this history. It is not that induction rules cannot work on a sufficient accumulation of well-tabulated data (but note that several questions are begged here), but that human ability to conjecture—well or badly—is based upon more than 'Bacon plus taxonomic heuristics'. A case in point is provided by a small study I conducted with some psychology students using an AI example. Michalski (1983) presented his program INDUCE with descriptions of constructed examples of cancerous and normal cells. The program successfully determined properties that differentiated the two classes of cells. Pairs of students were given the same problem using Michalski's diagrams (1983, p. 118) of the cells as their data. One pair adopted the machine approach, tabulating features and seeking rules. A second pair worked on the hypothesis that

Table 4 'Observations' (from Thagard and Nisbett, 1982)

1. Three instances of a new species of bird—the shreeble—all are blue.
2. Three instances of a new metal—fluoridium—all three heated produce a blue flame.
3. All three observed shreebles use baobab leaves as nesting material.
   How confident are you in the following generalizations:
1. All shreebles are blue.
2. All fluoridium burns with a blue flame.
3. All shreebles use baobab leaves as nesting material.

cancerous cells should show several pairs of similar features to facilitate readiness to split and proliferate. The third pair, wrongly assuming that the numbering of the four cells in each group indicated time-ordered snapshots of just two cells growing, sought a developmental rule to distinguish the two classes. The fourth pair worked on an alleged 'evolutionary' principle that cancer was more likely to develop in more complex cells. None of these students was a biologist, yet had they been working on real data about cells, the developmental and evolutionary 'theories' used by the latter three pairs might have succeeded where unguided taxonomic principles operating upon unselected data might have failed. At least, the four pairs of Ss offered four different views of 'expertise' for the problem on offer.

As with all the formalisms that psychology has flirted with there are various diagnoses, but none such as to wholly excuse our subjects for their failings, nor such as to excuse us our exaggerated trust that the technical disciplines capture a wider cognitive intelligence. Thagard (1982, p. 32), discussing the discrepancies between human inferential practice and logical norms exposed in our studies of reasoning and probabilistic thinking, characterized three possible conclusions as follows:

(1) People are dumb. They simply fail to follow the normatively appropriate inferential rules.
(2) Psychologists are dumb. They have failed to take into account all the variables affecting human inferences, and once all the factors are taken into account it should be possible to show that people are in fact following the appropriate rules.
(3) Logicians are dumb. They are assessing the inferential behaviour of human thinkers with respect to the wrong set of normative standards.

Thagard adopted 'the egalitarian position that everybody gets to be dumb some of the time'. Perhaps we can summarize our understanding of intelligence by the following generalizations:

1. People are clever, at least some of the time.
2. Some people are experts and are very clever for some professional situations.
3. Formalisms are very clever for some well-constructed problems.

Ultimately, a machine intelligence is by definition 'a formalism', but it is not evident that the available formalisms are adequate to the task of representing some human and especially expert clevernesses. If anything simple may be concluded, current machine intelligence is very good at the things we are not very good at, but there is much space left in the shell for offerings from cognitive psychologists.

Moonbeams

Whereas use of the expression 'old lamps' was meant to induce an impression of well-worn instruments of perhaps fading power, the term 'moonbeams' indicates an innocent, gentle light attempting to penetrate darkness. I am alluding here to my observation of the high hopes that cognitive psychologists bring to the financial trough of IT about the power of traditional models and principles and their readiness for machine implementation. One source of over-optimism is a failure of interdisciplinarity among psychologists. In a science policy study conducted by the Economic and Social Research Council a number of cognitive psychology and cognitive science journals were studied over a recent five-year period. Using the Institute of Scientific Information (ISI) data base, it was found that articles in cognitive psychology stayed very much within traditional bounds, only rarely referencing the AI literature on topics which both literatures addressed. Next, the most recent survey of the use of computers in departments of psychology (Burton, 1985) shows that while 'appreciation of AI modelling' is given as the most common reason for teaching computer programming, the clear predominance of BASIC, FOR-TRAN and Pascal languages suggests that serious AI modelling has not yet penetrated the teaching. With this background one cannot be too surprised at the naïvety of some research proposals from younger psychologists.

In the preceding section I have repeatedly noted that a major disappointment in the drive towards expert systems is the extent to which general or content-free processes fail to be anything but weak heuristics when compared with the content-bound principles that seem to be at the root of much expertise. We might note, for example, how long it has taken to develop chess-playing machines to their current level of competence. Yet in conventional problem-solving terms chess is regarded as a 'well-defined problem'. Certainly the initial state, the goal state(s) and the permissible operators are very clearly defined. The generation and examination of possibilities, even for the combinatorial explosion of board positions, is also something to which, in principle, a machine process is well suited. There remain, however, several problems. Not even the biggest and best of the current machines could maintain the pace at which the best humans must operate in competitions if they (the machines) were to be programmed to explore all possible prospective positions and lines of play. While programs use evaluation functions to compare paths of limited extent in the reduced space of heuristic searches, there are doubts that human experts do it this way. Indeed, the best current chess programs embody deep knowledge of openings and of endings and much else that is specific to chess. Envisioning advantageous board positions is also a feature of expert play. Analogous outcomes would seem to apply to physics expertise (e.g. Larkin, 1981), and to problem-solving in general (e.g.

Chi, Glaser and Rees, 1982). As a result of these kinds of studies I find current claims about expert system shells for reasoning rather shallow. For example, not untypical is the report by Becker (1985) that: '. . . an expert system giving advice on bank loans could use exactly the same shell as one which diagnoses faults in washing machines'. Differences in ethical implications apart, I find this kind of statement incredible; or else many person-years will be needed to massage the different 'knowledge bases' into shape for the shells to operate effectively.

The next mode of attack by the innocents is 'knowledge engineering': if the general structures for reasoning lack content, let us dig it out of the experts. So run several research proposals I have viewed; and that is how the proposals begin and end. Psychologists are not alone in their optimism. Commercial claims, including job advertisements, would have us believe that there is a new breed of person called a 'knowledge engineer'. The judgement must be that such people still operate with hard hat, firm boots and a shovel rather than with theodolite, map and calculator. Knowledge engineering is at the coal-face rather than in the electronics factory. Even given 'shells', many person-hours are required to fill them out. There is much room, therefore, for further study of the nature of expertise and the knowledge structures of experts, ahead of computational modelling.

Work by Collins and his co-workers offer two cautionary tales about the 'elicitation' of expert knowledge. Collins (1974, 1985) found that scientists who wished to replicate a new piece of equipment failed to do so even though the originators of the equipment had written down all they knew about it to the best of their ability. The length of an electrical lead turned out to be a critical datum. The experts who had successfully built the equipment in the first place might never have recognized this item to be significant had it not been for the failure of others to reproduce it. Collins, Green and Draper (1985) took on different roles in a study of semiconductor crystal growing. One interviewed the expert in the subject. They achieved, in essence, a fairly systematic textbook account of a practical process for their pains. Another author underwent a practical apprenticeship with the expert and a prototype expert system was developed. While this was immediately more workable than the textbook account, even this knowledge contained some rules of thumb that turned out, upon reflection, not to be as relevant, helpful or justifiable as other rules about the physical system. These the expert had not previously recognized.

One lesson concerns the existence of tacit knowledge in experts and its transmission. This knowledge could be either: (a) knowledge which the expert does not know he has, (b) knowledge which the expert might have long presumed to be common knowledge among those to be taught or advised, or (c) knowledge which the expert never had and never needed because details of his practices had always successfully avoided the problem. Collins, Green and Draper (1985, p. 111) draw another lesson in their conclusions: 'So long as human knowledge is thought of as being fully exhausted by information and heuristics many of the general features of the development of expert systems, and some particular features of the process of knowledge elicitation will remain puzzling.'

In application for research funds, newcomers sometimes offer that they will proceed by building programs that develop expertise for themselves. Not only have they not surveyed the AI literature on current attempts to do this, but they seem not to appreciate how much our traditional work on learning principles, concept identification and rule induction depend upon assumptions about the prior skills of Ss, their cultural commonalities and their willingness and ability to conform to peculiar strategic demands. Again, they claim too much for general processes which purport to apply to a wide range of knowledge, but lack sufficient definition in particular knowledge domains. Just the same thing happened during the phase in which Skinnerian principles were being applied to programmed learning devices, the previous machine revolution. The real task turned upon the analysis of knowledge, theoretical components, such as reinforcement, its nature and scheduling, turned out to be the less critical design features for achieving practical results. The analysis of knowledge lacks elaborated theory. Knowledge structures have replaced the older conceptions of 'intelligence' and 'learning' as the Holy Grails of psychology. Earlier analyses in terms of general processes seem to offer no short cuts.

Overall we should note that by various estimates it takes about 10 years or 4000 hours for expertise to develop. It is not evident that this is due merely to a lack of general-purpose logical or statistical structures in humans. It is certainly worth speculating why it takes so long. Human modes of achieving concepts and rules, of structuring knowledge, of search and retrieval, of generating inferences, of handling uncertainties and of envisioning possibilities, whether in chess or physics, war or medicine, remain much under-explored in conventional cognitive research. Our immediate task is to review all the *old* issues from the newer computational perspective.

REFERENCES

Becker, J. (1985). How to bridge the gap left by the top experts. *Expert System User*, **1985** (July/August), 26.

Braine, M. D. S. (1979). On some claims about if-then. *Linguistics and Philosophy*, 3, 35–47.

Burton, A. M. (1985). Computer use in British departments of psychology. *Bulletin of the British Psychological Society*, **38**, 1–5.

CCTA (1985). *Expert Systems: Some Guidelines*. London: Central Computer and Communications Agency, HM Treasury.

Chi, M. T. H., Glaser, R. and Rees, E. (1982). Expertise in problem solving. In R. J.

Sternberg (ed.) *Advances in the Psychology of Human Intelligence*, Vol. 1. New Jersey: Lawrence Erlbaum Associates.

Collins, H. M. (1974). The *TEA*-set: tacit knowledge and scientific networks. *Science Studies*, **4**, 165–86.

Collins, H. M. (1985). *Changing Order: Replication and Induction in Scientific Practice*. Beverly Hills and London: Sage.

Collins, H. M., Green, R. H. and Draper, R. C. (1985). Where's the expertise?: Expert systems as a medium of knowledge transfer. In M. Merry (ed.) *Expert Systems 85* (Proceedings of the Fifth Technical Conference of the British Computer Society Specialist Group on Expert Systems). Cambridge: Cambridge University Press, pp. 323–34.

Fox, J. (1980). Making decisions under the influence of memory. *Psychological Review*, **87**, 190–211.

Fox, J. (1984a). Language, logic and uncertainty. Unpublished paper. London: Imperial Cancer Research Fund Laboratories.

Fox, J. (1984b). Formal and knowledge-based methods in decision technology. *Acta Psychologica*, **56**, 303–31.

Gentner, D., and Stevens, A. L. (1983). *Mental Models*. New Jersey: Lawrence Erlbaum Associates.

Jevons, W. S. (1870). *Lessons in Logic: Lessons in Logic*. London: Macmillan (reprinted 1948).

Johnson-Laird, P. N. (1983). *Mental Models*. Cambridge: Cambridge University Press.

Johnson-Laird, P. N., and Wason, P. C. (1977). *Thinking: Readings in Cognitive Science*. Cambridge: Cambridge University Press.

Kahneman, D., and Tversky, A. (1982). Variants of uncertainty. In D. Kahneman, P. Slovic and A. Tversky (eds) *Judgement Under Uncertainty: Heuristics and Biases*. Cambridge: Cambridge University Press.

Larkin, J. H. (1981). A model for learning to solve physics problems. In J. Anderson (ed.) *Cognitive Skills and their Acquisition*. Hillsdale, NJ: Lawrence Erlbaum Associates.

Mamdami, A., Efstathiou, J. and Pang, D. (1985). Inference under uncertainty. In M. Merry (ed.) *Expert Systems 85* (Proceedings of the Fifth Technical Conference of the British Computer Society Specialist Group on Expert Systems). Cambridge: Cambridge University Press, pp. 181–94.

Michalski, R. S. (1983). A theory and methodology of inductive learning. In R. S. Michalski, J. G. Carbonell and T. M. Mitchell (eds) *Machine Learning: An Artificial Intelligence Approach*. Palo Alto, California: Tioga Publishing Co.

Neisser, U. (1967). *Cognitive Psychology*. New York: Appleton-Century-Crofts.

Newell, A. (1981). The knowledge level. *AI Magazine*, **2**, 1–20.

Simon, H. (1983). *Reason in Human Affairs*. Oxford: Blackwell.

Sommers, F. (1978). The grammar of thought. *Journal of Social and Biological Structures*, **1**, 39–51.

Sperber, D., and Wilson, D. (1986). *Relevance: Communication and Cognition*. Oxford: Blackwell.

Thagard, P. (1982). From the descriptive to the normative in psychology and logic. *Philosophy of Science*, **49**, 24–42.

Thagard, P., and Nisbett, R. E. (1982). Variability and confirmation. *Philosophical Studies*, **42**, 379–94.

Modelling Cognition
Edited by P. Morris
©1987 John Wiley & Sons Ltd.

2

Questions and thought

ROGER C. SCHANK
Yale University

Creativity means asking questions. If we ever want a machine to be creative, to think on its own, it must be aroused by what it perceives—it must wonder about its world. The process of wondering is one of asking questions. This chapter attempts to address the problem of asking good questions. We begin by considering the intimate relationship between understanding and asking questions, critiquing two earlier approaches to understanding. We then examine the process of question transformation: how, given a set of experiences, some questions are answered and others are raised. We consider the relationship of questions to explanation, and hypothesize that questioning is a step in the explanation process. We finally attempt to categorize questions and question transformations, providing a sketchy model of wondering.

IPP AND CYRUS

In 1980 two students at Yale produced Ph.D. theses that exemplified the ideas that were around our laboratory at that time. These programs were intended to illustrate the issues of how a dynamic memory would alter our conceptions of natural language understanding. The underlying premise in each of these programs is that understanding was a phenomenon best done in a real context. Previously, we had built programs that attempted to apply static knowledge structures to written text. The older programs interpreted the texts that they read by making inferences using those knowledge structures.

After our initial successes in applying static knowledge structures, it became clear to us that since people were not static, our programs should not be static either. In other words, when a person reads a story about terrorism, it is read within the context of previous stories that he has read. He is, in some sense, changed by reading the new story. His memory helps him to interpret the new story, and in so doing, is altered by the experience. Thus, what we needed was a dynamic memory, one that changes as it is used.

In a book that I wrote around that time (Schank, 1982), a theory about how such a dynamic memory might operate was developed. The two programs of which I speak, IPP (Lebowitz, 1980) and CYRUS (Kolodner, 1980), were attempts to make a first pass at how a dynamic memory might operate.

Here is some sample output from each program:

*(PARSE S1-7)

(10 9 79) SPAIN

(STEPPING UP EFFORTS TO DERAIL A BASQUE HOME RULE STATUTE THAT WILL BE PUT TO A REFERENDUM THIS MONTH BASQUE GUNMEN IN SAN SEBASTIAN SPRAYED A BAR FREQUENTED BY POLICEMEN WITH GUNFIRE WOUNDING 11 PERSONS)

(IN PAMPLONA ANOTHER BASQUE CITY TERRORISTS MURDERED A POLICE INSPECTOR *COMMA* KILLING HIM AS HE DREW HIS OWN WEAPON IN SELF-DEFENSE)

>>> Beginning final memory incorporation . . .

Feature analysis:	EV1 (S-DESTRUCTIVE-ATTACK)	
RESULTS	HEALTH	−10
	AU	HURT-PERSON
	HEALTH	−5
	5	
VICTIM	NUMBER	MANY
	ROLE	AUTHORITY
TARGET	PLACE	BAR
ACTOR	NATIONALITY	BASQUE
METHODS	AU	$SHOOT-ATTACK
LOCATION	AREA	WESTERN-EUROPE
	NATION	SPAIN

Indexing EV1 (S1-7) as variant of S-DESTRUCTIVE-ATTACK

>>> Memory incorporation complete

(5 15 80) SPAIN

(A BASQUE SEPARATIST GUERILLA SHOT TO DEATH THREE

YOUNG NATIONAL POLICEMEN AT POINT BLANK RANGE
THURSDAY AS THEY DRANK THEIR MORNING COFFEE IN A
BAR)

>>> Beginning final memory incorporation . . .

Feature analysis: EV5 (S-DESTRUCTIVE-ATTACK)
   TARGET   PLACE   BAR
   VICTIM   GENDER   MALE
               ROLE   AUTHORITY
   ACTOR   NATIONALITY BASQUE
               DEMAND-TYPE SEPARATISM
   METHODS   AU $SHOOT-ATTACK
   LOCATION   AREA   WESTERN-EUROPE
               NATION   SPAIN

Creating more specific S-DESTRUCTIVE-ATTACK
   (G1-1: BASQUE-GEN) from events EV1 (S1-7)
   EV5 (S1-6) with features:

VICTIM	(1)	GENDER	MALE
		ROLE	AUTHORITY
ACTOR	(1)	NATIONALITY	BASQUE
METHODS	(1)	AU	$SHOOT-ATTACK
LOCATION	(1)	AREA	WESTERN-EUROPE
		NATION	SPAIN
TARGET	(1)	PLACE	BAR

>>> Memory incorporation complete

'Terrorist attacks in Spain are often shootings
  of policemen in bars by Basques'

    IPP was written by Michael Lebowitz as part of his Ph.D. thesis at Yale.
The major intention of IPP was to add to its knowledge structures by forming
new structures as a result of what it read. Above, the program makes a new
generalization about Basque terrorist attacks which it constructed for itself
after reading the above three stories.
    CYRUS was a memory program that received from FRUMP (De Jong,
1979) all the stories it could find about Cyrus Vance, who was Secretary of
State at the time (it later had to switch to MUSKIE). It compiled a history of
Cyrus Vance, both professional and personal. We did this as an attempt to
begin to model the memory of a particular individual. We wanted the
program constantly to change itself on the basis of its new experiences.

@CYRUS

ARE YOU INTERESTED IN MUSKIE OR VANCE? (M OR V):
*VANCE

*(DIALOG2)

>When was the last time you were in Egypt?

    inferring a diplomatic trip
    answering question using time context

ON DEC 10 1978.

>Why did you go there?

    answering question using previous context

TO NEGOTIATE THE CAMP DAVID ACCORDS.

>Who did you talk to there?

    inferring undifferentiated political meeting
    answering question using previous context

WITH ANWAR SADAT.

>Has your wife ever met Mrs Begin?

    inferring a social political occasion

YES, MOST RECENTLY AT A STATE DINNER IN ISRAEL IN
JAN 1980.

>What heads of state have you met?

    inferring a diplomatic meeting
    searching directly for $MEET
    . . .

    applying strategies to search memory
    . . .

    searching for sM-CONFERENCE
    . . .

    searching for sM-VIPVISIT
    searching sM-VIPVISIT instance for $MEET
    . . .

    searching for I-NEGOTIATE
    . . .

KING HASSAN, MENACHEM BEGIN, MUSTAFA KHALIL, IAN SMITH, PRESIDENT ASSAD, KING HUSSEIN AND ANWAR SADAT.

>Last time you went to Saudi Arabia, where did you stay?

inferring a diplomatic trip
answering question using time context

IN A PALACE IN SAUDI ARABIA ON SEP 23 1978.

>Did you go sightseeing there?

answering question using previous context

YES, AT AN OILFIELD IN DHARAN ON SEP 23 1978.

CYRUS was written by Janet Kolodner as part of her Ph.D. thesis at Yale. Perhaps the most interesting thing to point out about CYRUS was its ability to answer questions about which it had no direct information. When CYRUS responded above that Mrs Begin had met Mrs Vance it was actually just guessing. It figured that if it could find a situation when both women were likely to be present then it could assume that they had met. It thus looked for social situations (to which wives might have been invited) that occurred on trips that either one of the men might have made with his wife to the home of the other. Finding a state dinner in Israel that occurred during a trip where Mrs Vance did accompany her husband, it assumed the rest.

On a crude level, both CYRUS and IPP could get reminded of a previous story, and compare the two in search of some general characteristics. For example, IPP came to some generalizations on its own derived from what it read. It decided that every terrorist attack in Ireland was by the IRA; in every terrorist attack in New Zealand the weapon was a boomerang; and that every time there was a hijacking in Lebanon it was in protest of the disappearance of a Shiite Muslim leader. But more and more, we came to realize that scripts, plans, goals and cross-textual referencing were not the only crucial elements of an understanding system. Understanding a story can involve everything a person has ever known. We began to realize the importance of a *dynamic* memory, one that changes every time it understands a story.

A dynamic memory would be able to find experiences in its past to help it understand a new event. A program equipped with such a memory would read a story differently each time it saw it, since it would be updating memory the first time, but be bored the second time. Or alternatively, it might learn more from it the second time, if it had gathered many new experiences that related to the subject of that story in the interim. Our early programs never changed their processing structures as a result of reading a new story.

The key point about those programs is that they were changed to some extent by their experiences and that they used their experiences to interpret their domains. They each had a serious theoretical flaw however. This was not a flaw that one can attribute to poor thinking or programming on the part of their authors. Rather, their flaw was the kind of flaw we often see in AI, one of the inadequate development of a theory because of the lack of perspective.

In other words, when one is trying to remedy problems with programs and ideas that have come before, one can try so hard to remedy those problems that one creates new problems. Sometimes these problems are simply conceptual ones. That is, you fail to see the forest because you are so involved with the trees.

Well then, what is the main problem with IPP? Below is the classic example from which it was decided to work on IPP:

An Arabic-speaking gunman shot his way into the Iraqi Embassy here (Paris) yesterday morning, held hostages through most of the day before surrendering to French policemen and then was shot by Iraqi security officials as he was led away by the French officers.

The premise here was simple enough. I was reading the *New York Times* one morning, read this story, and wondered how we could get a computer to have the same kind of reaction to it that I had had. I was amazed that the Iraqi security guards had shot the terrorist *after* he had been captured by French police. I expected no such thing. My problem was: how to get the computer to know enough to be able to read the story and understand it up to the point where the unexpected event occurs. At that point, we would expect that a sophisticated program would be amazed and surprised by the subsequent events. To do this, we needed a theory of expectation-based top-down processing that could, in some sense, turn around and be bottom up in attempting to understand something for which it could not have had expectations.

IPP was an attempt to implement a theory about how this was done, which also attempted to integrate parsing and memory operations. The idea was that if we knew enough about terrorism we would know how to quickly process common, everyday events that were expected and we could attempt to learn something new from items that were different in that they were unexpected, by storing them and comparing them to other expectation violations of a similar type.

Well, that was the idea anyhow.

Today, I am perplexed by a different problem. It is a problem which comes from the work that has followed the development of IPP and which has made me go back and think about that program again.

After IPP and CYRUS were finished, students at our lab began an effort aimed at attacking, in turn, the problems of reminding, explanation, indexing and learning. Let me explain why these problems came up so that it will be clear where what I am about to propose fits in.

REMINDING

It became clear to us, while we were working on problems of language understanding, that memory phenomena had to be considered in the overall understanding process. After all, people do not understand things in a vacuum. They relate what they know to what they are trying to find out. One way in which they exhibit their ability to do this is expressed by their capacity to be *reminded*.

In our progression from the use of static knowledge structures (such as scripts) towards our use of dynamic memory structures (such as MOPs and TOPs; see Schank, 1982) in our programs, the phenomenon of reminding stood out. Sometimes, we are simply reminded, during the processing of a current event, of an event almost identical to it. Often, this becomes the prototype for events of that kind, and we can interpret the new event *in terms of* the prototype. This is, of course, a type of reminding.

Often, however, not all of the remindings we experience are so straightforward. We might be reminded of an event that is superficially unlike the event being processed, but resembles it in a deeper way. Data that we collected over a period of years indicated that a surprisingly large percentage of remindings of this type were grounded in *expectation failures*. That is, our memories had created a set of expectations (from the standard prototype for the event being processed), and one of these expectations had failed in the sense that something entirely different occurred.

My favorite example of this type of reminding is the 'Steak and the Haircut' story from Schank (1982):

The Steak and the Haircut

X described how his wife would never make his steak as rare as he liked it. When this was told to Y, it reminded him of a time, 30 years earlier, when he tried to get his hair cut in England and the barber just wouldn't cut it as short as he wanted it.

The key issue that reminding examples like this bring up is the problem of indexing and explanation. It seems clear enough why we get reminded. We get reminded so that we can compare old experiences to our current experience. In that way, instead of using a prototype that has been found to be in error (an expectation has failed after all) we can use in its place an experience from memory that is much more like the current experience. Not only that, but it is like it in that the same kind of expectation failed in it as well. So, not only do we process more intelligently in this way, we also learn from our experiences.

Getting reminded is useful since new expectations can be generated and, more importantly, by comparing the two experiences (the remindee and the remindand), something new can be learned. That is, the combination of the two can allow for new generalizations to be made that capture the expectation failures in each, creating a new memory structure that has correct expectations in it for what can now be seen as a new situation, different from the previous prototype which contained the failed expectation.

The principle of dynamic memory which the phenomenon of reminding illustrates is that, in the process of understanding, we are changed by what we have understood. Understanding is, in essence, a learning process.

EXPLANATIONS AND INDEXING

Work in reminding and dynamic memory systems that change as they understand, led naturally into our current work on explanation. Not only do failed expectations match across remindings, but the explanations of why the expectations failed also matched. Thus, the explanation in the 'Steak and the Haircut' story is the same for the remindee and the remindand, namely, *the person in the service role must have believed that what was requested was too extreme to actually do*.

From that point we embarked on a series of projects that exemplified the human ability to construct explanations. When a football coach uses a play and it does not work, he must construct an explanation of why it did not work. Similarly, when a chef creates a new recipe that does not work, or when a predictor of horse races, weather or the stock market makes a prediction that is wrong, he must revise his current theory. In each case, what is required is an explanation of why what he thought before did not work.

Here again we can see the valuable role of reminding. In constructing an explanation of why a particular plan failed, the explanation itself can bring to mind another similar plan that failed. Those two plans, taken together, can form the basis of a new plan that would be an improvement on the old.

The cycle is: failure, explanation, reminding, generalization.

Seen this way, the role of reminding is as conscious *verification* for a subconscious explanation. That is, in constructing an explanation what we are doing is creating an hypothesis about why something did not work. Often, we cannot state these explanations and we barely have conscious access to them. These hypotheses can be verified and brought to our active conscious processing, if additional evidence can be found. That is where remindings come in.

One of my favorite examples of this explanation/reminding cycle is in the *Puerto Rican Hotel and Connecticut Road Signs* example:

> I was walking along the beach in Puerto Rico and noticed signs saying that it is unsafe to swim yet everyone is swimming and it is clearly safe.

I explained this to myself, after seeing a second sign of a different sort, warning about the dangers of walking in a given place, by assuming that the hotel that put up these signs was just trying to cover itself legally in case of an accident.

At this point, that is, after the explanation, I was reminded of signs in Connecticut that say 'road legally closed' when the road is in full use. I had previously explained these signs to myself in the same way.

The hard part in all this is the problem of indexing. It is clear that we need to find specific memories to help us in processing current events. The question is how to find them. It seems that the answer may well be in the explanation process. If memories have little tags or labels on them that help us retrieve them, those tags would appear to be strongly related to explanations. That is, if we find memories when we have constructed an explanation, it would seem obvious that the explanation itself is one possible index to that specific event in memory. Explanations are not the only possible indices into memory, but they are certainly an important type.

In any case, the indexing problem is critically important since finding a relevant memory to compare to the current event is a critical aspect of understanding. Any system has to employ indices that are somehow related to the goals that it has. In other words, we should label an incoming event by the features of that event that interest us. The features that interest us obviously relate to our particular goals. This theme is discussed some with respect to TOPs in Schank (1982) and I will not pursue it here.

Explanations, remindings and indexing are, in part, goal-based. But, most of our understanding programs failed to have any real goals of their own. Or, to put this another way, what is it that IPP was trying to find out when it was reading about terrorists? Or perhaps more interestingly, what was *I* trying to find out when I read about *the Arabic-speaking gunman in Paris*?

CYRUS

Now I would like to digress for a moment and talk about CYRUS, a program that was done at the same time as IPP, whose underlying philosophy is fairly similar.

CYRUS was an attempt to model one particular individual's memory, to the extent that that could be done. It got its data from news stories about Cyrus Vance and then attempted to place these stories in a dynamic memory structure that would enable them to be found again. CYRUS was not an understanding program since the stories had already been processed for it (either by hand or by FRUMP, another of our text-understanding programs (DeJong, 1979). Rather, it was a new kind of storage and retrieval program, one that employed a dynamic memory similar in philosophy to that used in IPP.

One area of particular interest in CYRUS was how it answered questions.

Its job was to answer questions about the experiences of Cyrus Vance as he traveled around the world in his role as Secretary of State. To do this, the program has to invent and reinvent categories in memory in which to place new stories as they became available. Since one could not easily anticipate everything that Cyrus Vance might ever experience, these categories had to be created dynamically as new stories were received.

Consequently, when answering a question about Cyrus Vance, CYRUS had to be able to reformulate the question in its own terms. That is, CYRUS knew where it had stored given stories and when it was asked about one of them it had to determine exactly which story it knew about that was germane to the answer and where it might find that story in its memory.

Because of this, CYRUS wound up doing something which was quite interesting. The question-answering module in CYRUS had to be written in such a way as to enable it to take a question, determine whether it could answer that question directly, and if it could not, it would have to reinterpret that question as a question that it believed that it could answer. This *question transformation process* is a crucial aspect of understanding.

To illustrate what I am talking about, consider the following I/O from CYRUS:

>Has your wife ever met Mrs Begin?
YES, MOST RECENTLY AT A STATE DINNER IN ISRAEL IN
JAN 1980.

The question is, how did CYRUS answer this question? In fact, CYRUS did not have the information contained in its answer in its memory in any way. Nevertheless it was able to answer the question. It did so by transforming the question into a series of questions, as follows:

Q1: Did your wife ever meet Mrs Begin?

  Q2: Where would they have met?

    Q3: Under what circumstances do diplomat's wives meet?

      Q4: Under what circumstances do diplomats meet?

      A4: On state visits to each other's countries.
          At international conferences.

    A3: When they accompany their husbands on these visits.

    Q3a: When did Vance go to Israel?
    Q3b: When did Begin go to the US?

    A3a/A3b: Various dates can now be retrieved from memory.

Q3c: Did their wives accompany any of them on any of these trips?
A3c: A trip where this happened is found.

Q2a: During what part of a trip would wives meet?
A2a: During a state dinner.

Final revised question: Was there a state dinner on May 24, 1977 during the diplomatic visit that Vance made to Israel with his wife?

Answer (A1): Probably on May 24, 1977 in Jerusalem at a state dinner in which they were both present.

The point here is that the question transformation process is a way of getting an answerable question from an unanswerable one. The original question is unanswerable because it gives no help as to where in memory we might search for the relevant facts. Through a series of transformations, this original question is changed into one about the dates of diplomatic visits and state dinners, both of which the program knows to have been used as categories in which to store information.

CYRUS seems smart because it can answer questions. Now this may seem like an obvious thing that most AI understanding programs can do. And, in fact, it is fairly easy to get a program to retrieve facts from a data base and thus answer questions. Actually, any intelligence attributed to CYRUS should be because it could *ask* questions. Asking questions is at the heart of intelligence.

IPP REVISITED

So, how does CYRUS compare to IPP? CYRUS is, in some sense a far more interesting program because it knows more about what it knows and it can ask about what it does not know. My problem with IPP (in principle that is, the same is true of all of our understanding programs) is that it does not *ask*, in any profound way. CYRUS does not ask all that much, but it is capable of posing answerable questions to replace unanswerable ones. Thus, it seems to want to know things more than IPP does. To what extent does IPP ask questions? To what extent does this matter in its attempt to be a model of an understander?

The major problem with IPP is that IPP never was actually astonished by the shooting of the Iraqi gunman after he had been captured by the French police. True, IPP was able to produce a sentence that voiced its *surprise* saying essentially that it did not have any expectations or knowledge structures available for interpreting this part of the event. Thus an expectation violation had occurred.

An expectation failure occurs when something that is expected fails to appear or when something occurs that was not anticipated. Either way, the terrorism MOP can be altered with a notation that a gunman had been shot by his own people, so that next time it would be able to be reminded of this by a similar kind of experience, thus allowing us to alter the terrorism MOP accordingly.

In essence, what IPP was capable of doing was to characterize an odd circumstance in such a way that it was possible to find it again when a similar circumstance arose. This is the indexing problem and is the significant issue in IPP.

Recently I read this story to someone who was reminded of how Israelis attempt to shoot Palestinian terrorists in similar situations on the grounds that if they were captured by the French, for example, the French would more than likely be too nice to them (from the Israeli point of view). It is quite possible to be reminded of such a fact and to determine that in this case it is not too relevant.

The issue here, however, is that, in the absence of the type of reminding mentioned above, a reader has an uneasy feeling about this story. Certainly I was quite fascinated by it when I read it. I wanted to know why the gunman was shot. It is true that I was surprised by the ending of the story, but that is really not what is so interesting about it. After reading it I found myself speculating about it. I wondered why they did that.

I began to create hypotheses:

- Maybe the French intended to release the Iraqi. (This is the Palestinian reminding case.)
- Maybe the Iraqis were afraid that this guy would say something damaging to them.
- Maybe they were afraid that he would be used as a *cause célèbre* by some dissident group.

No matter what the true answer, there is reason to believe that the Iraqi security guards had some underlying motive.

When we see something in a story that we could not have anticipated, we can safely assume that the event under consideration had some justification or purpose. We do not simply assume that expectation failures are random events not to be further bothered about. We assume, especially when the unexpected event involves a plan on the part of other people, that they had some motives and intentions and we wonder about what they were. Thus, a great deal of what understanding is about, in principle, is our ability to comprehend an unexpected event by making a hypothesis that accounts for how and why that event happened.

But this is very different from what IPP was doing. IPP was attempting to account for what was happening by finding previous events that were like the current one and comparing the two. This is, of course, a method that is quite useful. It forms the basis for dynamic memory as proposed in Schank (1982).

The idea is simply that by being reminded of one experience by a like experience, we can compare the two experiences and see what they have in common, thus allowing us to create better expectations in the future.

But we are capable of creating explanations *de novo*. We can come up with an explanation without coming up with an initial reminding. In fact, reminding often serves as a *verification* of an explanation, (see Schank, 1984). It seems obvious that we do come up with explanations just by looking at the facts, utilizing whatever principles are relevant to that process.

The key point here is that the program has to have, in some sense, a healthy curiosity. It has to want to know about things. In this instance, it has to care about the motivations of people and the specific plans used by terrorist, police, governments and so on. It has to care about these things in some non-artificial sense.

What we are talking about here is justifying actions of characters that we are hearing about by having a hypothesis for what motives them. Having a sense of understanding why a character in a given role does what he does is critical to understanding. In IPP this sense of the plans for characters it knew about was rather superficial, enough so that when a character acted differently from the norm it had no ability to question it. An understanding program should have a series of questions that are always ready to go. For example:

Why is this character doing what he is doing?
What are his motivations?
What are his plans?
What is his intention?

IPP should have wanted to know why the Iraqi gunman was shot. And, in wondering about it, it should have begun to speculate about it, to hazard some guesses.

Now, it should not have to ask that about every action that occurs in a story. It should not be wondering why a terrorist was armed because it would have already explained such things to itself after having encountered its first terrorism story.

What we mean when we say that we have understood something is that we have been able to either find an explanation that we have previously stored (either gotten whole from someone else or constructed on our own), or that we have successfully constructed an explanation of an event for which we had no relevant prior experience.

That is, to understand something means to be able to *re-cognize* it as something that has been *cognized* before. In a sense we are saying that, yes, I have already explained this before, so I will not have to explain it again. Understanding means having already explained it, and being able to access that explanation. In the case where you have not already explained an event like it, when something is novel in that sense, the issue becomes:

What questions are extant in my memory and how do those questions relate to the depth of the explanation that is required in this case?

In other words, you might explain the Iraqi security guards' actions by saying that they are just people with guns who shoot everything, or that they do not like this guy, or that he had hurt them during the time that he held hostages and that they were taking retribution. These are fairly superficial explanations.

Actually, as understanders, we look for more complicated, in-depth explanations. However, in order to get in-depth explanations you have to have been asking in-depth questions. The question of why the security guards did what they did can be answered at a rather simplistic level. But, of course, the issue in enhancing computers with a real understanding capability is to get them to ask questions of a much greater complexity.

For example, we might wonder about what this event tells us about the nature of security guards, or about the nature of the political relationship between Iraq and France. We might wonder about the increasing acceptability of terrorism in embassies throughout the world, or about the feelings and attitudes of people who have been held hostage. Each of these questions, once posed, causes us to construct an explanation that has that question at its base. That is, the question, once posed, biases the answer. Or, to put this another way, when there is a difficulty in understanding, the questions that are already present in our minds will direct the explanation process.

Suppose, for example, that the Iraqi security guards who did the shooting were the ones held hostage by the gunman. Then, certainly, retribution would have been a reasonable explanation of the subsequent shooting. So, it seems fairly important to pose the question of whether or not that were the case before deciding upon an explanation of the event. Issues such as what the actors may have been feeling, or what the gunman's fellow travelers might have done to relatives of the guards are relevant here. In other words, in order to understand fully, we have to call to mind knowledge of what revenge is about. Or, we have to be able to speculate that the action by the guards might be viewed as heroic action within the Iraqi culture. Perhaps when guards behave in this fashion they are considered to be 'heroes of the revolution'.

In order to create such explanations it is necessary to have the capability of making the inquiry that fosters the explanation. The explanation you create for yourself depends upon the questions that you ask. It is the question that is key here, not the answer. So, the question for us is, in this example, how do you pose the question, *could retribution have been a factor?* Unfortunately, we seem to have a vicious cycle here. The only way one could possibly pose a question about whether retribution might have been a factor is to somehow have had access to the idea that retribution might be a possible explanation. Which comes first?

THE RELEVANCE OF EXPLANATION PATTERNS

The basic cycle that I have in mind here is:

BASIC OPERATING QUESTIONS
FAILURE QUESTIONS
EXPLANATION PATTERNS
SPECIFIC QUESTIONS
EXPLANATIONS

To explain what I mean by this, we must diverge slightly to discuss explanation patterns.

An explanation pattern is a fossilized explanation. It functions in much the same way as a script does. When it is activated, it connects a to-be-explained event with an explanation that has been used at some time in the past to explain an event similar to the current event.

Explanation patterns are stored together with the failure questions that they answer. These questions are very standard prototypical questions, not specific to any given situation. They are, however, present because of the existence of the goals that are likely to be operative during processing. In other words, they are questions about why the goals that were being pursued did not work out quite the way they were supposed to.

Once a failure question is deemed to be of interest, various indices associated with the event to be explained can be used to activate one or more explanation patterns that may apply. Some failure questions that illustrate this process are:

1. What are the immediate consequences of this event?
2. What factors in the nature of the society in which we live might have caused this event to occur?
3. What group is the actor a member of that might have allowed us to predict this action because it is common to members of the group?
4. Are there other groups like the one to which the actor belongs that might shed light on the action of this group?
5. Did some physical event cause this action?
6. Are there unknown strategies that are standard in certain groups?
7. Was this action part of a counterplan to block some foreseen action?

The above questions are part of a standard set of questions that are used to help in explanations (Schank *et al.*, 1985). They tend to be relevant across domains for explaining expectation failures. Simply put, the idea is that these questions are normally fired off when a goal is unclear. They, in turn, have fairly standard answers.

A failure question can be best understood by analogy to the primitive actions in Conceptual Dependency Theory (Schank, 1975). The real value or meaning of the primitive actions was the set of inferences that they fired off. When a primitive action represents a part of an event, its real value is in the creation of a set of other actions which are also likely to be true.

The same situation exists with failure questions. The real import of these questions is in the fact that their answers are fairly standard. Explanation patterns are indexed under each question and these patterns fire off as likely hypotheses when various conditions are present.

To put this another way, in the case of question 1, various explanation patterns can be caused to 'come to mind' to be used in the current case, if they are indexed correctly. An explanation pattern is a standard stereotyped answer, with an explanation, to a question. For example, question 1 has within it the concept of a BENEFICIARY of the action. Thus the index BENEFICIARY OF DEATH might point to an explanation pattern asserting the death was caused by someone who would benefit by it. Many more specific questions are indexed under the standard failure question. In this case, the question is:

Who would benefit from the gunman's death?

For example, a standard explanation pattern for such a question relates to money. We know that one beneficiary of a death is someone who might inherit the deceased's money. We also know that another beneficiary of a death is someone who has an insurance policy made out to him on the life of the dead person. Both of these explanation patterns seem fairly irrelevant in this case. Nevertheless, they can be thought up and 'tried on for size' to see how well they work. Creating the hypothesis that the guards stood to inherit the gunman's estate may seem bizarre, but it is the beginning of a creative explanation, and that is what we are after. Why this one seems so wrong is also part of the issue to be dealt with. What is important here is that we have a procedure to create such hypotheses.

An explanation pattern consists of a number of parts. First, we have an index to the pattern. This index is made up of a combination of states and events. The next part is essentially a little story, a carefully constructed causal chain of states and events that starts with the premise of achieving the combination of states and events in the index and presents a plan of action for achieving that combination.

Essentially, the failure poses a question, and the explanation pattern answers that question. But, this question is in the most general terms. The question is not about the gunman's death, but about beneficiaries of death in general. The answer is not about the gunman, but about prior experiences with the general phenomenon. In the next step in the process, the particulars of the event are matched. So, if the proposed hypothesis is silly, it can be discarded.

Explanation patterns, then, are standard explanations. They are stored in terms of the failure questions, but there are a great many patterns per question. Indices are needed to get a relevant pattern out after having established a pertinent question. For the questions listed above, here are some explanation patterns:

1. What are the immediate consequences of this event?
   Index—beneficiary: killed for the insurance money.
   Index—employees: under orders to kill the opposition.
2. What factors in the nature of the society in which we live might have caused this event to occur?
   Index—embassy: increasing violence in embassies must be discouraged.
   Index—Arabic: fanatic Muslim leaders were making revolution.
3. What group is the actor a member of that might have allowed us to predict this action because it is common to members of the group?
   Index—enemy of Iraq: bringing the war home.
   Index—Arab terrorist: kill him before he is used for a protest.
4. Are there other groups like the one to which the actor belongs that might shed light on the action of this group?
   Index—guard: the police always overreact.
   Index—Arabic, France: the Algerians are still protesting against France.
   The Iraqis do not trust the French either.
5. Did some physical event cause this action?
   Index—time of month: maybe there was a full moon.
6. Are there unknown strategies that are standard in certain groups?
   Index—police: the Iraqis wanted to intimidate the French.
7. Was this action part of a counterplan to block some foreseen action?
   Index—police: the police are too lenient, they would let him go.

These are some examples of standard patterns, that is, ones that would have been compiled from previous experiences in different situations, that might be called up here as candidates to help make an explanation here. The role of explanation patterns is both to be useful in the circumstances for which they were originally intended, as well as to come to mind as hypotheses in situations that are only somewhat related.

TWEAKING REMINDINGS

To summarize: explanation patterns are standard, stereotypical explanations. These *old standards* are stored away, indexed to various standard questions that come up when an explanation is needed. This method of beginning the explanation process is analogous to methods of planning that occur in daily life. We do not plan out new strategies for attaining new goals. Rather, we first attempt to recall previous plans that have worked for achieving goals similar to those we now have in mind. To create a new plan, we modify an old one. (Quite a few computer programmers will admit to writing new programs in this fashion.)

The problem in planning, in this view, is to get reminded of an old plan. Just finding a relevant old plan can be quite difficult. Once one is found, however, the problem in planning is reduced to taking the old plan and modifying it to the task at hand. The adage I have developed therefore is:

> *To plan, get reminded, then, tweak the reminding.* The point here is that the same is true of explanation: *to explain something new, find an old explanation that has worked, and tweak it.*

So, in this example, we are trying to find an explanation pattern, that is, we need to get reminded and modify what we find. If we find an old example where retribution was an appropriate explanation, we must test the various aspects of that explanation to see if it still makes sense after it has been examined in more detail.

> First, we have the standard question, for example: *why do people commit what seems to be unjustified and uncalled-for violence?*
> Second, standard patterns indexed off that question come to mind (i.e. the retribution pattern).
> Third, we must attempt to see if we can reconsider the event in question to see if indeed the old retribution pattern can be made to fit. This means generating one or more additional questions about what events the gunman might have been involved in previously, what the guards were like, who paid them and what instructions were given to them and so on.

All of these questions are derived from the specifications of the old pattern as it applies to the new situation. Thus, if, in order for there to be retribution a prior evil had to be committed, we must ask if the hostage-taking qualified as such an act, or if there were some even more dastardly act in the gunman's past. A great many questions are thus generated in this fashion, each from the combination of a different standard failure question and the pattern that is fired off from it, together with the aspect of pattern that is being called into question.

The role of the standard questions and patterns therefore is to generate new questions. The task is to make the program or the person look at the situation and ask if this could be an example of retribution. Then, many specific questions are generated by accessing the explanation patterns and treating it as a hypothetical explanation. The hypothetical explanation is used to match against the current situation. To the extent that it matches, that match generates questions about whether the match is appropriate; whether the circumstances are very different; or whether some other explanation pattern should be sought.

The generation of a question is the most significant phenomenon that is

going on. It is the questions that we ask that allow for us to be clever enough
to create interesting answers. General questions are indexed under explanation patterns. Specific questions come from there.

THE UNDERSTANDING CYCLE

Returning to IPP for a moment, it is clear that IPP was missing what we can
now term *the basic understanding cycle*. That is, to really understand we must
be able to ask questions, in other words, to wonder about the things we are
reading or hearing about. We must be able to take phenomena that are out of
the domain of our prior experiences and find remindings of two types. First,
and best, we must be able to find remindings that are quite close in spirit to
the experience that we are currently processing. When this is not possible,
that is, when there does not exist a specific relevant memory, indexed under
an explanation of an expectation failure that we construct in an *ad hoc*
manner, or we cannot find that memory, we must be able to take more
neutral, that is less specific, more standard explanation patterns and derive a
set of questions from them.

In a sense, the first kind of reminding is a shortcut, an easy method of
processing a new situation by finding a very closely related old one to contrast
it against. When that path is not open to us, usually because such a memory
simply fails to come to mind, then we must take a more active role. We must
find vaguely related explanation patterns and allow those explanation patterns to drive the questioning process. Or, to put this another way, we must
try to get reminded.

The essence of my hypothesis here is that it is through the creation of these
questions that we understand. IPP, or any understanding program, has to be
operating under a set of questions. Its driving force, so to speak, has to be the
desire to know the answers to questions that are generated during the process
of understanding. That means that if you are going to read a terrorism story,
you have to have some questions which are driving the process. That is, there
has to be some reason why you have begun to read this story in the first place.

Why does one read a story in the newspaper? This may seem like a
whimsical question but a program that is intended to understand a story at
anything more than a superficial level must have some idea about what it
wants to know. When one reads a story like the one about the Iraqi gunman,
one is not just reading it to find out what happened in the Iraqi Embassy in
Paris, one is reading it for some set of personal reasons having to do with
one's cares and concerns about the world. Otherwise there is no reason to
read the story.

So when the story about terrorism comes by, you have to have had a
question in mind such as *I wonder why there is so much terrorism today?* or
What is going on in Paris? or *I wonder if I can find some new material for a*

joke in tonight's monologue? or *How can I better come to understand the world situation by seeing what is going on with terrorism?* or even *I feel the need to know about blood and gore, give me all the details so I will know how to act if it happens to me.* There are all kinds of reasons to read a newspaper story.

It might seem, at first glance, that a person can pick up a newspaper and just read the articles to kill the time, or amuse oneself or whatever. What happens then? Actually what is going on there is that you are letting your background questions take over. There are things you always want to know or always are curious about; hundreds of them, maybe thousands. You do not have to be thinking of them explicitly when you pick up the newspaper. They are there all the time, ready to be answered.

In other words, we cannot expect to build an understanding program that has no reason to read. It can have specific information it wants to find out, but then it will not find out anything else. I do not think that it is really possible to build a newspaper reader that does not have some questions it is trying to answer that are at a level greater than that of the specific article it is considering at any given time. Such a program would fail to make use of anything at all unusual in what it read.

If we were to start work on a new understanding program, one of the main issues would be how to have it approach every situation with a set of questions. Now this may remind you to some extent of FRUMP (DeJong, 1979) which, I believe, was methodologically correct as a program in the sense that it did have questions. These questions were not posed in the form of questions. They were posed as requests or conditions. The requests, translated into English questions, were *What was the Richter scale reading in the earthquake?*; or *How much damage did it cause?*; or *How many people died?*

These are questions, but they are too simplistic. I do not think people who read earthquake stories really spend their time asking about the Richter scale reading in any significant sense. We may have a bottom-up routine that says *if it is over 7 take note and recall the San Francisco earthquake of 1906.* In any case, these are fairly dull questions. FRUMP's problem was that it worked on dull stories.

If we were to attempt to make it work on interesting stories, or if we were going to attempt to do earthquakes in an interesting way, we would want to be able to start the understanding process with a hypothesis. The next generation of newspaper-reading programs will have to have a set of questions at their heart that drives the understanding process. They are, in essence, the reason that the program is reading the story. These questions would have to be more profound than *How many people died?* or *What is the latest news, I want to summarize it.* Such an attitude is all right for transmitting information but it is not good for absorbing information. The difference between transmitting information and absorbing information is profound.

Any program has to have a set of questions that constitute its starting point. They would have been generated as the result of previous experiences (other news stories perhaps) that raised these questions but failed to answer them. In some sense then, the input to the understanding process is the story *and* a set of questions. And the output is another set of questions. In the process of understanding, we answer some questions and raise others. This is not an infinite loop because, presumably, the questions that are being raised are somewhat more sophisticated than those that are being answered.

Thus, what we need to get real understanding is what I will call *question-driven understanding*. These questions can come from all kinds of areas. For example, they can come from old stories, that is, old remindings that you wonder about with incompletely understood parts. The Iraqi gunman story, if no certain explanation were arrived at, would become a set of questions which may drive the understanding of another story related to those issues. That is what reminding is really all about. The question in that case, is: *are there any other instances of this bizarre behavior that might help me better understand that story?* That kind of question might lay around passively, for years, waiting for an answer. Questions such as this wait, under the surface, looking for an answer. And, of course, there are questions that lie right at the surface, questions that we explicitly and consciously worry about. Lastly, there are underlying thematic questions that you are kind of always looking for the answer to consciously in the sense that you know you are looking for them, but unconsciously in the sense that there are not on your mind all the time. The distinction between these types of questions and the specific embodiment of each of them, is necessary in any understanding program we might develop.

SOME QUESTIONS

Viewing IPP in terms of the questions that it could ask (and therefore could answer), we can see that IPP functioned at what we might call the *journalist level*. It asked *who, what, where and when* questions. This is not terribly surprising—after all, it was reading newspaper stories. These journalist-level questions were programmed as expectations (or requests) and they were part of an overall system that also had the task of doing the basic language analysis.

It seems safe to say that people do have these journalist-level questions in mind when they read a story. (That is why journalists seek to answer them in their pieces, after all.) When one hears a story that does not present all the above information, one is very likely to attempt to fill in the roles and slots either by inference or by specifically asking (in the case of an interactive situation) so that one can know who did what, when and where. The major problem, from one point of view, with IPP is that these questions were not self-generated. In other words, IPP did not *want* to know these things.

Rather, it was told to ask about them (by the programmer). Quite naturally, this is true about all our programs. Such questions are put in the program (although not always in the form of questions), before the program actually attempts to read a story. We inform the program that reading means attempting to answer these questions. But what we do not do is tell the program to inquire about what it needs to know.

Now, there is a subtle difference between these two things. Asking a question comes from a need to know. It comes from wondering about something, or being interested in some aspect of something. The argument here is that you really cannot get a program to understand in any deep sense unless it is interested in what it is reading about.

You can say the same thing about people. It is not really possible for a person to really understand what they are reading unless they are really interested in it. A good example of this is a typist who is typing something from a dictaphone or tape recorder. The typist needs to hear the words but does not need to understand in any deep sense. The typist is not expected to understand what is being typed, and will not, unless the typist happens to be interested in the subject matter. The typist is unlikely to even try to understand it. As I have said, interest is derived from having a set of questions.

One of the reasons why a typist or a translator (this is another example of the same phenomenon) is unlikely to really understand what they are typing or translating is because it is likely they are not interested in it. A translator at the UN might be interested in international events to some extent, but in pursuit of their job as translator there is some question as to whether they can even *try* to understand what they are translating. It goes by too fast, and they have too much to do, to consider allowing their minds to begin to question what they are hearing.

Thus, what happens is that they really do not understand what they are hearing or reading. Now, I am not suggesting that they could not tell you a little about what was said or answer a few questions. Rather, they would not naturally be able to ask questions. The asking is of paramount importance. Now, of course, IPP could be reformulated so that it was capable of asking questions. The problem would be whether or not those questions would be heart-felt. That is, would it really want to know the answers?

This may seem a little silly since it is difficult to establish the true feelings of a machine and one is inclined to assume that the default answer is that there are not any feelings there at all. The more sensible thing to demand is that the questions be self-generated. That is, were the questions there prior to seeing the story or after seeing the story?

Instead of demanding *Does the program* really *want to know the answer*, we can investigate *How did the program come to want to ask the question?* If it were just told to ask the question, that might be a nice simulation but it would somehow be different from having generated the question on its own. We can tell a child, or a student, a reporter, what questions to ask; it is when they ask them on their own that we feel we have accomplished something. The program has to really want to know; it must generate its own questions.

How would a program get to *genuinely want to know*? In order to want to know, you must have a set of goals. There must be something driving the system so that there is some end that is in mind. In a sense, I am arguing that what was really wrong with IPP was that IPP (or FRUMP or SAM) did not start from a set of BASIC OPERATING QUESTIONS which they needed to answer. All their questions were very specific to their domains. They did not have a set of hypotheses that were driving them. (This is not a criticism of these works, of course, but merely an expansion of them. The goals of the designers of these programs were to test out basic ideas for the first pass at automated story understanding. All I am saying is that now it is time for a second pass.)

Of course, one could simply give IPP a set of hypotheses. One can attempt to develop a theory of terrorists—who they are, what they do, why they do it, and we can attempt to predict how a given terrorist will act, or where terrorism might be likely to occur.

In that case, such a program might not pay attention to the article we are considering—being shot by the Iraqi security guards. It might not find it interesting with respect to an overall hypothesis about terrorism on which it was working. On the other hand, maybe it would be. Maybe what we really want to do in a hypothesis-driven system is to be able to generate any possibly relevant question every time. We might find a program saying, of each event, *Is this of interest to my goals? How can I relate this to my goals?* If the goal is to track terrorists, to make predictions about terrorists, then the issue is, for any given action involving a terrorist, the extent to which that action relates to the overall theory.

The issue then is, what kinds of questions should we be asking? Journalistic-level questions are really the lowest level of questions to ask. The second level of questions, again at a very low level in the sense that they are fairly primitive to the concept of understanding, are those such as: *How does this action affect me? How does the action affect my goals? How is the action related to my goals?* The goals we are talking about here are those of the reader, so the argument here is simply this: you cannot write a very effective language-understanding program unless it has goals or interests of its own, that cause it to question what it reads with respect to those goals or interests.

TYPES OF QUESTIONS

We ask all kinds of questions all the time. To teach machines (and possibly also people) to ask these questions, we need to have a good sense of the kinds of questions that there are to ask. I have divided up the questions that I believe to be of significance to a creative and analytical understanding system into four broad levels.

Questions: Level One

The first type of questions, which I call **level one questions**, are the type of questions that no one needs to be taught to ask (except maybe a machine). By and large they are the kind of questions that programs such as IPP have, implicitly or explicitly, been asking all along. Any planning system must ask them as well.

They are questions that one asks naturally, that are essential to being alive. Some of these questions are to some extent forgotten as a person gets older. Some should continue to be asked—for example, basic assumptions about how things work, which are taught to children as a religion, not to be questioned, ought to be re-asked from time to time. The primary point is that people do ask these questions, although they often get afraid to ask them. Young children ask them all the time, but less so as they get older. Machines will have to learn to ask them too, but these are the least of the problem in asking questions since they are the simplest questions to ask.

First-level questions: Self-centered

Why does this matter to me?
How would this affect me or those close to me?

First-level questions: Plans of Others

Why did he do that? (What is in it for him?)
What are his intentions towards me?
What is he trying to communicate?

Questions: Level Two

Second-level questions are those that one is taught to ask in the normal course of a standard education. Not everyone learns to ask these questions because not everyone gets a decent education; however, learning to ask these questions is what a basic education is all about. The reason we learn to write essays or participate in arguments or debates is partially so that we can learn to do the kind of reasoning implicit in the asking of these questions.

Second-level questions: Journalism

Who did it?
Where did he do it?

When did he do it?
What did he do?

Second-level questions: Causality

What circumstances could be the case such that that would happen?
Are the facts consistent?

Second-level questions: Argumentation/Rhetoric

What evidence would support that argument?
What counterexamples are there to that premise?
What would have to be true in order for that to follow?

Questions: Level Three

Third-level questions are those that people are rarely taught to ask. The fact that machines should be taught to ask them might seem questionable in that case. But, in some sense, we are demanding that machines reach a level of understanding that is fairly complex. Many people have failed to achieve this level of understanding. These questions form the basis of a fundamental analytical mind. Scientists and scholars learn to ask these questions, but they often so engross themselves in the answer to any one of them that they forget to continue asking more of them. Machines, if they are to be good thinkers, must learn to ask them too. The trick, of course, is to learn when to ask them and when not to ask them.

Third-level questions: Understanding/Coherence

What other event do I have in memory that is like the current one?
What information am I missing that would make these events coherent?
What other events like the current one would cause me to rethink a basic hypothesis?
What would make me believe that a given action makes sense (when it does not seem to right now?)

Third-level questions: Prediction-making

What theory of that event would I have had to have had in order to have correctly anticipated that outcome?
What plan was being pursued that, had I known it, would have made a given action predictable?
What states of the world would have had to have been the case in order for a given event to have followed naturally from them?

Third-level questions: Strategies

Why would someone do something one way when another way seems better?
How do we determine the ultimate cost and benefits of an action?
How can you get someone to believe something that will enable your action to
    succeed?

Third-level questions: History/Epistemology

How can someone who has asserted a fact have come to have known that
    fact?
Who would they have to have known in order to have known that?
How could they possibly be in a position to have come to know that?
Where were they when they found that out?
What kind of analysis could they have used in order to be able to figure out
    that kind of thing?

Third-level questions: Economics/Sociology

How could a more equitable distribution have been made?
What kinds of things can be done to make things fairer?
Why were not things done to ensure fairness?
Who profits from the current state of affairs?

Third-level questions: Anthropology/Physics

Why was any given planned state of the world planned the way it was?
What do various states of the planned world tell us about the people who did
    the planning?
What do various states of the physical world tell us about the rules that govern
    our lives?

Questions: Level Four

Fourth-level questions are really those upon which the essence of creativity
hinges. These can be very basic or very obtuse. They often differ in different
fields of inquiry, sometimes bringing one field of inquiry's standard set of
questions to another field of inquiry to which they are not ordinarily applied.
Machines will have to learn to ask these kinds of questions as well.

Fourth-level questions: Appearances

How can we cast a given action in such a way that it appears to be something
    other than what it is?

How can we get someone to support something that they otherwise would not?

Fourth-level questions: Creativity by Alternation or Experimental Design

What other situations can I set up, that have the properties of the one under consideration, so that I can stress the absurdity of the original?
What other situations can I set up, that have the properties of the one under consideration, so that I can stress the validity of the original?
What other situations can I set up, that have the properties of the one under consideration, so that I can find the generalizations that hold between the two?

Fourth-level questions: Human Issues

What makes a person worthy of emotional support?
What makes an action good or bad?

Fourth-level questions: Rules for Success

How do certain people build up successful rules for coping with the world?
How and why do other people avoid those rules? Do they succeed as well?

TRIGGERS

The key issue in all this is fairly simple to state. It is very nice to have all these questions available to a system. If we were to go through every one of them every time we perceived an event, we probably would never get through the first event. The event, together with inferences about the causes and effects of that event, would, after having all these questions applied to them, cause a combinatorial explosion.

So, the issue is **triggers**. What causes one or more of these questions to be brought into consciousness? Just when should we consider what?

Types of triggers

There are three different types of triggers that we shall talk about here. The first, which I shall label TRIG-0, are those which one need not learn about in any complex way. These triggers are either innate, or else are learned quite easily in the first year of life. Of course, their nature is quite important to determine, and they certainly must be taught to a machine if it is to attempt to understand people and if it is to have any conscious life of its own. Essentially they are about the very nature of the thing being observed and relate in some

way to expectation failures arising from processing the action under observation.

The second, which I shall label TRIG-1, are those we learn fairly early on in
life, but which might not have been learned by everyone. Often these are rules
of thumb that are taught in school. They tend to relate to events that are being
processed second hand, without the benefit of first-hand observation.

The third, which I shall label TRIG-TBL (for To Be Learned), are those
which embody the essence of the learning problem. If, in order to be smart, as
we have claimed, it is necessary to constantly be asking questions, then the
triggers that one learns are an important part of that process. Learning to
trigger questions can be an important part of learning. It is important for both
people and machines to learn how to trigger new questions. But, learning
takes place in one's own personal context, so TRIG-TBLs tend to be
goal-related.

Initially, of course, one can simply be taught the appropriate triggers. Using
them at the right time is a matter of experience. Thus, it is the compilation of
information about the appropriate use of triggers that is the significant part of
learning from experience.

So, for example, the first-level questions have the following triggers:

First-level questions: Self-centered

Why does this matter to me?

TRIG-0:   observing a physical action headed your way (basically innate).
TRIG-1:   being told about an event (because there is the implication that
             the teller is telling it to you because he thinks it matters to you)
TRIG-TBL: observational (because observations may matter that do not
             appear to matter at first glance)

In other words, every animal knows TRIG-0. Over time, he must refine
what he knows on the basis of experience. This means knowing the answer to
the specific question generated by the general question that has been triggered. The process has the trigger causing the general question:

Why does this matter to me?

to be generated. This question is then transformed into a specific question,
i.e.:

Why does this wild animal heading towards me matter to me?

The answer to the specific question would presumably be encoded in such a
way as to include an action that has worked before in preventing any danger
that might be assumed to be a potential result of the ongoing action.

For TRIG-1, the situation is a bit more complicated. When we are told about an event as a child, it is precisely because this event had direct relevance to us. As we get older, information gets imparted to us that is only indirectly of relevance. TRIG-1 causes us to trigger the question:

Why does this matter to me?

and then decide whether to pursue thinking on that question until some personal relevance is gathered. For example, if you hear, on the news, that the Cardinals beat the Phillies 5–3, you would ask yourself, in some sense, whether or not you cared about that. You would if you were a Cardinal or Phillie fan. You would not if you were not a baseball fan, unless of course, you knew someone who was and cared about them in general, or had some specific reason (like an impending visit to a Phillie fan) to care at this time. If you were a Met fan, for example, you might care about this news if the Mets were tied in the standings with one or the other of these teams, or were about to face one of them and so on.

The point is that for any given input received in this way (i.e. passively), we attempt to determine its relevance. Through the process of question trans-formation that we saw with CYRUS, the task is to convert the triggered question:

Why does this matter to me?

to one that is directly answerable, such as:

Will the result of that game affect a team I care about?
Will the result of that game affect a person I care about?

Generating this question is of key significance. To do this, it is necessary to use one of many question-transformation rules (Q-T rules). For example, the Q-T rule applicable here is:

Q-T1: For TRIG-1 with respect to the results of an athletic contest:

transform into

question about the possible relationship to the results of other athletic contests

or

question about affective states of individuals associated with the teams in the contest.

Notice that the rule here is rather specific. We would expect to find rather specific rules because once we learn to know what we care about in a given context, we can easily get to that issue. In essence what we are saying here is that for any new event one transforms general questions about personal relevance into specific questions that one has learned to ask about that kind of situation. In other words, Q-Ts are triggers to activate questions one has previously thought about in contexts where they are relevant.

Now, let us consider what happens when the information that causes TRIG-1 to fire is told directly to you. That is, suppose that someone walks over to you and says something to you. Let us assume that he either tells you a fact about himself or about something not directly related to either of you. For example, assume he has said either:

My wife woke up sick this morning.

or

The Iranians have bombed Baghdad.

The problem is to figure out what the relevance of these remarks is to you. A number of different Q-T rules apply:

Q-T2: For TRIG-1 with respect to illness:

transform into

(a) question about the possible contagion of the illness;
(b) question about the possible effects of the illness on the individual causing the lack of availability of that individual;
(c) questions about the possible effects on other individuals upon whom you rely of the difficulties of the ill person.

Now, this may seem a rather egocentric set of questions, but recall that that is precisely what *Why does this matter to me?* is all about. The problem here is to generate a set of questions from the original question. Not all the question types we have discussed are all active all the time. But, level-one questions such as this one are always active.

The Q-Ts for the bombing of Baghdad are:

Q-T3: For TRIG-1 with respect to war in foreign countries:

transform into

(a) question about the possible spread of the war to other countries;
(b) question about the possible effects of the war in terms of the production of commodities used by you.

The Q-Ts mentioned above are all rather typical. For a variety of given specific areas of knowledge, we have developed a set of standard ways of determining the relevance of events in those areas to ourselves. Thus we learn to ask certain questions when these events occur.

Naturally, these Q-Ts look a great deal like inferences or requests that might have been generated by FRUMP or IPP. That is because they are at the simplest level of understanding. My point here has been to attempt to raise the level of understanding by having the machine generate questions that it itself was interested in or at least that it knew how to ask.

In general, such questions come about in two different ways. Either they come from the TRIG-TBL, or they come from the higher-level questions (levels three and four). To see what I mean here, consider the TRIG-TBL for the above first-level question.

Even though the first-level question: *Why does this matter to me?* is rather unsophisticated as questions go, there can be a strong learning aspect to that question. When one observes an event that is not overtly threatening, one can still learn quite a bit from the event. TRIG-TBLs cause one to ask of a given event whether it is unusual enough to merit further study. In other words, for TRIG-0 and TRIG-1, we know that there is direct relevance to us. The task is to determine what the relevance is. For events other than those that are coming right at us or those that someone has decided we ought to know about, we have to determine for ourselves how important they may be to us.

To do this, we must compile a complex data base of knowledge about the world that enables us to determine if an event is unusual. Unusualness is actually fairly difficult to determine. If a new building is being constructed near one's home, is that unusual? It may be unusual enough that we would want to consider how it might affect us.

The task for a computer is to learn, by asking about the possible effects of every action that it processes, which actions can potentially affect its goals. Here we are again then, at goals. One cannot determine if an event is worth examining fully unless one has a set of goals in terms of which to examine the event. IPP and CYRUS had no such goals and thus were incapable of really generating their own questions to follow.

Goal-based triggers

Let us consider an example level-three question and an example level-four question in terms of the triggers that would make those questions fire off and in terms of the goals that would have to be present in order to force those triggers. As examples, let us consider the following:

Third-level questions: Strategies

Why would someone do something one way when another way seems better?
How do we determine the ultimate cost and benefits of an action?
How can you get someone to believe something that will enable your action to succeed?

Fourth-level questions: Appearances

How can we cast a given action in such a way that it appears to be something other whan what it is?

How can we get someone to support something that they otherwise would not?

The triggers for the first third-level question are as follows:

TRIG-0:   expecting an alternative plan.
TRIG-1:   being told about an alternative plan.
TRIG-TBL: goals: theory of actor, theory of plan selection.

Essentially what these say is that when an action fails to fit into an anticipated set of actions in service of a known goal, TRIG-0 fires. Another way to put this is that someone did something towards an end that you expected, but in a way that you did not expect. TRIG-0 causes the third-level question that it indexes to fire. The question might then be subject to some Q-Ts. The question that fires is: *Why would someone do something one way when another way seems better?* Q-Ts can only be applied in real contexts, so let us reconsider our example from before: *The Iranians have bombed Baghdad.*

The issue here is to get yourself to ask a question that might cause you to think about something, in a creative way, that arises from the new information. TRIG-0 would only fire in this instance if you had some expectation about the event. In other words, interest is reflected in expectations that fire, and further interest is generated by questions that come from the trigger.

So, in order for TRIG-0 to have fired here some expectation that the Iranians would not bomb Baghdad would have had to have been around. Thus, the Q-T depends upon the failed expectation.

Q-T4: For TRIG-0 with respect to the actions in a war, when expectations were present that such actions would not be taken:

transform into

(a) question about what new goal may be held by the actor that this plan serves;
(b) question about what conditions changed in the war;
(c) question about leadership changes that may have occurred.

These transformations produce, in this case:

(a) Do the Iranians now believe that Tehran is completely defensible? (This is based on the assumption that the failed expectation was derived from an assumption that the reason not to bomb Baghdad was so as to prevent an escalation that could harm Iran.)

(b) Are the Iranians getting desperate because they believe they cannot go on much longer?
(c) Is the Ayatollah Khomeini no longer in full charge of his government?

My point here has been that it is in the generation of such questions that the answer to learning lies. These questions can either be easily rejected or indexed so they can be tested in future cases. They are, in essence, hypotheses that should be generated by an understander in response to his attempt to process a new event.

For TRIG-1 to fire, it is necessary for the event being processed to be presented together with an alternative. Thus, TRIG-1 fires when two plans are under consideration, and where the one that has been pursued seems to be the less likely of the two. Q-T5 therefore, transforms

Why would someone do something one way when another way seems better?

into

(a) Did the actor believe that plan A was better than plan B?
(b) Are there negative side-effects of plan B for the actor?
(c) Was the actor unable to execute plan B for some reason?

For TRIG-TBL to fire, we need specific goal matches. Our question:

Why would someone do something one way when another way seems better?

is transformed into:

(a) What properties of the actor make him unlikely to follow the plans I expect him to follow? (This fires when the actor is marked as interesting to the processor.)
(b) What properties of the plan in question have I failed to think about? (This fires when the plan is marked as inherently interesting.)
(c) Do actors acting under a given goal behave differently for specific goals? (This fires when the goal is marked as inherently interesting.)

The point here is that for a processor that has the goal of becoming more knowledgeable about a given actor, plan or goal, questions such as these would fire when the interest matches with a failed expectation about the interest. The intention here is to learn more about a subject of interest when one's expectations are unsatisfied.

AT THE FOURTH LEVEL

Now, let us consider the other example in the context of a fourth-level question. The sentence:

My wife woke up sick this morning.

can have numerous subplots to it. An interested understander begins to think about these extra issues to the extent that he has reason to believe any of them.

We have the following triggers:

TRIG-0:   negative effects of action; blame falls on you.
TRIG-1:   having an action presented to you in the opposite way than you would have expected.
TRIG-TBL: goals, rhetorical: need to convince someone of a point of view

TRIG-0 fires when a reason can be inferred whereby the action in question causes potential blame to the hearer. This is a paranoid-type interpretation and should only fire when the processor has some reason to be paranoid.

Thus, you should ask the question:

How can we cast a given action in such a way that it appears to be something other than what it is?

when you have reason to be suspicious that the event under discussion in some way is being related to you. The task before you is to generate a question that enables you to say or do something that turns the situation around.

Q-T6: For TRIG-0 with respect to an event being blamed on you:

transform into

(a) question about how the event is really a positive event;
(b) question about how to make it appear as if the event in question could not have happened;
(c) question about who else can be blamed.

Again, as with most TRIG-0 firings, the questions generated are known to most children. They rarely have to be taught them. But, level-four questions even for TRIG-0, have some creativity to them.

The questions actually generated would be, for example:

(a) What will the positive effects of this sickness be for the husband? (This could be generated without blame being assigned of course.)
(b) What reasons would his wife have for faking this illness?
(c) Who else could have been responsible for this event? (This might be an important question if the sickness were 'morning sickness' and this really as an accusation.)

Here again, these questions are only the beginning, but the answer can be easily generated so as to help create good responses to the initial remark if it were found that it was appropriate to do so.

We fire TRIG-1 when there is some expectation about the event being discussed, but where the expectation that is violated is about how that information is being presented. In other words, if you knew that the speaker's wife was unhappy and he was told that she was sick, the issue is why the information was presented in this peculiar way.

Q-T7 therefore transforms the original question into:

(a) Why did the speaker decide not to tell me what I thought he would?
(b) What actually has happened (as opposed to what I was told)?
(c) Why does the speaker perceive the consequences of one event as being more significant than the other?

For TRIG-TBL, the issue is to be able to recast a given event in terms of one's own goals. This would be fired if one's point of view were at odds with a given assertion. Thus the triggers to be learned depends upon one's ability to test a given assertion to see if it is at odds with one's assumptions on the subject. The question:

How can we cast a given action in such a way that it appears to be something other than what it is?

is transformed by Q-T8 when an event is presented that conflicts with one's own viewpoint and one has the opportunity to make a rejoinder.

Q-T8: For TRIG-TBL:

transform into

(a) question about how the event could be portrayed as part of a plan to achieve ends opposite from those that are obvious;
(b) question about how to make it appear as if the negative aspects of the event were really neutral or beneficial;
(c) question about the evidence behind the basic assumptions of even causing aspects of it, such as who really did the planning, the acting and so on.

CONCLUSION

The details of all this are so large in scope as to make a complete paper on this subject prohibitive in size (and beyond belief in complexity and dullness). The point here is that creativity means asking questions. If we want a machine to be creative, to think in any significant sense of that term, then it must be aroused by what it perceives so as to wonder about it.

Much of this wondering is fairly prescribed. We know what to wonder about at a certain basic level. After that, we are taught what to wonder about. Beyond that there is a level at which we wonder truly new things. But, whether new or old, we learn certain tricks about how to wonder and at what level to wonder.

My claim is that we must teach machines to wonder too. To do so, they must be given very detailed ideas about what to wonder about in specific domains, as well as a set of algorithms about how to wonder in general. In addition, they must be given personalities of a sort. That is, one tends to wonder idiosyncratically. One wonders about things in a way that reflects one's own personal experiences and knowledge about a domain. I have attempted to present some of the rules for this process here, in a fairly sketchy form. There are undoubtedly more questions to ask and more ways to decide when to ask them. But this is a beginning.

ACKNOWLEDGMENTS

This work was supported in part by the Advanced Research Projects Agency of the Department of Defense and monitored under the Office of Naval Research under contract N00014-85-K-0108 and contract N00014-82-K-0149, National Science Foundation IST-8120451, and the Air Force contract F49620-82-K0010.

REFERENCES

DeJong, G. (1979). Skimming stories in real time: an experiment in integrated understanding. Ph.D. thesis, Yale University, May.
Kolodner, J. L. (1980). Retrieval and organizational strategies in conceptual memory: a computer model. Ph.D. thesis, Yale University, November.
Lebowitz, M. (1980). Generalization and memory in an integrated understanding system. Ph.D. thesis, Yale University, October.
Schank, R. C. (1982). *Dynamic Memory: A Theory of Learning in Computers and People.* Cambridge University Press.
Schank, R. C. (1984). *The Explanation Game.* Technical Report 307, Yale University Department of Computer Science, March.

Modelling Cognition
Edited by P. Morris
© 1987 John Wiley & Sons Ltd.

3

Coping with novelty and human intelligence

ROBERT J. STERNBERG
Yale University

Nothing is so certain in life as the existence of uncertainty. From the day of birth, the human infant is required to process and somehow cope with an environment that is strange, uncertain and largely unpredictable. The infant's ability to adapt to the new environment outside the womb is critically dependent on that infant's ability to cope with the novel aspects of the environment. To the extent that there are individual differences among infants and among older individuals in the ability to cope with novelty, so there will be differences in that individual's ability intelligently to adapt to the array of environments that the individual will confront during the course of his or her life span. This fact has led us to conclude that the ability to cope with novelty may be an important source of continuity in intellectual development (Berg and Sternberg, 1985). Indeed, our review of the research literature led us to conclude that among cognitive tests administered to infants, the only ones that provide consistently substantial prediction of later intelligence are those tests that measure, in one way or another, the infant's ability to cope with novelty. The purpose of this chapter is to present some cognitive models of coping with novelty, and to discuss how this ability to cope relates to intelligence.

The idea that intelligence involves the ability to deal with novel task demands is far from novel (see, e.g., Cattell, 1971; Horn, 1968; Kaufman and Kaufman, 1983; Raaheim, 1974; Snow, 1981; Sternberg, 1981, 1982). Sternberg (1982) has suggested, in fact, that intelligence is best measured by tasks that are 'nonentrenched' in the sense of requiring information processing of kinds outside people's ordinary experience. The task may be nonentrenched in the kinds of operations it requires or in the concepts it requires the subjects to utilize. According to this view, then, intelligence involves

> not merely the ability to learn and reason with new concepts but the ability to learn and reason with new kinds of concepts. Intelligence is not so much a person's ability to learn or think within conceptual systems that the person has already become familiar with as it is his or her ability to learn and think within new conceptual systems, which can then be brought to bear upon already existing knowledge structures (Sternberg, 1981, p. 4)

It is important to note that the usefulness of a task in measuring intelligence is not a linear function of task novelty. The task that is presented should be novel, but not totally outside the individual's past experience (Raaheim, 1974, 1984). If the task is too novel, then the individual will not have any cognitive structures to bring to bear upon the task, and as a result the task will simply be outside of the individual's range of comprehension. Calculus, for example, would be a highly novel field of endeavor for most five-year-olds. But the calculus tasks would be so far outside their range of experience that the tasks would be worthless for the assessment of the intelligence of five-year-olds. In Piaget's (1972) terms, the task should primarily require accommodation but must require some assimilation as well.

Implicit in the above discussion is the notion that novelty can be of two kinds, either or both of which may be involved in task performance. The two kinds of novelty might be characterized as involving (a) comprehension of the task, and (b) acting upon one's comprehension of the task. Consider the meaning of each of these two kinds of novelty.

Novelty in comprehension of the task refers to the novelty that inheres in understanding the task confronting one. Once one understands the task, acting upon it may or may not be challenging. In essence, the novelty is in learning how to do the task rather than in actually doing it. Novelty in acting upon one's comprehension of the task refers to novelty in acting upon a problem rather than in learning about the problem or in learning how to solve it. The genre of task is familiar, but the parameters of the particular task are not. It is possible, of course, to formulate problems involving novelty in both comprehension and execution of a particular kind of task and to formulate problems that involve novelty in neither comprehension nor execution. The present account suggests that problems of these two kinds might be less satisfactory measures of intelligence than problems involving novelty in either comprehension or execution, but not both. The reason for this is that the former problems might be too novel, whereas the latter problems might not be novel enough to provide optimal measurement of intelligence.

The notion that intelligence is particularly aptly measured in situations that require adaptation to new and challenging environmental demands inheres both in experts' and laypersons' notions of the nature of intelligence (Intelligence and its measurement, 1921; Sternberg *et al.*, 1981). The idea is that a person's intelligence is best shown not in run-of-the-mill situations that are encountered regularly in everyday life, but rather in extraordinary situations that challenge the individual's ability to cope with the environment. Almost everyone knows someone (perhaps oneself) who performs well when confronted with tasks that are presented in a familiar milieu, but who falls apart when presented with similar or even identical tasks that are in an unfamiliar milieu. For example, a person who performs well in his or her everyday environment might find it difficult to function in a foreign country, even one that is similar in many respects to the home environment. In general, some people can perform well, but only under situational circumstances that are highly favorable to their getting their work done. When the environment is less supportive, their efficacy is greatly reduced.

Essentially the same constraints that apply to task novelty apply to situational novelty as well. First, too much novelty can render the situation nondiagnostic of intellectual level. Moreover, there may exist situations in which no one could function effectively. Second, situational novelty can inhere either in understanding the nature of the situation or in performing within the context of that situation. In some instances, it is figuring out just what the situation is that is difficult; in others, it is operating in that situation once one has figured out what it is.

It is important to take into account the fact that tasks or situations that are novel for some persons may not be novel for others. Thus, a given task or situation will not necessarily measure 'intelligence' to the same extent for some people that it does for others. Similarly, people vary widely in the extent to which various kinds of situations are novel in their experience. Not only do task and situation interact with person, but they can interact with each other as well. A task that is novel in one situation might not be novel in another situation. Finally, at the level of 'third-order' interaction, a task may be novel (or mundane) for some persons in one situation but not in a second situation, whereas the same task would be novel (or mundane) for other persons in the second situation but not in the first. In sum, one needs to take into account interactions among these variables as well as their main effects.

In a series of experimental investigations, my collaborators at Yale and I have sought to study the roles of comprehension of novel tasks and of acting upon one's comprehension of these tasks in human intelligence. This chapter will review the evidence that these investigations have provided regarding the nature of the ability to cope with novelty, and its role in human intelligence.

Before discussing our experimental investigations, it will be useful to provide a brief sketch of my triarchic theory of human intelligence, and of the role of coping with novelty in that theory. According to the triarchic theory, intelligence can be understood in terms of three interactive subtheories regarding its nature and function. These three subtheories are the componential, the contextual and the experiential subtheories of intelligence, respectively.

The componential subtheory seeks to understand the relation of intelligence to the internal world of the individual—what goes on 'inside a person's head' when that person thinks intelligently. This subtheory specifies the information-processing components of human intelligence, as well as the strategies into which these components combine and the mental representations upon which they act. According to the subtheory, intelligent information processing can be understood in terms of three basic kinds of information-processing components: metacomponents, performance components and knowledge-acquisition components. Metacomponents are used to plan what one is going to do, to monitor it while one is doing it, and to evaluate it after it is done. Such components have been called by a variety of names, such as 'executive processes' or 'metacognitive processes', but regardless of what they are called, they are responsible for the higher-order information processing that is needed in order to regulate human mental functioning. Performance components are the mental processes that act upon the instructions of the metacomponents. They are responsible for accomplishing what the metacomponents dictate needs to be done. Knowledge-acquisition components are responsible for learning how the thing is to be done in the first place. These three kinds of components are interactive, with metacomponents providing direction to the performance components and knowledge-acquisition components, and the performance and knowledge-acquisition components providing feedback to the metacomponents.

The contextual subtheory specifies the relation between intelligence and the external world of the individual. It specifies the functions that the components of intelligence serve when applied to intelligent behavior in the everyday world. According to the contextual subtheory, there are three such functions: adaptation, selection and shaping. Adaptation to the environment involves the regulation of one's behavior so as to make it suitable for a given environment in which one finds oneself. The individual effects changes in him- or herself that render him or her responsive to the demands of the given environment. At most points in one's life, the intelligent thing to do is to adapt. However, there are points at which it can actually be maladaptive to adapt. If one's interests, aptitudes, values or needs do not fit with the environment in which one finds oneself, one may choose to select another environment in which to reside. For example, one may decide that a given job is a poor fit to one's abilities, that the mores in a particular community do not fit one's values, or that one is unhappy with a particular course of study in college. In such cases, it may be preferable to select a new environment rather than attempting to adapt oneself to the old one. However, one does not select a new environment every time one discovers some degree of misfit between oneself and the environment. Before attempting such selection, or possibly even before entertaining the idea of the selection of a new environment, one may attempt to shape the environment in which one resides, attempting to change the environment to conform to one's abilities, interests, values or needs, rather than attempting to change oneself to conform to the environment. For example, one may attempt to restructure one's job, or to find a subgroup of people within the community in which one lives whose values better conform to one's own. Alternatively, one may attempt to select a new environment before shaping the old one, and then resort to shaping only if selection fails.

The ability to apply the three kinds of components of intelligence to the three functions of adaptation to, selection of, and shaping of, environments is mediated by one's experience in the world. In other words, one learns how to adapt, select and shape environments through one's experience in life. The experiential subtheory provides the mediation between the relation of intelligence to the internal world of the individual and the relation of intelligence to the external world of the individual. According to this subtheory, there are two regions of experience with tasks and situations that are particularly important with respect to the role of experience in intelligence: the region of relative novelty of tasks and situations, and the region of automatization of information processing within a given task or situation. Initially, a new task or situation requires one to cope with the novel element within that task or situation. It is at this point that the ability to cope with novelty comes into play. After some amount of time goes by within which one gains experience with the task or situation, one may start to automatize processing of that task or situation, rendering the controlled unconscious, automatic and subconscious. The efficacy of this automatization will determine how well one can perform in the long run, and also how many mental processing resources will be freed to deal with further novelty in the environment. In sum, one's ability to apply the components of intelligence to the environmental context in which one lives will be mediated by the ability to cope with novelty and by the ability to automatize information processing.

In this chapter, I will concentrate upon the ability to cope with novelty, and its role in human intelligence. The remainder of the article will describe four sets of experiments that have sought to study the ability to cope with novelty, and will then discuss the general findings that emerge from these sets of studies.

The first part of the experiential subtheory deals with individuals' ways of responding to novelty. It was noted earlier that novelty can inhere primarily either in task performance or in understanding how to perform the task. Both of these kinds of cases will be considered below.

NOVELTY IN TASK PERFORMANCE: A MODEL OF INSIGHT

Novelty can inhere in task performance for any of a number of reasons. A particularly important class of tasks involving novelty in task performance is the class of insight tasks. Insight tasks require one to find a novel and unobvious solution to a problem that may or may not, on the face of it, seem difficult. Such tasks may be quite easy to understand, but quite difficult to perform. Conventional views of insight fall into two basic camps—the special-process views and the nothing-special views. Consider each of these views.

Conventional views of insight

According to 'special-process' views, insight is a process that differs in kind from ordinary kinds of information processes. These views are often associated with the *Gestalt* psychologists and their successors (e.g., Kohler, 1927; Maier, 1930; Wertheimer, 1959). Among these views are the ideas that insight results from extended unconscious leaps in thinking, that it results from greatly accelerated mental processing, and that it results from a short-circuiting of normal reasoning processes (see Perkins, 1981). These views are intuitively appealing, but seem to carry with them at least three problematical aspects. First, they do not really pin down what insight is. Calling insight an 'unconscious leap in thinking' or a 'short-circuiting of normal reasoning' leaves insight pretty much a 'black box' of unknown contents. Even were one of these theories correct, just what insight is would remain to be identified. Second, virtually all of the evidence in support of these views is anecdotal rather than experimental, and for each piece of anecdotal evidence to support one of these views, there is at least one corresponding piece of evidence to refute it (Perkins, 1978). Finally, the positions are probably not pinned down sufficiently as they stand to permit empirical test. As a result, it is not clear that the positions are even falsifiable. It is this characteristic of nonfalsifiability that probably resulted in the death of *Gestalt* psychology: its propositions were simply not testable.

According to the 'nothing-special' views, insight is merely an extension of ordinary processes of perceiving, recognizing, learning and conceiving. This view, most forcefully argued by Perkins (1978), would view past failures to identify any special processes of insight as being due to the (alleged) fact that there is no special process of insight. Insights are merely significant products of ordinary processes. We can understand the kind of frustration that would lead Perkins and others to this view: after repeated failures to identify a construct empirically, one can easily be tempted to ascribe the failure to the nonexistence of the construct. One cannot find what is not there! But I am not yet ready to abandon the notion that there is something special about insight, any more than I am ready, on the basis of Mischel's (1968) devastating critique of the trait literature, to abandon the notion of personality traits. Arguments for the 'nothing-special' views are arguments by default—because we have not identified insight processes, they have no independent existence—and I do not accept such arguments because I believe we can create positive arguments for the existence of insight processes.

Proposed view of insight

Sternberg and Davidson (1982, 1983) have proposed that a main reason psychologists (and others) have had so much difficulty in isolating insight is that it involves not one but three separate though related psychological processes given under the headings below.

1. Selective encoding

An insight of selective encoding involves sifting out relevant information from irrelevant information. Significant problems generally present one with large amounts of information, only some of which is relevant to problem solution. For example, the facts of a legal case are usually both numerous and confusing: an insightful lawyer must figure out which of the myriad facts confronting him or her are relevant to principles of law. Similarly, a doctor or psychotherapist may be presented with a great volume of information regarding a patient's background and symptoms: an insightful doctor or psychotherapist must sift out those facts that are relevant for diagnosis or treatment. A famous example of what we refer to as an insight of selective encoding is Alexander Fleming's discovery of penicillin. In looking at a Petri dish containing a culture that had become moldy, Fleming noticed that bacteria in the vicinity of the mold had been destroyed, presumably by the mold. In essence, Fleming encoded the information in his visual field in a highly selective way, zeroing in on that part of the field that was relevant to the discovery of the antibiotic.

2. Selective combination

An insight of selective combination involves combining what might originally seem to be isolated pieces of information into a unified whole that may or may not resemble its parts. Whereas selective encoding involves knowing which pieces of information are relevant, selective combination involves knowing how to put together the pieces of information that are relevant. For example, the lawyer must know how the relevant facts of a case fit together to make (or break!) the case. A doctor or psychotherapist must be able to figure out how to combine information about various isolated symptoms to identify a given medical (or psychological) syndrome. A famous example of selective combination is Darwin's formulation of the theory of evolution. It is well known that Darwin had available to him for many years the facts he needed to form the basis for the theory of natural selection. What eluded him for those years was a way to combine the facts into a coherent package.

3. Selective comparison

An insight of selective comparison involves relating newly acquired information to information acquired in the past. Problem-solving by analogy, for example, is an instance of selective comparison: one realizes that new information is similar to old information in certain ways (and dissimilar from it in other ways) and uses this information better to understand the new information. For example, an insightful lawyer will relate a current case to legal precedents; choosing the right precedents is absolutely essential. A doctor or psychotherapist relates the current set of presenting symptoms to previous case histories in his or her own or other's past experiences; again, choosing the right precedents is essential. A famous example of an insight of selective comparison is Kekulé's discovery of the structure of the benzene ring. Kekulé dreamed of a snake curling back on itself and catching its tail. When he woke up, he realized that the image of the snake catching its tail was a metaphor for the structure of the benzene ring.

Tests of the model of insight

Adult subjects

Preliminary data testing the theory of insight are encouraging.

In one study (Sternberg and Davidson, 1982), we presented 30 adults from the New Haven area (who were not Yale-connected) with unlimited time to solve 12 insight problems chosen to require little background knowledge. Some examples are:

1. If you have black socks and brown socks in your drawer, mixed in the ratio of 4 to 5, how many socks will you have to take out to make sure of having a pair of socks the same color?
2. Suppose you and I have the same amount of money. How much must I give you so that you have 10 dollars more than I?
3. Water lilies double in area every 24 hours. At the beginning of the summer there is one water lily on a lake. It takes 60 days for the lake to become covered with water lilies. On what day is the lake half-covered?
4. A farmer has 17 sheep. All but 9 broke through a hole in the fence and wandered away. How many were left?

Of these particular problems, the first emphasizes selective encoding, the second emphasizes selective combination, the third emphasizes both of these processes and the fourth emphasizes neither of these processes. Rather, it is a 'trick' problem that requires one to read the problem and question very carefully. The difficulty of the problem is in encoding, but not in *selective* encoding of relevant versus irrelevant information. Incidentally, the answers to the problems are 3, 5, 59 and 9 respectively; proportions of subjects getting each of these particular problems correct were 0.43, 0.40, 0.40 and 0.57 respectively. Overall proportion correct for the full set of twelve problems was 0.37.

Performance on the complete set of problems was correlated 0.66 with Henmon Nelson IQ; 0.63 with inductive reasoning, as measured by 'letter sets' from the French Kit of Reference Tests for Cognitive Factors (French, Ekstrom and Price, 1963); and 0.34 with deductive reasoning, as measured by 'nonsense syllogisms' from the French Kit. In a second (as yet unpublished) study, performance of 30 different individuals (again not Yale-connected) on 20 insight problems such as those above was correlated 0.55 with Henmon Nelson IQ, 0.51 with inductive reasoning (letter sets), and 0.42 with deductive reasoning (nonsense syllogisms). In both studies, an examination of point-biserial correlations between item scores and IQ revealed that the highest correlations tended to be for items that clearly measured either selective encoding, selective combination or both. Trick problems, such as the 'sheep' problem (no. 4 above), tended to have relatively lower correlations with IQ.

In the second study, we also investigated subjects' relative uses of the processes of selective encoding and selective combination. By far the most successful strategy was to use both of these processes in solving an insight problem. Using just selective encoding tended to result in a lesser degree of success, and using just selective combination resulted in the least degree of success. Unfortunately, this last strategy (as determined by analysis of subjects' written protocols while they solved the problem) was common.

A third study investigated the selective comparison process. Subjects were again New Haven area adults who were not Yale-connected at the time of testing. Each subject was assigned to 1 of 4 experimental conditions and received 12 insight problems divided into 2 sets of 6 problems each. There were 4 types of conditions. In 1 of the 4 conditions, subjects received example problems that were relevant to solving half of the test problems prior to receiving the actual test problems. The relevance of the examples for the test problems was not pointed out, however. In a second condition, subjects received the same examples and test problems, except that the relevance of the samples for the test problems was pointed out to them. In a third condition, subjects received example and actual test problems, but the example problems were not directly relevant to the solution of the test problems. In the fourth condition, subjects received no example problems at all.

Subjects performed best when they received relevant example problems and the relevance of the examples was pointed out to them, second best when they received relevant problems but without the relevance of the problems being pointed out to them, and worst in the two conditions where there were no relevant examples. Moreover, the effect was isolated only in the particular half of the problems for which the examples had been relevant. Performance on the problems for which the examples were not relevant was the same in all of the groups that received any examples, and these means did not differ from the nonexamples group either. These results indicate that subjects can peform an insight of selective comparison in solving the test problems, bringing to bear information from the examples when it is relevant. But as might be expected, subjects do even better when they are 'given' the insight and told the examples are relevant rather than having to figure out this fact for themselves.

Performance in all kinds of conditions was highly correlated with psychometric test scores, as in the preceding two studies. The median correlation with IQ was 0.77; with inductive reasoning, it was 0.70; and with deductive reasoning, it was 0.56. Insight problems thus appear to overlap with whatever it is that IQ tests measure but to measure other skills as well that are not measured by IQ tests.

From these three studies, we drew four primary conclusions that are relevant here. First, subjects use selective encoding, selective combination and selective comparison in the solution of insight problems. Second, insight problems measure skills that are related, but not identical, to what it is that IQ tests measure. 'Trick' problems, however, do not provide good measurement either of insight or of IQ. Third, subjects differ in the extent to which they use the various kinds of insights in solving a given problem. Finally, failures in past research to isolate a process of insight may stem in part from failure to realize that insights can be of at least three kinds. Providing one kind of insight for subjects may not be sufficient for problem solution if other kinds of insights are needed as well.

Child subjects

We have also sought to test our theory of insight on fourth-, fifth- and sixth-grade normal and gifted subjects (Davidson and Sternberg, 1984). The subjects, students in an upper-middle-class suburban school district, had been identified as either gifted (minimum IQ 140) or nongifted on the bases of IQ test scores, Torrance creativity test scores, teacher recommendations and achievement test scores. Three experiments were performed—examining, respectively, the nature of selective encoding, selective combination and selective comparison—using both mathematical and verbal problems (sentence completions). Because we experienced ceiling effects on the part of the gifted with respect to the verbal problems, I shall confine my discussion to results from the data for the mathematical problems. In addition to the insight problems, subjects were also given a test battery including mystery problems (requiring subjects to figure out how a detective knew the identity of the perpetrators of various crimes), inductive reasoning problems and deductive reasoning problems. We also had available IQ test scores for all of the subjects on a group-administered IQ test. The mathematical insight problems were similar to those described earlier—for example, 'If you have black socks and brown socks in your drawer, mixed in the ratio of 4 to 5, how many socks will you have to take out to make sure of having a pair of socks the same color?'

I think it important to note that the kinds of problems we have used to date in our studies of insight clearly depart from the kinds of large-scale scientific, mathematical, literary and other problems that give rise to major intellectual insights. Thus, the data I report here can be regarded as only of the most preliminary kind. They very much need to be followed up by data based upon problems requiring much more significant kinds of insights. Our present work is, we hope, headed in this direction.

Our first concern was whether performance on the insight problems showed a predicted pattern of convergent–discriminant validation. In particular, we expected performance on the insight problems (a) to be better for gifted children than for nongifted children, and (b) to correlate most highly with performance on the mystery stories, which require insights; next most highly with inductive problems, which require the subject to go beyond the information given; and least highly with deductive problems, which provide all information needed for solution. In fact, the respective mean numbers of problems correct (out of 15 possible) were 8.45 for the gifted children and 5.36 for the nongifted children, a difference that was statistically significant for the 86 children involved in this comparison. Correlations with the respective reference tests were 0.56 with mysteries, 0.53 with letter sets and 0.43 with nonsense syllogisms. The correlation with a group IQ test administered by the school was 0.55. Although the differences between correlations were not significant, they seemed at least to fall into the pattern we had expected.

In a first experiment, which investigated selective incoding, subjects were either precued as to what information in each of a set of insight problems was relevant for problem solution or not so precued. For example, the following problem would either be given in normal form or with solution-relevant parts underlined, as follows: 'A farmer buys 100 animals for $100. *Cows are $10 each*, sheep are $2 each, and pigs are 50 cents each. *How much did he pay for 5 cows?*' Eighty subjects participated in this experiment: all of them received half of the problems with cueing and half without. Which problems were or were not cued was counterbalanced. In addition, some of the problems were designated as 'encoding' problems, in that they contained both relevant and irrelevant information; other problems contained only relevant information, and were thus designated as 'nonencoding' problems (because selective encoding was not needed). When these problems were presented in cued form, the entire problem was underlined.

There were five major predictions regarding the results. First, it was predicted that gifted children would perform better than nongifted ones. This prediction was confirmed, with respective mean insight-problem scores (out of 12 possible) of 4.08 and 2.45. Second, it was predicted that performance on the cued problems would be better than performance on the uncued problems. This prediction was also confirmed. Mean scores were 3.63 for cued problems and 2.89 for uncued problems (out of 12 possible). Third, it was predicted that encoding problems, for which the underlining manipulation would be expected to provide facilitation, would be easier than nonencoding problems, for which the underlining manipulation would be expected to provide no facilitation. Again, the prediction was confirmed: respective means were 3.42 for encoding problems and 3.10 for nonencoding problems (out of 12 possible). Fourth, it was predicted that there would be a significant cueing × encoding interaction. This interaction would follow from cueing having more of a facilitatory effect for encoding problems (where only some information was underlined) than for nonencoding problems (where all information was underlined). If the cueing information did genuinely facilitate selective encoding, then this interaction should be significant. This prediction was also confirmed. Means were 2.99 for uncued nonencoding problems, 3.22 for cued nonencoding problems, 2.80 for uncued encoding problems and 4.04 for cued encoding problems (all out of 6 possible). Finally, it was predicted that there would be a significant group × cueing × encoding triple interaction. Such an interaction would follow if there was a greater facilitation by cueing for encoding than for nonencoding problems, and if this facilitation was greater for nongifted than for gifted subjects. We expected such a difference across groups in facilitation in that, according to our view of giftedness, the primary difficulty of the nongifted subjects in solving insight problems is in having the proper insight. Thus, providing them with the insight should be quite helpful, as the gifted subjects are more likely to have the insight without cueing. This prediction, too, was confirmed. Examination of the eight relevant means confirmed that the interaction resulted from the predicted pattern of results. In this experiment and in the ones that follow, differential performance of gifted and nongifted was not due to ceiling effects, which did not occur in any of the experiments with mathematical insight problems.

To conclude, the results of the selective encoding experiment were wholly consistent with our five major predictions. The results thus supported the proposed role of selective encoding as critical to solution of insight problems and as an important factor in distinguishing the performance of the gifted from the nongifted.

Our second experiment had as its target the role of selective combination in insightful problem-solving. The 74 subjects in the experiment received mathematical insight problems presented either in the standard format or with cueing intended to facilitate selective combination processes. Consider an example of a problem and how it was cued.

There are five people sitting in a row at a table at a dinner party:

Scott is seated at one end of the row.
Ziggy is seated next to Matt.
Joshua is not sitting next to Scott or Ziggy.
Only one person is sitting next to Walter.
Who is sitting next to Walter?

In its uncued form, the problem was presented just as above. In its cued form, the subject was shown a horizontal grid of five contiguous rectangles. The name 'Scott' was written in the leftmost rectangle. The subject was thereby both shown how to form a grid that would represent the table arrangement and was given a clue as to the location of one individual at the table. Again, all subjects received both cued and uncued problems in a counterbalanced order.

Three major predictions were made regarding the results. First, it was predicted that the gifted subjects would perform better than the nongifted. This prediction was confirmed. Respective means (out of 16 possible) were 6.50 and 4.16 for the gifted and nongifted subjects. Second, it was predicted that performance on the cued problems would be superior to performance on the uncued problems. This prediction, too, was confirmed. Mean scores were 5.82 on the cued problems and 4.84 on the uncued problems (out of 8 possible). Finally, it was predicted that there would be a significant group × cueing interaction, with the nongifted group profiting more from the cueing than the gifted group. This prediction, too, was confirmed. Relevant means were 6.56 for the gifted on uncued problems, 6.44 for the gifted on cued problems, 3.11 for the nongifted on the uncued problems and 5.20 for the nongifted on the cued problems (all out of 8 possible). Thus, once again, the nongifted profited more from receiving the insight than did the gifted.

In sum, the selective combination experiment also supported our theory. In particular, selective combination appears to play an important role in solving insight problems (not all of which involved seats at a table, as did the sample). Moreover, it appears to be a primary source of difficulty for nongifted but not for gifted subjects: Gifted subjects did not benefit from cueing, whereas nongifted ones did.

Our third experiment was designed to assess the role of selective comparison in insightful problem-solving. In this experiment, most subjects received two different example problems prior to receiving the insight problems. For example, the subject might see as an example: 'You are flipping a fair coin. So far, it has come up heads ten times and tails one time. What are the chances that it will come up tails the next time that you flip the coin?' After subjects read the example problems, the nature of the problems was explained to them, and they were given a fairly detailed explanation of how to solve each problem. Later, subjects received a set of insight problems. Some of these problems, in fact, drew upon the principle taught in one example; other problems drew upon the principle taught in the second example; still other problems drew upon neither principle. Problem-solving would clearly be facilitated if the subject recognized (via selective comparison) that one of the examples was relevant to solution of certain ones of the test problems. For instance, a test problem corresponding to the above example would be: 'There are an equal number of red, white and blue gum balls in a penny gum machine. Sandy spent six pennies last week and got five red gum balls and one white one. What are the chances that if she puts in one penny today she will get a red gum ball?'

The experiment actually involved four conditions of item presentation. In one condition, 'No examples', subjects received no examples prior to the actual test problems. In a second condition, 'examples—no relevance information', subjects received two example problems that they could later draw upon in their solution to test problems. They were not told, however, that the examples would later be directly helpful to them. In a third condition, 'Examples—limited relevance information', subjects received two relevant examples and were further told that the examples were relevant to the solution of some of the test problems. They were not told, however, to which test problems each of the examples was relevant. In the fourth condition, 'Examples—full relevance information', subjects were given two examples, told that they would be relevant to their solution of some of the test problems, and were explicitly told to which problems each example was relevant.

There were three main predictions in this experiment. First, it was predicted that gifted children would perform better than nongifted ones. This prediction was confirmed. Mean scores (out of 6 possible) were 4.08 for the gifted children and 3.17 for the nongifted children. Second, it was predicted that problems would become easier as more selective comparison information was provided to the subjects. This prediction, too, was confirmed. Relevant means (all out of 6 possible) were 1.63 for the 'No examples' condition, 3.76 for the 'Examples—no relevance information' condition, 4.32 for the 'Examples—limited relevance information' condition, and 4.79 for the 'Examples—full relevance information' condition. Finally, it was predicted that there would be a significant group $\times$ condition interaction, with the nongifted benefiting more than the gifted from successive amounts of relevance information. This prediction, too, was confirmed. Respective condition means (for the four conditions of successively more information) were 1.82, 4.60, 5.00 and 4.91 for the gifted subjects, and 1.44, 2.92, 3.64 and 4.67 for the nongifted subjects (all out of 6 possible). Note that the gifted benefited only from the receipt of examples. Relevance information seemed to have little or no further effect upon their performance. The nongifted, in contrast, benefited incrementally as each further amount of information was given them.

In sum, the third experiment supports our contention of the importance of selective comparison in insightful problem-solving as well as its role in differentiating the performance of gifted from nongifted subjects. In particular, gifted subjects seem to perform spontaneously the selective comparison that nongifted subjects perform only when prompted.

To conclude, then, the results of our experiments are wholly consistent with our information-processing theory of insight. Of course, the theory needs to be tested on more consequential kinds of insight problems before any strong conclusions can be drawn.

One could argue that the ability of the nongifted but not the gifted to profit from being given the insights was somehow artifactual. One possibility, of course, would be ceiling effects—that the gifted were doing so well on the insight problems to begin with that there simply was not much room for improvement. However, there were no ceiling effects in any of the data. Another possibility would be simply that the nongifted would profit from essentially any instruction at all, whereas the gifted would not so profit from instruction. In order to test this possibility, we did a fourth experiment. In this experiment, insight problems were precued, but with precuing that did not involve handing over the insights. Instead, it involved providing relevant formulas that could be used in task solutions to problems. This noninsightful form of precuing did not aid either the gifted or the nongifted. In other words, the interaction between the gifted and nongifted with respect to benefiting from precuing was limited to precuing that involved insights. Hence, it appears that the crux of the difference between the performance of the two groups was in *insightful* problem-solving, rather than in problem-solving in general.

THE ROLE OF SELECTIVITY IN COPING WITH NOVELTY

In the Davidson and Sternberg (1984) research, the importance of selectivity to encoding, combination and comparison was clear. But it was not clear just how this selectivity was exercised, either by the gifted or by the nongifted students. A study by Marr and Sternberg (1986) sought to investigate the way in which gifted and nongifted children exercise selectivity in their information processing. In particular, the study examines the amount of attention that intellectually gifted and nongifted students in grades 6, 7 and 8 devoted to relevant and irrelevant novel and familiar information, and the accuracy with which they processed this information.

Subjects were 161 sixth-, seventh- and eighth-grade students from two public intermediate schools in southeastern Connecticut. Eighty of the subjects were males, and 81 were females. The gifted sample consisted of students who had already been identified by the schools as eligible for enrollment in their gifted classes.

A self-paced, microcomputer-administered verbal analogies test was developed for this study. Each of 72 simple verbal analogies was paired with three-word precue statements, which contained either novel or familiar, and either relevant or irrelevant information about the third term in the analogy. Thus, 18 precued analogies were written for each of four item conditions: (a) novel relevant precued items; (b) novel irrelevant precued items; (c) familiar relevant precued items; and (d) familiar irrelevant precued items. Examples of each of this types of items are shown in Table 1.

Two test forms were constructed from the 72 items and precues. Each test form presented 36 of these items with precue statements (9 precues and analogies in each of the four conditions shown in Table 1). The remaining 36 items (9 from each condition) were presented without their precue statements (yielding estimates of each subject's solution time and accuracy in the absence of precue information). The items presented with precues in form A were presented without precues in form B, and vice versa. Within each school and subgroup (gifted or nongifted), half of the subjects received form A, and half received form B. Within each test form, presentation order of the 36 items was randomized for every student. Item conditions were not blocked.

In addition to the experimental task, each student also received a seven-

Table 1   Sample items from the four novelty/relevance conditions

Item category	Precue	Analogy	
Novel relevant	Radishes are candies	Pretzel is to salty as radish is to	
		Crunchy	Sweet[a]
		Bitter	Tasty
Novel irrelevant	Lemons are animals	Lime is to green as lemon is to	
		Hard	Red
		Yellow[a]	Round
Familiar relevant	Pistols are weapons	Dagger is to knife as pistol is to	
		Outlaw	Gun[a]
		Holster	Steel
Familiar irrelevant	Zebras are wildlife	Leopard is to spot as zebra is to	
		Stripe[a]	Hoof
		Tail	Mark

[a]Indicates keyed response.

item subset of the insight problems for Davidson and Sternberg (1984), as well as the verbal analogies and number series subtests of the cognitive abilities test. In school no. 1, teachers' ratings of general intelligence, verbal ability and quantitative ability were obtained for every student. Such ratings were not available for students in the second school.

The critical finding in this study was a significant three-way interaction of novelty by relevance by giftedness. We found that intellectually gifted students were more sensitive to the relevance of novel information than were nongifted students. The gifted and nongifted students did not differ in their attention to novelty unless the relevance of the novel stimuli was taken into account. In particular, the gifted and nongifted students in the study differed substantially in their attention to irrelevant novel information, but not in their attention to relevant novel information. Gifted students allocated approximately the same amount of time to relevant novel information as did nongifted students, but quickly dismissed irrelevant novel information. Nongifted students, however, allocated as much time to irrelevant novel information as they did to relevant novel information.

We also found significant correlations between the precued verbal analogies and the abilities tests. These correlations were 0.40 with the insight problems, 0.39 with the psychometric verbal analogies and 0.31 with the psychometric number series. Scores on the precued verbal analogies were also correlated with teachers' ratings of general intelligence in school no. 1. The overall correlation was 0.40. However, this correlation was due to the relationship between analogy scores and ratings for the gifted, but not for the nongifted group. The correlation for the gifted group was 0.56, whereas the correlation for the nongifted group was a trivial 0.15. In other words, teachers' ratings of general intelligence seem to take into account the students' ability to deal with novelty as measured by the precued verbal analogies task only for the gifted students.

In conclusion, then, gifted students are more selective than nongifted students in processing information for reasoning: they better allocate their time in focusing on relevant rather than irrelevant information for problem-solving.

NOVELTY IN TASK UNDERSTANDING: A MODEL OF CONCEPT PROJECTION

Whereas the studies described above focussed upon the role of novelty in task performance, the studies described below focused on the role of novelty in task understanding. From the standpoint of the comprehension of novelty, there are five critical processes in the understanding of a novel task in which an individual must mentally move from a conventional conceptual system to a novel one. The critical processes are:

1. *Encoding the expectation of a change in conceptual system.* This process entails recognition on the part of an individual that a novel conceptual system will be required that is different from the one the subject is using in his or her current information processing.
2. *Accessing a novel conceptual system.* This process requires an individual to go from the current and conventional conceptual system to a new and novel one.
3. *Finding an appropriate concept in a new conceptual system.* This process requires an individual to find the appropriate concept within the now-accessed novel conceptual system.
4. *Allowing for a nonentrenched relationship.* This process requires an individual to process a concept in a new conceptual system that is different in kind from the kinds of concepts with which the individual is familiar in the conventional conceptual system.
5. *Responding to a violation of an expectation of a change in conceptual system.* On occasion, an individual may expect there to be a change in conceptual system, but this expectation proves to be incorrect. This process requires recovery from this incorrect expectation so that the individual is again able to function in the conventional conceptual system.

The concept projection task

I have studied people's responses to novelty in understanding or learning how to perform a new kind of task through a 'concept projection task' (Sternberg, 1981, 1982). In order to understand the model of concept projection, it is necessary to understand something about the kind of task used to measure this skill. The task is quite complicated, but this complication is deliberate. Remember that the goal here is for the task to require response to novelty in task understanding, although not necessarily in task performance.

The main novel or 'nonentrenched' task I have studied is one that requires the individual to make a projection that characterizes the state of an object at some future time on the basis of incomplete information about the state of the object both at that time and at some earlier time. The projection task was studied with four different 'surface' structures having very similar 'deep' structures. Consider the first instantiation of the task, which requires projection of the color an object will appear to be at a future time.

In the first instantiation of the task, subjects were presented with a description of the color of an object in the present day and in the year 2000. The description in each case could be either pictorial—a green dot or a blue dot—or verbal—one of four color words, namely, *green*, *blue*, *grue*, and *bleen*. An object was defined as green if it appeared physically green both in the present and in the year 2000. An object was defined as blue if it appeared physically blue both in the present and in the year 2000. An object was defined as grue if it appeared physically green in the present but physically blue in the year 2000 (i.e. it appeared physically green until the year 2000 and physically blue thereafter). An object was defined as bleen if it appeared physically blue in the present but physically green in the year 2000 (i.e. it appeared physically blue until the year 2000 and physically green thereafter). (The terminology is based upon Goodman, 1955.)

Because each of the two descriptions (one in the present and one in the year 2000) could take one of either two pictorial forms or four verbal forms, there were 36 (6 × 6) different item types. The subject's task was to describe the object in the year 2000. If the given description for the year 2000 was a pictorial one, the subject had to indicate the correct verbal description of the object; if the given description for the year 2000 was a verbal one, the subject had to indicate the correct physical description of the object. There were always three answer choices from which the subject had to choose the correct one.

Subjects were alerted to a complexity in the projection task that applies to the real world as well. When one observes the physical appearance of an object in the present day, one can be certain of its current physical appearance but not of what its physical appearance will be in the year 2000. Hence, all descriptions given for the present day could be guaranteed to be accurate with respect to physical appearance in the present, but they could not be guaranteed to be accurate with respect to their implications, if any, regarding physical appearance in the future. For pictorial descriptions of objects as they appear in the present, this complexity presents no problems, since the pictorial description of an object (a green dot or a blue dot) carries no implications regarding the future physical appearance of the object. For verbal descriptions of objects as they appear in the present, however, this complexity does present a problem. The verbal descriptions *green* and *blue* imply constancy in physical appearance (*steady-state words*), whereas the verbal descriptions *grue* and *bleen* imply change (*variable-state words*). Unfortunately, all one can infer with certainty from these verbal descriptions is the current physical appearance of the object. The implication for the future physical appearance of the object can only be a guess, which may be right or wrong. This complexity ceases to exist for the observer in the year 2000 because at this point all of the evidence is in. The observer in the year 2000 knows for certain what the physical appearance of the object is in 2000 and also knows for certain what the physical appearance of the object was in what was once the present. Hence, the second description, that of the object in the year 2000, is guaranteed to be correct both with respect to the object's appearance in 2000 and the object's appearance in what was once the present. (The one exception to this guarantee is a certain problem type referred to as 'inconsistent', as described below.)

To summarize, pictorial descriptions, which carried no implications for what an object would look like at another time, were always accurate in all respects. Verbal descriptions, which did carry an implication for the appearance of an object at another time, were always accurate with respect to the physical description they implied for the object at the time at which the description was given (except for inconsistent items), but in the present, they might not be accurate with respect to the physical description they implied for the year 2000.

Some examples of actual items will illustrate a few item types (see Sternberg, 1981, 1982, for further examples). In these examples the letters G and B are used to represent the colored dots (green or blue) that were used to indicate the physical appearances of the actual objects. The letter I stands for 'inconsistent'. Recall that items could consist of either two verbal descriptions, a pictorial description and a verbal description, a verbal description and a pictorial description, or two pictorial descriptions.

Blue Blue (GBI)

In this example, an object is described verbally as blue in the present and as blue in 2000. Clearly, its physical appearance in 2000 is B. This was an easy item, with a mean response latency of 1.5 seconds.

Blue Green (IBG)

In this example, an object is described verbally as blue in the present but as green in 2000. These two items of information are inconsistent with each other, and hence the correct answer is the letter I. If the physical appearance of the object changes from blue in the present to green in 2000, the appropriate verbal description of the object in the year 2000 is bleen. If the physical appearance of the object does not change, the appropriate verbal description in the year 2000 is blue. But an object cannot correctly be described as green in the year 2000 if its physical appearance was formerly blue. This item was moderately difficult, with a mean response latency of 2.5 seconds.

G Grue (GBI)

In this example, an object is described as physically green in the present but as verbally grue in the year 2000. The object thus must have appeared physically green in the present and physically blue in 2000. The correct answer is B. This item was also moderately difficult, with a mean solution latency of 3.1 seconds.

Bleen B (Green Bleen Blue)

In this example, an object is described verbally as bleen in the present and physically as B in 2000. One can infer that its physical appearance remained in 2000 what it was in the present, blue. The prediction that the object would change in its physical appearance was incorrect. The correct answer is blue. This was a very difficult item, with a mean solution latency of 4.3 seconds.

BG (Bleen Green Grue)

In this example, an object is described physically as B in the present and as G in 2000. The correct verbal description of the object in 2000 is bleen. This was a difficult item, with a mean solution latency of 3.5 seconds.

Consider the second instantiation of the projection task, which was seen by subjects different from those participating in the first experiment (instantiation). In this experiment, based on appearances of objects on the planet Kyron, an object was described as plin if it appears solid north of the equator and solid south of the equator, as kwef if it appears liquid north of the equator and liquid south of the equator, as balt if it appears solid north of the equator but liquid south of the equator, and as pros if it appears liquid north of the equator but solid south of the equator. In each case, subjects were told that knowledge about an object was obtained first regarding its state north of the equator and then regarding its state south of the equator. Hence, 'north of the equator' corresponds to 'the present' in the first experiment, and 'south of the equator' corresponds to 'the year 2000' in the first experiment. Pictorial representations of objects were either a filled dot (for solid physical appearance) or a hollow dot (for liquid physical appearance). Two experiments were conducted with this instantiation. The second one was added to the first because some subjects had difficulty with the complexity of the instructions in the first of the two experiments using this instantiation.

In the third instantiation of the projection task, which was seen by still different subjects, the words, *plin, kwef, balt* and *pros* were again used, but their meanings were different. Four types of persons were alleged to live on the planet Kyron. A person was described as plin if the person was born a child and remained a child throughout his or her life span. A person was described as kwef if the person was born an adult and remained an adult during the course of his or her life span. A person was described as balt if the person was born a child but became an adult during the course of his or her life span. And a person was described as pros if the person was born an adult but became a child during the course of his or her life span. A stick figure of a little person was used for the pictorial representation of a child; a stick figure of a big person was used for the pictorial representation of an adult.

In the fourth instantiation of the projection task, which was seen by a new set of subjects, the same four words were again used, but their meanings were different again. Subjects were told that a chemist had discovered four new chemicals that look and smell exactly the same. He had found, however, that each chemical had a different effect on the freezing (or melting) point of H_2O (the chemical formula for both water and ice). To test these effects, he added each chemical to a sample of H_2O at time 1 and then placed the H_2O in either a warm oven (in one condition) or in a cold icebox (in the other condition). Subjects received items only in one of the two conditions. One day later, at time 2, the chemist examined the H_2O. He learned that when the chemical plin is added to ice at time 1, the H_2O is still ice at time 2; when the chemical kwef is added to water at time 1, the H_2O is still water at time 2; when the chemical balt is added to ice at time 1, the H_2O becomes water at time 2; and when the chemical pros is added to water at time 1, the H_2O becomes ice at time 2. In these experiments the chemist never added kwef or pros to ice, nor plin nor balt to water, because he had previously found that doing so produced a volatile reaction, resulting in a dangerous explosion. For pictorial descriptions, a filled circle was used to represent ice and a hollow circle was used to represent water. Note that this surface structure has a certain ecological validity lacking in the previous experiments: it deals with the here and now on earth rather than the distant future or an indeterminate time, whether on earth or some other planet.

Model of concept projection

The proposed model will be described with reference to the following problem from the child–adult task, balt plin CAI (where I stands for 'inconsistent').

According to the proposed model, subjects initiate the problem solution by *identifying proposition 1*, which is *balt* (born a child and becomes an adult) in the sample problem. Next, they *access the conceptual system* appropriate for understanding this proposition, which is *variable-state words* in the case of the example. The other two possible states in the present set of problems are *steady-state words* and *pictures*. If the first proposition is a word, subjects *decode the stated physical representations for states 1 and 2*, which in the sample item are C, A (where C refers to a picture of a Kyronian in the childlike state and A refers to a picture of a Kyronian in the adultlike state). If the word is a variable-state word, subjects *encode the expectation of a changed physical representation in state 2*: $\langle C-A \rangle$ in the sample item. Next, regardless of whether or not the first proposition was a word, and, if so, whether or not it was a variable-state word, subjects *store the physical representation* of the first proposition in working memory, for example, $\langle C-A \rangle$.

Now, subjects *identify proposition 2*, which is *plin* in the example item (born a child and remaining a child). If this proposition uses a *new conceptual representation*, that is, a conceptual system different from the one required by the first proposition, subjects *access the new conceptual system*, which is *steady-state words* in the present example; otherwise, subjects stay with the same conceptual system that they had previously assessed (which would have been [*variable-state words*] in the example). If the second proposition takes the form of a word, subjects *decode the stated physical representation for states 1 and 2* as implied by the second proposition, ⟨C–C⟩ in the present example.

Now, subjects are ready to *compare the physical representations in states 1 and 2*. This comparison involves the first item in the first representation, C in the example, and the second item in the second representation, also C in the example. If the relationship between these two items is nonentrenched with respect to subjects' experience, then subjects *allow for a nonentrenched relationship*. This is the case in the example because retention of the childlike state over a long period of time is nonentrenched with respect to our experience. If there is a *change in physical representation* between these same two items, then subjects *find the appropriate variable-state concept* to describe the change. In the example, there is no change in physical state. A change can be recorded even for an inconsistent item if the physical state represented by the second term is different from that represented by the first. If there is no change in physical representation, subjects further query whether there is a *violation of an expectation of change*, that is, whether the first proposition led one to expect a change that did not in fact occur. If there is a violation, subjects *allow for lack of change in the physical representation*. In the example, there is such a violation. *Balt* leads one to expect a change (from the childlike state to the adultlike state), but in fact no change occurred. Thus, the retention of the childlike state (indicated by the second item in the representation of the second proposition) is allowed despite the expectation of a change to the adultlike state (indicated by the second item in the representation of the first proposition).

Regardless of the outcomes of the previous tests, subjects are now ready to *read the answers* presented for the problem. In the example, these are C, A and I. If the answers are words, which they are not in the example, the subject *decodes the meanings* of the words. Subjects now *check their representations for inconsistency* by comparing the first item in the representation for the first proposition with the first item in the representation for the second proposition. If these items do not match, subjects *respond with inconsistency*. If the representations are consistent, subjects query whether the *second proposition is a word*. If so, subjects *respond with the correct picture*, which is the picture that matches the second item in the second representation. If the second proposition is not a word, subjects *respond with the correct word*, which is the word that corresponds to the conjunction of the first item in the first representation and the second item in the second representation. Note that in all cases the final representation is' sufficient to determine whether the problem is consistent and, if so, which picture or word provides the correct response.

Tests of the model of concept projection

Each of approximately 25 adult subjects was tested in each of 5 experiments. Testing consisted of a number of projection-task items followed by standardized tests of inductive reasoning ability from widely used tests of general intelligence. In the last experiment, deductive reasoning tests were also used. Each subject in each experiment saw each of the 36-item types three times, once with the correct answer in each of the three possible ordinal positions. Subjects also received tests of inductive reasoning ability in all of the five experiments and received a test of deductive reasoning ability in the last experiment.

Mean latencies were 3.02 seconds for the green–blue task, 5.44 and 3.89 seconds for harder and simpler versions of the liquid–solid task, 4.15 seconds for the child–adult task and 5.54 seconds for the water–ice task. These means differed significantly. Latencies were highly correlated across experiments (using item types as observations), suggesting that similar information processing was involved in all four instantiations. The information-processing model of task performance accounted for 0.94, 0.92, 0.91, 0.92 and 0.84 of the variance (as measured by squared multiple correlations, or R^2) in the green–blue, liquid–solid (two versions), child–adult and water–ice tasks respectively. Root-mean-square deviations (RMSDs) for the respective tasks were 0.20, 0.43, 0.30, 0.29 and 0.42 second. Residuals were significant only in one variant of the second (liquid–solid) task and in the water–ice task, indicating that the model did an exceptionally good job of accounting for the task latencies.

Global correlations of task scores with psychometically measured induction scores (averaged over psychometric tests) were −0.69, −0.77, −0.61, −0.48 and −0.62 for the five respective experiments. These correlations are not only significant, they are quite substantial. The correlations are thus consistent with the notion that performance on nonentrenched tasks is related to intelligence in a particularly central way. Moreover, the task appears primarily to measure inductive rather than deductive reasoning skills. In the last experiment the correlation with deductive reasoning was −0.43. When deductive reasoning was held constant in a partial correlation of task scores with inductive reasoning, however, the first-order partial was a significant −0.50. When inductive reasoning was held constant in a partial correlation of task scores with deductive reasoning, however, the first-order partial was a nonsignificant −0.10. Patterns of correlations of parameter scores with the psychometric scores also made sense. Parameters representing dealing with novelty were the ones that tended to be responsible for the high levels of correlation with the global scores, whereas parameters representing operations dealing with conventional concepts were only trivially correlated with psychometric test scores.

MODELS OF NONENTRENCHMENT

The studies described above suggested the importance of the ability to deal with novelty, or 'nonentrenchment', in intelligence. A further set of studies was undertaken by Tetewsky and Sternberg (1985) in order to clarify the nature of nonentrenchment. A reasoning task was designed in which the naturalness of a concept and the type of name used to define that concept could be independently varied. A conceptual system was found in which the content could be expressed in four different forms, so the two levels of concepts (natural or unnatural) could be crossed with two levels of names (familiar or novel). The underlying assumption for this design was that these two variables might be important in distinguishing between entrenched and nonentrenched concepts.

In the first experiment to be described, subjects were required to solve reasoning problems in which they had to select among alternative projections about occurrences in the environment that relate to seasonal changes. It is quite natural for the leaves to change color in accordance with the seasons (at least in New England!). However, it is not at all natural for us to think that rocks will change color according to a seasonal pattern. Analogously, seasons can be identified by the names *summer*, *fall*, *winter* and *spring*, or they can be given novel names, such as *soob*, *trit*, *blen* and *mave*. By using these two sets of concepts and names, the following four situations were constructed: (a) familiar season names describing states of the leaves; (b) novel season names describing states of the leaves; (c) familiar season names describing states of the rocks; and (d) unfamiliar season names describing states of the rocks. In the second experiment, subjects were required to make projections about events in the environment that relate to periods of the day. In this context, it is natural to identify a period of the day by noting the position of the sun relative to the horizon and it is quite unnatural to expect that minerals will change shape as the day progresses. Also, the periods of the day can be identified by the names *daytime*, *dusk*, *night time* and *dawn*, or they can be given novel names such as *trofar*, *bren*, *stobe* and *kovit*. By using these two sets of concepts and names, a set of four situations was constructed that was structurally equivalent to that describing seasons in the first experiment.

Subjects in each of these conditions were given descriptions of the beginning and the end of a season (or the beginning and end of a period of the day) and were required to make inferences regarding the events that occurred. The problems were presented individually as 'selection task items'. The ease with which subjects made these judgments was measured by both latency and error indices. A model of information processing was also tested for the latency data obtained in each of the four tasks. In addition to providing an empirical analysis about the nature of nonentrenched concepts, these experiments also required subjects to solve a set of novel reasoning problems, which were of varying degrees of difficulty. They therefore provided a way to assess the extent to which intelligence is associated with the ability to reason within new conceptual systems.

These experiments presented an opportunity to compare different structural models for nonentrenched concepts. The potential effects of linguistic familiarity and conceptual naturalness on nonentrenchment can be described in terms of five basic models, which are shown in Table 2. Analysis-of-variance contrast weights are used to represent the patterns of reaction time and error rates that characterize each of these models.

Model 0

In model 0, the null case, there is no effect for either linguistic unfamiliarity or conceptual unnaturalness. This model implies that there is no psychological

Table 2   Models for nonentrenched concepts

	Linguistic familiarity		Conceptual naturalness
	Familiar	Unfamiliar	
Model 0	0	0	Natural
	0	0	Unnatural
Model 1	−	−	Natural
	+	+	Unnatural
Model 2	−	+	Natural
	−	+	Unnatural
Model 3	− −	0	Natural
	0	+ +	Unnatural
Model 4	−	+	Natural
	+	−	Unnatural

reality in the nonentrenchment construct. In essence, this model represents the null hypothesis.

Model 1

In model 1, the locus of nonentrenchment can be found entirely in conceptual naturalness; according to this formulation, linguistic unfamiliarity does not contribute to nonentrenchment.

Model 2

Model 2 shows the complementary situation, in which the locus of nonentrenchment can be found entirely in linguistic unfamiliarity; according to this formulation, conceptual unnaturalness does not contribute to nonentrenchment.

Model 3

Model 3 is essentially an extension of models 1 and 2, in that it describes the situation in which linguistic unfamiliarity and conceptual unnaturalness are both important, such that their effects are additive. Model 3 distinguishes between two levels of nonentrenchment. On one level (represented by '0' in the table), nonentrenchment is characterized by using either familiar names to denote unnatural occurrences or unfamiliar names to denote natural occurrences—at this level, there is no predicted difference in difficulty between these forms of nonentrenchment. At a second level, there is a more difficult form of nonentrenchment that involves using unfamiliar names to denote unnatural occurrences.

Model 4

Finally, model 4 describes the situation in which nonentrenchment is defined by an interaction between linguistic unfamiliarity and conceptual unnaturalness. According to this model, there are two equivalent types of nonentrenched concepts, one in which familiar names denote unnatural occurrences, and another in which unfamiliar names denote natural occurrences. The locus of difficulty is in pairing the familiar (either concepts or language) with the unfamiliar (again, either concepts or language).

In a first experiment, subjects were 96 Yale undergraduates who participated for course credit, monetary payment or both. Subjects were randomly assigned to one of four conditions, with 24 subjects in each condition. A separate group of 25 undergraduates taking a developmental psychology course at Yale gave responses to a set of background survey questions.

The basic materials were selection-task items presented via a tachistoscope and psychometric inductive and deductive ability tests presented in a paper-and-pencil format. In addition to the standardized ability tests, subjects were given a set of problems that have previously been used to study insight (Sternberg and Davidson, 1982).

In the selection task, items were modeled on previous problems used by Sternberg (1982). Items were developed in which a common 'deep' structure was used to generate four different 'surface' structures. In each of the four sets of items, the problems were based on the initial premise that the seasons of the year allow one to predict certain occurrences in nature and that, in turn, these occurrences identify what a given season is. Each problem contained two pieces of information. The first piece of information described a situation at the beginning of a season and the second piece of information provided 'follow-up' data from the end of the same season. Because each of the four variations of the task were similar, only one version will be described in detail. The other variations will be described more briefly.

The premise that served as the model for the other three versions of the task stated that in New Haven, the beginning and end of each season is marked by the fact that the leaves will be either green or brown. In summer, the leaves are green at the beginning and at the end of the season. In fall, the leaves are green at the beginning of the season but are brown at the end. In winter, the leaves are brown at both the beginning and end of the season. And, in spring, the leaves are brown at the beginning of the season but are green at the end. Subjects were required to use this information to solve a series of reasoning problems.

Each problem was presented on one card. Each term of a problem could contain one of two forms of information. The description could be either a picture of the leaves, indicated by a green or brown circle, or the name of a season that represents a decision about what season it is, based on the color of the leaves at the time the observation was made. Information about the leaves at the beginning of the season appeared on the left and information about the leaves at the end of the season appeared on the right. Because each of two descriptions of the leaves (one at the beginning of the season and one at the end) could take either of two physical forms (brown or green) or four verbal forms (an inference based on a season name), there were 6 × 6, or 36, distinct items.

The subject's task was to describe the leaves at the end of the season, based on the information provided in the problem. If the given description for the end of the season was a picture of the leaves, the subject had to indicate the correct name of the season. If the given description for the end of the season was a name, the subject had to indicate the correct color of the leaves. There were always three choices, from which the subject had to choose the correct one. These alternatives appeared below the problem stem.

There were four different types of problems. Items either had two season names, a picture followed by a season name, a season name followed by a picture, or two pictures. In the first two types of problems, subjects had to determine the color of the leaves at the end of the season. In the other two problems, subjects had to give the name of the season consistent with the given information. Subjects were alerted to a further complexity in the selection task, which also applies in the real world. At the beginning of a season, it is impossible to distinguish summer from fall or spring from winter, if the only available information is the initial color of the leaves. Also, the names 'summer' and 'winter' imply that the leaves will remain the same color, whereas the names 'spring' and 'fall' imply that the leaves will change color by the end of the season. For problems in which the first term was the name of the season, this name correctly described the color of the leaves at the beginning of the season, but only predicted what color the leaves would be at the end. This prediction might not correspond to the color that was described by the second term. Thus, it was not possible to know for certain the color of the leaves at the end of the season or to know for certain the true season. When the first term of the problem was a picture of the leaves, this complexity did not exist, because a physical description carries no implication regarding the future physical appearance of the leaves.

Although this uncertainty in prediction did not exist for information describing the leaves at the end of the season, there was a related problem associated with the second term. When a season name described the leaves at the end of the season, it could be assumed to provide correct information about both the beginning and ending color of the leaves, because assessments of season made late in the season were based on observations of the leaves throughout the entire season. For the problems in which the second term was a name, however, this season name could be 'inconsistent' with the starting color of the leaves, as defined in the first term of the problem. For example, if the first term was 'summer', this name means that the leaves were green at the beginning of the season and predicts that they would be green at the end. If the second term was 'spring', this name means that the leaves were brown at the start of the season and eventually turned green. Because the leaves cannot be both brown and green at the beginning of the season, this problem describes an inconsistent situation; as a result, it was impossible to determine the color of the leaves at the end of the season. The correct answer was thus 'inconsistent'.

To summarize, physical descriptions, which carried no necessarily correct implication for what the leaves would look like at another time, were always accurate with respect to the appearance of the leaves at the time of the description. However, they might not be accurate with respect to the appearance of the leaves at the end of the season.

This experiment attempted to assess the extent to which various conceptual systems are more or less 'entrenched' by comparing how different problem contents and forms affect reasoning. In the form mentioned above, subjects were required to reason within an 'entrenched' framework. The other three forms of this task varied either the 'naturalness' of the concepts or the type of language used, or both. It is expected that leaves will alternate between green and brown as the seasons change. However, it is not at all normal to expect that rocks will change from orange to blue with the passage of seasons. Similarly, the terms summer, fall, winter and spring carry certain connotations about the season they name, but the neologisms soob, trit, blen and mave do not carry any unequivocal information about the physical world. Because there are two types of concepts (natural and unnatural) and two types of names (familiar and novel), there are 2 × 2 or 4 possible versions of the season—color information.

In a second condition, subjects were told about the distant country of Latzania, where the leaves change color just as they do in New Haven, but the seasons are called trit, blen, mave and soob. In a third condition, subjects were told about the planet Kyron, where the seasons are called summer, fall, winter and spring, but are marked by the fact that rocks change from blue to orange or from orange to blue. In the fourth condition, subjects were told about the planet Kyron, where the seasons are called trit, blen, mave and soob, and can be distinguished by the fact that the rocks vary from orange to blue, according to a systematic pattern.

Using each of the conditions described above, 3 more sets of 36 problems were generated that were structurally identical to those described for the case of New Haven. The only difference among the four tasks involved the extent to which the conceptual system was 'entrenched' as defined by a particular concept–language combination. This manipulation of content made it possible to identify the locus of 'nonentrenchment'.

The ability tests that were used included geometric series completion (abstract reasoning) from the Differential Aptitude Test (Bennett, Seashore and Wesman, 1973), letter and number series completions (reasoning) from the SRA Primary Mental Abilities, adult level (Thurstone and Thurstone, 1962), and deductive syllogisms (subtest 3) and confirming the validity of conclusions (subtest 9) from the Watson–Glaser (1964) Critical Thinking Appraisal.

The survey requested subjects to rate how common it is, in their experience, for either leaves or rocks to change colors with the seasons. In addition, subjects were given an array with the names 'summer', 'fall', 'winter' and 'spring' on one side and the four possible blue–orange or brown–green pairings on the other side. Their task was to match one season name with one of the four physical occurrences. Subjects answered questions about either leaves or rocks, but not both.

The overall design placed subjects within a 2 × 2 between-subjects factorial arrangement. The primary dependent variable was solution latency; a secondary dependent variable was error rate. In item construction, independent variables were the six possible state descriptions (e.g. in the case of New Haven, summer, fall, winter, spring, G [green circle], and B [brown circle] crossed with the two possible times of occurrence [the beginning and end of a season]). All subjects saw each of the 36 possible item types three times, with the correct option in a different location each time. The items in each task variant were grouped into three blocks so that a subject had to complete an entire set of 36 items before seeing an item for a subsequent time.

Each subject was randomly assigned to one of the four versions of the selection task. For items in which subjects had to determine the color of the leaves at the end of the season, distractors consisted of an incorrect picture and an 'indeterminate' (I) option, to correspond to the possibility that the information in the problem could be describing a self-contradictory and hence, indeterminate situation. For the items that required subjects to determine the name of the season, distractors consisted of two of the three possible word distractors balanced over the three replications of the task for a given experiment. Thus, each possible word distractor appeared equally often across item replications. In the three versions that described the seasons in Latzania or on Kyron, four counterbalanced forms of the items were constructed so that each season name was paired with each of the four physical occurrences (two concepts describing a physical change and two concepts describing constant physical states) only once. For example, in Latzania, the season that would correspond to summer was soob in form A, trit in form B, blen in form C and mave in form D. The scheme was followed for each of the other three seasons. This method of counterbalancing was not applied to the New Haven scenario, however, because this scenario did not have any possible alternative forms. Subjects who filled out the survey were given one of two alternative forms of the questions. The forms differed in the order that the season names were listed, so that subjects would not be biased in favor of choosing a particular season name for any one color change.

Selection-task items were administered on an Iconix tachistoscope with attached millisecond timer. Subjects signaled their responses by pressing the button corresponding to the appropriate answer option. Psychometric ability tests, insight problems, and the survey were all administered in written form.

The instructions for the experiment were rather lengthy and required that subjects learn how to solve an entirely new set of reasoning problems. Because of the complexity of the task, after each subject finished reading the instructions, the experimenter reviewed the essential elements involved in each of the four types of problems. Then subjects received eight practice items, two of each of the four types of problems described earlier. When needed, extra practice items were provided until subjects were able to give correct responses and to demonstrate that they were aware of the different requirements of each problem. Subjects were instructed to solve the items as rapidly as they could under the constraint that they be as accurate as possible. After the practice trials were over, subjects received three randomized blocks of 36 problems, each of a different type. Each of the 36 problem types appeared once in each of the three blocks. Items were drawn on separate 6 × 9-inch cards. Each answer option was correct equally often in each block (twelve times per block). The experimenter initiated each trial. The milli-second clock started as soon as the subject pressed one of the three answer buttons. In general, feedback was not provided during selection-task trials, unless subjects made three errors in a row. This feedback was given to ensure that subjects were aware of the various intricacies involved in the different types of problems. Of the 96 subjects who participated in this experiment, 12 were given feedback. The selection task usually took about one hour to administer.

The ability tests were administered at a later time in small groups. All tests were timed and subjects were told to complete the tests as quickly and accurately as possible. The various tests were always presented in the follow-ing order, under the specified time constraints: (1) letter series ($2\frac{1}{2}$ minutes); (2) deductive syllogisms (6 minutes); (3) number series ($2\frac{1}{2}$ minutes); (4) confirming the validity of conclusions (4 minutes); (5) abstract reasoning (12 minutes); and (6) insight problems (20 minutes).

The critical finding in this study was that the data supported model 4: the mean reaction times were 3.83 seconds for group 1, 4.18 seconds for group 2, 4.80 seconds for group 3, and 3.76 seconds for group 4. Error rates showed the same pattern as the solution latencies. In other words, the locus of the nonentrenchment effect was not in linguistic difficulties *per se*, nor was it in conceptual difficulty *per se*, but it was in the integration of linguistic with conceptual information. In other words, subjects found it difficult to process the conceptual-projection items when novel concepts were paired with famil-iar linguistic tokens, or when novel linguistic tokens were paired with familiar concepts. They did not find difficult problems in which the linguistic tokens and the concepts underlying these tokens were either both novel or both nonnovel.

A second experiment was designed to replicate and generalize the findings of the first study. The major differences involved the content of the concep-tual system and the words used to describe this content. Subjects were 80 Yale undergraduates. They were randomly assigned to one of four conditions, with 20 subjects in each condition. The same ability tests and insight problems were used as in the preceding experiment. The selection-task items used in this experiment were structurally identical to those used previously, differing only in content. The premise that serves as the model for the other three versions of the task stated that, in New Haven, the beginning and end of each period of the day is marked by the fact that the sun is either above or below the horizon. At dawn, the sun starts out below the horizon but eventually ends up above the horizon. In daytime, the sun is above the horizon at the beginning and at the end of this period. At dusk, the sun starts out above the horizon but eventually ends up below the horizon. And in nighttime, the sun is below the horizon at the beginning and at the end of this period.

In order to parallel the first experiment, the period of the day had to be characterized by an 'unnatural' occurrence. Because it is not at all normal for the periods of the day to be characterized by minerals that change shape from oval to rectangular, this occurrence served as the unnatural concept. In one variation, subjects were told about the Hafo Indians of western Canada, who use the names stobe, kovit, bren and trofar to describe the daily pattern of changes in the position of the sun. In another version, subjects were told about the planet Kyron, where the periods of the day are called dawn, daytime, dusk and nighttime, but are marked by the fact that a certain type of mineral changes from rectangular to oval shape or from oval shape to rectangular shape. In the final variation, subjects were told about the planet Kyron, where the periods of the day are called stobe, kovit, bren and trofar, and can be distinguished by the fact that a certain kind of mineral changes shape from rectangular to oval, according to a systematic pattern. All stimuli were presented on a cathode ray tube screen.

The results of this experiment replicated the results of the preceding experiment. Once again, it was found that the locus of nonentrenchment lies in mapping unnatural occurrences onto familiar names or natural occurrences onto novel names. These data suggest that people have difficulty reasoning with new information because it is both similar to and different from the knowledge they already possess. The entrenchment construct shows that prior knowledge can both facilitate and impede our attempts to understand the world.

To conclude, I have argued in this article that the ability to cope with novelty and, especially, relevant novelty, is an essential aspect of intelligence. Four series of experiments have been presented in support of this position, each making this argument in a somewhat different way. The experiments have elaborated on the information-processing bases of the ability to cope with novelty, pointing out that this ability is not a unitary one. Rather, the ability involves component subskills requiring both comprehension of novelty and reasoning with the information comprehended. Of course, the ability to cope with novelty is not all there is to intelligence. The triarchic theory of human intelligence (Sternberg, 1985) specifies other aspects of the construct. But the ability to cope with novelty enters into so many aspects of intelligent performance that it seems clear that we will not be able fully to understand intelligence until we understand this very basic ability.

ACKNOWLEDGEMENT

Preparation of this article was supported by Contract N00014783K0013 from the Office of Naval Research and Army Research Institute.

REFERENCES

Bennett, G. K., Seashore, H. G. and Wesman, A. G. (1973). *Differential Aptitude Tests*. New York: The Psychological Corporation.

Berg, C. A., and Sternberg, R. J. (1985). Response to novelty: Continuity versus discontinuity in the development course of intelligence. In H. Reese (ed.) *Advances in Child Development and Behavior*. New York: Academic Press.

Cattell, R. B. (1971). *Abilities: Their Structure, Growth, and Action*. Boston: Houghton-Mifflin.

Davidson, J. E., and Sternberg, R. J. (1984). The role of insight in intellectual giftedness. *Gifted Child Quarterly*, **28**, 58–64.

French, J. W., Ekstrom, R. B. and Price, I. (1963). *Kit of Reference Tests for Cognitive Factors*. Princeton, NJ: Educational Testing Service.

Goodman, N. (1955). *Fact, Fiction, and Forecast*. Cambridge, MA: Harvard University Press.

Horn, J. L. (1968). Organization of abilities and the development of intelligence. *Psychological Review*, **75**, 242–59.

Intelligence and its measurement: A symposium. (1921). *Journal of Educational Psychology*, **12**, 123–47, 195–216, 271–5.

Kaufman, A. S., and Kaufman, N. L. (1983). *Kaufman Assessment Battery for Children* (K-ABC). Circle Pines, Minn. American Guidance Service.

Kohler, W. (1927). *The Mentality of Apes*. New York: Harcourt, Brace.

Maier, N. R. F. (1930). Reasoning in humans: I. On direction. *Journal of Comparative Psychology*, **12**, 115–43.

Marr, D. B., and Sternberg, R. J. (1986). Analogical reasoning with novel concepts: Differential attention of intellectually gifted and nongifted children to relevant and irrelevant novel stimuli. *Cognitive Development*, **1**, 53–72.

Mischel, W. (1968). *Personality and Assessment*. New York: John Wiley.

Perkins, D. (1978). *The Mind's Best Work*. Cambridge: Harvard University Press.

Piaget, J. (1972). *The Psychology of Intelligence*. Totowa, NJ: Littlefield, Adams.

Raaheim, K. (1974). *Problem Solving and Intelligence*. Oslo: Universitesforlaget.

Raaheim, K. (1984). *Why Intelligence is not Enough*. Bergen, Norway: Sigma Forlag.

Snow, R. E. (1981). Toward a theory of aptitude for learning: I. Fluid and crystallized abilities and their correlates. In M. Friedman, J. P. Das and N. O'Connor (eds) *Intelligence and Learning*. New York: Plenum Press.

Sternberg, R. J. (1981). Intelligence and nonentrenchment. *Journal of Educational Psychology*, **73**, 1–16.

Sternberg, R. J. (1982). Natural, unnatural, and supernatural concepts. *Cognitive Psychology*, **14**, 451–88.

Sternberg, R. J. (1985). *Beyond IQ: A Triarchic Theory of Human Intelligence*. New York: Cambridge University Press.

Sternberg, R. J., Conway, B. E., Ketron, J. L. and Bernstein, M. (1981). People's conceptions of intelligence. *Journal of Personality and Social Psychology*, **41**, 37–55.

Sternberg, R. J., and Davidson, J. E. (1982). Componential analysis and componential theory. *Behavioral and Brain Sciences*, **53**, 352–3.

Sternberg, R. J., and Davidson, J. E. (1983). Insight in the gifted. *Educational Psychologist*, **18**, 52–8.
Tetewsky, S. J., and Sternberg, R. J. (1986). Conceptual and lexical determinants of nonentrenched thinking. *Journal of Memory and Language*, **25**, 202–225.
Thurstone, L. L., and Thurstone, T. G. (1962). *Tests of Primary Mental Abilities* (revised). Chicago, Ill. Science Research Associates.
Watson, G., and Glaser, E. M. (1964). *Watson–Glaser Critical Thinking Appriasal*. New York: Harcourt Brace Jovanovich.
Wertheimer, M. (1959). *Productive Thinking* (revised). New York: Harper & Row.

Modelling Cognition
Edited by P. Morris
© 1987 John Wiley & Sons Ltd.

4

Cognitive principles in the design of computer tutors

JOHN R. ANDERSON, C. FRANKLIN BOYLE, ROBERT FARRELL and BRIAN J. REISER
Advanced Computer Tutoring Project, Carnegie-Mellon University

In this chapter a set of eight principles are derived from the ACT* theory for designing intelligent tutors: use production system models of the student, communicate the goal structure of the problem space, provide instruction on the problem-solving context, promote an abstract understanding of the problem-solving knowledge, minimize working memory load, provide immediate feedback in errors, adjust the grain size of instruction according to learning principles, and enable the student to approach the target skills by successive approximation. These principles have guided our design of tutors for LISP and geometry.

There has been and continues to be a great deal of hope for the role of computers in education (Cohen, 1982; Papert, 1980; Taylor, 1980). The actual record of accomplishment is still quite modest, however. Most computer education takes the form of simple drill and practice and is often not as effective as classroom drill and practice. There has always been the hope that artificial intelligence techniques would illuminate computer instruction. The buzz word of a decade ago was 'intelligent computer assisted instruction' or ICAI (Carbonnel, 1970). The relative lack of progress in that field led to a disenchantment with that expression, and we now see new descriptors. The basic problem with the earlier work was lack of a clear paradigm for bringing intelligence to bear in delivering instruction. A current belief is that the most promising paradigm for bringing intelligence to bear is to emulate a private human tutor. This is the intelligent tutoring paradigm (Sleeman and Brown, 1982). The basic observation that motivates the intelligent tutoring approach is the great effectiveness of private human tutors over either classroom instruction or standard computer education. Bloom (1984) reports that 98 percent of students instructed by private tutors performed better than the average student in the classroom. In an experiment reported at the end of this chapter, we found private tutors were able to bring students to the same level of achievement in perhaps as little as a quarter of the time that was needed in the classroom. The hope of intelligent tutoring is to find some way of 'bottling' the skill of the human tutor and putting it in a computer tutor.

The most straightforward application of artificial intelligence techniques to intelligent tutoring would be an expert systems approach. In this approach, one would treat the human tutor as the expert whose knowledge has to be extracted and build an expert system to apply that knowledge. Work such as that of Stevens, Collins and Goldin (1982) on teaching topics such as rainfall seems to have this character. However, human tutoring does not have the characteristics of a domain that proves susceptible to the expert system methodology. It is not a clearly circumscribed knowledge domain, it is heavily dependent on natural language understanding, and human tutors show enormous individual differences in their tutoring styles. Thus, it seems unlikely that there is a well-defined expertise to be captured and emulated.

It is probably for this reason that most approaches to intelligent tutoring have not tried to really emulate human tutors (see the papers in Sleeman and Brown, 1982). Rather they have tried to identify abstract principles of effective tutoring and design tutors that embody these principles without concern with whether these tutors emulate humans. While the tutoring system is not itself an expert system, an intelligent tutor often has an expert system as a submodule for solving problems in the domain to be tutored. For instance, Brown, Burton and DeKleer (1982) include an expert circuit analysis system as part of their SOPHIE tutor for troubleshooting circuits. Such a system can reason correctly about the domain and thus provide the correct answer, which is, of course, an important piece of information in instruction.

We feel that the actual pedagogical design of the tutor must be based on detailed cognitive models of how students solve problems and learn. The state of the art in cognitive science has reached the point where we now are able to produce theories capable of applications to intelligent tutoring. In this paper we would like to develop a set of principles for computer tutoring based on the ACT* theory of cognition (Anderson, 1983). This theory has been developed at a sufficient level of detail that it is possible to produce simulations of the theory that actually solve problems the way students would solve problems and which learn from problem-solving much as students learn. These simulations form the core of our tutorial efforts because part of every tutor is what we call an *ideal* model, which models how successful students solve problems in the domain. Such models have an additional requirement not found in the expert systems of most tutors. Not only must they be able to solve the problems in the domain, they must be able to solve them the way students do. For instance, Clancey (1983) has found it necessary to rework mycin in order to build a tutor for medical reasoning.

The major portion of this paper will be devoted to identifying and justifying eight principles for doing intelligent tutoring. Then the last two sections of the paper will describe two tutors we have built partially embodying these principles. One is a tutor for the LISP programming language and the other is a tutor for high-school geometry. However, before embarking on any of this we should state a major limitation on the principles that we will articulate. We can only defend their application to a relatively restricted set of topics—those for which we can develop ideal student models. These include the domains of high-school and early-college math and introductory programming. These domains are relatively sparse in their importation of extra-domain knowledge, and thus the ideal model need only address domain knowledge. It is possible to develop much more articulate tutors for domains for which one has precise student models. If one does not know exactly what it is the student is supposed to do, it forces one to back off into a different tutoring strategy.

Throughout this paper we will be making reference to observations we have made of high-school students learning geometry and college students learning to program in LISP. We have observed four students spend approximately 30 hours studying beginning geometry and three students similarly spending 30 hours learning LISP. These sessions have all been recorded and have been subjected to varying degrees of analysis. Some of these analyses have been reported in a series of prior publications (Anderson, 1981a,b; 1983; Anderson, Farrell and Sauers, 1984; Anderson, Pirolli and Farrell, in press). This data base of protocols has served as a rich source of information about the acquisition of problem-solving skill and has heavily influenced design of our computer tutors. In addition to gathering this protocol data, we have performed a good number of more analytic experiments which we will refer to throughout this chapter.

REVIEW OF THE ACT* THEORY

Before turning to the cognitive principles it is useful to give a brief review of the ACT* theory on which they are based. This theory has been embodied in computer programs which have successfully simulated many aspects of human cognition (Anderson, 1983). The ACT* theory is an attempt to identify all the principal factors that affect human cognition and organize them into a complete cognitive theory. The ACT* theory is quite complex, consisting of a set of assumptions about a declarative memory and a procedural memory. However, it appears that only certain aspects of the theory are relevant to the tutoring of cognitive skills: in particular, the procedural assumptions. The procedural component in the ACT* theory takes the form of a production system. Much of human cognition appears to unfold as a sequence of actions evoked by various patterns of knowledge. Productions attempt to capture this by pattern–action pairs describing individual steps of cognition. The actual productions are implemented in a computer system that simulates human cognition. An 'Englishified' version of a production from one of the ACT* simulations is:

IF the goal is to prove $\triangle UVW \cong \triangle XYZ$
THEN set as subgoals to
1. Prove $\overline{UV} \cong \overline{XY}$
2. Prove $\overline{VW} \cong \overline{YZ}$
3. Prove $\angle UVW \cong \angle XYZ$

This is a backwards chaining rule that embodies the SAS (side–angle–side) rule of geometry. If the goal is to prove two triangles congruent, it sets as a subgoal to prove two sides and an included angle congruent. One can also have forward inference rules such as:

IF the goal is to make in inference from the fact that $\overline{XY} \cong \overline{UV}$
and it is true that $\angle XYZ \cong \angle UVW$
and it is true that $\overline{YZ} \cong \overline{VW}$
THEN infer that it is true that $\triangle UVW \cong \triangle XYZ$
because of the side-angle-side postulate.

As these examples illustrate, productions in the ACT* theory are *goal-factored*. That is, they make reference in their condition to a specific goal to which they are relevant. These productions can only be evoked when that goal is active.

The conditions of these productions are patterns that match to information being held in working memory. The ACT* theory assumes people have only a limited capacity to keep information active in working memory. It is possible that the capacity will be exceeded in a problem, and critical information for the matching of a production will be lost. This can result in the failure to execute the appropriate production or the execution of an inappropriate production. A good many errors of learners are due to working memory failures rather than failures of understanding (Anderson and Jeffries, in press).

Knowledge compilation

Key to any theory of tutoring are the learning mechanisms by which new procedures (productions above) are acquired. Knowledge compilation is a major mechanism for procedural learning in ACT*. Elsewhere (Anderson,

1983) I have argued that knowledge compilation and production strengthening account for all forms of procedural learning. There are two subprocesses involved in knowledge compilation. The first, proceduralization, creates productions that eliminate the retrieval of information by pattern matching of a production condition. Proceduralization builds that information into the proceduralized production. One example of this involves retrieval of information from long-term memory about LISP programming. In ACT* there is a production that will retrieve function definitions from long-term memory and apply them:

> IF   the goal is to code a relation defined on an argument
>   and there is a LISP function that codes this relation
> THEN   use this function with the argument
>   and set a subgoal to code the argument

In this production, *relation* and *function* are variables which allow the production to match different data. The second line of the condition might match, for instance, 'CAR codes the first member of a list'. If this rule is proceduralized to eliminate the retrieval of the CAR definition, it becomes:

> IF   the goal is to code the first member of a list
> THEN   use the CAR of the list
>   and set as a subgoal to code the list

This is achieved by deleting the second clause that required long-term memory retrieval from the first production. In addition, the rest of the production is made specific to the relation *first element* and the function CAR. Now a production has been created which can directly recognize the application of CAR. This will result in a reduction in the amount of long-term memory information that needs to be maintained in working memory.

Composition involves collapsing a number of successful operators into a single macro-operator that produces the same overall effect as the sequence of individual operators. As an example of this from LISP, suppose one wanted to insert the first member of List1 into List2. Then the following two operators would apply in sequence:

> IF   the goal is to insert an element into a list
> THEN   CONS the element to the list
>   and set as subgoals to code the element
>   and to code the list

> IF   the goal is code the first member of a list
> THEN   take the CAR of the list
>   and set as a subgoal to code the list

The first rule above would apply and bind *an element* to 'the first member of List1' and *a list* to 'List2'. The second production would apply and bind *a list* to 'List1'. A simple case of composition would involve combining these two productions together to produce:

IF   the goal is to insert the first member of one list into another list
THEN   CONS the CAR of the first list to the second list
       and set as subgoals to code the first list
       and to code the second list

Such composition would collapse repeated sequences of coding operations to create macro-operators. The result would be a speed up in coding because problems could be coded in fewer steps. McKendree and Anderson (in press) provide evidence for such speedup of frequently repeated combinations of LISP functions.

We have briefly reviewed four features of the ACT* theory (use of productions, goal structure, working memory limitations and knowledge compilation) that prove to be key to the cognitive principles that we will be describing.

STATUS OF THE COGNITIVE PRINCIPLES

Before describing our principles of computer tutoring, it is important for us to clarify the relationship among these principles, our ACT* theory, and various empirical results. Each principle is in fact derived from the ACT* theory. However, the derivation is not always transparent, and in fact it was often a discovery for us that ACT* implied these principles. This is frequently the relationship between a scientific theory and design principles based on it. The theory is typically cast to predict what the results will be of particular manipulations, not to predict what manipulations will achieve a particular optimal outcome. Also, these principles often have boundary conditions—it is not the case that in all circumstances a particular manipulation is optimal.

The ACT* theory has a fair degree of empirical support (e.g. Anderson, 1983) but, as with any psychological theory, hardly has the status of an established fact. Therefore, we would like to have more evidence for those principles than simply that they are implied by ACT*. We will also describe empirical evidence consistent with these principles. In fact, one of the major reasons for our interest in tutoring research is to gather further empirical evidence for these principles and hence for the ACT* theory on which they are based.

Principle 1: Represent the student as a production set

Probably the most important role for a cognitive theory in tutoring is to provide explicit process models of how the ideal student should behave and of how the current student is behaving. The process model of the ideal student allows one to be very precise about instructional objectives. The process model of the current student allows one to be very precise about the current state of the student and how he or she deviates from the desired state. The current student model also allows one to interpret the student's behavior.

The implications of the ACT* theory for student models are, of course, that they should be cast as production systems. Much of our success in constructing tutors is to be credited to this design choice. It is an interesting question what the evidence is for production systems. The hypothesis of a production system is too abstract to be put to direct empirical test. Rather, the evidence for production systems comes from their success as the basic formalism for developing explanations of human problem-solving (e.g. Newell and Simon, 1972). It is also the case that numerous other efforts in the general domain of intelligent tutoring have taken to representing the to-be-tutored skill as a production set (e.g. Brown and Van Lehn, 1980; O'Shea, 1979; Sleeman, 1982).

Production systems not only enable the system to follow student problem-solving, but the individual productions define an appropriate grain size for instruction. Each production is a package of knowledge that can be communicated to a student in one interaction. Basically, a tutoring system monitors whether a student has the correct form of each rule, and the system provides missing rules and corrects buggy rules. Also, as emphasized by Brown and Van Lehn (1980), student misconceptions or bugs can be organized as production rules which are perturbations of correct rules. For example, a buggy rule may be missing a condition, resulting in an over-general rule that applies in incorrect situations.

Principle 2: Communicate the goal structure underlying the problem-solving

According to the ACT* theory, and indeed most cognitive theories of problem-solving, the problem-solving behavior is organized around a hierarchical representation of the current goals. It is important that this goal structure be communicated to the student and instruction be cast in terms of it. Below we discuss the fact that it is not communicated in typical instruction for LISP or geometry and some of the unfortunate consequences of this fact.

Geometry

Figure 1 shows the two-column proof form that is almost universally used in geometry. It is basically a linear structure of pairs where each pair is a statement and justification. Typical instruction encourages the belief that the goal structure of the student should mimic this linear structure—that at any point in the proof the student will have generated an initial part of the structure and the current goal is to generate the next line of the structure.

Figure 1 also illustrates the typical instruction that is given about how to generate a proof. This is all the instruction a student receives from the textbook about how to generate a proof, and many teachers provide no more in their classroom instruction. Clearly, there is very little identification of the goal structure a student should assume in generating a proof.

Figure 2 illustrates the mental representation that we believe a successful student creates for the proof of a geometry problem. The conclusion to be

---

1-7 *Proofs in Two-Column Form*

You prove a statement in geometry by using deductive reasoning to show that the statement follows from the hypothesis and other accepted material. Often the assertions made in a proof are listed in one column, and reasons which support the assertions are listed in an adjacent column.

EXAMPLE. A proof in two-column form.

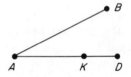

Given: *AKD; AD = AB*

Prove: *AK + KD = AB*

Proof:

STATEMENTS	REASONS
1. *AKD*	1. Given
2. *AK + KD = AD*	2. Definition of between
3. *AD = AB*	3. Given
4. *AK + KD = AB*	4. Transitive property of equality

Some people prefer to support Statement 4, above, with the reason *The Substitution Principle*. Both reasons are correct.

The reasons used in the example are of three types: *Given* (Steps 1 and 3), *Definition* (Step 2), and *Postulate* (Step 4). Just one other kind of reason, *Theorem*, can be used in a mathematical proof. Postulates and theorems from both algebra and geometry can be used.

Reasons Used in Proofs

Given (Facts provided for a particular problem)
Definitions
Postulates
Theorems that have already been proved.

Figure 1. An example of the instruction about a two-column proof used in high-school geometry from Jurgensen *et al.* (1975).

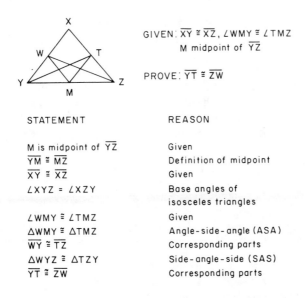

GIVEN: $\overline{XY} \cong \overline{XZ}$, $\angle WMY \cong \angle TMZ$
M midpoint of $\overline{YZ}$

PROVE: $\overline{YT} \cong \overline{ZW}$

STATEMENT

M is midpoint of $\overline{YZ}$
$\overline{YM} \cong \overline{MZ}$
$\overline{XY} \cong \overline{XZ}$
$\angle XYZ = \angle XZY$

$\angle WMY \cong \angle TMZ$
$\triangle WMY \cong \triangle TMZ$
$\overline{WY} \cong \overline{TZ}$
$\triangle WYZ \cong \triangle TZY$
$\overline{YT} \cong \overline{ZW}$

REASON

Given
Definition of midpoint
Given
Base angles of
isosceles triangles

Given
Angle-side-angle (ASA)
Corresponding parts
Side-angle-side (SAS)
Corresponding parts

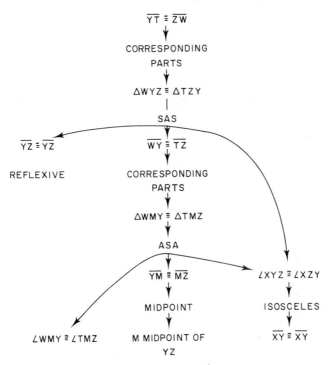

Figure 2. (a) A proof problem; (b) a representation of the
logical structure of inferential support.

proven is related to the givens of the problem by a hierarchical structure. In that structure rules of geometry relate givens to intermediate statements and these statements to the conclusion. Hopefully, the readers will find nothing surprising in this representation of the logical structure of the proof, but it needs to be emphasized that conventional instruction does not communicate this structure and students hardly find it obvious when they first encounter such proofs (Anderson, 1981a,b).

Figure 3 illustrates the proof in Figure 2 embedded in a set of additional

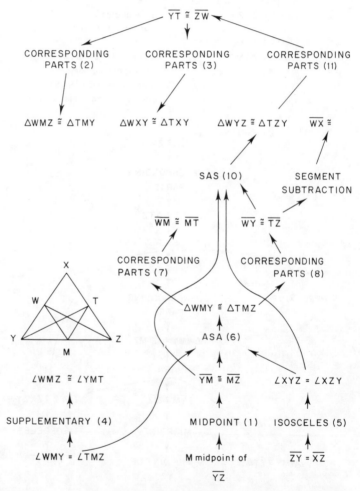

Figure 3. A representation of the order of inferences made in discovering the proof in Figure 2.

inferences generated by one of the authors (J.R.A.) in constructing the proof. The inferences are numbered in the order that they were made. The structure includes many inferences that were made in an attempt to construct the proof but were not part of the final proof. These extra inferences reflect some of the search that was involved in producing the final proof. Because standard pedagogy fails to communicate either the proof structure or the search based upon it, there is no way to provide instruction about this critical aspect of the learning process. This aspect is entirely a matter for the student to induce. Thus, typical instruction focuses only on the desired results without explaining the mental planning required to generate such a result. Given its complexity, it is no wonder that students have the difficulties they do with geometry proofs.

LISP programming

As in geometry, the goal structure underlying writing a LISP function does not correspond to the syntax of the problem solution and yet instruction is usually cast in terms of the syntax. Our studies indicate that generating a LISP program is largely a top-down planning process (Anderson, Farrell and Sauers, 1982; Anderson, Pirolli and Farrell, in press). The surface form of most programming languages involves a linear sequence of symbols. Thus, there is the natural danger of casting instruction in the terms of this linear structure. Fortunately, more enlightened instruction does emphasize a hierarchical, structured program. There is evidence that this is a better instructional mode (Shneiderman, 1980) although it is notoriously difficult to prove obviously correct hypotheses in this field with conventional experimental methodology (Sheil, 1981).

While structured programming is definitely a step in the right direction, it only ameliorates the basic problem. As Soloway, Bonar and Ehrlich (1983) show, the structured program itself is only a syntactic object which will have an imperfect correspondence to the structure of the programmer's plan. Consider an example we have studied at length (Anderson, Pirolli and Farrell, in press) from learning to program recursive functions, a recursive function that calculates the intersection of two lists:

```
(defun intersection (set1 set2)
    (cond ((null set1) nil)
          ((member (car set1) set 2)
           (cons (car set1)
                 (intersection (cdr set1) set2)))
          (t (intersection (cdr set1) set2))))
```

From a syntactic point of view, this function consists of a conditional structure that is composed of three clauses, each consisting of a condition and an action.

The student is encouraged to believe that it is just a matter of 'programmer's intuition' that leads to the division of the conditional into the right set of three conditions and actions. Instruction is largely focused on explaining how the code works rather than on how to write it. As an instance of the kind of discussion that can be found in many texts, Siklossy (1976, p. 55) gives the following explanation of intersection:

> The simplest case occurs when one of the sets, say Set1, is the empty set (). The intersection is then the empty set. In the next simplest case, Set1 could be a set with only one element, for example (HAYADOIN). If the element HAYADOIN is a MEMSET of SET2, then the intersection is the set (HAYADOIN). On the other hand, if HAYADOIN is not a MEMSET of SET2, then the intersection is the empty set (). In the general case, we move down SET1 (taking CDR's) and accumulate those elements of SET1 which are also MEMSETs of SET2.

Clearly no algorithm is specified for deciding how to generally break such a function into cases.

However, there are very precise principles that underlie the division of this code into its components (Soloway, 1980; Rich and Shrobe, 1978). This is an example of what we call the CDR-recursion plan. This plan applies when an argument of the function is a list such as *set1*. The plan involves coding a terminating case for when the list is *nil* and a recursive case that relates the result of the function applied to the tail (*cdr*) of the list to the result of the function applied to the full list. In the code above, the first clause of the conditional implements the terminating case and the second and third clauses perform the recursive step. So, the plan that generated the conditional consists of two major subgoals, not three. However, it is necessary to break the recursive step into two subcases—one to deal with the situation where the first element is in the list and one where it is not. This division is dictated by a standard list search plan.

We have evidence (Pirolli and Anderson, in press) that students learn significantly faster when told about the CDR-recursion plan and encouraged to use it rather than having recursive evaluation explained to them. Our protocol studies (Anderson, Pirolli and Farrell, in press) show the extreme cost of not informing students of such goal structures. We have seen students work for ten hours with some popular LISP texts on problems like *intersection* and not figure out the CDR-recursion plan. Rather, they pay attention to surface characteristics of the examples and fail to identify the powerful principles for coding recursive functions. As a consequence, they were still floundering after the ten hours.

Summary

Traditional instruction does not explain the goal structure of the problem-solving plan nor the search involved in the problem-solving. Private human tutors often communicate this information as they direct and assist students' problem-solving. For instance, all three of the LISP tutors we observed in our protocols suggested dividing the code into terminating and recursive cases. A computer tutor should strive to communicate the goal structure to the student as this is absolutely critical to effective problem-solving.

Principle 3: Provide instruction in the problem-solving context

Students appear to learn information more effectively if they are presented with that information during problem-solving rather than during instruction apart from the problem-solving context. For example, providing a student with hints or answers to confusions is much more effective while the student is trying to solve a problem, as opposed to prior to the problem-solving or following it. That this should be true is a direct consequence of ACT*'s knowledge compilation mechanism. Because knowledge compilation only works on traces of problem solutions, productions are only acquired in the process of problem-solving; they cannot be learned in the abstract. In all of our studies of skill acquisition (see Anderson, 1981a,b), we have noted a great speedup after the first few problems. Detailed analyses of protocols suggest that students are compiling domain-specific productions from this experience with the first few problems, and that they did not have these productions prior to solving the first problems. Thus it seems that ACT* is correct in its basic claim that skill is only acquired by doing. Instruction should be most effective if given in the context of the problem-solving while the student is forming these productions.

In addition to this basic reason, there are four other reasons for believing instruction will be more effective when provided in context. First, there is evidence that memories are associated to the features of the context in which they were learned. The probability of retrieving the memories is increased when the context of recall matches the context of study (Tulving, 1983; Tulving and Thomson, 1973). An extreme example of this was shown by Ross (1984) who found that secretaries were more likely to remember a text-editor command learned in the context of a recipe if they were currently editing another recipe.

Second, it is often difficult to properly encode and understand information presented outside of a problem context. Thus the applicability of knowledge might not be recognized in an appropriate problem context. For instance, students may not realize that a top-level variable is really the same thing as a function argument in LISP even though they are obliquely told so. As another example, many students reading the side–angle–side postulate may not know what *included angle* means and so misapply that postulate.

Third, even if students can recall the information and apply it correctly, they are often faced with many potentially applicable pieces of information and do not know which one to use. We have frequently observed students painfully trying dozens of theorems and postulates in geometry before finding the right one. The basic problem is that knowledge is taught in the abstract and the student must learn the goals to which that knowledge is applicable. If the knowledge is presented in a problem-solving context its goal relevance is much more apparent.

Fourth, we do not want to overload the student by providing in advance every possible hint and explaining every possible pitfall. But we do not know in a classroom lecture or in writing a textbook what help the student will need. In fact, the students in listening to a lecture may not know what help they will need either. If we wait until the problems arise, we can provide just the information that is needed.

Private human tutors characteristically provide information in the problem-solving context. Some, but not all, of the tutors we observed gave almost nonstop comment as students tried to solve problems. They take great advantage of the multi-modality character of the learning situation—with the student solving the problem in the visual modality and their instruction in the auditory modality. Although it would be difficult for a computer tutor to be as interactive as these human tutors and take full advantage of multi-modal processing, we shall see that it is possible to partially achieve this by providing appropriate instruction tailored to the students' current goal context.

Principle 4: Promote an abstract understanding of the problem-solving knowledge

Students differ in the level of abstraction at which they bring knowledge to bear in problem-solving. Pirolli and Anderson (in press) compared the approaches of three students to writing recursive programs. One student wrote such programs by literally copying code from an example program. Another student focused on a more abstract representation of the syntax of the condition–action structure. A third student relied on an even more abstract representation of division into terminating and recursive cases. In terms of ability to transfer to coding other recursive functions, ACT* simulations of these three students learned the least in the first case and the most in the last case, as did the actual students. The reason for the ACT* behavior was that the most abstract representation corresponded best to the right problem-solving organization.

Again in geometry, student success is ordered by the level of abstraction at which they solve problems. For instance, some students will represent the side–angle–side postulate as involving only the lower left angle because that is the way it is illustrated in the book. Thus, they learn an overly specific rule, which leads to later difficulties in problem-solving.

It is much easier for a student to encode knowledge concretely but much less effective to do so. A good tutor should see to it that a student achieves the right level of abstraction. It should be noted, however, that this principle does not deny the usefulness of concrete examples. As noted with respect to Principle 3, it is much easier to understand an abstract principle when one sees it applied to a concrete example. The recommendation here is that students should be encouraged to produce the right abstract encoding of that concrete example. For example, in the case of recursion they should represent an example function according to its division into terminating and recursive cases.

Principle 5: Minimize working memory load

As mentioned earlier, a principal source of learner errors in ACT* is loss of critical working memory information. Anderson and Jeffries (in press) provide evidence that almost all of the errors in the first few hours of LISP are from this source.

A good human tutor can recognize errors of working memory and typically provides quick correction (McKendree, Reiser and Anderson, 1984). Tutors realize that there is little profit in allowing the student to continue with such errors. However, human tutors really have no easy means at their disposal for reducing the working memory load. This is one of the ways we think computer tutors can be an improvement over human tutors—one can externalize much of working memory by rapid updates in the computer screen. This involves keeping track of partial products and visually presenting the goal structures.

Working memory errors increase the time to solve a problem but also, according to ACT*, limit what can be learned from a problem. If students cannot hold the key factors to a solution in working memory, they cannot build them into the compiled productions.

Principle 6: Provide immediate feedback on errors

Novices make errors both in selecting wrong solution paths and in incorrectly applying the rules of the domain. Errors are an inevitable part of learning, but the cost of these errors to the learner is often higher than is necessary. They can severely add to the amount of time required for learning. More than half of our subjects' problem-solving sessions were actually spent exploring wrong paths or recovering from erroneous steps.

According to the ACT* theory, it is difficult for a student to learn the correct production from an episode involving applying the wrong production, applying a sequence of other productions predicated on the wrong production, hitting an impasse, evetually finding the difficulty, and correcting it. The student needs to represent in working memory all of this complex sequence of events in order to be guaranteed successful compiling of a correct production.

Obviously, representing so much information can pose a severe information-processing load. ACT* predicts best learning of the correct operator if students are told immediately why they are wrong and what the correct actions are.

Of course, the student can learn something from the error episode, if not what the correct production was. The student can learn how to diagnose and correct error states. For instance, one normally learns to debug programs by making errors in one's own program. Given that debugging is a valuable skill, time should be set aside to teach it. However, the prescription of the ACT* theory is that it should be taught in the same way as programming. That is, there should be an ideal cognitive model for debugging, and the student should be given immediate feedback when his or her behavior seriously deviates from the ideal model.

We have found our emphasis on immediate feedback to be the most controversial of our principles. One reason for the controversy is just a misunderstanding. This is the belief that we are advocating that it is not important to learn to identify and correct errors. The other reason reflects a fundamental disagreement. Many people have strong beliefs that we learn better when we discover our errors rather than when we are told about them. However, it needs to be emphasized that the importance of immediacy of feedback to skill acquisition is one of the best documented facts in psychology (e.g. Bilodeau, 1969; Skinner, 1958). Much of this research has been with somewhat simpler skills than the complex cognitive skills we have studied. However, we have shown the same principle in a complex problem-solving domain (Lewis and Anderson, in press). Subjects learned more slowly when they were allowed to go down erroneous paths and were only given feedback at delay. This is despite the fact that these students spent much more time in the learning situation than the immediate feedback students because it took them longer to solve the same number of problems.

Another cost of errors is the demoralization of the student. These are domains in which errors can be very frequent and frustrating. We believe that much of the negative attitudes and math phobias derive from the bitter experiences of students with errors. It is hard to convey on paper the emotional tone of some of the protocols we have gathered, but below are the excerpts from students struggling with LISP errors:

> . . . No, I need another set of parentheses, and I think I want it around—but I can't do that—that's got to be—damn!—I think the first argument of CONST has to be a list . . . and why is that? No—I don't need *const*!! What am I talking about?! I need to use Union! . . . No, no! That didn't work before because . . . oh (groan) . . . let's see . . . I don't know what I'd use the Union of! . . .

> . . . I don't know. I lost where I am. That's usually what happens when I do that—when I slow down and stop—'cause I forget what I am doing. Err . . . It's taken that much time!! Ok. Geez! Ugh . . . I guess I will have to go back to it again . . .

... I'm just so slow today. Damn! ... so that means if this element of *set1* is in *set2* ... the value of *setdiff* is gonna be ... the ... the ... Union of Cons? ... Doesn't matter what I guess ... So it's gonna be *setdiff* of ... is it that simple!? ... something with the *cdr* of *set1* with ... the *cdr* of *set1* and *set2* ... Let me see if that works ... Is that right? If that's right, I'll be p ... ed. God, I hate myself. I can't even think about it 'cause I'll be so p ... ed. But I have got to think about it ...

The potential advantages of a private tutor are clear in this regard. The tutor can prevent the student from wasting inordinate amounts of time searching wrong paths. The tutor can both provide immediate feedback when errors are made and point out to the students which aspects of the problem solution are correct and which are in error. Actual human tutors vary in how much feedback they give (McKendree, Reiser and Anderson, 1984). Typically, they point out immediately what they perceive to be slips. They may allow a more conceptual error to pass if they believe the subject may be able to detect it. However, they tend to be very concerned about the emotional tone of the learning situation, and if the subject is frustrated they will gently put the subject back on the right track.

Principle 7: Adjust the grain size of instruction with learning

The productions in the ACT∗ theory define the grain size with which a problem is solved. Because of the knowledge compilation process, this grain size will change with experience. As an example from LISP, a novice approaches each symbol in the definition syntax as a separate subgoal. Later the student writes out the whole structure as a unit. As another example, geometry students come to recognize that they can apply a whole sequence of inference steps. Clearly, if the tutor is going to be helpful, the tutor will have to adjust instruction with the growing grain size of the instruction.

Human tutors often adjust their instruction according to individual differences between students and advances in the student's performance during a lesson. One of the things the tutor does is to chunk the instruction, thus stopping the student before taking in too much material to practice. For example, on encountering a page of new LISP functions, one tutor stopped his student after the first function in order to insure that the student understood that function before continuing with the rest of the functions. Prior to this the student had had a difficult time understanding the basic LISP structures, and presumably the tutor calculated that simply reading through the descriptions of each of the functions would not be very effective until the student saw one of these functions working and was able to understand the basic idea of LISP operations.

We have also observed students getting into trouble when their tutors have made incorrect assumptions about the level of instruction appropriate. For example, one tutor we observed explained the details of the LISP read–

eval–print loop (the internals of LISP's interactive system) when the student did not understand about when function arguments needed to be quoted. Although the student appeared at first to have understood this explanation, he made several quote errors in later problems until the tutor then decided to work through an example concerning quotes in more detail.

Principle 8: Facilitate successive approximations to the target skill

Students do not become experts in geometry or LISP programming after solving their first problem. They gradually approximate the expert behavior, accumulating separately the various pieces (production rules) of the skill. It is important that a tutor support this learning by approximation. It is very hard to learn in a situation that requires that the whole solution be correct the first time. The tutor must accept partial solutions and shape the student on those aspects of the solution that are weak.

Generally, it is better to have the early approximations occur in problem contexts that are as similar to the final problem context as possible. It is a consequence of the ACT* learning mechanisms that skills learned in one problem context will only partially transfer to a second context. Students are learning features from early problems to guide their problem-solving operators. If these features are different from the final problem space the problem-solving rules that the students learn will be misguided. For instance, early problems in geometry tend to involve algebraic manipulations of measures. Consequently, the student learns to always convert congruence of segments and angles into equality of the measure of the parts. Later problems such as those involving triangle congruence do not involve converting congruence of sides and angles into equality of measures. Students frequently carry over their over-general tendency to convert and get into difficulties because of this. This is just what the ACT* learning process would do given this experience.

It is often extremely difficult for students starting out to solve the kind of problems that they will eventually have to solve. For instance, in geometry students cannot initially generate proofs. To deal with this, standard pedagogy often evolves intermediate tasks such as giving reasons for the worked-out steps of a proof. The problem is that the process of finding reasons for the steps of a proof is different from the process of generating that proof. In our ACT* simulations of these tasks, there is almost no overlap between the productions involved in reason-giving and proof generation. As another example, in programming students are often given practice evaluating recursive functions as preparation for writing recursive functions. Again, these are separate tasks. Both in the geometry case and the programming case we have shown that there is not much transfer from one task to another. Neves and Anderson (1981) found no transfer from ten days of reason-giving to proof generation. McKendree and Anderson (in press) found no transfer from four days' practice of function evaluation to the task of generating the LISP code.

The advantage of private tutors is that they can help the student through problems which are too difficult for the student to solve entirely alone. Thus, it is common to see a sequence of problems where the tutor will solve most of the first problem with the student just filling in a few of the steps; the tutor will help less with the second problem, etc., until the student is solving the entire problem. Consequently, the tutor can enable the student's early learning to be in problem contexts very similar to the more advanced problem contexts.

ISSUES OF HUMAN ENGINEERING

We have tried to achieve the principles enumerated above in our development of computer tutors. However, many of the problems that we face in creating actual computer tutors were not with seeing how these principles should apply but were at a level which might best be called human engineering. This refers to issues of designing the interface and the natural language dialogue so that information exchanges occur that satisfy our cognitive principles. If one cannot communicate the knowledge effectively, the cognitive bases for these systems will become lost. Our human-engineering efforts have been somewhat guided by what we know from cognitive psychology, somewhat guided by results in the literature on the human–computer interface, but largely the result of trial and error exploration. This human-engineering aspect is far from trivial. Before we are going to have a good theory of intelligent tutors, we will need a good theory of their human engineering.

In the remaining two sections of this paper we will describe our geometry tutor and our LISP tutor. We will try to show how these tutors approximate the design criteria we have set forth. We will also try to communicate some of our experience with the human-engineering problems.

THE GEOMETRY TUTOR

High-school geometry has all the characteristics of a topic which should be amenable to the intelligent tutoring approach. Of all the high-school math courses, it is most frequently rated as the least liked, although students who go on to have successful mathematical careers often rate it as their favorite (Hoffer, 1981). So there is a wide range of educational outcomes and a real need for improvement. The most difficult part of geometry is doing proofs. While proof generation in general is hard, high-school proof problems are within the range of artificial intelligence techniques. Therefore, it appears that intelligent methods might make an impact on this most difficult aspect of this most difficult of the high-school math subjects. Our geometry tutor (Boyle and Anderson, 1984) is focused on teaching students how to generate proofs.

A geometry proof problem as stated in a high-school geometry text (see Figure 1) consists of three ingredients—a diagram, a set of givens and a to-be-proven statement. Despite claims to the contrary, the diagram plays a critical role in many high-school geometry proofs. Frequently (although this not the case in Figure 1), the diagram is the only source of critical information about what points are collinear and which points are between which others. This information often is not provided in the givens. Most other information which can be read off the diagram, such as relative measure, is not to be taken as true in general. It is a rare high-school proof problem that involves constructions or creating new entities not in the diagram. Indeed, some geometry textbooks have a policy of never requiring the student to do proofs by construction although all conventional texts must use proof by construction in establishing theorems for the student. Therefore, to a good approximation, the student's task is to find some chain of legal inferences from the stated givens and the givens implicit in the diagram to the conclusion.

The ideal model

Consider the problem in Figure 4. There are a set of forward and backward deductions that can be made. Forward deductions take information given and note that certain conclusions follow. So, we can infer from the fact that the M is the midpoint of $\overline{AB}$ that $\overline{AM} \cong \overline{MB}$. We can also infer from the vertical angle configuration that $\angle AMF \cong \angle BME$. Backward inferences involve noting that a conclusion could be proven if certain other statements were proven. So, we could prove M is the midpoint of $\overline{EF}$ if we could prove $\overline{EM} \cong \overline{MF}$. We could prove the latter statement if we could prove $\overline{EM} \cong \overline{AM}$ and $\overline{MF} \cong \overline{AM}$.

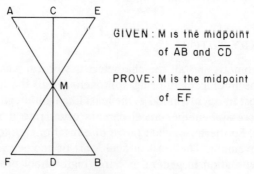

Figure 4. A relatively advanced proof problem
for high school geometry.

As these examples illustrate, sometimes forward and backward inferences are part of the solution and sometimes they are not. In challenging problems the student cannot always know whether an inference is part of the solution. Rather, the student must make heuristic guesses about which inferences are likely. We saw this with respect to Figure 3.

In our view, the ideal student extends the proof backward from the to-be-proved statement and forward from the givens until there is a complete proof. At each point the ideal student makes the heuristically best inference where this is defined as the inference most probably part of the final proof. 'Most probable' depends on some induction over the space of high-school problems. Currently, we have no formal definition of the probability that an inference will be part of a proof, but our intuitions are usually quite defensible. So, we create the ideal student model as a set of rules that seem heuristic. For instance, one rule is that when vertical angles are parts of to-be-proven congruent tirangles, infer that they are congruent but not otherwise. Basically, the rules all take the form of 'apply a particular rule of inference when such and such conditions prevail'. These conditions refer to properties of the diagram, givens, established inferences, and goals set in backward inference. These rules can be represented as production rules; for example:

IF $\triangle$XYZ and $\triangle$UVW are to-be-proven congruent triangles
      and $\overline{XYW}$ and $\overline{ZYU}$ are intersecting lines
THEN   infer $\angle$XYZ $\cong$ $\angle$UYW because of vertical angles.

We have developed a set of 194 such production rules which seem to be sufficient for the problems in the first four chapters of Jurgensen *et al.* (1975), which is what our geometry tutor covers (about half of a high-school course). Many such rules can apply at any point in time, and the conflict-resolution principle selects the most highly rated rule to apply. Given this organization, we are able to solve all the problems in the text, develop proofs that strike us as the same as what we would do, and generate such proofs rapidly.

The proof graph

As noted earlier, standard instruction does a very poor job of communicating the goal structure to the student. Therefore, our first human-engineering problem was to find a way of communicating this information to the student. We decided to use a graphical formalism in which the to-be-proven statement was at the top and the givens were at the bottom. A proof is created as a logical network connecting the givens to the to-be-proven statement. The basic unit of this network is a structure connecting one or more givens to a conclusion through a rule of inference. Figure 5 shows four states of the proof network from beginning to end for the problem in Figure 4. The network can

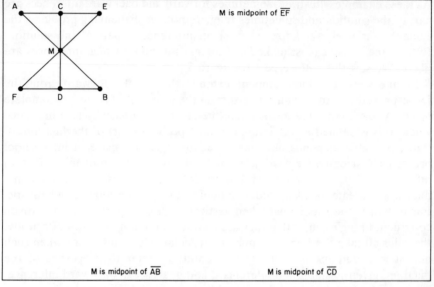

(a)

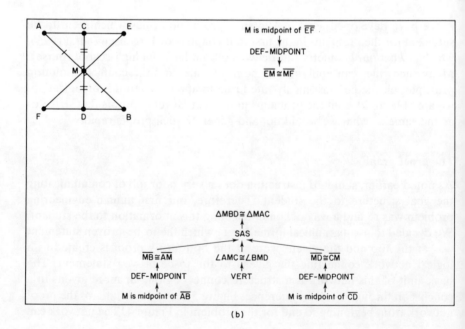

(b)

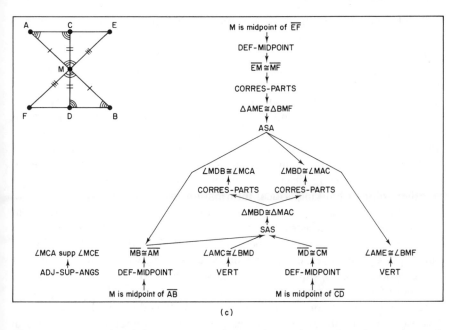

(c)

Figure 5. Four states of the tutor screen in a students construction of a graph proof for the problem in Figure 5.

be grown from the bottom by forward inference or from the top by backward inference. As Figure 5 illustrates, it is certainly possible to generate inferences off the correct path. We have testimonials from three pilot students that they better understood both the structure of the proof and nature of our proof generation because of the graphical formalisms of the proof structure.

Interacting with the system

The basic cycle of interaction with the system is as follows. The student points to one or more statements on the screen from which he or she wants to draw an inference. Pointing causes these statements to blink. If at least one legal inference can apply to these statements, the system asks the student for the rule of inferent that applies. The student then types in the rule of inference. If it is applicable to these statements the system will prompt the student for the conclusion that follows. The student either types in the conclusion or points to it if it is on the screen. If correct the student can now initiate another cycle of interaction with the system, which will result in the posting of another deductive inference. This continues until a complete proof has been generated.

The human engineering of the system has involved a lot of trial and error to decide issues such as how to position the graph, what abbreviations to use, when to correct misspellings, how to let the student point, and how to relate the proof structures to the diagram. We have also found it useful to have the student spend an hour with a warm-up system that uses the same graphical conventions but with the familiar domain of arithmetic. The student can learn to use the system much more rapidly if this learning is decoupled from learning to do proofs in geometry. One problem with a complex screen is that the student may not notice when new information is added. We have found that color and motion are fairly effective ways of capturing attention. We we have taken to changing the colors of the windows, bringing up new windows in another color or blinking critical information.

For the accomplished geometry student, this system is a convenient and efficient vehicle for constructing proofs. It serves as an external memory so that forgotten information can be quickly recovered. It also catches slips of mind quickly. However, more is needed when dealing with a novice. The most basic problem for a student is not knowing how to proceed. There are a number of ways that our system helps students during problem-solving. Most directly the student can ask the system for help. Less directly, the student may choose to make inferences off nodes from which no inferences or no useful inferences follow. In either case, the system will provide the student with a hint in the form of suggesting the best nodes from which to infer.

The student may be uncertain about what inference rule to apply or how to apply the inference rule. He can manifest this again by asking for help or by inappropriately applying a rule. In this case windows can be brought up to display which rules of inference are currently applicable and to display a definition of each rule of inference. When the student displays a known bug, such as applying the side–angle–side postulate when the angles are not included by the sides, a window will appear explaining why the student's choice is not correct.

Students get in ruts in which they try to make an inference from an inappropriate set of statements over and over again or apply the same rule over and over again. In such cases, the system will interrupt and display what it regards as the next best inference step and interrogate the student to make sure that the step is understood.

An interesting property of the graphics screen is that the student has no access to solutions of previous problems. Therefore, it is very difficult to do any problem solution by copying parts of prior solutions—an unfortunate tendency of many students in the conventional classroom. When the students gets instruction, the instruction is about the inference rules in the form of general problem-solving operators. For instance, the system will give the following statement of the corresponding parts rule when it is evoked in backward inference to prove two sides congruent:

IF   you want to prove the conclusion $\overline{UV} \cong \overline{XY}$
THEN   try to prove the premise $\triangle UVW \cong \triangle XYZ$

along with a pattern diagram to help the student instantiate the abstract terms in this statement.

It is difficult to get access to high-school students, but we have looked intensively at three students working with the system—one with above-average ability, one of average ability and the other of below-average ability (as defined by their math grades). The below-average student came to us for remedial purposes having failed tenth-grade geometry. The other two students were eighth graders with no formal geometry experience. We can only report that the system works, i.e. all students learned with it and without great difficulty. We think they learned faster than with traditional instruction, but we have no way to document this belief. All students were able to do problems that local teachers consider too difficult to assign to their tenth-grade classes. They also all claimed to like the subject of geometry, which seems an important outcome given the negative ratings geometry typically gets.

Design principles in the geometry tutor

It is worth reviewing how the geometry tutor does and does not realize the design principles set forth in the beginning of this chapter.

1. As we have noted, we have an ideal model represented as a production system. We have yet to integrate a similar model of student bugs into the tutor.
2. The proof graph is an attempt to reify the goal structure and communicate it to the student.
3. The postulate, definition and theorems of geometry are taught in the context of their use in problem-solving.
4. The problem-solving is guided by abstract instruction, not by superficial properties of examples.
5. Working memory load is minimized in a number of ways. The proof graph is an attempt to represent subgoals. A color-coding scheme facilitates integration of the diagram and the abstract statements. This involves marking congruence on a diagram in the same color that they are displayed in the proof graph.
6. The system does provide immediate feedback on logical errors. It does not yet provide much strategic feedback about inferences that are logically correct but do not lead to proofs. We have observed students seriously flounder as a consequence. Providing such strategic advice is a current research goal.

7. Another deficit of the tutor is that it does not adjust grain size to reflect the level at which the student is working. Its grain size always corresponds to a single step of inference. However, beginning students need to be led through some inferences in mini-steps, while advanced students prefer to plan in multi-step inferences.
8. The system is a beautiful illustration of how a tutor can enable a skill to arise through successive approximation. Students start out relying on the tutor to provide almost all of the steps of the proof but reach the point where they are doing proofs completely on their own, proofs that school-teachers consider too difficult to assign to conventional classes.

THE LISP TUTOR

Our work on the LISP tutor is based on earlier research (Anderson, Farrell and Sauers, 1984; Anderson, Pirolli and Farrell, in press) studying the acquisition of basic LISP programming skills by programming novices. Given standard classroom instruction, a programming novice typically takes over 40 hours to acquire a basic facility with the data structures and functions of LISP. At the end of this period they can write basic recursive and iterative functions. In this time the student has probably not written a LISP program more than three functions deep and still does not know how to use LISP for interesting applications.

We believe that the LISP tutor will be able to cover *the same material* in under 20 hours (we are currently over halfway there). After this point the tutor would step back and become an 'intelligent editor' which could help the student create programs and catch obvious slips, but would no longer instruct. Besides the desire to have a manageable project, we do not feel we are capable of modeling the problem-solving that occurs after learning the basics of LISP.

The ideal model

Brooks (1977) analyzed programming into the activities of algorithm design, coding and debugging. We are currently focusing on algorithm design and coding. Our past research on LISP involved creating simulations of both errorful and ideal students in the algorithm design and coding phases. Brooks characterized programming as first designing an algorithm and then converting it into code. However, the break is seldom so clean. The student alternates between algorithm design and coding, sometimes omitting the algorithm design altogether and going directly from problem statement to code. Often novices and experts differ as to whether there is a distinct algorithm design stage. One example we have studied involves writing LISP code to take a list and return that list with the last element removed. A number of experts

generated (reverse (cdr (reverse lis))) immediately upon hearing the statement, whereas some novices went through a ten minute phase of means–ends
analysis to come up with the algorithm.

The ideal model for code generation, both for experts and novices, involves
a top-down generation of the code. Figure 6 illustrates the goal structure
underlying the generation of the code for the function *powerset*, which takes a
list and returns the list of all sublists. This is recognized as involving recursion
on the list and subgoals are set to code the terminating step and the recursive
step of the recursion. Both of these steps are broken down into algorithm
design plus code generation. Writing the code for the recursive step involves
writing a 'helping function' *addto* that will add an element to each list in a list
of lists.

The actual code generated along with the goal structure in Figure 6 is:

```
(defun powerset (list)
    (cond ((null list) (list nil))
          (t (append (powerset (cdr list))
                     (addto (car list) (powerset (cdr list))))))
    )).
```

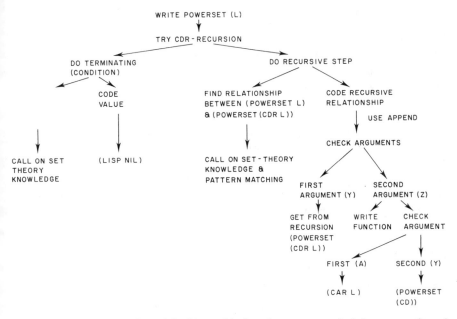

Figure 6. A representation of the hierarchical goal structure underlying generation of
the LISP function to calculate POWERSET.

There are a number of features to note about the goal decomposition shown in Figure 6. First, code is generated top-down. Second, there is alteration between algorithm design and code generation. Third, the encoding of the embedded function, *addto*, is postponed until the top function is coded.

It is difficult to develop ideal models for the algorithm design aspect of the problem-solving. Students can potentially bring any of their past experiences and prior knowledge to bear in designing an algorithm. With each problem we have to specially provide the ideal model with potentially relevant prior knowledge. So, for instance, to model the creation of a graph search function we had to provide the system with knowledge of the fact that paths in a graph can loop (Anderson, Farrell and Sauers, 1982).

Interacting with the LISP tutor

Figure 7 illustrates a typical state of the screen in interacting with the tutor. We used the hierarchical structure of LISP to support representation of the top-down structure of the programming activity. At all times during the problem the code window displays the part of the problem that has been coded. Placeholders are used to indicate the structures requiring top-down expansion: e.g.:

(defun rotator (lis)
    (append (last $\langle 3 \rangle$) $\langle 2 \rangle$))

where the symbols $\langle 2 \rangle$ and $\langle 3 \rangle$ denote the points for top-down expansion. The tutor moves the student to the next symbol for expansion, and the student types the code to replace this symbol. So, at this level the system is just a structured editor for creating the code.

In some cases, the hierarchical structure of the LISP code does not correspond to the goal structure. A good example of this was the intersection function discussed earlier where the COND structure had three clauses but the goal structure for CDR-recursion just involved one goal for doing the terminating case and one goal for doing the recursive step. In such cases we have the subject generate the code according to the underlying goal structure rather than the syntax of the LISP code. The placeholder symbols indicate the conceptual breakdown of the problem before they are transformed into LISP code. Thus, for instance, at one point in *powerset* the code is displayed

(defun powerset (lis)
    (cond $\langle$TERMINATING-CASE$\rangle$
          $\langle$RECURSIVE-CASE$\rangle$))

Sometimes, the student has to branch into algorithm design where the problem-solving will not correspond to the hierarchical structure of the code. In this case the tutoring window is used to work out a successful algorithm.

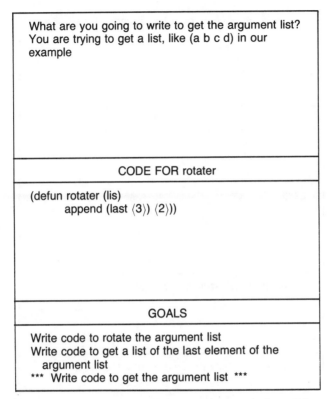

Figure 7. A typical state of the tutor screen in interacting with a student. The tutor's query is displayed at the top of the screen. The 'code' window displays the current code, and the 'goals' window summarizes the problem solving so far and indicates the current goal.

Figure 8 illustrates the tutor in the algorithm-design mode. The final product of the algorithm design ing will be some specific code that must be mapped into the abstract code of the function. So, for instance, if the student needs to design an algorithm for returning a list of all but the last of the *lis*, we will have him work out a solution for a concrete instance of *lis*, say lis = (a b c d). The final product in this case would be:

(reverse (cdr (reverse '(a b c d))))

which can be mapped into the abstract function to produce:

(reverse (cdr (reverse lis)))

Again, when doing the recursive step for *powerset* (see Figure 6) with the

a

What can we do to change (a b c d) into (a b c)?

PRESS   IF YOU WANT TO:
1   Get each element of (a b c d) and put them in a list.
2   Remove d from (a b c d).
3   Have the tutor choose.
PLAN CHOICE: 2

CODE FOR ROTATER

```
(defun rotater (lis)
    (append (last lis) ⟨2⟩))
```

PLAN

Transform (a b c d) into (a b c)

---

b

What function will remove d from (a b c d)?

FUNCTION: cdr

CODE FOR rotater

```
(defun rotater (lis)
    (append (last lis) ⟨2⟩))
```

PLAN

Transform (a b c d) into (a b c)

c

> You can use CDR to remove the first item of a list,
> but in this case, d is the last element. So, to use
> CDR we have to get d into the first position. How can
> we do this?
> PRESS   IF YOU WANT TO:
> 1   Flip the list so that d becomes the first item.
> 2   Go down the list until we get d.
> 3   Let the tutor choose.
> PLAN CHOICE: 1

CODE FOR rotater
(defun rotater (lis)   (append (last lis) $\langle 2 \rangle$))

PLAN
Transform (a b c d) into (d . . .)

Figure 8(a, b, c). Three stages of the tutor screen during the
tutoring of the algorithm. Note the description of the algorithm as applied to a concrete example. The 'plan' window
summarizes the current plan for the example.

specific list (A B C), the final result in the algorithm window would be:

(powerset '(a b c)) =
(append '(() (c) (b) (b c)) '((a) (a c) (a b) (a b c)))
and
(powerset '(b c)) = (() (c) (b) (b c))

We feel that the code window and the algorithm window do a good job of
communicating the hierarchical structure of the programming activity as well
as the separate status of algorithm design.

We feel we have been successful in structuring the interface for the input of
code. However, generating and understanding a dialogue with the student
about algorithms are much more difficult. The most obvious method is to have
the student type in an English description of his algorithm and for our tutor to
try to understand that. The program has only the task of categorizing the

student's description into one of the algorithm categories it is prepared to process. Even with this considerable constraint, we have only had modest success at language comprehension. One of the frequent student complaints about earlier versions of our tutor is its inability to understand algorithm descriptions. In part this is due to the tutor's limited natural language understanding and in part this is because students often only have vague ideas of algorithm choices. Our solution to both difficulties has been to implement a menu system to replace the need for natural language parsing.

Our menus are generated dynamically from the instantiations of productions in the ideal model. The menus contain English descriptions of all the algorithmic variations, correct and buggy, that we are prepared to process. Menu selection is technically simpler than language comprehension. It is an issue for further research as to which is more effective. We were surprised by how well students appear to adapt to menu selection. This may be simply that it is much easier to pick a menu entry than to generate a description.

As in the geometry system, there are general help facilities so that the student can bring up information. Again, the information is given in terms of abstract problem-solving operators. For example, rather than showing how *cons* is used in a specific program, *cons* might be explained: 'If you want to insert an element into a list use the functions *cons*' with an example to instantiate the explanation.

Novices are prone to a substantial set of misconceptions and slips in writing LISP programs. One of the strengths of the system is that we have created recognizers for a great many of the possible bugs and provided for appropriate feedback on the errors. In our pilot study, we have discovered a number of other stereotypic errors which we have also entered into the system with appropriate feedback. We are able to recognize 80 per cent of the errors our students make once we have the errors carefully catalogued.

The rightp problem

Table 1 presents a dialogue which is focused on teaching a student how to decompose a problem into a set of subfunctions. It is impossible in this limited space to present the tutor as it really appears. Instead, Table 1 is essentially a 'teletype' version of the student–tutor interactions. The actual interactions involve use of several windows displayed on the terminal screen: a code window in which the student types the code, a tutoring window in which tutoring feedback is displayed, and a goals window in which reminders are displayed about the current portion of the problem. In the 'teletype' versions that we present, the tutor's output is given in normal roman characters, while the student's input is shown in bold characters. This table presents 'snapshots' of the interaction—each time the student provokes a response from the tutor we have listed the student's input and the tutor's response (numbered for

Table 1   rightp

Define rightp. It takes three arguments, side1, side2 and side3, which represent the lengths of the three sides of a given triangle, where side3 is the longest side. The function rightp tests whether the three sides form a right triangle. In a right triangle, the sum of the squares of side1 and side2 is equal to the square of side3. However, your function should allow for a measurement error of 2 percent. In other words, your function should return *t* if the sum of the squares of the first two sides is within 2 percent of the square of the third side.

For example (rightp 3 4 5.01) = *t*, because 3 squared + 4 squared = 25, which is within 2 percent of 5.01 squared.

1. **(defun rightp (side1 side2 side3) (cond***))*

      Yes, you could use COND here, but there is a much easier way to test if the sum of the squares of the first two sides is within 2 percent of the square of the third. You can use a predicate, since we only have one test to do.

2. *(defun rightp (side1 side2 side3)*
    (lessp (difference*)* $\langle NUM2 \rangle$*))*

      You want to code the amount of difference between the sum of the squares of the first two sides and the square of the third side, and you do NOT care which of these two numbers is larger. So we want to take the absolute value of their difference.

3. *(defun rightp (side1 side2 side3)*
    (lessp **(abs (difference** $\langle NUM3 \rangle$ $\langle NUM4 \rangle$**)))**
    $\langle NUM2 \rangle$*))*
    Which do you want to do first?
    PRESS: IF YOU WANT TO:
    1   Write code to get the sum of the squares of the first two sides
    2   Write code to get the square of the third side

    Menu choice: 1

4. *(defun rightp (side1 side2 side3)*
    (lessp (abs (difference **(plus)** $\langle NUM4 \rangle$*))*
    $\langle NUM2 \rangle$*))*
      No. You should create a helping·function for this code, rather than coding it directly. Our function, rightp, is now four levels of embedding deep, and the relation we are about to code—the sum of squares of two numbers— would be a useful helping function. Thus, let us code the sum of the squares of the first two sides using a helping function.

5. *(defun rightp (side1 side2 side3)*
    (lessp (abs (difference **(sumsq** $\langle ARGUMENTS \rangle$**))** $\langle NUM4 \rangle$*))*
    $\langle NUM2 \rangle$*))*
    What do you want the helping function sumsq to do?
    PRESS: IF YOU WANT TO:
    1   Takes two arguments, the square of the first side and the square of the second side. Computes their sum.
    2   Takes two arguments, the first side and the second side. Computes the sum of the squares of these numbers.

Table 1 (*continued*)

---

3   Have the tutor choose.
    Menu choice: 1
    No. We would not need a helping function JUST to compute the sum of
two numbers. You should create your helping function so that it does more
than just a sum.
    It would be better to define sumsq so that it takes two arguments, in this
case, [1] the first side, and [2] the second side, and computes the sum of the
squares of these numbers.
    Menu choice: 2

6. *(defun rightp (side1 side2 side3)*
    (lessp (abs (difference (sumsq **side1 side2**) **(times***)))*
    ⟨*NUM2*⟩*))*
    You should use a helping function that you have already coded, square.
Since this function computes the square of a number, you can use it to code
the square of the third side.

7. *(defun rightp (side1 side2 side3)*
    (lessp (abs (difference (sumsq side1 side2) **(square side3**))*
    (plus*)))*
    I do not understand that, Rob. How are you going to code 2 percent of
the square of the third side?
    [EXPLAIN]
    OK. I will explain what I wanted. You could either code this directly or
create a helping function here to code 2 percent of the square of the third
side. Let us create a helping function just to make things easier. We will call
this helping function percentage. We will define percentage when we are
finished coding rightp.
    What do you want the helping function percentage to do?
    PRESS: IF YOU WANT TO:
    1   Takes two arguments, one-hundredth of 2 and the square of the third
        side. Computes their product.
    2   Takes two arguments, 2 and the third side. Computes the given percen-
        tage of the square of its second argument.
    3   Takes two arguments, 2 and the square of the third side. Computes the
        given percentage of its second argument.
    4   Takes one argument, the square of the third side. Computes 2 percent of
        its argument.
    5   Have the tutor choose.
    Menu choice: 3

    Very good.

8. *(defun rightp (side1 side2 side3)*
    (lessp (abs (difference (sumsq side1 side2) (square side3)))
    (percentage 2 (square side3)*)))*
    OK. Now we have finished coding the function rightp. Let us now code the
helping function(s) we used but have not yet defined.
    Which do you want to do first?

Table 1 (*continued*)

PRESS: IF YOU WANT TO:
1   Define the helping function sumsq
2   Define the helping function percentage

Menu choice: 1

Define the helping function sumsq. It takes two arguments. (num1 num2) are the suggested names for the arguments, but you may name them whatever you wish. The function sumsq should compute the sum of the squares of num1 and num2.

9. **(defun sumsq (s y)**
    (plus (square s) (square y)))
    OK. Now we have finished coding the function sumsq. Let us now code the helping function(s) we used but have not yet defined.
    Define the helping function percentage. It takes two arguments. (pcnt total) are the suggested names for these arguments, but you may name them whatever you wish. Percentage should compute pcnt percent of total.

10. **(defun percentage (x y)**
    ⟨*PROCESS*⟩)
    [EXPLAIN]
    OK. I will explain what I wanted. Let us figure out how to code *x* percent of the second number. How can you code *x* percent of the second number?
    PRESS: IF YOU WANT TO:
    1   Multiply the second number by one-hundredth of *x*.
    2   Multiply the second number by *x*.
    3   Divide the second number by 100.
    4   Have the tutor choose.

    Menu choice: 1

    Good.

11. *(defun percentage (x y)*
    (times ⟨*NUM1*⟩ ⟨*NUM2*⟩**))**
    What do you want to do first?
    PRESS: IF YOU WANT TO:
    1   Write code to get one-hundredth of the first number.
    2   Write code to get the second number.

    Menu choice: 1

12. *(defun percentage (x y)*
    (times **(quotient** × **.01)** ⟨*NUM2*⟩**))**
    No, that is not the right number. How are you going to specify 100 in LISP?

13. *(defun percentage (x y)*
    (times (quotient × **100) y))**
    OK. Now we have finished coding the function percentage. There are no more helping functions to define.

---

convenience.) The total code as it appears on the screen is shown, although the student has added only what is different from the previous code, shown in bold face type. For example, in line 2 of Table 1 the student has typed '(**lessp** (**difference**' as an extension of the code in line 1. It is important to point out several things about these dialogues. First, the tutor balances parentheses and provides placeholders (e.g. ⟨CASE⟩, ⟨NAME⟩, ⟨NUM⟩) for portions of code that must be expanded. Second, although we are showing in some cases large portions of code being added from one line to the next, the tutor has understood each separate word or symbol the student has entered, and would have responded with an error message if it were necessary for any of those items.

Although the frequency of errors in this dialogue is somewhat greater than for the typical student, the dialogue is a good illustration of the various ways that the tutor responds to student errors and requests for assistance. As can be seen, the tutor allowed the student to input information until the student typed **cond**, at which point the system pointed out that a conditional structure

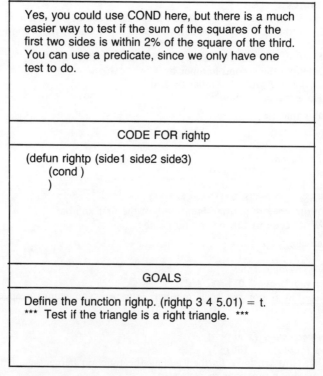

Figure 9. Screen configuration after line 1 in Table 1.

was not necessary. The actual screen image at this point in the interaction is shown in Figure 9. Line 2 illustrates that the student next types (**lessp** (**difference** and receives a hint which causes the student to correctly insert the absolute value function (**abs**) before **difference** in line 3. Note that the tutor presents a menu when it is uncertain what the student will do next. For instance, since the arguments to **difference** in **rightp** can be in either order, the tutor needs to know which the student will type next, and it asks the student via a menu after line 3.

After line 4 we see the tutor give the student information about when it is useful to code a separate helping function. The tutor queries the student after line 5 to make sure the student and tutor agree on what that helping function will compute. This is an example of the planning mode in the tutor. In this case, the student has a mistaken idea about what the subfunction should compute, which is then rectified by the tutor.

After line 7 the tutor detects that the student's code will not achieve the goal. However, this input does not match any of the buggy rules in the model, so the tutor provides minimal feedback: it indicates that it cannot understand the input, and queries the student to remind him about what he should be trying to code. This hint is not enough for the student who asks for an explanation by hitting a special key, whereupon the tutor helps the student specify another helping function *percentage*.

The final form of **rightp** is displayed in line 8. In line 9 the student defines the helping function **sumsq** without error and goes on to defining *percentage* in line 10. He is stuck as to what to do after typing the function body and requests an explanation. The tutor helps the student refine his algorithm. After this the student defines percentage with one error in line 12.

After defining **rightp** and its helping functions, the LISP tutor puts the student into a real LISP environment where the student can experiment with the functions that have just been defined, and can also try variations on those functions, perhaps to see what type of error would be produced by a function the student had in mind but was prevented from coding by the tutor. After the student has experimented to his satisfaction, the tutor provides the next problem in the lesson.

Evaluation

Because of the availability of the college population, we have been able to evaluate the quality of our LISP tutor more carefully than we have the geometry tutor. We have run a fairly robust version of the tutor that took ten students through basic LISP functions and data structures, function composition, function definition, predicates, conditional expressions, auxiliary functions and recursion. In a questionnaire administered to classes of students of comparable background, students reported an average of 43 hours spent studying this material, attending class and (the bulk of the time) solving problems. We ran two comparison groups of ten subjects each. One group, the human-tutor group, had private human tutors to help them work through the material. The other group, the 'on-your-own group', read the instructional material written for the other groups and solved the same sequence of problems on their own with help from a proctor only when they really got stuck (average amount of help = 6 mins/hour). In all three groups the majority of the time was spent solving problems, not reading instructions. Subjects solved 20 problems not involving function definition and 38 function definition problems spread over six lessons, one per day.

Not all subjects were able to solve the recursion problems in the allotted time, so we extrapolated how long it would have taken them to finish. Averaging the actual and extrapolated times, subjects took 11.4 hours with a human tutor, 15 hours with the computer tutor and 26.5 hours in the on-your-own condition. The difference between the computer-tutor condition and the human condition is not statistically reliable, but both are faster than the on-your-own condition.

We compared their performance on a test just before the recursion exercises. In a series of small problems the human-tutor subjects got 56 percent correct, the computer-tutor subjects got 65 percent correct and the on-your-own subjects got 64 percent correct. There are no significant differences. We also asked them to recall all the functions they could and describe what these functions did with a simple example. Subjects in the human-tutor condition recalled 22.1 functions; in the computer-tutor condition, 19.3 functions; and in the on-your-own condition, 19.3 functions. In terms of percentage of these functions given correct definitions, the results were human tutor, 82 percent; computer tutor, 77 percent; and on-your-own, 75 percent. Again there are no statistically significant differences.

To summarize, both human and computer tutors take significantly less time to bring subjects to the same criterion as the on-your-own condition. However, there is no difference in final level of knowledge. It is interesting that the on your own estimate (26.5 hours) is less than the class estimate (43 hours). This may reflect an overestimate by class students or the better design of our instructional material.

Cognitive principles in the design of the LISP tutor

As with the geometry tutor, it is worth reviewing how the LISP tutor does and does not achieve the cognitive-design principles set forth earlier:

1. In this system we represent both the ideal student model and the bugs as production rules.
2. We try to reify the coding goal structure in the code and placeholder

symbols. We have been less successful with communicating the goal structure behind the algorithm design but do try to communicate it by the hierarchy of menus.

3. All of the instruction about LISP is provided in the context of writing LISP code.
4. As with the geometry tutor, we try to focus the student on the critical abstract properties of problems and not on their superficial properties. For instance, error messages are general descriptions of the relevant issues.
5. There are a number of ways we try to minimize working memory. The annotated code that we display is an attempt to represent the goal structure. When students are working on examples all relevant information in these examples is kept displayed in an example window.
6. The system does provide immediate feedback on errors.
7. As with the geometry tutor, a serious deficit of this tutor is that it does not adjust grain size with the student's development.
8. As for the issue of successive approximation, the LISP tutor has had one success case and one failure case. The failure case was from a demonstration in the summer of 1984. Many students complained that they were moved onto more advanced topics before mastering easier ones. Partly in response to that we instituted more practice problems for a demonstration in the fall of 1984. In this case, students were able to successively approximate more and more advanced problem-solving skills.

FINAL CONCLUSIONS

This is a report of work in progress. We have yet to get our tutors for geometry or LISP into their final states. We have yet to completely formalize our general methodology for creating tutors. Our evaluation is still preliminary, both of the general methodology and of the specific tutors. However, we believe that the results are sufficiently encouraging to present at this time. The basic result is that it does seem possible to create computer tutors that are capable of making a major improvement in the education for at least some topics. An important additional observation is that the computer technology to deliver these tutors is rapidly becoming economically feasible. For example, the personal computers soon to be distributed to each undergraduate student at Carnegie-Mellon University are powerful enough to run our tutors.

REFERENCES

Anderson, J. R. (1981a). Tuning of search of the problem space for geometry proofs. In *Proceedings of IJCAI-81*, pp. 165–70.
Anderson, J. R. (1981b). *Acquisition of Cognitive Skill*. ONR Technical Report 81-1. Carnegie-Mellon University, Pittsburgh. Pa.

Anderson, J. R. (1983). *The Architecture of Cognition*. Cambridge. Mass.: Harvard University Press.
Anderson, J. R., Farrell, R. and Sauers, R. (1982). *Learning to Plan in LISP*. ONR Technical Report ONR-82-2. Carnegie-Mellon University.
Anderson, J. R., Farrell, R. and Sauers, R. (1984). Learning to program in LISP. *Cognitive Science*, **8**, 87–129.
Anderson, J. R., and Jeffries, R. (in press). *Novice LISP Errors: Undetected Losses of Information from Working Memory. Human–Computer Interaction.* ⎫
Anderson, J. R., Pirolli, P. and Farrell, R. Learning recursive programming. In forthcoming book edited by Chi, Farr and Glaser.
Bilodeau, I. McD. (1969). Information feedback. In E. A. Bilodeau (ed.) *Principles of Skill Acquisition*. New York: Academic Press.
Bloom, B. S. (1984). The 2 sigma problem: The search for methods of group instruction as effective a one-to-one tutoring. *Educational Researcher*, **13**, 3–16.
Boyle, C. F., and Anderson, J. R. (1984). Acquisition and automated instruction of geometry proof skills. Paper presented at the 1984 AERA meetings.
Brooks, R. E. (1977). Towards a theory of the cognitive processes in computer programming. *International Journal of Man–Machine Studies*, **9**, 737–51.
Brown, J. S., Burton, R. R. and DeKleer, J. (1982). Pedagogical, natural language and knowledge engineering techniques in SOPHIE I, II and III. In D. Sleeman and J. S. Brown (eds) *Intelligent Tutoring Systems*. New York: Academic Press, pp. 227–82.
Brown, J. S., and Van Lehn, K. (1980). Repair theory: A generative theory of bugs in procedural skills. *Cognitive Science*, **4**, 379–426.
Carbonell, J. R. (1970). AI in CAI: An artificial intelligence approach to computer-aided instruction. *IEEE Transactions on Man–Machine Systems*, **11**, 190–202.
Clancey, W. J. (1983). The epistemology of a rule-based expert system—a framework for explanation. *Artificial Intelligence*, **20**, 215–51.
Cohen, V. B. (1982). Computer software found weak. *New York Times* (20 April), **C4**. Summary of a research.
Halasz, F., and Moran, T. P. (1982). *Analogy Considered Harmful*. Technical Report. Proceedings of the Human Factors in Computer Systems Conference, 15–17 March. Gaithersburg, Md.
Hoffer, A. (1981). Geometry is more than proof. *Mathematics Teacher*, **1981** (January), 11–18.
Jurgensen, R. C., Donnelly, A. J., Maier, J. E. and Rising, G. R. (1975). *Geometry*. Boston, Mass.: Houghton Mifflin.
Kant, E., and Newell, A. Problem solving techniques for the design of algorithms. *Proceedings of the symposium on the Empirical Foundations of Information and Software Science*. Atlanta. (Ga.)
Lewis, M., and Anderson, J. R. (in press). The role of feedback in discriminating problem-solving operators. *Cognitive Psychology*.
McKendree, J., and Anderson, J. R. (in press). Frequency and practice effects on the composition of knowledge in LISP evaluation. In J. M. Carroll (ed.) *Cognitive Aspects of Human–Computer Interaction*.
McKendree, J., Reiser, B. J. and Anderson, J. R. (1984). Tutorial goals and strategies in the instruction of programming skills. *Proceedings of the Sixth Annual Conference, Cognitive Science Society*. Boulder, Colo.
Neves, D. M., and Anderson, J. R. (1981). Knowledge compilation: Mechanisms for the automatization of cognitive skills. In J. R. Anderson (ed.) *Cognitive Skills and their Acquisition*. Hillsdale, NJ: Erlbaum.
Newell, A., and Simon, H. (1972). *Human Problem Solving*. Englewood Cliffs. NJ: Prentice-Hall.

O'Shea, T. (1979). A self-proving quadratic tutor. *International Journal of Man–Machine Studies*. **11**(1), 97–124.

Papert, S. (1980). *Mindstorms*. New York: Basic Books.

Pirolli, P., and Anderson, J. R. (in press). The role of learning from examples in the acquisition of recursive programming skills. *Canadian Journal of Psychology*.

Rich, C., and Shrobe, H. (1978). Initial report of a LISP programmers' apprentice. *IEEE Trans. Soft. Eng.*, **SE-4:6**, 456–66.

Ross, B. H. (1984). Remindings and their effects in learning a cognitive skill. *Cognitive Psychology*, **16**, 371–416.

Sheil, B. A. (1981). The psychological study of programming. *Computing Surveys*, **13**, 101–20.

Shneiderman, B. (1980). *Software Psychology*. Cambridge. Mass.: Winthrop.

Siklossy, L. (1976). *Let's Talk LISP*. Englewood Cliffs, NJ: Prentice-Hall.

Skinner, B. F. (1958). Teaching machines. *Science*, **128**, 889–977.

Sleeman, D. (1982). Assessing aspects of competence in basic algebra. In D. Sleeman and J. S. Brown (eds) *Intelligent Tutoring Systems*. New York: Academic Press.

Sleeman, D., and Brown, J. S. (eds) (1982). *Intelligent Tutoring Systems*. New York: Academic Press.

Soloway, E. (1980). *From Problems to Programs via Plans: The Context and Structure of Knowledge for Introductory LISP Programming*. COINS Technical Report 80-19. University of Massachusetts at Amherst.

Soloway, E., Bonar, J. and Ehrlich, K. (1983). Cognitive strategies and looping constructs: An empirical study. *Communications of the ACM*, **22**, 853–60.

Stevens, A., Collins, A. and Goldin, S. E. (1982). Misconceptions in student's understanding. In D. Sleeman and J. S. Brown (eds) *Intelligent Tutoring Systems*. New York: Academic Press.

Taylor, R. (1980). *The Computer in the School: Tutor, Tool, Tutee*. New York: Teachers College Press.

Tulving, E. (1983). *Elements of Episodic Memory*. London: Oxford University Press.

Tulving, E., and Thomson, P. M. (1973). Encoding specificity and retrieval processes in episodic memory. *Psychological Review*, **80**, 352–73.

Van Lehn, K. (1983). *Felicity Conditions for Human Skill Acquisition: Validating an AI-based Theory*. Technical Report CIS-21, Xerox Parc. Palo Alto, Calif.

Modelling Cognition
Edited by P. Morris
© 1987 John Wiley & Sons Ltd.

5

Initial skill learning: an analysis of how elaborations facilitate the three components

DAVIDA H. CHARNEY and LYNNE M. REDER
Carnegie-Mellon University

1. INTRODUCTION: SKILL LEARNING AND THEORIES OF COGNITION

Understanding the processes by which people learn is fundamental to any theory of cognition. Accounting for learning adds constraints to theories of cognition; not only must a theory account for adult capacities, but it must also posit mechanisms for acquiring new capabilities as adult learners do. Although the study of how information is acquired has been central in memory research, only a few theories of cognition, problem-solving and the like (e.g. Anderson, 1983; Kieras and Polson, 1985; Hayes and Simon, 1974) have been concerned with specifying how a skill or procedure is initially acquired.

It seems natural and desirable to try to apply what we have discovered about acquiring factual information to the study of how people learn new skills or procedures. However, while the findings from the memory domain are certainly relevant to the study of skill acquisition, they fall short of what is needed. At the very least, the standard performance measures for fact learning (e.g. recognition judgments, binary-choice decision tasks and recall protocols) are inappropriate for measuring skill learning, which requires the learner to *apply* his or her knowlege. Consider a budding scientist who has studied inferential statistics in order to determine the reliability of experimental results. A fair test of how well this student has learned the various statistical tests is not whether she can recall their formulae, but rather whether she can select the appropriate test and use it correctly to analyze the data.

Presented with two samples to contrast, the student must remember that there is a test called the Student t-test and decide that it is an appropriate test for the data at hand. Then she must retrieve the formula for the test, find and plug in values for the variables in the formula correctly, and solve for the correct result.[1]

This example illustrates that although skill learning and fact learning both involve the acquisition of new information, they differ in the types of information that must be learned and the ways in which the learner uses the information. The first obvious difference between fact learning and skill learning is that a skill has an *execution component* that is quite specific to that skill and the requirements for execution vary considerably from skill to skill. The output for many skills comes in the form of complex motor activity, such as pressing a certain sequence of keys or fitting together the parts of a device. In contrast, the output modes for demonstrating mastery of a fact are general, simple and well-learned: the learner vocalizes or writes the fact that is retrieved from memory or signals whether the retrieved representation meets some criterion (e.g. recognition or paraphrase match).

One reason for the variation is that skills are often built up out of component skills, which are called on in the manner of 'subroutines'. For example, performing a t-test involves at least two component skills: finding the mean and the standard error of a sample. A different procedure might involve finding a different mean, but using some of the same values to determine the error term. The relationship between facts in a domain seems qualitatively different from the relationship between subroutines embedded in a procedure. While it is common to 'unpack' a concept by retrieving related concepts, the process is seldom as routine and unvarying as performing a fixed subroutine.

Another difference between skill learning and fact learning is that the context in which a fact is retrieved can facilitate access to the learned information. A learner demonstrates fact learning by retrieving a fact in response to a query. The query not only provides a retrieval cue, but it also provides an appropriate occasion for retrieving that particular fact. In other words, a person can be considered to have mastered a fact if he or she can recall it when specifically queried. But recall of procedures when queried is not sufficient for mastery of a skill. Knowing how to perform a skill requires that the learner understand and appreciate the contexts in which a particular procedure is appropriate. In the case given above, deciding to use the t-test rather than some other test depends on knowing something about the function of the t-test and something about the data to be analyzed. Granted, it is just as important to know when to use a fact as when to use a procedure.

---

[1] Remembering that the name of the test is 't-test' is not critical in this case, but in other skill tasks (such as using a computer or constructing a proof), remembering the name of a procedure can be quite important.

The difference is, however, that learning a skill means knowing when to use the acquired procedures but learning a fact does not. A test of skill learning should measure the learner's ability to choose procedures appropriately.

In addition to differences in what must be learned, there are also differences in how we view 'mastery' of a fact versus a skill. Although facts can vary in learnability and strength, we usually do not judge 'how well' a fact is recalled when it is recalled. In contrast, procedures not only vary in ease of learning, but most require practice for any degree of competence to be attained. That is why in skill domains, we classify practitioners as experts, novices or intermediates. We do not say that someone is 'skilled' in a particular domain until she can execute the procedures rapidly and rather effortlessly. A person who is slow to execute basic procedures or who rehearses the requisite steps 'declaratively' is usually judged to be a novice.

Because skill learning involves different output requirements and different standards for proficiency, we need new, more sensitive measures in order to study skill learning. But, more importantly, we need to consider closely the cognitive mechanisms of skill learning and how they interact with those of fact learning. If skill learning draws heavily on declarative knowledge, then we might expect factors that affect encoding, retention and retrieval from declarative memory to be important for skill learning. Conversely, if skill learning and fact learning involve largely independent processes, then we might not expect conditions that facilitate fact learning to have much benefit for skill learning.

One model of cognition that carefully considers where declarative knowledge interacts with procedural knowledge is Anderson's (1983) ACT* model. Anderson follows Fitts (1964) is positing that learners initially acquire a skill in declarative form, usually from oral or written instructions. Procedural knowledge of the skill, in the form of a production system, arises only after hands-on practice. At first, in order to approximate the required skill behavior, the learner uses a set of general-purpose productions to retrieve segments of the declarative representation of the instructions, and translate them into a series of actions. With additional practice, the learner gradually constructs a set of skill-specific productions that directly incorporate the relevant declarative knowledge, eliminating the extra step of retrieving this information from declarative memory. As the productions are compiled and tuned, skill performance improves dramatically; performance becomes much more efficient and requires much less conscious attention.

In this model, declarative knowledge becomes increasingly superfluous to skill performance as learners gain expertise, but the declarative representation is critical to the initial stages of skill learning. We might expect, then, that factors influencing the formation of the declarative representation would strongly influence initial skill performance. In particular, the form of the verbal instructions on which the declarative representation is based is clearly quite important. If the learner cannot extract an adequate declarative representation of what to do from the instructions, it is unlikely that he or she will be able to approximate the skill, except perhaps through trial-and-error or some other problem-solving heuristic. Further, since the initial productions are based on the learner's early approximations of the skill performance, the form of the verbal instructions may critically influence what the skill-specific productions look like. Surprisingly the issue of how verbal instructions influence the initial acquisition of procedures is only beginning to receive attention in the literature (e.g. LeFevre, 1985; Kieras and Polson, 1985; Hayes and Simon, 1974).

This chapter, then, is concerned with the initial stage of cognitive skill acquisition; that is, how a novice learns a skill well enough to use it. We mean to distinguish this stage, in which the learner acquires the bare essentials of a cognitive skill, from later stages in which the learner becomes proficient. Theories concerned with proficiency (e.g. the dynamics of speedup with practice) have been developed by a number of researchers (e.g. Anderson, 1982; Newell and Rosenbloom, 1981; Rosenbloom and Newell, in press; Schneider and Shiffrin, 1977; Shiffrin and Dumais, 1981; Shiffrin and Schneider, 1977). Rather than trying to understand the development of cognitive expertise, our goal is to explore more carefully the requisite components of initial cognitive skill acquisition and what features of the initial verbal instruction facilitate each component.

We will begin by outlining three components that we consider crucial for initial skill learning. Then we will describe three types of elaborations that we believe facilitate learning and illustrate the ways in which they facilitate the components of skill learning. Finally, we will summarize our view as to where elaborations are beneficial and where they are not.

2. A TRIPARTITE MODEL OF COGNITIVE SKILL ACQUISITION

We conceive of initial skill learning as consisting of three critical components:

(a) learning novel concepts and the functionality of novel procedures,
(b) learning how to execute the procedures;
(c) learning the conditions under which a procedure is applied; and remembering the best procedure to execute in a given situation.

In other words, learning a skill means knowing what procedures exist for accomplishing various goals, knowing how to carry out the procedures, and knowing under what circumstances to apply them (including remembering to use them when the situation warrants). Each of these components can be learned independently and each component can be a 'bottleneck' to acquiring a skill. Furthermore, the relative importance of the components may vary, depending on the type of skill being learned: assembling a piece of equipment, operating a device, using a computer system, solving problems. This section will consider the requirements of each component in more detail.

2.1. Learning novel concepts and the functionality of procedures

For someone learning an entirely new skill, the idea of what kinds of things can be accomplished and what objects the procedures act on may be entirely unfamiliar. Consider someone who is learning to use a computer text-editor (e.g. EMACS) for the first time. A proficient typist who has never used a word-processor will consider it a novel concept to insert a word into a string instead of erasing a line and retyping it. Features such as automatic line wrapping, multiple windows into the same file, keyboard macros and kill buffers are other concepts that will be entirely new. In addition to novel concepts such as these, the novice user must also find out what things can and cannot be done with a text-editor. That is, the learner needs to know what distinct procedures (in this case, what commands) are available in the text-editing system and understand what each one does.

It is important to distinguish between learning a procedure's functionality and acquiring a 'mental model' of the system that uses these procedures. Learning the concepts and the function of individual procedures does not entail acquiring a mental model of a system (i.e. its components and how they interact). Although a *sophisticated* understanding of the concepts and procedures may involve the construction of a mental model, a mental model is not always necessary for proficient skill performance. For example, many experienced drivers have little more than a crude idea of how a car works. The value of a mental model to the novice learner depends on the type of skill being learned. As Kieras (1985) points out, a mental model of how a device works is only likely to improve performance if the procedures for operating or assembling the device can be inferred from knowing how the parts interact. In a computer-operating system, the syntax and the names of commands are oftentimes chosen arbitrarily, so having a mental model of how a computer works is not likely to help people learn and remember how to execute the commands. On the other hand, when the goal is to *trouble-shoot* the system, having a mental model can be very helpful. That is, when the computer is not responding in the expected way, it is much easier to diagnose the trouble if one has a mental model of what the computer does under various circumstances.

2.2. Learning how to execute new procedures

It is often crucial in skill learning to remember fairly arbitrary associations of objects and functions (e.g. which button on a control panel produces the desired state) and to be able to reproduce exact sequences of symbols and actions. In this respect, skill learning is quite different from fact learning. When seeking declarative information, people are usually highly tolerant of gist reporting, paraphrasing and even slips of the tongue. It is irrelevant for most purposes whether a fact presented in one syntactic form (e.g. passive) is stored or retrieved in another (e.g. active). In contrast, there is low tolerance for such variation in most cognitive skill domains. For example, computers cannot commonly recognize a wide range of synonyms or abbreviations of crucial terms. In fact, computers are notoriously 'literal-minded': when a user presses the wrong key, the computer at best responds with an error message, and at worst performs an undesired action. The computer has little or no capacity to infer what key the user intended, even if the key he typed had a similar label or was physically near the correct key. Given the current technology, learners must strictly adhere to the vocabulary and syntactic rules of whatever system, language or program they are using. Equally strict conditions on the sequence of operations and the use of symbols are imposed in many noncomputer skill domains.

The complexity of the execution component depends on the nature of the procedure and the skill domain itself. In many domains, the task of learning to execute a procedure consists of learning three elements:

(a) the name of the procedure;
(b) the rule describing a sequence of operations; and
(c) the method of binding variables in the rule to objects in that problem space.

These three elements can be illustrated most clearly in the case of computer commands. Suppose that a learner is given the task of renaming a file. To execute the procedure, the learner must first remember the name of the command (e.g. RENAME). Then he must reproduce the sequence of arguments that the RENAME command requires (e.g. type the name of the command, then the current name of the file, then the desired name of the file). In this sequence, the name of the command (RENAME) is a constant term, but the present and desired names are variables. The learner must determine the values of these variables for the present situation, and plug the values into the correct places in the sequence.

The first and third elements, learning the name of a procedure and learning to bind variables, are not required in all skills. They are most often required in skills like using a computer that involve a set of general, multi-purpose procedures. Whereas the procedures in a computer manual can be used over and over in novel combinations to accomplish a wide variety of goals, the goal is fairly fixed in an assembly task or a device operation task. For example, when one is learning to put together a stereo phonograph system, there is a specific, known object that a closed set of pieces is going to form. In this case, the descriptions of the procedures can be completely explicit, naming the exact parts that are involved at each stage. Each step in the assembly is performed only once. Under these circumstances, there are no variables and the procedures need not be named.

The second element, the rule or sequence of operations, can take many different forms. Commonly, the sequence of operations comes in the form of an ordered list such as a cookbook recipe, each step of which may refer to distinct subprocesses (e.g. sautéing vegetables as part of a recipe for making spaghetti sauce). However, a list format is not appropriate to all skills. Mathematical formulaes and computer commands have a formal syntax which may be expressed abstractly in the form of a rule or template. To illustrate the diversity of these abstract rules, we provide three examples below. The first is a formula for the t-test for single mean (compared to a specified constant). The second is the syntactic rule for the command to rename files on the IBM-PC. The third is a template for defining functions in the computer language LISP:[2]

$$t = \frac{X - \mu}{s/\sqrt{N}} \qquad (1)$$

where s is an estimate of the population standard deviation.

REN[AME] [*d:*][*path*]*filename*[*.ext*]   *filename*[*.ext*]   (2)

(DEFUN ⟨function name⟩   (3)
　　　(⟨parameter 1⟩ ⟨parameter 2⟩ . . . ⟨parameter n⟩)
　　　⟨process description⟩

To execute the procedures for the t-test, one finds values for all of the variables mentioned in the rule, performs the arithmetic calculations signaled by the mathematical symbols and solves for a numeric solution. This procedure is quite different from the use of a syntactic rule or template. The sequence of operations for generating a RENAME command or defining a LISP function from a template is to type a sequence of symbols that matches the template in structure, in which each constant term (e.g. DEFUN) and each symbol (e.g. parentheses, colons, spaces) appears in the appropriate location and each variable is replaced by the appropriate value.

The degree to which the rule for a procedure must be internalized depends on the task. For many skills, executing the procedures should be automatic. For example, once learners know how to use a computer text-editor, they use the manual mainly to learn new features or to solve some unexpected problem or for an occasional reminder. They should not have any difficulty executing the standard set of commands without much conscious attention. On the other

---

[2] The rule for the rename command was taken from the official Disk Operating System (DOS) manual (Anonymous, 1983). The LISP template is taken from Winston and Horn (1981).

hand, factors such as the number and complexity of the procedures, their importance or their frequency of use may require learners to depend on written instructions each time they perform a task. For example, airplane pilots review printed check-lists each time they fly.

2.3. Learning conditions for application

As argued above, having a skill means knowing when to apply particular procedures. In some cases, the conditions for application are perfectly straightforward. For example, when the procedures come in a strictly ordered sequence, the precondition for any given procedure is the result of correctly executing the previous procedure. The conditions for application may be much more complex, however. In skills such as using a computer, there may be multiple ways to accomplish a goal. Under certain conditions, one procedure might be much more efficient or advantageous than the rest. If novices do not appreciate the conditions under which the procedures are most useful, they might overlook procedures that would be very useful to them. Instead, they might always choose to use some inefficient procedure that they happened to learn first or that may initially be easier to remember.

Card, Moran and Newell's (1983) study of experienced users of text-editing system demonstrated that experts have well-defined rules for selecting between procedures. The text-editor involved offered two basic methods of moving the cursor: searching for a specified string of characters or moving the cursor up or down a line at a time. The subjects had consistent strategies for choosing between these methods (e.g. use the search method if the target location is more than three lines away, use the line-feed method otherwise). Presumably, these computer users developed their strategies themselves, but their early learning was not observed. At least some of the subjects had developed fairly inefficient strategies. For example, one subject never used the string search method; she used some variation of the line-feed method even when the target location was over ten lines away.[3]

If we wish learners to use a repertoire of procedures appropriately, it may be necessary to *motivate* the use of some procedures by demonstrating the advantages they have in particular situations. Acquiring a repertoire goes beyond the ability to decide between specified procedures on demand. Even if a person can, when queried, consistently judge which of two procedures is more efficient in a given context, he may not always select the most efficient one in *real* situations. The learner may fail to ask (or be unwilling to ask) for each subgoal, 'which procedure is optimal here?' Computing the relative costs

---

[2] Card, Moran and Newell successfully modelled how the experts used selection rules, but they were not interested in the relative efficiency of the rules their subjects had come up with nor in how the subjects had acquired their rules.

of procedures can be time consuming and tedious, and not without its share of the costs. Therefore, unless a procedure easily 'comes to mind', it may remain unused. This means that skilled performance involves not only the ability to recognize the situations in which a given procedure is optimal, but the ability to retrieve the best procedure easily and rapidly when necessary.

It is worth noting that learning sophisticated selection strategies is probably unnecessary for skill tasks such as learning to assemble a device or operate a piece of equipment. Since the procedures in these tasks are less multipurpose, they are also less interchangeable. It is more likely that the conditions for application in these tasks grow out of ordering constraints rather than considerations of efficiency.

2.4. The independence of the three components of skill learning

The three components of skill learning that have just been described are fairly independent of one another. A learner may know that a specific procedure exists for solving a problem without knowing or remembering how to apply it. For example, a child knows what shoe-tying is and when it needs to be done, but lacks the ability to carry out the procedure. Similarly, by rote learning, one may learn to perform a series of steps without knowing what the steps are for. Finally, one may understand what a procedure does and how to carry it out, but not know when or why to use it. This situation often arises when novices consult computer manuals: they finish reading a description of a command, understand more or less what it does and how to issue it, but lack the slightest inkling as to when they would ever want to use it or how it relates to other commands they have learned. Since each of the three components is necessary to skill learning, each can constitute a 'bottleneck' for acquiring a skill.

3. THREE TYPES OF ELABORATIONS FOR FACILITATING SKILL LEARNING

The question we address in the remainder of this chapter is how the presentation of information in an instructional text can facilitate learning in the three components just described. We will focus on a particular aspect of instructional texts, namely the degree to which the main points are elaborated.

The effect of elaborations on the acquisition of information from a text has been the topic of considerable speculation and research (Reder, Charney and Morgan, in press; Anderson and Reder, 1979; Reder, 1976, 1979, in press; Weinstein, 1978; Mandl and Ballstaedt, 1981; Mandl, Schnotz and Tergan, 1984; Bransford, 1979; Chiesi, Spilich and Voss, 1979; Craik and Tulving, 1975). In the view of most researchers, there are several reasons why elaborations should help subjects learn and remember the main ideas of a text. Elaborations provide multiple retrieval routes to the essential information by creating more connections to the learner's prior knowledge. If one set of connections is forgotten, it may be possible to retrieve the desired information another way. Further, if the learner forgets an important point, it may be possible to reconstruct it from the information that is still available. Not all the evidence on elaborations is positive, however. Reder and Anderson (1980, 1982) found that elaborations can impair learning and retention of the main points of a textbook chapter as compared to studying a brief summary of the main points. In contrast, Reder, Charney and Morgan (in press) found that when the goal is to use the information in a skill-learning task, elaborations can improve performance.

This section defines the essential characteristics of three types of elaborations that we think are especially important for skill learning: analogies and two types of examples (simple instantiations and situation examples). After these types of elaborations are defined, the next section will describe how they may specifically contribute to skill learning.

3.1. Analogy

An analogy draws a comparison between a concept that a person wants to learn and concept in a different domain that the learner is already familiar with. In Gentner's (1983) terminology, the former is the 'target concept' and the latter is the 'base concept'. Gentner proposes that the quality of an analogy depends on what type of information can be mapped from the base to the target construct. Good analogies map across relationships between objects rather than specific attributes of objects. For example, in the familiar analogy between the solar system and the structure of the atom, the attributes of the sun (HOT and YELLOW) are not mapped to the nucleus of the atom. What is mapped is the relationship of the sun to the planets (i.e. the sun is MORE MASSIVE THAN the planets and the planets REVOLVE AROUND the sun).

We suspect that analogies reduce the processing load during learning by facilitating chunking of the information in the target domain. That is, the structure of concepts and relations from the base domain can be used to provide temporary labels on components of the target idea while the problem or task is being solved. Since the base labels are well understood, the pointers to the relevant structure(s) in memory are not lost while the learner works through the critical new aspects of the target domain.

3.2. Exemplification

Like analogy, exemplification involves a mapping between two concepts, but the mapping is more tightly constrained. We will follow Hobbs (1978) in defining exemplification as a relationship between a rule (or generalization) and a specific instance (or example) for which the rule holds true. The rule and the example are related by sharing the same underlying proposition. In other words, the relationships beween objects in the general construct must map across to the specific construct. Unlike analogy, however, exemplification also constrains the mappings of object attributes. The objects in a rule are abstract, general categories. The objects in an example are more specific members of those general categories. That is, an example can be constructed by substituting one or more specific, concrete terms for general terms in a rule. To see how this works, consider the following generalization–example pair (taken from Charney, 1985):

> Lawsuits are now pending which seek to hold handgun manu-   (4)
> facturers and distributors liable for the damage caused by their products.

> The family of James Riordan, a Chicago police officer killed by   (5)
> a handgun, is suing Walther, the West German maker of the gun and International Armament Corporation, its American distributor.

Statement (4) is a generalization that asserts the existence of a new type of lawsuit, initiated against manufacturers and distributers of handguns by people who have been hurt by the handguns. Statement (5) is an example of this generalization. It asserts the existence of a particular lawsuit, initiated against a specific manufacturer (Walther), and a specific distributor (the International Armament Corporation), by the Riordan family, who were hurt when James Riordan was killed by a handgun.

The class/member constraint on examples leads to an important difference between analogy and exemplification. The base and target concepts in an analogy come from different domains: a familiar base and an unfamiliar target. In exemplification, on the other hand, the rule and the example are both from the same domain, the domain of the skill to be learned. Since both constructs are relatively unfamiliar, there is the danger that the learner will not understand the rule well enough to make the appropriate mapping to the example.

Despite this danger, exemplification may aid learning in several ways. First, seeing typical objects that the rule might operate on can clarify the general terms in the rule. The general terms are linked to more concrete and specific concepts. Second, seeing a variety of examples and counterexamples can help the learner define the scope of the rule's application (Nitsch, 1977; Tennyson, 1973; Tennyson, Woolley and Merrill, 1972). Third, examples may have an important role for establishing the validity or the utility of a rule (Perelman and Olbrechts-Tyteca, 1969; Schoenfeld, 1979; Mandl, Schnotz and Tergan, 1984; Gilson and Abelson, 1968). Finally, learners can use examples of correctly solved problems as models for solving new problems (e.g. Anderson, Sauers and Farrell, 1984).

With this last use of examples (serving as models for solutions to new problems), the boundary between analogy and exemplification begins to blur. On the one hand, using examples as models is analogic in that there is a specific-to-specific mapping between the constructs (the example and the new problem). Furthermore, as we would expect in an analogy, the 'base' example is more familiar than the target problem by virtue of having been seen or worked on before. On the other hand, unlike analogy, the examples that are used as models are often introduced to the learner in the context of a general principle of rule. Further, the model problems come from the same unfamiliar domain as the novel problems they are mapped to. Consider, for example, the problems that are laid out in the course of a mathematics chapter. A general formula or algorithm is exemplified with specific problems that can then be used as models for the chapter-end exercises. Anderson, Farrell and Sauers (1984) explicitly combine general-to-specific and specific-to-specific mappings in their analysis of subjects learning to write LISP functions. The subjects were presented with an abstract template for defining a function in LISP along with an example of a correct function definition. On the basis of protocol analysis, Anderson *et al.* conclude that subjects first make the exemplification mapping between the template and the example, then analogize between the example and the new problem. In spite of the dual nature of this type of learning, we will use the term exemplification whenever a general principle or rule or procedure is instantiated with a specific example within a prescribed domain, even when we assume that the example is later used as a model.

3.3. Situational examples

We will single out *situational examples* as an especially rich type of example. Situational examples differ from other kinds of instantiations in that they illustrate the contexts in which a procedure applies rather than simply illustrating the details of how to execute an abstract procedure. The distinction we are drawing between simple instantiations and situational examples is similar to that drawn by Mandl, Schnotz and Tergan (1984) between 'illustrative examples' and 'application examples'. Both types of examples provide specific instances of the general terms of a rule, but the types differ in what other kinds of information they provide.

To illustrate the two kinds of examples, consider the following three sentences. The first is a rule from a text for teaching students to improve their writing style (Williams, 1981). The second simply instantiates the concepts in the rule, and the third is a situational example:

> When a nominalization follows an empty verb, change the nom-   (6)
> inalization to a verb that replaces the empty verb.

> For example, nominalizations such as *investigation*, *inquiry* or   (7)
> *response* often follow empty verbs such as *make* or *conduct*. Use
> the verbs *investigate*, *inquire* or *respond* instead.

> For example, change the sentence 'The police conducted an   (8)
> extremely thorough investigation into the incident', to 'The
> police investigated the incident extremely thoroughly.'

The example in statement (7) instantiates the general terms 'empty verb' and 'nominalization' but does not provide a context in which they might occur. The situational example (statement 8) instantiates the general terms within a specific context. The context illustrates something about the situations in which the rule should apply: the nominalization need not follow the empty verb directly. It also illustrates something about how to carry through the solution: changing a noun to a verb can necessitate changes to other parts of the sentence.

If instantiation is the major contribution of an example, then both types of examples should aid performance to the same degree. But if it is important to use the example as a model or to motivate the use of a procedure, then seeing a situational example should improve performance more than seeing a conceptual example. Situational examples may also help people remember a rule when they are working on a task, because seeing the task may remind them of the example (Ross, 1984). Finally, situational examples may be better for demonstrating the utility of the rule, by showing rather than just asserting that following the rule leads to a desirable outcome.

4. THE INTERACTION OF ELABORATION TYPES AND THE COMPONENTS OF SKILL LEARNING

In this section, we recapitulate the three components of skill learning and analyze the potential benefits that specific types of elaborations may have for learning a specific component. In particular, we claim that situation examples are the most useful for skill learning because each example can contribute to learning in all three components. On the other hand, while analogies can be constructed to illustrate each component, they are more likely to help people learn the functionality of a procedure than how to execute it or when to select it. We will begin by briefly discussing the role of analogies in skill learning, describing their benefits and limitations. Subsequent sections will show in more detail how examples can contribute to the three components of skill learning.

4.1. The role of analogies in skill learning

Initially, one might expect analogies to be the most helpful form of elaboration for learners since, unlike examples, they involve constructs in a base domain that are highly familiar to the learner. As such, analogies may be very useful for clarifying unfamiliar concepts. Suppose a novice computer user is learning to use a personal computer with floppy disk drives. The following analogy can help the user anticipate some features of diskettes:

> A diskette is similar to a small, flexible phonograph record, ex-   (9)
> cept that instead of storing sounds, it contains information
> that the computer can read, add to or delete.

By mapping information from his previous knowledge of phonograph records, the user may anticipate that diskettes are used in a horizontal orientation and that it is unwise to let the surface of the diskette become dirty or scratched. The usefulness of the analogy is somewhat limited, however. Learners may draw spurious assumptions from the analogy, e.g. that information is stored on a diskette linearly, as it is on a phonograph record. Or they may assume that, like phonograph records, diskettes must be removed from their protective covering when they are used.

Analogies may also be constructed for motivating the use of some procedures. One procedure that many computer users must learn is how to specify the location of the file or directory they want to work on. The following analogy attempts to motivate the choice between two options for specifying the 'path' through a directory structure. The choice arises in the DOS operating system because paths optionally begin with a backslash symbol (\). The backslash signals that the path is to start at the top-level (or 'root') directory. If the backslash is omitted, the path is assumed to start at the current directory (which may or may not be the top-level directory). This analogy compares the specification of a file in a directory structure to dialling a local or long-distance telephone call.

> When should you specify a path that begins at the root direc-   (10)
> tory? It may be useful to draw an analogy to using the tele-
> phone to make long-distance calls. When you are calling a
> number within the current area code, you do not have to dial or
> specify your own area code. You just dial the number you want.
> This is like leaving off the first backslash in a path; the computer
> assumes you want to stay within the current directory. However,
> if you want to call someone outside the current area code, you
> dial '1' and then the new area code and then the number. The
> '1' that you dial first is analogous to the backslash for the root
> directory, and the new area code is analogous to the name of

another subdirectory where the files (or phone numbers) are stored.

This analogy clarifies the concept of a path and the appropriate circumstances for starting the path at the root directory. Again, however, the analogy is fairly fragile. For instance, the computer allows you to 'overspecify' the location of a file, but the phone company does not. That is, you can specify a path to any file starting at the root directory, even a file in the current directory. This would be analogous to dialling '1' and your own area code. The analogy also breaks down in a very common circumstance: when the current directory is the root directory and you wish to specify a path to a subdirectory within it, no backslash is needed. If all exceptions have to be explained to the user, the analogy may be more trouble than it is worth.

A more important drawback of the analogy is that it does not help the learner acquire the particular procedures needed for using the operating system. That is, knowing that an area code is analogous to a directory name does not help the learner master the system-specific conventions for specifying a path through a directory structure. So even if the analogy were more robust, learners would still have to rely on other means to learn how to execute the procedures.

As this discussion illustrates, it is possible to construct analogies for various components of skill learning, but the benefit of analogies is limited. Analogies can clarify unfamiliar concepts and procedures, but often cannot hold up at the level of detail to which learners must understand and apply the concepts. Analogies are probably least appropriate for elaborating on the execution component of a skill. We believe that examples drawn from the domain under study, though less familiar than the base domain of an analogy, are more useful to the learner in the long run. If examples are carefully constructed, they may simultaneously clarify the function of a procedure, how to execute it and when to select it.

4.2. The role of examples for conveying functionality and motivating procedures

Below we introduce two new concepts from computing to illustrate how situational examples can motivate us well as explain a concept or procedure. To give more force to our claim that rich situational examples are best for introducing or teaching these concepts, we will present the concepts first with the impoverished examples and then with richer ones.

4.2.1. Command editing

At the time of this writing, using a command editor within an operating system is a relatively novel concept, even for people familiar with computers, since this feature is not available on many operating systems. Command editing refers to the ability to retrieve commands that were already issued to the system and then use them again, either reissuing them verbatim or issuing a modified (edited) version of the command. The functionality of command editing can be conveyed with rather straightforward examples; however, if the examples do not illustrate the *motivation* for its use, learners will not appreciate the feature and when it is most useful. Consequently, they will not use the procedures regularly and will probably forget all about them fairly rapidly.

Consider the following example that explains what command editing means, but fails to motivate its use (the example pertains to a modified VMS operating system):

> Suppose you have typed the following sequence of commands (11) into your computer—
>
> $dir
> $finger
> $go .chap
>
> The first command in this sequence produces a listing of the contents of the current directory; the second, a listing of the people currently using the machine, and the last requests that the current directory be changed to a subdirectory called 'chap'.) Now suppose you want to list the contents of the 'chap' subdirectory. Using command editing, you press the up-arrow a few times so that *$go .chap*, then *finger*, then *$dir* appear on the command line. Now you need only press the return key to reissue the *$dir* command for the .chap subdirectory.

The above example is sufficient for explaining the functionality of the command editing procedure, but is poor for motivating its use in that it provides little or no savings in keystrokes over typing a new *dir* command. In such an example, the usefulness of the procedure is obscured and no novice would see the need to spend time learning it. The following example, in contrast, should make much clearer the usefulness of the command editor.

> Suppose, for example, you want to copy a number of files from (12) someone else's account on another system. To copy the first file (called 'draft1.mss'), you must specify a long path to the relevant directory in your friend's account on the other machine.
>
> $copy cmpsyb::[wells.papers.curchap]draft1.mss *.*
>
> Suppose you want to copy another file called 'final.mss' from

that same location. One way to do so would be to type a new copy command that would look exactly the same as the command above, except that 'final.mss' would appear in place of 'draft1.mss'. However, retyping the command will require 58 keystrokes for each file you want to copy. And if you enter the command with unnoticed typing mistakes in the path or the filename, you will have to type the entire command again. Command editing saves you all of this retyping. Instead of retyping, you simply 'recall' the last copy command and edit it to change the name of the file. Typing the up-arrow key brings back the last command. Then, by striking the left-arrow key, you can move the cursor leftward to the specific characters in the filename that must be changed. When you are finished changing the name of the file, press RETURN to issue the modified command. By editing and reusing your first copy command, you save nearly 40 keystrokes for each file you have to copy and you reduce the chances of error in retyping the whole command.

Both examples clarify the concept of reissuing a command. By specifying the sequence of keys that must be typed, both examples also instantiate the rules for executing the command-editing procedures. Only the situation example, however, illustrates the conditions under which the command-editing procedure is more desirable than the procedure for issuing a new command. In particular, command editing is worthwhile when you must type a number of long, similar commands. We will return to the issue of learning when to use a procedure in section 4.4 below.

4.2.2. Subdirectories

Consider another example from the same general domain. We have mentioned subdirectories in the course of the preceding example. This construct may also be unfamiliar to many readers of this chapter. Simply stating that a directory can be divided into subdirectories is sufficient for 'explaining' the concept, but it is unlikely that the user will be sufficiently motivated to acquire the cluster of skills needed to make use of such a facility.

The following example, taken from the IBM DOS Manual (Anonymous, 1983), illustrates the concept more fully along with some rationale for the usefulness of subdirectories, but adds little to the reader's sense of how subdirectories might facilitate day-to-day activities on the computer.

DOS Version 2.00 gives you the ability to better organize your   (13)
disk by placing groups of related files in their own directories
—all on the same disk. For example, let us assume that the XYZ

company has two departments (sales and accounting) that share
an IBM Personal Computer. All of the company's files are kept
on the computer's fixed disk. The local organization of the file
categories would be viewed like this:

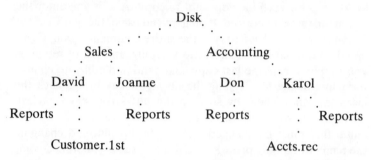

With DOS Version 2.00, it is possible to create a directory structure that matches the file organization. With this ability, all of
DAVID's report files can be grouped together in a single directory (called REPORTS), separated from all the other files on
the disk. Likewise, all of the accounts receivable files can be in
a unique directory, and soon.

    The example above implies that subdirectories are only useful when
different people are using the same disk. Even then, it does not illustrate the
advantage subdirectories have over a single directory for any given user. In
order to convey the usefulness of subdirectories, the learner might be shown a
'one-level' directory filled with many unrelated files and told to imagine trying
to find a file for which the name can be recognized but not easily recalled. The
figure below is an example of a listing of files in a flat or one-level directory.

Directory __CMPSYB::PSY$USER:[ANON]

2APA.REF;6	2SCS.DAT;1	ABHRTR3.MSS;7	APAREF.LIB;1
CAU.M88;15	CHP2BIB.AUX;1	CHP2BIB.MAK;3	CHP2BIB.MSS;10
CHP6BIB.MAK;3	CHP6BIB.MSS;12	CHP7BIB.MAK;1	CHP7BIB.MSS;14
CIANCI.MSS;3	COLDSA.DAT;1	COPING1.DAT;1	DEBBIB.AUX;1
DEBBIB.MSS;3	DEBBIB.OTL;1	DOCU.MDR;1	DOCU.MSS;1
EMACSINIT.;1	FILE2.OUT;3	FMC.DAT;1	FORM.ERR;2
FORM.LET;1	FPRO.DAT;2	FRDPRO.LNO;1	FRDPRO.MSS;1
FREUD.LNO;2	FREUD.MSS;13	FREUD2.LNO;1	FREUD2.MSS;1
GPSCIBIB.AUX;3	GPSCIBIB.MSS;4	GRADE.BAS;1	HEARTBIB.AUX;1
HEARTBIB.MAK;10	HEARTBIB.MSS;19	HEARTBIB1.MSS;3	HRTBIBADD.MAK;3
HRTBIBADD.MSS;2	IMP.FRM;2	IMPFRM.MSS;8	INST.MSS;1
INTERR.SPS;1	JPAREV.MSS;1	JUNK.DT;1	JUNK2.DT;1
LMFF.MSS;1	LOGIN.COM;6	LOT.OTL;1	LOT.OU1;1
LOT2.OTL;10	LOT2R.OTL;5	LOTA.MSS;8	LOTREF.AUX;19
LOTREF.MSS;18	LOTREF.OTL;14	LOTTAB4.MSS;13	MAIL.MAI;1

MALIAS.;4	MBOX.;2	METHOD.MSS;4	MFSBIO.MSS;9
MIKE.MSS;2	MIKE.OU1;1	MYAPA.LIB;2	MYAPA.REF;2
MYREG.CON;1	MYREG2.CON;1	NETLOGIN.COM;2	NETSERVER.LOG;15
NEWSCS.DAT;2	NOTES.MSS;2	NYEAR.;1	P1.MSS;30
P2.MSS;51	P3.MSS;11	PCORR.SPS;1	PFU.MSS;20
PILL.CON;1	PILL.DT;1	PILL2.DT;1	PLAN.;2
POSURG.DAT;1	PRE2.MSS;4	PREFACE.MSS;3	PRETEST.MSS;9
PROO.DAT;1	PROT.DAT;1	QUES.;1	QUEST.;1
QUEST.MSS;6	RA.MSS;1	RALOT.SPS;1	REG.MSS;1
REV1.;1	SA3.DAT;1	SA3.SRT;3	SAMPLE.MSS;1
SAREF.MSS;3	SAREF.OTL;3	SCHBIB.MSS;28	SCORES.DT;1
SCRIBE.LOG;1	SCRIPT.MSS;1	SCS.MSS;4	SECOND.QUE;6
SEVEN.QUE;4	SF2F.SPS;3	SHVITA.MSS;31	SHVITA1.MSS;1
SIG.LET;1	SIGMA1.MSS;1	SIGNUP.;1	SIX.LPT;1
SIX.QUE;1	SOCANX.DAT;1	SOCSUP.MSS;3	SPSS.TXT;1
SPSS1.TXT;1	SPSS2.TXT;1	STATE.;2	SUM.MSS;1
SUM1.MSS;4	SUP.;1	SUPPORT.MSS;9	TA.;3
TAB7.MSS;3	TABLE1.MSS;1	TABLE2.MSS;1	TABLE4.ERR;1
TABLE4.MSS;1	VCR.;1		

Total of 134 files.

Often people forget the exact name they gave to a file. They correctly believe that they can often recognize the name from a complete listing of the file names; however, in a directory such as the one above, as many as 134 filenames might have to be inspected. Contrast the directory listing above with the one below:

Directory __CMPSYB::PSY$USER:[NEAT–NIK]

COURSES.DIR;1	EMACSINIT.;1	EXPER.DIR;1	INFO.DIR;1
LOGIN.COM;57	MALIAS.;6	MAIL.;17	MISC.DIR;1
MSS.DIR;1	PLAN.;1		

Total of 10 files.

Each of the subdirectories (i.e. the entries with dir suffixes) may contain files and still deeper subdirectories (e.g. under 'courses' are subdirectories for specific courses, and under 'exper' are subdirectories with the data and materials for specific experiments.) Searching for a particular file may still take some looking around; however, assuming the user knows the category of the file, the number of individual filenames that must be inspected is much smaller.

By contrasting the situations for finding a file with and without subdirectories, the pair of example directories above clarifies what subdirectories are, as well as motivating the circumstances for their creation (e.g. whenever a user has a large number of files that an be categorized fairly easily.) Carefully constructed situational examples can thus illustrate both why the feature is useful and when it is most appropriate or efficient to use.

4.3. The role of examples for learning how to execute procedures

We believe that examples can give the learner the most concrete, most specific picture of exactly what to do while executing a procedure and making the necessary adjustments to specific task situations. The procedures that benefit most from exemplification are those that involve the interpretation of a general rule. An unelaborated rule, with its special notation, variables, symbols, general terms, etc., is usually too abstract for learners to comprehend. In this section, we will describe various ways in which examples can facilitate execution, including clarifying the spirit of a rule and providing a model for future solutions.

4.3.1. Learning to integrate a collection of operations: command editing

Command editing, a procedure introduced in the last section, is not a difficult concept to grasp; however, whether or not it is easy to execute depends on the nature of the system implementation. Both the DOS and VMS operating systems have command-editing features, but the implementations differ in several important respects, such as providing external cues to relevant operations. For example, on the IBM-PC, the key that recalls the previously issued DOS command is the F3 button. Of the ten function keys on the keyboard, there is no obvious reason why the desired key should be F3. Once the previous command is recalled, the user may edit it using a key labeled 'Ins' that toggles the system between insert and overwrite modes, and a key labeled 'Del' that puts the machine into delete mode. In contrast, it may be easier to remember how to initiate command editing in VMS because there are up-arrow and down-arrow keys that are uniquely associated with going back over a buffer of previously issued commands. Once a command is recalled, however, it may be harder to remember how to toggle from insert mode to overwrite mode because there are no overt function keys; the relevant sequence of keystrokes is the non-mnemonic control-a.

Command editing thus consists of a collection of operations for viewing and retrieving items in a buffer and changing the mode or state of the computer. The operations themselves are fairly simple: usually consisting of a single keystroke. As a result, the execution component of command editing is not easily described with a general rule; rather, learners must remember all the component operations and determine how to sequence them. Situational examples that show learners a complete interaction should be very valuable.[4]

The most difficult aspect of learning to execute this type of procedure may be remembering the arbitrary association of a key and a function. An

---

[4] The situational example about command editing presented earlier (example 12) provides much of the necessary description. To have fullest effect, the editing operations should probably be described more fully and should be set off from the body of the text.

additional benefit of examples may be to strengthen memory traces for such associations through repetition in a concrete context.

4.3.2. Learning to generate instances of a rule: renaming files

Among the types of procedures that are hardest to learn to execute are those that require the learner to generate a particular instance of an abstract rule. Examples of these procedures were provided earlier: learning to perform a t-test, learning to issue computer commands, or defining a function in a programming language. As discussed above, executing this type of procedure requires that the learner remember the name(s) of the procedure, the details of the rule or sequence of operations and how to assign values to any variables that appear in the rule.

Examples can help people learn this type of procedure in several ways. Consider the following typical example that was intended to help learners parse a rule, in this case, a rule for renaming files on the IBM-PC. In the manual, the example in (15) follows the general rule in (14).

REN[AME] [*d*:][*path*]*filename*[.*ext*]   *filename*[.*ext*]   (14)

For example, the command:

REN   B:ABODE   HOME   (15)
renames the file ABODE on drive B to HOME.

The example clarifies some notational aspects of the rule. Elements that appear in square brackets in the rule are optional; in the example, the last three letters of the name of the command and the path are omitted. One problem with the example is that it does not clarify under what conditions the optional elements can be omitted. A series of situational examples that contain different combinations of optional elements might be necessary to illustrate these points. The example does begin to illustrate the distinction between constant terms and variables. Elements in the rule that are printed in italics are variables. In the example, the italicized elements have been replaced. The *d*: is replaced by B: and the first instance of *filename* is replaced by ABODE.

One serious problem with this example is that the filenames ABODE and HOME do not seem very typical of real filenames and, more importantly, they do not signal which is the *old* name and which is the *new* name of the file. If learners have trouble figuring out and remembering the order of the arguments in the rule, remembering this example is unlikely to help them. Some manuals attempt to solve this problem with examples like the following:

RENAME   OLDFILE   NEWFILE   (16)

While the 'filenames' in this example do signal the function of the arguments, they are far from typical examples of filenames. Since real filenames do not typically refer to functions in rules, using this type of example may ultimately confuse the learner. The filenames are poor illustrations of what the 'fillers' of the argument slots may look like. The following situational example is better:

> Suppose you have a file called BUDGET that contains your   (17)
> budget for 1986. Now you want to create a new budget for
> 1987, but you need a way to keep the files for the two years
> distinct. The command:
>
> RENAME   BUDGET   BUDGET.86
>
> changes the name of the existing file BUDGET to
> BUDGET.86. Now you can create a file for the new budget
> called BUDGET.87, and it will be easy to distinguish the two
> files.

In addition to clarifying aspects of notation, this example also clarifies the functions of the two ordered arguments or parameters in the rule: the first is the old name and the second is the new name. The example also helps to motivate the use of the RENAME command, by presenting a situation in which renaming a file makes sense. As mentioned above, additional examples of the same sort may be needed to illustrate other aspects of rule.[5]

The results of Reder, Charney and Morgan (in press) suggest that rich examples of correct commands help people learn to generate their own commands. Indeed, elaborations on the execution of procedures proved to be more important to learners than elaborations on the function and motivation of the commands. We systematically varied whether or not a computer manual contained *syntactic* elaborations (e.g. examples of syntactically correct commands to illustrate more abstract rules for the commands) or *conceptual elaborations* (e.g. analogies illustrating the basic concepts, examples of situations in which a command would be useful). Factorially combining the two types of elaborations produced four versions of the manual. Figures 1 and 2 are corresponding excerpts from two of the manuals, describing the CHDIR ('Change Directory') command; Figure 1 contains just conceptual elaborations and Figure 2 contains just syntactic elaborations.

---

[5] The rule itself, taken from the DOS manual, is not very informative about the function of the arguments (or parameters). The following statement of the rule might be better:

    RENAME   *[location and current name of file]*   *[new name of file]*

Research suggests, however, that even this form of the rule benefits from exemplification (Reder, Charney and Morgan, in press).

CHANGING THE CURRENT DIRECTORY – CHDIR

The CHDIR command allows you to designate a directory as the "current" directory for a drive, so that the computer will automatically look there for files or sub-directories mentioned in your commands. You can designate a current directory for each disk drive independently.

FORMAT

CHDIR   [loc and name of new current directory]

You can use the abbreviation CD in the command instead of typing CHDIR.
[Location of new current directory] refers to the path to the directory you want to designate as the new current directory. The last directory name on the list should be be the name of the directory you want to designate.
For example, the command below designates a subdirectory called PASCAL as the new current directory in drive B:

A⟩ CHDIR B:\PROGRAMS\PASCAL   ⟨ENTER⟩

The first symbol in the path is a backslash (\). This means that the path to the new current directory starts with the root directory of the diskette in drive B. The path indicates that the root directory contains a subdirectory called PROGRAMS, and that PROGRAMS contains PASCAL, the directory you want to designate as the "new" current directory. As usual, the amount of location information you need to provide depends on which directory was last designated as the current directory for the drive.
To change the current directory back to the root directory, give a command like the following:

A⟩   CHDIR   B:\   ⟨ENTER⟩

The backslash (\) in the commands above symbolize the root directory. So the command above changes the current directory for drive B to the root directory.
If you forget which directory is the current directory, the computer can remind you. Enter a CHDIR command without specifying a location. The computer will display the path from the root directory to the current directory or a backslash if you are still in the root directory.

Figure 1. Excerpt of manual illustrating RICH SYNTAX elaborations.

After they studied a version of the manual, subjects were asked to carry out a set of ordinary tasks on the computer, without referring back to the documentation. The subjects who had studied manuals containing syntactic elaborations worked significantly more quickly and issued significantly fewer commands. The conceptual elaborations did not significantly improve performance, perhaps because the selection of appropriate commands was fairly obvious for this particular set of tasks.

There is other evidence that examples strongly influence subjects' interpretation of procedural rules. LeFevre and Dixon (1984) and LeFevre (1985)

CHANGING THE CURRENT DIRECTORY – CHDIR

The CHDIR command (short for "change directory" allows you to designate a directory as the "current" directory for a drive so that the computer will automatically look there for files or subdirectories mentioned in your commands. You can designate a current directory for each disk drive independently. Changing the current directory on the diskette in drive A does not affect the current directory on drive B.

The root directory is automatically designated as the current directory for each drive when you first start up the computer. It is useful to designate a subdirectory as the current directory when you will be working primarily on the files in that subdirectory. Then you won't have to specify the path to the subdirectory in each command you issue.

FORMAT

The format of the command is:

CHDIR   [[d:]path]

You can use the abbreviation CD in the command instead of typing CHDIR.

If you designate a subdirectory as the new current directory, the computer will carry out all the subsequent commands within that directory, unless you specify a path to another directory. To change the current directory back to the root directory, use a backslash as the path.

If you forget which directory is the current directory, the computer can remind you. Enter a CHDIR command without specifying a location. The computer will display the path from the root directory to the current directory, or "\", if you are still in the root directory.

Figure 2. Excerpt of manual illustrating RICH CONCEPT elaborations.

conducted research on instructions for solving analogy problems. They found that when verbal instructions for how to solve a problem (i.e. rules) were *contradicted* by a situational example, subjects tended to execute a procedure that was consistent with the example rather than one consistent with the rule. We suspect that because the examples were concrete and specific, subjects mistrusted their intepretation of the more abstract rule and reinterpreted the rule to conform to the operations illustrated in the example. In any case, the results underscore the importance of choosing examples carefully.

4.4. The role of examples for learning and remembering to select the best procedure

Various factors may cause a learner to select a less than optimal procedure for solving some problem. The learner may know that one procedure is more appropriate for a problem than another, but if she only remembers how to execute the suboptimal one, that is the one she will end up using. In this sort of situation, the learner has mastered the selection problem; she simply needs more help with the execution of the procedures she has learned. In contrast, the situations we are mainly interested in concern people who do not think of using a procedure that they would acknowledge to be more appropriate and people who have not learned to judge between alternative procedures.

We believe that *situational examples* can play a dual role in procedural selection. First, they can provide the relevant stimulus cues to help the user 'think of' the right procedure for a specific situation, and second, they can help people learn or induce a generalization for when a given procedure is better than some alternative.

4.4.1. Increasing the salience of alternative procedures: command editing

Consider again the *command editing* procedure. It is quite possible for a user who knows what command editing is and who remembers how to bring back previous commands, to type in a long command instead of modifying and reissuing a similar command that he recently issued. The procedure simply may not have been sufficiently salient that it occurred to the user at the appropriate time. If a person only thinks of one procedure to achieve a specific goal then the problem of *selection* does not arise.

It is interesting to speculate on what aspects of a hypothetical situation example are most likely to increase salience and facilitate retrieval of the procedure in a real problem situation. Retrieval is probably most likely when the example and the problem are identical or very similar. Under these circumstances, many elements in the problem situation may remind the learner of the example, and hence the procedure used in the example. Unfortunately, since the procedures in a computer-operating system can be used in such a wide variety of contexts, it is highly unlikely that the problems users face will be exactly like the examples in the manual, even if the examples are carefully chosen.

What happens, then, when the actual problem situation does not perfectly match the example? In part, this will depend on how the example is represented in memory and how good the example is at illustrating the relevant dimensions of the situation to encode. We believe that the same examples that best motivate *why* a person should want to use the command-editing facility will also be best for reminding a person to use it because these examples highlight those elements of the problem situation that make the command most appropriate. As long as a problem situation matches the example on those dimensions, the example may serve as a good retrieval cue, in spite of other differences between the situations. On the other hand, it is possible that a learner will only store a *superficial* representation of the example; in this case, examples that *literally* match aspects of the current situation will be better memory cues.

To illustrate these two possibilities, consider again the two examples on command editing that were provided earlier (examples 11 and 12), in the light of the following 'real-world' problem. Suppose your friend Smith has a subdirectory called 'upkeep' on his computer that contains files with helpful information about maintenance and repair people. Smith has given you permission to browse through his files from your account on another computer. To see what files are available in the subdirectly, you type a relatively long command, such as the following:

$dir onion::[Smith.home.upkeep]

To read the contents of any file in the 'upkeep' directory, you will have to issue commands of the form:

$type onion::[Smith.home.upkeep]plumbers.mss.

The question is, will you be more likely to remember to use command editing in this situation (i.e. changing the *dir* command into the needed *type* command and reissuing it), if you had previously seen example (11) or example (12) in the manual? Example (11) superficially resembles the problem situation, in that both involve typing and later reissuing a *dir* command. Example (12) showed how to avoid retyping a different command, the *copy* command. However, the point of this example was to motivate *why* one would want to bother with command editing: to save keystrokes by avoiding retyping a very long file specification or 'path' to a file. So despite the greater superficial similarity of example (11) to the problem situation, example (12) should be a better cue to a user's memory. This assumes that users represent tasks and goals at a deeper level, e.g. 'My goal is to save keystrokes and reuse the expression that I already typed.' It is obviously an empirical question how users tend to encode the examples they read in a manual.

4.4.2. *Learning to judge when one procedure is better than another: command editing*

Skill learners should be familiar with a repertoire of procedures and should be able to select the most appropriate procedure for any given situation. An obvious question is what makes a procedure most appropriate? At various points in this chapter, we have described situations in which one procedure is 'better' than another. In most cases, we have justified this valuation in terms of efficiency: one procedure saves the user keystrokes (e.g. command editing) or reduces the size of the search space (e.g. creating subdirectories). Often, of course, the choice between procedures is not so clear-cut. Consider the choice between procedures for writing a computer program: e.g. should the programmer write a recursive program or an iterative one? It may be easier to write a computer program one way, but the program may be more computationally efficient another way. To the extent that the considerations for choosing between procedures can be specified, we are interested in how instructional texts can help learners acquire such selection strategies.

As we argued in the preceding section, situational examples highlight those characteristics of a situation that make a particular procedure highly appropriate. Consider again the two examples used to illustrate the command-editing procedure. Example (11) illustrated a situation in which command editing was no more efficient than typing a new *dir* command. In example (12), however, command editing was by far the more efficient procedure, because the user could avoid typing a number of *copy* commands that all contained the same long path specification. We can use this characteristic of the task situation to formulate a generalization about when to choose command editing:

> If you must issue a number of very long, similar commands, it is more efficient to edit the commands than to type new ones.

One way to convey a selection principle such as this would be to state it explicitly in a computer manual or instructional text. As with any generalization, a selection principle can be illustrated with examples, in this case, situation examples. Since, as we have seen, situation examples can also be used to exemplify syntactic rules for issuing computer commands, situation examples have the potential of simultaneously illustrating two sorts of rules: rules for executing procedures and generalizations for when to select the procedures. Of course, it may not always be necessary to state the selection principle explicitly. We speculate that learners who see a number of situation examples can often induce the generalization independently.

The extent to which learners need help choosing between alternative procedures is a question which requires further research. We have found that learners can often choose the most efficient computer command without the benefit of explicit advice, whether exemplified or not (Reder, Charney and Morgan, in press; Charney, 1985). It may be that instruction is needed more in more complex skill domains, such as programming.

4.5. Some potential drawbacks to situational examples

Our analysis suggests that situational examples must be chosen carefully to illustrate the conditions under which a procedure should be applied. The example must make salient the underlying *goal* of the procedure as well as illustrating a situation where it is used. If the examples are poorly constructed, they can actually interfere with good performance. When subjects only see impoverished examples, that fail to emphasize the conditions that make one procedure more appropriate than another, the subjects may draw spurious conclusions about when to use the procedures.

Consistent with this analysis, Ross (1984) found that superficial similarities between the problem that subjects are currently working on and examples they previously saw in the instructional materials influenced their choice of procedure. Ross's subjects learned pairs of alternative procedures for using a computer text-editor. In the instructional materials, each procedure was illustrated with a different superficial situation. For example, one procedure for inserting a word was illustrated in a task involving a shopping list. The example for the other word-insertion procedure involved a course listing. When subjects subsequently worked on editing a shopping list, they tended to use the procedure they had seen associated with a shopping list, even though either procedure would have worked equally well. As Ross points out, this effect of 'reminding' has potentially adverse consequences: in subsequent studies, Ross found that subjects tended to use the procedure they were reminded of, even if it was inappropriate for the problem at hand. Further research is needed to determine whether rich situational examples that clarify conditions on application can overcome the effect of reminding.

There is another problem with examples that we have thus far not addressed: people vary in their willingness to read and work through them. Some subjects in our studies on computer manuals told us that they do not like to read any more prose than they have to; they search for the examples and rely heavily on those. Other people do not want to be bothered reading examples, especially drawn-out situational examples that take some effort to comprehend. To accommodate both sorts of readers, we intentionally set off the examples in this chapter, so that readers could easily identify them as such. We believe that one's understanding of the paper will be greater if an attempt is made to 'work through' the examples, but we know that not everyone will do so. Indeed, lack of motivation to read elaborations may have been part of the reason why Reder and Anderson found that subjects learned the main points of a textbook chapter better in summary form, when all elaborations were omitted (e.g. Reder and Anderson, 1980, 1982; Allwood, Wikstrom and Reder, 1982). Examples, therefore, must satisfy one further constraint: they must seem sufficiently interesting to capture the reader's attention or the text must convince the reader that he cannot understand the material without reading the examples.

5. CONCLUSION AND FURTHER REMARKS

In this chapter, we outlined three basic components of skill learning: learning what kinds of procedures are available in the skill domain and what objects they operate on; learning how to execute procedures; and learning the conditions under which procedures can and should be applied. We discussed various types of elaborations and speculated about what types of elaborations in an instructional text might facilitate each component most. We argued that situational examples are likely to be the most useful sort of elaboration since they can perform triple duty, facilitating learning of each of the three components. However, since learners tend to rely on examples as models, it is very important to choose examples with great care and to provide enough examples to illustrate the range of application of a rule. Otherwise, learners may not interpret the rules correctly or they may make spurious assumptions about the conditions under which a rule applies.

Finally, we think it is interesting to note that our conception of the necessary requirements for skill acquisition resembles McGuire's (1961) theory of stimulus–response learning. McGuire's theory was developed to account for data from a paired-associate learning paradigm of almost half a century ago, in which either the stimulus or the response term could be a *cvc* nonsense syllable, and learners needed to know which response *cvc* went with a given stimulus *cvc*. McGuire's theory posits three components to learning a particular association: the learner must learn to discriminate the stimulus from competing stimuli, learn the response and then learn to link the two together. Despite the difference in domains, one can draw the parallels to our view of skill acquisition. The learner must understand the functionality or nature of the procedure (learning or discriminating the stimulus), learn the exact sequence of actions for executing a procedure (learning the response), and execute the correct procedure for a specific situation (learn to link the stimulus and response terms). Linking the stimulus and response terms is like learning the best procedure for a given situation because understanding the functionality of a procedure entails the recognition that it is appropriate in certain contexts.

ACKNOWLEDGEMENTS

The work reported here was sponsored by the Office of Naval Research, Contract No. N00014-84-K-0063, Contract Authority Identification Number NR667-529, and in part by Grant BNS-0371 from the National Science Foundation to the second author. The authors would like to thank C. Neuwirth and G. Wells for their comments on the manuscript.

REFERENCES

Allwood, C. M., Wikstrom, T., and Reder, L. M. (1982). Effects of presentation format on reading retention: superiority of summaries in free recall. *Poetics*, **11**, 145–153.

Anderson, J. R. (1982). Acquisition of cognitive skill. *Psychological Review*, **89**, 369–406.

Anderson, J. R. (1983). *The Architecture of Cognition*. Cambridge, Mass.: Harvard University Press.

Anderson, J. R., Farrell, R. and Sauers, R. (1984). Learning to program in LISP. *Cognitive Science*, **8**, 87–129.

Anderson, J. R., and Reder, L. M. (1979). An elaborative processing explanation of depth of processing. In L. S. Cermak and F. I. M. Craik (eds) *Levels of Processing in Human Memory*. Hillsdale, NJ: Erlbaum.

Bransford, J. D. (1979). *Human Cognition: Learning, Understanding and Remembering*. Belmont, Calif: Wadsworth.

Card, S., Moran, T. & Newell, A. (1983). *The Psychology of Human Computer Interaction*. Hillsdale, NJ: Erlbaum.

Charney, D. (1985). The role of elaborations in instructional texts: Learning to use the appropriate procedure at the appropriate time. Unpublished doctoral dissertation, Carnegie-Mellon University.

Chiesi, H. L., Spilich, G. J. and Voss, J. F. (1979). Acquisition of domain-related information in relation to high and low domain knowledge. *Journal of Verbal Learning and Verbal Behavior*, 18, 257–73.

Craik, F. I. M., and Tulving, E. (1975). Depth of processing and the retention of words in episodic memory. *Journal of Experimental Psychology: General*. 104, 268–94.

Disk Operating System Manual (1983).

Fitts, P. M. (1964). Perceptual-motor skill learning. In A. W. Melton (ed.) *Categories of Human Learning*. New York: Academic Press.

Gentner, D. (1980). *The Structure of Analogical Models in Science*. Technical Report 4451. Bolt Beranek and Newman.

Gentner, D. (1983). Structure-mapping: A theoretical framework for analogy. *Cognitive Science*, 7, 155–70.

Gilson, C., and Abelson, R. (1968). The subjective use of inductive evidence. In P. C. Wason and P. N. Johnson-Laird (eds) *Thinking and reasoning*. Harmondsworth, Middlesex: Penguin Books.

Hayes, J. R., and Simon, H. A. (1974). Understanding written problem instructions. In L. W. Gregg (ed.) *Knowledge and Cognition*. Potomac, Md.: Erlbaum.

Hobbs, J. (1978). *Why is Discourse Coherent?* Technical Note 176. SRI International (November).

Kieras, D. (1985). *The Role of Prior Knowledge in Operating Equipment from Written Instructions*. Technical Report 19, University of Michigan (February).

Kieras, D., and Bovair, S. (1985). *The Acquisition of Procedures from Text: A Production-system Analysis of Transfer of Training*. Technical Report 16, University of Michigan (January).

Kieras, D., and Polson, P. (1985). An approach to the formal analysis of user complexity. *International Journal of Man-Machine Studies*, 22, 365–394.

LeFevre, J. (1985). A model of the use of instruction and example information on a simple inductive-reasoning task. Master's thesis, Department of Psychology, University of Alberta (Spring).

LeFevre, J., and Dixon, P. (1984). Do written instructions need examples? Unpublished manuscript, University of Alberta.

McGuire, W. J. (1961). A multi-process model for paired-associate learning. *Journal of Verbal Learning and Verbal Behavior*, 62, 335–47.

Mandl, H., and Ballstaedt, S. (1981). Effects of elaboration on recall of texts. Paper presented at the International Symposium on Text Processing, Fribourg (September).

Mandl, H., Schnotz, W. and Tergan, S. (1984). On the function of examples in instructional texts. Paper presented at the AERA meeting, New Orleans (April).

Microsoft, Inc. (1983). *IBM Personal Computer Language Series, Disk Operating System, Version 2.00*. Boca Raton, Fla.: IBM.

Newell, A., and Rosenbloom, P. S. (1981). Mechanisms of skill acquisition and the law of practice. In J. R. Anderson (ed.) *Cognitive Skills and their Acquisition*. Hillsdale, NJ: Erlbaum.

Newell, A., and Simon, H. A. (1972). *Human Problem Solving*. Englewood Cliffs, NJ: Prentice-Hall.

Nitsch, K. E. (1977). Structuring decontextualized forms of knowledge. Unpublished doctoral dissertation, Vanderbilt University.

Perelman, C., and Olbrechts-Tyteca, L. (1969). *The New Rhetoric: A Treatise on Argumentation*. Notre Dame, Ind.: University of Notre Dame Press.

Reder, L. M. (1976). The role of elaborations in the processing of prose. Doctoral dissertation, University of Michigan. Available through University Microfilms, Ann Arbor.

Reder, L. M. (1979). The role of elaborations in memory for prose. *Cognitive Psychology*, **11**, 221–34.

Reder, L. M. (in press). Beyond associations: Strategic components in memory retrieval. In D. Gorfein and R. Hoffman (eds) *Memory and Learning: The Ebbinghaus Centennial Conference*. Hillsdale, NJ: Erlbaum.

Reder, L. M., and Anderson, J. R. (1980). A comparison of texts and their summaries: Memorial consequences. *Journal of Verbal Learning and Verbal Behavior*, **19**, 121–34.

Reder, L. M., and Anderson, J. R. (1982). Effects of spacing and embellishment on memory for the main points of a text. *Memory and Cognition*, **10**, 97–102.

Reder, L. M., Charney, D. and Morgan, K. (1986). The role of elaborations in learning a skill from an instructional text. *Memory and Cognition*, **14**, 64–78.

Rosenbloom, P. S., and Newell, A. (in press). Learning by chunking: A production system model of practice. In D. Klahr, P. Langley and R. Neches (eds) *Self-modifying Production Systems: Models of Learning and Development*. Cambridge, Mass.: Bradford Books/MIT Press.

Ross, B. (1984). Remindings and their effects in learning a cognitive skill. *Cognitive Psychology*, **16**, 371–416.

Schneider, W., and Shiffrin, R. M. (1977). Controlled and automatic human information processing. I. Detection, search, and attention. *Psychological Review*, **84**, 1–66.

Schoenfeld, A. (1979). Can heuristics be taught? In J. Lockhead and J. Clements (eds) *Cognitive Process Instruction*. Philadelphia: Franklin Institute Press.

Shriffrin, R. M., and Dumais, S. T. (1981). The development of automatism. In J. R. Anderson (ed.) *Cognitive Skills and their Acquisition*. Hillsdale, NJ: Erlbaum.

Shriffrin, R. M., and Schneider, W. (1977). Controlled and automatic human information processing: I. Detection, search, and attention. *Psychological Review*, **84**, 1–66.

Tennyson, R. (1973). Effect of negative instances in concept acquisition using a verbal learning task. *Journal of Experimental Psychology*, **64**, 247–60.

Tennyson, R., Woolley, F. and Merrill, M. (1972). Exemplar and nonexemplar variables which produce correct concept classification behavior and specified classification errors. *Journal of Experimental Psychology*, **63**, 144–52.

Weinstein, C. E. (1978). Elaboration skills as a learning strategy. In H. F. O'Neil, Jr (ed.) *Learning Strategies*. New York: Academic Press.

Williams, J. (1981). *Style: Ten Lessons in Clarity and Grace*. Glenview, Ill.; Scott, Foresman.

Winston, P., and Horn, B. (1981). *LISP*. Reading, MA: Addison-Wesley.

Part 2: Theoretical issues

Modelling Cognition
Edited by P. Morris
© 1987 John Wiley & Sons Ltd.

6

Simple models for experimentable situations

DONALD BROADBENT
Department of Experimental Psychology, Oxford

This paper presents a case for replacing the verbal theories of traditional experimental psychology by small-scale computational models. The argument is that verbal theorizing about cognition is much too ambiguous and imprecise; but that on the other hand the full power of main-frame computing takes one immediately beyond the limits of operational testing. The policy being urged, therefore, is to use models of a size that can be implemented on a personal computer.

If we open most journals of experimental psychology, we find ourselves nowadays looking at descriptions of experiments that have considerable precision of technique and of statistical analysis. The necessary precautions and controls needed in sentence verification tasks, in lexical decision, in tests of recognition memory, in categorization, in same–different judgements, in visual search, and in many other situations, have been developed to a very high level. On the whole, the standard of repeatability of experiments is probably higher than at any time in the past; provided that one repeats exactly the procedure given in the paper.

If one varies the experiment even slightly, however, the results are liable to be quite surprising. The theoretical statements that sum up the experiments are sufficiently vague that one cannot easily make out whether or not some change of conditions is crucial. Terms are used such as 'access to the lexicon', 'automatic processing', 'central executive', 'resources'; formal definitions of such terms are rare, and even rarer are statements of the rules supposed to be governing their interaction. As a result one is left unclear about exactly what kinds of experimental data would invalidate such theories, and whether or not they are intended to apply to some new experimental situation. It could well be held that the standard of precision in theoretical statements in the experimental journals is now markedly lower than it was at the height of the Hullian movement 40–50 years ago.

In the literature of computational modelling, on the other hand, one finds much more clarity about the meaning of the theoretical statements. There is no problem about understanding what is meant by a subroutine, by a loop that iterates a fixed number of times, or by a loop that continues until a condition is fulfilled. The interaction between these concepts is also fairly clear, so that we know that a system possessing those three kinds of operation can in principle model any specifiable behaviour.

The problem in this case is that the systems are too powerful. They can parse sentences that are multiply embedded, although human beings have great difficulty with such a task. They can create structures to store information about past episodes, in which a central node in the network corresponds to the verb of a sentence describing the episode; and yet we know that for humans the verb is often greatly inferior to the subject or the object as a retrieval cue for the episode. So, we know already that cognitive operations are certainly not performed in some of the ways in which an unrestricted computational model can perform them. The discrepancy arises because these very powerful models deal with processes on which experiment is difficult. It would be very hard to take a series of subjects to a sample of restaurants, drive-in movies, crematoria and battlefields. In order to see how their behaviour is altered in accordance with the particular frame they encounter. So, the models are made to perform cognitive operations that square with the investigator's memory of everyday experience rather than with less subjective data. Precision of theory is gained at the expense of lack of contact with the real world.

Neither of these outcomes is satisfactory, though I think there is less excuse for the vague verbal theories that go with most laboratory experiments. There is a genuine difficulty of principle in experimenting on large cognitive structures; there is no such difficulty in being precise about one's terms. In principle, most experimenters have had access for many years to computers that would be capable of implementing theories of the low degree of complexity used in most verbal discussions. There has admittedly been a practical problem that using, say, a PDP-8 was less convenient than using the back of an envelope; you could hardly keep it at home, and if you tried to write a psychological theory on the one in your lab, somebody would be likely to complain that the machine was wanted to do some psycho-physics.

All this has now changed. There is no practical difficulty any longer in keeping a microcomputer standing idle at the bedside ready to record your latest insight; and remember, even the smallest micro possesses the three crucial properties mentioned earlier. So, it ought to be able to implement your theory, if you can manage to get the theory into a precise form. We are not used to thinking of such small machines as capable of anything interesting in the way of AI, and of course there are many things they cannot do. But they can out-perform ordinary language. The best way of arguing this is to give concrete examples, and that is what the rest of this paper attempts.

Most of the results that I am going to discuss have been obtained on a Sinclair QL, which is a slightly luxurious machine by the standards of the private owner. But each of the three programs was first implemented on a prehistoric Acorn Atom, rejoicing in an absolute maximum of 12k of memory. You should be able to replicate the results by borrowing from your nearest teenager the machine usually used for playing space invaders.

VISUAL AND MEMORY SEARCH

For nearly 20 years the experimental literature has been greatly concerned with data on speed of search. Sometimes the subject is asked to remember a list of items, and then shown an item and asked if it was in the list. Sometimes the subject is given a target item, and then asked to look for its presence or absence among a number of other items that are shown simultaneously. In either case, the number of non-target items that are being considered may have an effect on the speed with which a decision is made; though it may not. There are four main patterns of results, each of which is held to argue for a different kind of mechanism.

First, there is the case in which the time taken to give an affirmative response increases linearly with the number of items being considered; while negative responses show a parallel increase, usually beginning from a slower starting-point (see Figure 1a). This kind of result is characteristic of the case in which the set is held in memory and a single target is presented for a recognition decision (Nickerson, 1972; Sternberg, 1975).

Second, there is the case in which the time for an affirmative response increases linearly as before; but the time for a negative response increases much more steeply, often at about twice the slope found for the affirmative (see Figure 1b). This kind of result has been found when a visual display is being scanned for the presence of a target that is defined by having a conjunction of two sensory features, the non-targets each having one but not the other (Treisman and Gelade, 1980). For example, the task might be to search for a pink O among green Os and pink Ns.

Third, there is the case in which the two kinds of response slow down as the size of the set increases, and do so at different rates; but the slopes are not in a two-to-one ratio, and the two functions may not be strictly linear. If so they may well have a decelerating shape, increases in set size having progressively less effect as they accumulate (Figure 1c). This kind of result appears in visual search for a target defined by a single feature shared by none of the non-targets, especially if the subject has had a reasonable amount of practice (e.g. Treisman and Gelade, 1980).

Fourth, there is the case in which the response time is essentially indepen-

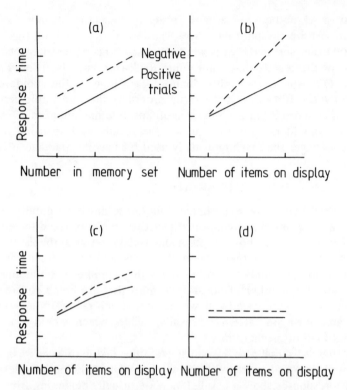

Figure 1. Four typical results found in: (a) speed of recognition of an item as present or absent in memory sets of various sizes; (b) speed of detection of presence or absence of a conjunctively defined target on a visual display with various numbers of items present; (c) speed of detection of a non-conjunctively defined target on a visual display; (d) speed of detection of a practised non-conjunctive target on a visual display.

dent of the size of set, at least for affirmative responses (Figure 1d). This kind of result applies to very highly practised search for targets that are not defined by a conjunction of features and that never in the experience of the subjects occur as non-targets (Schneider and Shiffrin, 1977).

These four patterns of results are often interpreted as requiring different mechanisms to explain them. The first pattern, for example, could be produced by a series of comparisons between the target and each of the other items in the set. If each comparison process took some constant unit of time, then one would get the linear increase as the number of items in the set increased; for the negative decisions, one would get such an increase, because the time to go through the set would go up by the same extent whenever the number of comparisons increased by the same amount. On the other hand, there is a problem about the affirmative responses, because the slope of the function is the same for them as it is for the negative ones. That is what would happen if every item was examined even if one of the comparisons had already come out positive. So, this pattern is explained by a *serial exhaustive* chain of comparisons.

If the mechanism was able to stop as soon as it reached a positive comparison, then the number necessary for an affirmative response would on average be only half that needed for a negative response to the same size of set. So, the slope of the positive function ought to be half that for the negative one. This of course is the second pattern of results, the one that one obtains with visual search for a conjunction target. This pattern is therefore interpreted as coming from a *serial but self-terminating* chain of comparisons.

Now suppose all the comparisons went on at the same time, and that there is a bit of randomness in the time taken for each of these parallel comparisons. In that case, the negative decisions would mean that you had to wait for the last of the whole set to finish, while the postive decisions would only take the average of the set. So, the negative decisions would be slower than the positive, and this would probably increase as the size of the set increased. The more processes, the bigger the chance of one very slow one. The same increased chance of an unlucky slow process might also generate an increase in the time for positive decisions, though smaller than the slope for negative ones. But the increase would be unlikely to be linear in either case. This can be called *variable parallel, exhaustive for negative and self-terminating for positive*. It is of course the pattern for moderate levels of practice with feature search.

I have passed over one possibility, which is that all comparisons are parallel and all take exactly the same time. In that case, the decision would of couse be independent of the number of comparisons. This would be true whether the decision was positive or negative. That is the pattern of results one obtains with visual search for highly familiar target and non-target sets. So, such a pattern is usually interpreted as requiring a *parallel* processing of each of the objects in the field. Because the time for each comparison would need to be the same regardless of what else was happening, the mechanism is also often described as *automatic*.

Many intelligent and respected psychologists therefore believe that these different findings require different mechanisms, sharply distinguished from each other. From the beginning there have been others who take a different view, and think that the same basic machinery could give any of these patterns under appropriate conditions. Mathematical psychologists in particular have repeatedly demonstrated that serial mechanisms could produce any of the patterns claimed as evidence for parallel processes, and conversely that parallel mechanisms could produce the patterns ascribed to serial ones.

Townsend (1971, 1974) for example, has discussed the matter on a number of occasions. Ratcliff (1978) has generated a parallel model for the memory-search data that had a very high degree of goodness of fit to particular experiments. Thus, the data do not strictly require any one of the mechanisms rather than another, even if one does make the assumptions that each process of comparison is separate, and that the only question is that of serial versus parallel.

Another line of attack is that one need not suppose separate processes of comparison at all, but rather a single process of decision between alternatives. Indeed, the approach of Ratcliff (1978) is really of this type rather than a set of independent parallel comparisons, and the model to be presented follows closely that of Ratcliff. In such a process the evidence in favour of one possibility rather than another builds up gradually, never reaching absolute certainty; and the criterion level that is demanded by the process determines both the total time and the probability of error. In the field of reaction time it was established in the 1960s that some such model is certainly correct, even though a number of details remain uncertain.

The reasons for being confident about the general approach have to do with the relative speed of errors and of correct responses, the fact that particular responses are likely to occur as errors and also have fast reaction times even when correct, and so on. The arguments in the reaction time area were reviewed by Broadbent (1971); the effect of practice was seen as reducing the level of 'noise' or randomness affecting the momentary level of certainty reached after any given time. It was not thought to require a change from one mechanism to another.

It is perhaps fair to say that these two lines of counter-argument have not had a great impact on experimenters, and that the different patterns of behaviour in search experiments have gone on being interpreted as evidence for different underlying mechanisms. Some distinction between 'automatic' and 'control' processes, for example, is widely accepted. The difficulty is probably that models such as Ratcliff's appear to have many free parameters, to require a good deal of curve-fitting, and that as a result they seem to some tastes less parsimonious than the assumption of simple mechanisms for each pattern of results. Furthermore, the statistical decision models lead to conclusions that are mathematically intractable, so that only a few firm predictions can be made. Sceptics could therefore deny that any single mechanism could produce such varied patterns of data.

The essential features of a statistical decision model can, however, be easily implemented on a personal computer. Suppose one creates an array of numbers, each corresponding to one of the items in memory or on the screen, depending on which kind of experiment one is considering. For brevity, let us call each of these numbers the 'strength' of the corresponding comparison. Then suppose that, at the start of the process, we increase by an amount D the strength of any positive comparison. At the same time, we reduce by the same amount D the size of every strength that corresponds to a negative comparison. It would then be clear whether any comparison is positive, and which it is. But suppose there is randomness in the system; suppose that each of the strengths has also had a different random number added to or subtracted from it. Say that an integer chosen from the range $+V$ to $-V$ has been added in each case. After one such operation, it may be very unclear whether there is one strength that is increasing, or whether they are all decreasing. So, we repeat the operation until there is enough evidence to show what is happening. How can we tell when that may be?

In the reaction-time field, Rabbitt and Rodgers (1977) have found that the speed of response sharply declines immediately after an error. They therefore suggested that the person controls the criteria for the decision by observing the frequency of errors; whenever a mistake is made, the criterion is moved sharply so as to demand much more evidence. It may then creep gradually back towards a more risky level as correct performance continues without errors. Let us therefore suppose that our computer model behaves in the same way. Whenever any of the strengths exceeds a criterion amount, the process stops and gives an affirmative output; but if it finds itself to be wrong, the criterion is increased by a large amount for the next decision. It then creeps back by a small amount on every subsequent trial, until some other error is made. For the negative decisions, there is another criterion such that when all the strengths are simultaneously below that criterion, the process stops and reports that no target is present. Again if the decision turns out to be wrong, this criterion also moves sharply downwards so as to make such an error less likely in future; it then creeps in again on each subsequent trial.

The numbers are all in arbitrary units; so let us take the amount of creep of the criterion as the smallest, and call it 1. The constant amount D that is added to, or subtracted from, each strength ought to be bigger than the criterion-creep, so let us call it 5. We are then left with two more numbers to choose, the amount of randomness V added on every cycle of the process, and the jump which each criterion gives when there is an error. If we explore a range of values for each, it turns out that the size of the criterion-jump affects primarily the error rate, as you might expect. Actual experiments in visual and memory search tend to have error rates of about 5 per cent, so let us settle on a criterion-jump of 40, which gives such a rate regularly, within 0.5 per cent.

We are then left with the amount of randomness or noise. To look at the effect of a large amount of noise, let us try choosing the random component from a range of $+35$ to -35, and see how many cycles of the process are needed for various numbers of alternatives. The results are shown in Figure 2, and one can see that they are closely similar to those of Figure 1a. The decision time increases linearly with the number of alternatives, and does so at the same rate whether one is considering positive or negative decisions.

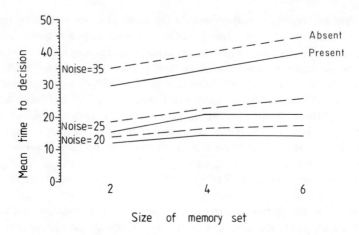

Figure 2. Results of 1000 trials of a random walk model of
parallel self-terminating search, with different noise levels.
Compare Figure 1(a) and (d).

The other lines in Figure 2 show what happens if the amount of 'noise' is
reduced; choosing the random addition on each cycle from $+25$ to -25, or
$+20$ to -20. The curves first become less linear, but then flatten out so that
there ceases to be much effect of the number of alternatives between which
choice is being made. Changing the noise level therefore turns the typical
memory-search result of Figure 1a into that more characteristic of subjects
highly practised with constant mapping, as in Figures 1c and 1d.

What about the type of result shown in Figure 1b that would be produced
by serial self-terminating search? There are two places where we have made
assumptions in the model that are fair for the typical memory-search experiment, but not for visual search. The most important of these concerns false
affirmative responses. In the model, false alarms result when one of the
strengths rises by chance above the affirmative criterion even though that
particular strength is on average declining. It is quite possible for this to
happen when the trial is a positive one, that is, when one of the *other* strengths
is on average increasing. In a memory experiment, if the probe is an item that
was actually in the memory set, and if the person gives an affirmative
response, neither experimenter nor subject would know if this response came
from the correct strength or not. Hence, the model was made to count such
responses as correct.

In visual search, however, the stimulus remains visible after the decision has
been taken; even if it is turned off by the overt response, we know from the
work of Rabbitt (1966) that subjects are often aware when they have made
error responses to visual stimuli. Hence, it would be more proper in that case
to change the model. We ought to count as a false affirmative any case in

which the criterion was exceeded by the wrong strength, even if there was some other comparison that was in fact positive. This simple change immediately causes the slopes of the functions to diverge. With the levels of noise we have been employing, they do not take up a two-to-one ratio (see Figure 3). Neither, quite often, do the slopes in visual search experiments for conjunctions: Egeth *et al.*, 1984.)

There is still another assumption we have made that is arbitrary, however. We assumed that all strengths that were declining would do so at the same rate. But this is not necessarily so, and especially not if the target shares one feature with half the non-targets and a different feature with the other half; as is true in the work of Treisman and Gelade (1980). Let us therefore suppose that the constant amount D which is subtracted on every cycle from all the strengths that are declining is different for each comparison, although remaining the same for any one comparison throughout the decision. Specifically, let us suppose that it is chosen randomly from 4, 5 or 6; rather than always being 5. This would be much more characteristic of a decision in which half the distractors were relatively easy to eliminate and the other half relatively difficult.

With these two changes, we obtain the curves shown in Figure 4. For the highest noise level, we have the data apparently explicable by a serial self-terminating search. As the noise reduces, the curves again flatten as they did for the 'memory-search' model.

Thus, if we construct and run an actual model, we find that a single mechanism is perfectly capable of producing all the patterns of results in the literature. The only differences are in the amount of information available to

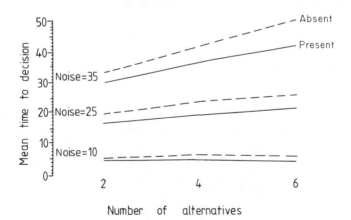

Figure 3. Results of 1000 trials of a similar model to Figure 2, but with a slight change to the definition of a 'false alarm'. See text and compare Figure 1(c).

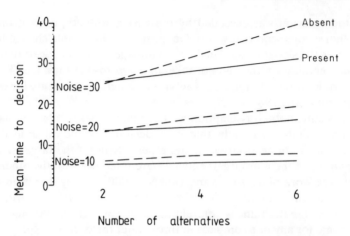

Figure 4. Results of 1000 trials of a model similar to Figure 3, but with a range of different possible drifts for the negative comparisons, i.e. as if some comparisons were harder than others. Compare Figure 1(b).

the person about their errors, the differences in discriminability between the target and different non-targets; and above all the level of uncertainty or noise in the process. The suggestion that the different experiments require different theories arises because of the inadequacy of verbal models.

In the terms in which the problem has usually been discussed, the model is one of self-terminating parallel comparison. Those terms are a little misleading, however, because the key point is that each comparison is not being made in isolation from the others, but is cumulating evidence towards a criterion set by the overall error rate; that is, the whole operation is in one sense a single process. It is certainly a mechanism of limited capacity even though it may under suitable conditions show no increases in search time as a function of the number of comparisons.

THE CATEGORY EFFECT

A second experimental paradigm that has often been discussed in terms of verbally formulated theories is that in which people are asked to look for visual letters or digits against a background of other letters or digits. It is often found that items drawn from one category are easier to see if the background consists of members of the other category. For example, Duncan (1983) asked people to name any digits present in a display of six characters; and, in another condition, to name all the characters on the display, including the letters. Sometimes three of the six were digits, and sometimes only one. It was considerably easier to do the partial task than that of complete report; and, when reporting only digits, to do so if there was only one digit. The interpretation of these results was that the category membership of each character in the display was available simultaneously and in parallel, and could be used to select the desired items to enter some late and limited mechanism for verbal report. This would be consistent with the suggestion of Duncan (1980), that the identity of each item is computed at an early stage.

An alternative view is that the process of identifying items perfectly is very demanding, and that this itself can only be undertaken for selected items. The selection, on this view, must be based on partial information that would be insufficient to identify the specific item. With some character sets, digits may be larger than letters, or have more curves, and this would make it easy to tell whether any particular item was not a digit, and therefore need not be identified. It was therefore a specially valuable feature of Duncan's experiments that the character sets were selected to examine this possibility. In set 1, the letters and digits were chosen so that no single feature of the characters could reliably separate the letters from the digits. In set 2, on the other hand, there was a vertical line in every letter but in no digit. Finally, in set 3, each letter was highly confusable with a particular individual digit. The advantage of partial report, and of having only one digit in the display, did not interact significantly with the character set being used (though set 3 was harder overall). Figure 5 shows typical error rates replotted from the data given by Duncan. Thus, on the face of it, the ease of identifying the category does not depend on featural differences between the categories.

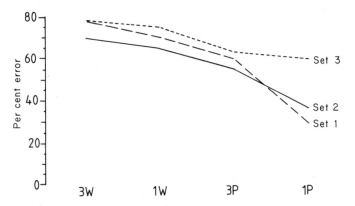

Figure 5. Mean per cent error in an experiment by Duncan (1983) in which people had to name the whole of a display of three digits and three letters (3W), the Whole of a display of one digit and five letters (1W), report partially the digits alone from the first display (3P), and from the second (1P).

The alternative view, however, does not necessarily argue that the discrimination of letters from digits is done by one single feature; only that *fewer* features of a character need to be taken into account in determining its category than in identifying it. In the face of Duncan's data, this may seem implausible. Simply looking at the character sets, or discussing them verbally, does not allow one to say confidently whether or not a mechanism that was selecting as efficiently as possible would in fact be able to tell that a character was a letter before it knew which specific letter it was.

As it happens, I have recently developed a very simple program at the bottom end of the class of 'expert systems', which will consider a set of alternatives and recommend the most efficient possible series of tests to decide which alternative is actually true. To take a concrete case, suppose you have a patient who may have one of several different diseases that are dangerous; or alternatively one of another class of diseases that are trivial and require no treatment. The program would ask the shortest series of questions about symptoms, first to identify which class the disease was in, and then, if it was the dangerous class, which disease it was.

The way the program works is this. It examines each possible symptom, counts how often that symptom occurs in the class of diseases of interest, counts how often the symptom occurs if none of that class of diseases is present; and then the program works out the information conveyed by knowledge about each of the symptoms. Finally, it picks the most informative, and suggests that you ask about it.

In the case of visual characters, the problem is to know what would count as a 'symptom' that a character is present. One possibility is to divide up the whole area occupied by the character into small squares, pixels, each of which is either black or white. One can then see which squares are occupied by a character, and treat each square as a symptom. John Duncan has been good enough to let me have detailed plots of the actual letters and digits that he used in his experiments. I was therefore able to construct lists of the squares occupied by each character, and to unleash my program at the same task that Duncan's subjects had to perform. The program would then 'look at' a series of points in the display, guiding its choice at each moment by picking the point that would get is as close as possible to knowing whether the character was a letter or a digit. Once it knows that the character is a letter, it stops; but if it is sure that the character is a digit, then it goes on to look at points that establish the exact identify of the digit.

The number of observations the program needs is shown in Figure 6 for each of Duncan's conditions. It is clear that the program can tell the category of a character with fewer tests than it needs to establish the identity; so, partial report of digits needs fewer 'looks' than whole report of letters and digits. Similarly, fewer 'looks' are needed for partial report of only one digit among five letters than for three among three. This is true for each of the three character sets, though as in Duncan's own results, set 3 is the hardest.

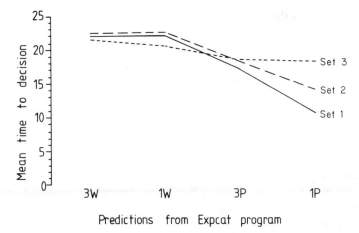

Predictions from Expcat program

Figure 6. Number of pixels tested by the Expcat program in looking at Duncan's characters to perform the same tasks as those of his subjects in Figure 5. In the P conditions, the program first determined whether each character was a letter or a digit, and only identified it further if it was a digit.

Of course, Duncan's choice of characters had indeed succeeded in choosing shapes where no single feature distinguished letters from digits. The average number of points needing to be examined before one was sure that a character was a letter was, for the hardest set 3, three; and the points were quite widely separated. To know the identity of each letter would, however, have needed still more tests. Hence it is clear in principle that, even with these character sets, a sophisticated processing system does not need to have the full identity of every presented item available in order to decide whether or not to react to it.

I think I ought to make it clear that John Duncan himself would argue that my program may not be using the visual input information that the human sensory apparatus makes available. That may well be so. The role of the computer model in this case is to provide an existence proof. There is in the visual display the necessary information to guide an early selection device, if the nervous system can use it. One is not compelled by Duncan's results to believe that the full identity of all visual inputs is computed before the selective system operates.

TEMPORARY MEMORY

The two foregoing examples have both been from search processes, and to some extent have been cases in which the computer is undertaking calculations rather than shedding light on flow of information from one part of a system to another. A third area is worth giving as an example even though it is still less developed than the two already given. This is the area of temporary or working memory.

During recent years there has been an explosion of important research, largely stemming from that of Baddeley and Hitch (1974), which has split the traditional concept of short-term memory into a number of different subsystems or components. One must distinguish, for example, an articulatory loop or component that is disrupted by asking the person to repeat irrelevant redundant items while memorizing. One must also distinguish a special memory for speech inputs that is selectively disrupted by hearing later speech even if one does not have to do anything about it. (At one time this system was often called a 'sensory' memory, but visual lip-read speech seems to enter it, so a different term is desirable.) Baddeley himself has published excellent comprehensive summaries, e.g. Baddeley (1984); a related classification, which I might as well use as I want to be critical, is that of Broadbent (1984). Each of these accounts is in fact somewhat ambiguous although the ambiguity can escape notice as long as the model is stated in words.

Suppose, for example, that one uses written verbal stimuli to exclude the speech input system mentioned earlier; memory can then be quite seriously disrupted by the articulatory suppression technique. But there is also a residue of material that can be recalled even despite the reduction of articulation. This is sometimes spoken of as in a 'central executive', or, in the terms I myself have used, an 'abstract working memory'.

There may be other forms of temporary memory also, such as the spatial 'scratch-pad' (Baddeley and Lieberman, 1980); but even for verbal materials there appear to be at least three distinguishable types. The relationship between these types raises fresh problems, which did not exist in the single temporary memory of theories a decade or so ago. What determines whether an item is reproduced from one form of storage or from another? Is the relationship between abstract storage and articulation one in which the former *controls* the latter as the term 'central executive' might imply? How is the output kept in the correct order? What happens when incoming material is 'chunked' by recognizing a sequence of several items as forming a familiar unit? It is not clear whether the existing formulations of working memory can be expanded to deal with these problems.

One way of seeing whether theories of working memory do offer a viable account of the experimental data is to try and translate them into a program. As a start, one obviously needs three distinguishable forms of storage, one for input memory, one for articulation and one for the abstract store. Following the verbal theories, it would seem plausible to make the input memory a single string which receives any item entered at the keyboard. Thus, entering a fresh item clears out the last. (If we wish, we could have some kind of stack, so that more than one item is held in sensory store, but let us start with one.)

Similarly, the articulatory loop could be represented as an array of strings, each having a maximum length corresponding to the time limit on the amount that can be held in articulation at one time. The abstract memory is more debatable; a way of implementing it that would be consistent with some of my own verbal statements would be to create an array with three entries. Each of these is capable of holding the address of a string rather than holding the string itself; this will allow the chunking effect at a later stage. For brevity, let us call the three components of memory I, A and W.

Now, the difficult bit; how should these components interact? One line of approach is to start with the problems of output; when the system is instructed to recall, what does it do? A reasonable method would be for it to consult in turn each of the entries in W, and to output whatever string is found at the corresponding address. When all three have been printed out, then as a last action the system should output the contents of I.

If that were the method of output, how then would the system act during the presentation of material? For short lists, the process is obvious; after arrival of each item in I, the contents of W should be examined in turn to see if there is a space with no address in it. When one is found, then the string in I is transferred to the next vacant space in A, and the address of that space is put in the vacant space in W. Thus after three items have been delivered they will each have been 'articulated' (transferred to A) and their addresses in A will exist in the right order in W. If we actually run this model, we shall find that it works nicely for four items. Nevertheless, we do seem to have developed a system of apparently unnecessary complexity to print out, say, four numbers that have been typed in.

The reason for the complexity appears when we input more than four items. Although the limit for 100 per cent accurate recall by people is only about four items, they can of course produce better than 50 per cent accuracy for much longer lists, with the conventional seven as the usual 50 per cent point. This seems to be done by some kind of chunking of the material into larger units (e.g. Broadbent, 1975). Suppose for instance that our program, after looking at W and finding no vacant space, looked at pairs of strings found from W, to see if the pair was still shorter than the articulatory loop. If it was, then the pair is combined into a single string in A, and only the address of the combination held in W. This will free a space in W and the contents of I can then be moved to A.

This kind of process will of course iterate; the way it is controlled is for the system to have an ordered list of conditional instructions through which it cycles until everything possible has been done to intake the item just received. This is in essence a production system, although that term normally implies something more computationally sophisticated (Newell and Simon, 1972).

When we look more closely at the detailed performance, however, there are discrepancies. What this program does is to perform perfectly for the early part of the list, then miss out items, and then give the contents of I. A little bit of random failure here and there would stop the sudden transition from perfection to total forgetting; but there is a more important problem. If the length of items is lengthened, or if the articulatory loop is shortened, there is a loss of recall from the part of the list that is not coming from I; that agrees with the empirical results of Baddeley *et al*. (1975). But the loss occurs at serial positions at the end of the part that is being successfully recalled with shorter items. The loss is therefore in the part of the list that is just before the final bit coming from input store I. But this is not in accordance with the results of experiment. I can suggest ways of altering the program so that it will fit the data; but the crucial point is that a simple verbal statement of 'central executive and articulatory loop' leads one naturally to a model that does *not* work.

CONCLUSION

We have seen three fields in which experiments are frequent but theories are not usually computational. In each case, using a micro-model shows that the computational approach has advantages. This intermediate level of theory is more precise than natural language, but sufficiently close to the data that experiment can be used, as in the last example, to develop the theory. It is to be hoped that more authors will use such micro-models.

REFERENCES

Baddeley, A. D. (1983). Working memory. *Philosophical Transactions of the Royal Society of London*, **B302**, 311–24.
Baddeley, A. D. (1984). The fractionation of human memory. *Psychological Medicine*, **14**, 259–64.
Baddeley, A. D., and Hitch, G. J. (1974). Working memory. In G. Bower (ed.) *Recent Advances in Learning and Motivation*. New York: Academic Press, pp. 47–90.
Baddeley, A. D., and Lieberman, K. (1980). Spatial working memory. In R. S. Nickerson (ed.) *Attention and Performance*, Vol. VIII. Hillsdale, NJ: Lawrence Erlbaum.
Baddeley, A. D., Thomson, N. and Buchanan, M. (1975). Word length and the structure of short-term memory. *Journal of Verbal Learning and Verbal Behavior*, **14**, 575–89.
Broadbent, D. E. (1971). *Decision and Stress*. New York: Academic Press.
Broadbent, D. E. (1975). The magic number seven after fifteen years. In A. Kennedy and A. Wilkes (eds) *Studies in Long Term Memory*. New York: John Wiley.
Broadbent, D. E. (1984). The Maltese cross: A new simplistic model for memory. *The Behavioral and Brain Sciences*, **7**, 55–94.
Duncan, J. (1980). The locus of interference in the perception of simultaneous stimuli. *Psychological Review*, **87**, 272–300.
Duncan, J. (1983). Perceptual selection based on alphanumeric class: Evidence from partial reports. *Perception and Psychophysics*, **33**, 533–47.
Egeth, H. E., Virzi, R. A. and Garbart, H. (1984). Searching for conjunctively defined

targets. *Journal of Experimental Psychology: Human Perception and Performance*, **10**, 32–9.

Newell, A., and Simon, H. A. (1972). *Human Problem Solving*. Englewood Cliffs, NJ: Prentice-Hall.

Nickerson, R. S. (1972). Binary-classification reaction time: a review of some studies of human information-processing capabilities. *Psychonomic Monograph supplements*, **4**, 275–318 (Whole Number 65).

Rabbitt, P. M. A. (1966). Errors and error correction in choice–response tasks. *Journal of Experimental Psychology*, **71**, 264–72.

Rabbitt, P., and Rodgers, B. (1977). What does a man do after he makes an error? An analysis of response programming. *Quarterly Journal of Experimental Psychology*, **29**, 727–43.

Ratcliff, R. (1978). A theory of memory retrieval. *Psychological Review*, **85**, 59–108.

Schneider, W., and Shiffrin, R. M. (1977). Controlled and automatic human information processing: I. Detection, search, and attention. *Psychological Review*, **84**, 1–66.

Sternberg, S. (1975). Memory scanning: New findings and current controversies. *Quarterly Journal of Experimental Psychology*, **27**, 1–32.

Townsend, J. T. (1971). A note on the identifiability of parallel and serial processes. *Perception and Psychophysics*, **10**, 161–3.

Townsend, J. T. (1974). Issues and models concerning the processing of a finite number of inputs. In B. H. Kantowitz (ed.) *Human Information Processing: Tutorials in Performance and Cognition*. Hillsdale, NJ: Lawrence Erlbaum.

Treisman, A. M., and Gelade, G. (1980). A feature integration theory of attention. *Cognitive Psychology*, **12**, 97–136.

Modelling Cognition
Edited by P. Morris
© 1987 John Wiley & Sons Ltd.

7

Schemas versus mental models in human memory

WILLIAM F. BREWER
Department of Psychology, University of Illinois at Urbana-Champaign

In recent years a number of new constructs have been developed to deal with the mental representation of complex phenomena: frames (Minsky, 1975); scripts (Schank and Abelson, 1977); schemas (Rumelhart, 1980); mental models (Johnson-Laird, 1980, 1983); causal mental models (Gentner and Stevens, 1983; de Kleer and Brown, 1981); and situation models (van Dijk and Kintsch, 1983). When the first attempts were made to develop forms of representation for molar phenomena theorists were pleased to be able to develop some form of representation for the problem at hand. However, it seems to me that we have now reached the point where there is considerable confusion about the nature and function of these different forms of representation. Certainly this has been true of the author of this chapter. Thus, it seems a good time to compare the alternate proposals and see if it is possible to work out the essential characteristics of these different theories.

This chapter examines the major proposals for representing complex knowledge domains and attempts to show that many of the crucial theoretical differences can be captured by an analysis in terms of: (a) a distinction between underlying knowledge structures and the episodic representations formed from these underlying structures; and (b) a distinction between representations which are derived from old generic knowledge and representations which are constructed at the time of use. This analysis is then used to clarify some of the confusions in the recent experimental literature and to suggest directions for future research.

SCHEMAS

The first form of knowledge representation to be examined will be schemas. In a recent theoretical paper (Brewer and Nakamura, 1984) we have argued that frames (Minsky, 1975), scripts (Schank and Abelson, 1977) and schemas (Rumelhart, 1980) are all examples of one general class of knowledge structure (to be referred to as 'schemas' in this chapter). We concluded that schemas are unconscious mental structures that underlie the molar aspects of human knowledge and skill. They are modular—different cognitive domains have schemas with different structural properties. Schemas interact with incoming episodic information to modify the generic information in the schema and to produce specific instantiated memory representations of the incoming episodic information. An instantiated schema is a specific cognitive structure that results from the interaction of the old information of the generic schema and the new information from the episodic input.

The schema construct as outlined above can account for a wide range of phenomena, such as the occurrence of inferences from generic memory (e.g. Brewer and Treyens, 1981; Graesser, Gordon and Sawyer, 1979; Sulin and Dooling, 1974) and for a variety of comprehension and memory phenomena (e.g. Bower, Black and Turner, 1979).

While schemas clearly serve a valuable role in mental life, a number of researchers have recently pointed out that they are inadequate to account for a wide range of phenomena. Human beings are capable of dealing with a great variety of complex situations that do not involve old generic information. Thus, we can understand actions that we have never seen carried out before; we can find our way around a town that we have never been in before; and we can understand an argument we have never heard before. Johnson-Laird (1980, 1983) has introduced the construct of the mental model to deal with these problems.

MENTAL MODELS

Johnson-Laird (1980, p. 98) states that a mental model 'represents a state of affairs and accordingly its structure is not arbitrary like that of a propositional representation, but plays a direct representational or analogical role. Its structure mirrors the relevant aspects of the corresponding state of affairs in the world'. He has emphasized that mental models are specific, not generic, representations (1983, p. 157) and has argued that they give rise to images (1983, p. 157).

Using this construct Johnson-Laird has been able to provide an account for a wide variety of phenomena, such as comprehension of texts involving spatial descriptions (Ehrlich and Johnson-Laird, 1982) and inferences derived from a particular mental model of a nongeneric situation (e.g. Bransford, Barclay and Franks, 1972). Thus, mental models, like schemas, capture an important component human cognition.

SCHEMAS VERSUS MENTAL MODELS

This section of the chapter compares schemas and mental models in an attempt to extract the theoretically crucial differences.

Clearly, both schemas and mental models are constructs that are meant to be mental representations of aspects of the external world, and some discussions of schemas have made the structural analogue hyopthesis explicit (cp. Brewer and Pani's, 1983, discussion of generic perceptual schemas). Thus it appears that schemas and mental models do not contrast on the characteristic of being structural analogues of the world.

Schemas and mental models do appear to differ in terms of the specific/generic dimension, but this is due to the fact that the comparison is made between the *generic* aspect of one form of knowledge representation and the *specific* aspect of the other form. Schemas are generic knowledge structures, while instantiated schemas are the specific knowledge structures formed from them. The case is similar for mental models. There must be some forms of generic knowledge structures that are used to construct mental models, even though the term 'mental model' is typically used by Johnson-Laird to refer to the specific representations that have been constructed by these underlying generic knowledge processes.

Next consider the issue of imagery. It is true that the recent schema literature is fairly silent on the issue of mental imagery. However, this is not a necessary consequence of the construct itself. In the original treatment of schemas, Bartlett (1932) was concerned with the issue of how generic knowledge structures can give rise to specific memory images (cf. the discussion of Bartlett's theory in Brewer and Nakamura, 1984); and more recently in a paper on the structure of human memory (Brewer and Pani, 1983) we developed an argument that, in certain content domains, instantiated schemas should be highly imageable. Thus, schemas and mental models may be parallel here: for both, the underlying knowledge structures are unconscious but the specific knowledge representations can give rise to phenomenally experienced imagery.

Thus, it seems to me that what distinguishes mental models from other forms of mental representations is not the set of features that Johnson-Laird emphasizes, but rather another aspect of the two forms of representation. In *schemas* the molar knowledge structures are old generic information while in *mental models* the global knowledge structures are constructed at the time of input. In other words, schemas are precompiled generic knowledge structures, while mental models are specific knowledge structures that are constructed to represent a new situation through the use of generic knowledge of space, time, causality and human intentionality.

CAUSAL MENTAL MODELS

The term 'mental model' has also come to be used for the forms of representation used in the modelling of physical systems. There has not been a systematic treatment of how the term 'mental model' is used in this area and so it will be necessary to work out a rough account from the individual investigators' usages. Gentner and Stevens, in the introduction to their 1983 book on mental models, state that the three key dimensions that characterize this research tradition are that the investigators study simple physical systems, that they use formalisms from artificial intelligence, and that they employ eclectic methodologies. Norman (1983, p. 7) points out that it is a basic assumption of workers in this area that 'In interacting with the environment, with others, and with the artifacts of technology, people form internal, mental models of themselves and of the things with which they are interacting'. A number of researchers in this area have made reference to the imaginal properties of mental models. For example, de Kleer and Brown (1981, p. 286) state that mental models are generated 'by running a qualitative simulation in the mind's eye', and Collins and Gentner (in press) state that people can 'construct mental models that have the introspective feel of manipulating images'. These quotes also point up another aspect of causal mental models that is often emphasized—they can be 'run'. Thus, Collins (1985, p. 80) states, 'Mental models are meant to imply a conceptual representation that is qualitative, and that you can run in your mind's eye and see what happens.' Several theorists in this area have argued that mental models underlie an individual's ability to give a causal account of a physical domain. For example, Williams, Hollan and Stevens (1983, p. 135) stated that, 'They can also be used to produce explanations or justifications'; de Kleer and Brown (1981, p. 286) make a similar point. There has been little or no explicit discussion in the causal mental model literature concerning the generic versus constructed nature of these forms of representation. However, it seems to me that researchers in this area will need to include both forms of representation. Thus, the representation for a well-learned domain, such as the rotation of the earth or the operation of an internal combustion engine, will presumably rely on precompiled generic knowledge structures. Whereas, the representation for a new episodic input such as 'Why is there iridium in the rocks during the period when the dinosaurs became extinct?' or 'Why are inert elements not really inert?' will have to be constructed at the time of input from whatever relevant knowledge the individual can bring to bear on the problem.

CAUSAL MENTAL MODELS VERSUS SCHEMAS AND MENTAL MODELS

It does not seem that causal mental models can be distinguished from schemas and mental models in their use of eclectic methodologies and formalisms from artificial intelligence since both of these characteristics are also true of some research in each of the other traditions. It is true that Johnson-Laird (1980, 1983) has criticized the use of propositional notation and argued for some form of representation that is a structural analogue of the world. However, Clement (1983, p. 337) makes a similar argument from within the causal mental model tradition. The hypothesized imaginal properties of some causal mental models do not distinguish them from the other forms of representation since, as argued above, both schemas and mental models may have imaginal properties. As discussed above, some causal mental models would seem to be based on generic precompiled knowledge, making them similar to schemas in this regard. Other causal mental models would seem to be constructed at the time of use, making them similar to mental models as the term is used by Johnson-Laird. The ability to 'run' causal mental models does not seem to be crucial, since certain classes of schemas (e.g. scripts) can also be run. It seems to me that the crucial aspect of the causal mental model research tradition is that it has focused on physical systems and that the underlying forms of representation for these systems include a domain-specific construct of causality, just as certain schema domains have an underlying construct of spatial relations (e.g. scene schemas) and certain mental model domains have an underlying construct of human intentionality (e.g. plans). the causality component of the causal mental models accounts for the ability of individuals to run these forms of representation and it also accounts for their use in giving explanations of physical phenomena. Thus, in summary, this analysis suggests that causal mental models are the domain-specific subclasses of schemas and mental models that use causal forms of representation to deal with physical systems.

SITUATION MODELS

Recently van Dijk and Kintsch (1983) have modified their earlier views on text comprehension (e.g. Kintsch and van Dijk, 1978) by adding a component they refer to as the 'situation model'. They state that a level of analysis such as the situation model is needed in a text comprehension theory in order to go beyond the structure of the text itself and represent what the text is about. When they introduce situation models (p. 12) they refer to Johnson-Laird's (1980) work on mental models as the historical precedent for their construct. However, close analysis of their theory makes it clear that van Dijk and Kintsch include under the term 'situation model' both instantiated schema *and* mental models as used by Johnson-Laird. For example, they state that 'a situation model is an integrated structure of episodic information, collecting previous episodic information about some situation as well as instantiated general information from semantic memory' (1983, p. 344). Thus van Dijk and Kintsch are asserting that the representation that an individual forms after reading a passage of coherent text is typically a mixture of instantiated schemas and constructed mental models.

TERMINOLOGY

This analysis of the forms of knowledge representation for dealing with complex phenomena suggests that there is a reasonable degree of conceptual coherence in these proposals. However, it appears that we are in real trouble with respect to the technical vocabulary used to refer to these constructs.

For schemas, the problem is not too severe (except for the 'schemas' versus 'schemata' problem!). We can use the term 'schema' to cover generic knowledge structures and use the modifier 'global' to indicate that we are restricting it to global precompiled knowledge structures. We can use the existing term 'instantiated schema' for specific knowledge structures derived from global schemas.

However, there is real trouble with the term 'mental model'. Throughout this chapter I have used the term 'causal mental models' for the construct used by researchers in the physical model research tradition, but, in fact, they themselves have used the term 'mental model'. Thus, the same technical term is currently being used to refer to two quite different forms of knowledge representation. This seems to me an impossible situation (although it will certainly make for great undergraduate exam questions for generations to come). Therefore, with some reluctance, I suggest that we give up the term 'mental model' as a technical term. I propose that the term 'episodic model' be adopted as the technical term for mental model as this construct was explicated above. The use of 'episodic model' reflects Johnson-Laird's desire to capture a specific, nongeneric form of knowledge representation. In fact, it will avoid one additional problem. The earlier explication of Johnson-Laird's use of the term 'mental model' focused on his discussion of the representations formed when reading text. However, there are a few places in Johnson-Laird's (1983) work where he uses the term to cover other forms of representation. For example, he states that mental models are the 'models governing domains of pure mathematics' (p. 11), yet this would seem to be a clear example of some form of generic knowledge structure. Thus, the use of 'episodic model' as the term for specific knowledge structures that are constructed to represent new situations would avoid any possible ambiguity in the term 'mental models' as used by Johnson-Laird.

There is currently no term for the generic knowledge structures that are used to construct the episodic models. I propose that we use the term 'local schemas' to indicate that these are local generic knowledge structures which can be used to build new representations for complex situations.

In summary, the terminology suggested here is that *instantiated schemas* are the specific knowledge structures that are derived from the generic knowledge

Table 1   Forms of knowledge representation for complex domains

Pre-existing knowledge	Global schema	Local schema
Episodic input	Global related	Local related
Resulting episodic knowledge structure	Instantiated schema	Episodic model

represented in *global schemas*; while *Episodic models* are the specific knowledge structures that are constructed to represent new situations out of the more specific generic knowledge represented in *local schemas*. Table 1 provides a summary of these suggestions.

In keeping with the decision to reduce confusion by abandoning the term 'mental model', it seems to me that constructs used by those researchers who deal with representations of physical systems could be distinguished by the use of the adjective 'causal'. Thus, one could refer to a *causal schema* or *causal episodic model*. If 'mental model' is to be used at all it could be used very generally (cf. Perrig and Kintsch, 1985, p. 503) to refer to all forms of mental representation, general or specific, from any domain, causal, intentional or spatial.

CONCEPTUAL CONFUSIONS IN RECENT WORK ON KNOWLEDGE REPRESENTATION

This section of the chapter shows some of the conceptual confusions that have resulted from not making the distinction between schemas and episodic models through an analysis of the recent experimental and theoretical work of one investigator, namely myself.

In our recent review of the scheme literature (Brewer and Nakamura, 1984) we define schemas in much the way they have been defined in this chapter. Yet, if you look at the details of some of the research we review you can see several blunders. For example, we review an early demonstration experiment by Bransford and Johnson (1972). We cover the 'washing machine' experiment, which showed improved recall for an opaquely written passage when it was given a title. We also cover the 'Romeo' experiment, which showed improved recall for a passage after seeing a relevant picture. The washing machine experiment clearly belonged in the schema chapter since it is a good example of the operation of an instantiated schema. However, the Romeo experiment simply does not meet our own definition of a schema and is an example of an episodic model. A good heuristic for distinguishing between instantiated schemas and episodic models is to ask yourself if the subject knew the relevant global knowledge structure before he or she came into the experiment. Clearly, the subjects in the passage title experiment knew about washing machines before they came into the experiment, but, equally clearly, the subjects in the picture experiment did not have generic knowledge about people who serenade women who live in tall buildings by using a balloon to carry the speaker of an electric guitar.

Next, we can apply the distinction between schemas and episodic models to several recent 'schema' experiments that have come out of our laboratory. Our naturalistic study of memory for rooms (Brewer and Treyens, 1981) does appear to be predominately a study of instantiated schemas. The books that the subjects gave as recall inferences in that study came from the subjects' generic knowledge of academic offices. However, other aspects of the study, such as the recall of the location of the desk on either the right or left side of the room, now seem better described as episodic model information.

Our naturalistic study of memory for subjects setting up a slide projector (Lichtenstein and Brewer, 1980) is probably a complex mixture of instantiated schema and episodic model information. In the area of human actions, *scripts* are the form of representation for global generic information, while *plans* are the form of representation used to construct episodic models for new intentional actions that are observed.

Finally, our study (Brewer and Dupree, 1983) of 'plan schemata' in memory for human actions now seems a clear example of the operations of an episodic model in memory. For methodological reasons in this study we carefully designed our actions to be *nongeneric*. For example, we had our actress pull out a ruler from a bookshelf in order to change the hands of a clock—not to draw a straight line. Thus, I know at least one cognitive psychologist whose thinking would have been much clearer if he had read this chapter before carrying out and interpreting all those experiments.

INSTANTIATED SCHEMAS VERSUS EPISODIC MODELS IN MEMORY AND COMPREHENSION

This section of the chapter briefly describes some of our recent empirical work directed at understanding the differences betwen instantiated schemas and episodic models. In order to carry out these experiments we developed a technique that makes it possible to construct instantiated schema passages, episodic model passages and control passages from the same set of experimental sentences and thereby hold sentence-level variables constant.

Instantiated schema passages

Most recent experiments that have used linguistic materials to study the operation of schemas in memory have confounded the recall of generic schema information with recall of true instantiated schema information. If a study on memory for scripts includes an item such as 'He paid his bill', one does not know if the subject recalling such an item is retrieving an episodic fact acquired in the experiment, or if the subject is simply retrieving information from a generic 'purchase script'. However, if the experiment used a true instantiated script item such as 'He paid his bill with his American Express card', and items are scored correct only if the subject includes the material about the American Express card, then one knows the subject is retrieving true episodic knowledge from the experimental passage. Note that the usual procedure of confusing generic schema information and instantiated schema information inflates the recall scores for the schema conditions since old generic information is scored as if it had been acquired in the experimental task.

The actual instantiated script materials used in these experiments consisted of a set of passages describing the actions of an individual carrying out a series of script-based activities that could be accomplished in the downtown area of a small town (e.g. mailing a package, cashing a check). A segment from one of the instantiated passages follows, with the experimental items in italic type:

> He went in and looked for the place to mail packages. *There are two people in front of him in the package line.* The line in front of him moved rapidly. *He gave a package of records to the postal worker.* The postal worker asked Philip how he wanted to send the package. *He told the postal worker that he wanted to mail his package 2nd class. The postal worker put his package on an old scale with weights. The package weighed 7 pounds.*

Episodic model passages

The episodic model materials were developed by designing an imaginary town with a number of buildings in it. Each building corresponded to the location of one of the scripts used in the construction of the instantiated script passages. Then passages were written in which a character walked a simple path among the buildings. At each building the character carried out one appropriate script activity. The sentence describing the script action was taken from one of the instantiated schema passages. For the resulting passages, it should be possible for a reader to develop an episodic model of the spatial and event information, but the reader would not have any pre-existing global schema information about the location of the buildings or the sequence of visits. A segment from one of the episodic model passages follows, with the experimental items in italic type:

> Upon leaving the movie theater, Philip was at the far south end of Main Street, so he crossed over to the west side of the street and went into the copy shop. *Philip went into the back room with the self-service IBM machines.* After leaving the copy shop Philip began walking north along the west side of Main Street and entered the post office. *He told the postal worker that he wanted to mail his package 2nd class.* Philip left the post office and continued walking north and entered the bank. *The teller asked him for his university ID.*

Control passages

Control passages were constructed from the episodic model passages by retaining the experimental items but eliminating the event sequence and spatial information that makes it possible for readers to construct an episodic model for the overall passage. The omitted spatial-event sentences were replaced with other irrelevant sentences.

I am currently carrying out a series of memory and comprehension experiments with Susan Perkins and Woo-Kyoung Ahn using materials of this type. Results of an initial memory experiment shows that both the instantiated schema structure and the episodic model structure improve recall of the specific episodic information in the passages. However, we believe that the episodic model group has to work much harder to construct their representation so we are investigating the amount of attentional resources needed by subjects to construct the two forms of representation.

CONCLUSION

The results of the analysis carried out in this chapter suggest that we have reached a new stage in theorizing about forms of representation for complex phenomena. Initially there was much excitement over the realization that research in many areas of cognitive science seemed to require molar knowledge structures. Now, we appear to moving toward a period when it is necessary to work out the relations between the various proposals and to provide more specific and detailed theories for each of the hypothesized forms of knowledge representation.

ACKNOWLEDGEMENTS

Preparation of this chapter was supported in part by National Institute of Education Contract No. HEW-NIE-C-400-76-0116. I would like to thank Ellen Brewer for commenting on an earlier draft of this paper.

REFERENCES

Bartlett, F. C. (1932). *Remembering*. London: Cambridge University Press.
Bower, G. H., Black, J. B. and Turner, T. J. (1979). Scripts in memory for text. *Cognitive Psychology*, 11, 177–220.
Bransford, J. D., Barclay, J. R. and Franks, J. J. (1972). Sentence memory: A constructive versus interpretive approach. *Cognitive Psychology*, 3, 193–209.
Bransford, J. D., and Johnson, M. K. (1972). Contextual prerequisites for understanding: Some investigations of comprehension and recall. *Journal of Verbal Learning and Verbal Behavior*, 11, 717–26.
Brewer, W. F., and Dupree, D. A. (1983). Use of plan schemata in the recall and recognition of goal-directed actions. *Journal of Experimental Psychology: Learning, Memory, and Cognition*, 9, 117–29.

Brewer, W. F., and Nakamura, G. V. (1984). The nature and functions of schemas. In R. S. Wyer, Jr, and T. K. Srull (eds) *Handbook of Social Cognition*, Vol. 1. Hillsdale, NJ: Erlbaum, pp. 119–60.
Brewer, W. F., and Pani, J. R. (1983). The structure of human memory. In G. H. Bower (ed.) *The Psychology of Learning and Motivation: Advances in Research and Theory*, Vol. 17. New York: Academic Press, pp. 1–38.
Brewer, W. F., and Treyens, J. C. (1981). Role of schemata in memory for places. *Cognitive Psychology*, **13**, 207–30.
Clement, J. (1983). A conceptual model discussed by Galileo and used intuitively by physics students. In D. Gentner and A. L. Stevens (eds) *Mental Models*. Hillsdale, NJ: Erlbaum, pp. 325–40.
Collins, A. (1985). Component models of physical systems. *Proceedings of the Seventh Annual Conference of the Cognitive Science Society*, pp. 80–9.
Collins, A., and Gentner, D. (in press). How people construct mental models. In N. Quinn and D. Holland (eds) *Cultural Models in Language and Thought*. London: Cambridge University Press.
van Dijk, T. A., and Kintsch, W. (1983). *Strategies of Discourse Comprehension*. New York: Academic Press.
Ehrlich, K., and Johnson-Laird, P. N. (1982). Spatial descriptions and referential continuity. *Journal of Verbal Learning and Verbal Behavior*, **21**, 296–306.
Gentner, D., and Stevens, A. L. (eds) (1983). *Mental Models*. Hillsdale, NJ: Erlbaum.
Graesser, A. C., Gordon, S. E. and Sawyer, J. D. (1979). Recognition memory for typical and atypical actions in scripted activities: Tests of a script pointer + tag hypothesis. *Journal of Verbal Learning and Verbal Behavior*, **18**, 319–32.
Johnson-Laird, P. N. (1980). Mental models in cognitive science. *Cognitive Science*, **4**, 71–115.
Johnson-Laird, P. N. (1983). *Mental Models*. Cambridge, Mass.: Harvard University Press.
Kintsch, W., and van Dijk, T. A. (1978). Toward a model of text comprehension and production. *Psychological Review*, **85**, 363–94.
de Kleer, J., and Brown, J. S. (1981). Mental models of physical mechanisms and their acquisition. In J. R. Anderson (ed.) *Cognitive Skills and their Acquisition*. Hillsdale, NJ: Erlbaum, pp. 285–309.
Lichtenstein, E. H., and Brewer, W. F. (1980). Memory for goal-directed events. *Cognitive Psychology*, **12**, 412–45.
Minsky, M. (1975). A framework for representing knowledge. In P. H. Winston (ed.) *The Psychology of Computer Vision*. New York: McGraw-Hill, pp. 211–77.
Norman, D. A. (1983). Some observations on mental models. In D. Gentner and A. L. Stevens (eds) *Mental Models*. Hillsdale, NJ: Erlbaum, pp. 7–14.
Perrig, W., and Kintsch, W. (1985). Propositional and situational representation of text. *Journal of Memory and Language*, **24**, 503–18.
Rumelhart, D. E. (1980). Schemata: The building blocks of cognition. In R. J. Spiro, B. C. Bruce and W. F. Brewer (eds) *Theoretical Issues in Reading Comprehension*. Hillsdale, NJ: Erlbaum, pp. 33–58.
Schank, R. C., and Abelson, R. P. (1977). *Scripts, Plans, Goals and Understanding*. Hillsdale, NJ: Erlbaum.
Sulin, R. A., and Dooling, D. J. (1974). Intrusion of a thematic idea in retention of prose. *Journal of Experimental Psychology*, **103**, 255–62.
Williams, M. D., Hollan, J. D., and Stevens, A. L. (1983). Human reasoning about a simple physical system. In D. Gentner and A. L. Stevens (eds) *Mental Models*. Hillsdale, NJ: Erlbaum, pp. 131–53.

Modelling Cognition
Edited by P. Morris
© 1987 John Wiley & Sons Ltd.

8

Making decisions under the influence of knowledge

JOHN FOX
Imperial Cancer Research Fund Laboratories, London

INTRODUCTION

Decision-making is pivotal to behaviour. The ability to make decisions does not seem to be a primary faculty like memory, perception or language, but neither is decision-taking merely another laboratory task like free recall, visual search or phoneme monitoring. It is a generic ability which is necessary for the successful realization of most cognitive skills. We make decisions when we interpret visual images, words, sentences and the behaviour of others. We make decisions when we decide on solutions to problems, on how to look for solutions, and indeed on what the problem was in the first place.

This centrality of decision-making recurs in computational studies of cognition. Decisions are made when programs adopt or eliminate hypotheses in understanding speech; when problem-solving strategies are selected or rejected; when moves are chosen in playing games, and when learning and discovery programs expand or restrict the hypothesis space they are searching. Decision-making is an explicit function of expert systems such as systems for medical diagnosis and treatment, which weigh evidence for the options or the likely desirability of the outcomes. Planning programs make decisions when assembling plans from candidate parts (e.g. in formulating travel plans or designing gene manipulation experiments) and so on.

The main type of decision, or at least the type that has received most attention in both the psychological and the artificial intelligence (AI) literature, is the decision which involves judgement. This is usually interpreted to mean decisions where the significance or consequences of the decision options are uncertain. All the examples given involve uncertainty.

How we treat uncertainty and its place in decision-making are the major themes of this chapter. A change of direction from traditional views of decision-making is urged, which marries models of decision-making with our growing understanding of the computational basis of knowledge-based skills. My thesis is that decision-making and coping with uncertainty are often knowledge-intensive processes.

The major theories of human decision-making and uncertainty are reviewed first. This reveals a preoccupation with mathematical interpretations of uncertainty, and a lack of concern with the obvious point that knowledge must be important somewhere. A knowledge-based interpretation of uncertainty is then presented, which shows one way in which uncertainty and hence decision-making processes may relate to other kinds of knowledge. Finally some historical, linguistic and theoretical arguments are presented to support the change of perspective from the predominantly mathematical view of uncertainty to one which recognizes the role of logic as well as numbers, and the meaning as well as the magnitude of uncertainty terms.

REVIEW OF MODELS OF UNCERTAINTY

Probability models

By the time that the psychological study of decision-making began to develop, the conceptual framework of probability theory and statistics was well established. It was therefore natural to investigate human decision-making within that framework. The study of decision-making within a normative statistical framework revealed significant weaknesses in human performance by the lights of the statistical decision analyst. By comparison with precise probabilistic calculation human decision-making is distinctly rough and ready.

At the end of the 1960s it was becoming clear that at least two important processes were influencing decision-making, both of which seemed to fall a long way short of the ideal decision-making process. On the one hand it was clear that people were strongly influenced by patterns (e.g. 'textbook patterns of symptoms'), and on the other by seemingly crude methods of weighing evidence. The so-called 'linear' models, in which decisions are made simply by adding up the pros and cons of different options, accounted for much of decision behaviour.

The conclusion from all this was unsettling. People are not, it seems, natural intuitive statisticians. Nevertheless, as we have seen, people must constantly cope with uncertainty; if they are not doing mathematics what are they doing?

Heuristics

From a cognitive perspective the mathematical models revealed little about what goes on in people's heads when decisions are made under uncertainty.

The realization that pattern recognition and other simple ways of aggregating information might be important led Tversky and Kahneman (1974) to their famous reformulation of the problem in terms of 'heuristics'. People are not, said Kahneman and Tversky, simply making feeble attempts to apply proper decision procedures and failing. On the contrary, 'people rely on a limited number of heuristic principles which reduce the complex tasks of assessing probabilities and predicting values to simpler judgemental operations'.

The three heuristics identified by Tversky and Kahneman were:

1. Representativeness, in which people rely on assessments of similarity or typicality in judging whether an 'object or event A belongs to a class or process B'.
2. Availability, in which people assess the frequency of a class or the probability of an event by the ease with which instances or occurrences can be brought to mind.
3. Adjustment and anchoring, in which people make numerical estimates by taking an initial value (a guess or quick calculation) and progressively adjust it to give a final, often wildly wrong, estimate.

Tversky and Kahneman concluded that: 'In general these heuristics are quite useful, but sometimes they lead to severe and systematic errors.'

The architecture of cognition

While the heuristic approach sheds light on broad features of decision-making under uncertainty, making reference to memory and other cognitive mechanisms, it says little about the details of these processes. It says little, for example, about the way in which the heuristics are represented or processed in computational terms (e.g. how adjustment and anchoring processes are implemented); how memory mechanisms influence the speed at which relevant material is retrieved (as in judging availability) or how categories or events are perceived as similar (as in representativeness).

About the time that Tversky and Kahneman were developing their ideas, computational models of cognition were also emerging (Newell and Simon, 1972). These were eventually to offer models of the 'architecture of cognition' (e.g. Anderson, 1983), which was a theoretical backdrop against which all cognitive processes like decision-making must be seen.

I have discussed elsewhere how decision-making might be understood within an architectural framework (Fox, 1980). I was interested in how easily the sort of heuristics that Tversky and Kahneman postulated might translate into an architectural model of cognition, and what if any advantages this would have over earlier mathematical approaches. Using a task modelled on medical diagnosis, a detailed set of simulations covering memory retrieval and rule-based components of decision-making was developed. The simulations provided a computational interpretation of such notions as 'availability' and a model of how parts of the cognitive architecture might interact to influence decision-making. It turned out that the interaction of these mechanisms could provide at least as good an account of decision-making under uncertainty as the traditional mathematical frameworks, and in some respects a better one.

Representational models

Although Tversky and Kahneman's heuristics and their exploration within an architectural framework seem to be useful steps on the way to a cognitive account of decision-making they share an important feature. They treat the management of uncertainty as a side-effect of cognitive mechanisms. They do not treat it as something which is explicitly represented in our thinking. Yet it is obvious that at some level we represent uncertainty explicitly. We claim to 'feel uncertain' and, more convincingly, the vocabulary of natural language is littered with specialized terms that describe it. Words like 'possibility' and 'plausibility', 'suspicion' and 'doubt', 'conceivability' and 'expectation' and many others seem to suggest that uncertainty is to some degree an explicit part of our representation of the world, not merely an implicit feature of the cognitive architecture.

What exactly is the representation underlying such terms? Some people have attempted to develop an explicit representation which takes a probabilistic view of human decision-making, but at the same time accounts for our statistical inadequacies. A device often used is to represent terms like 'likely', 'possible' and so on, as intervals on the probability scale (e.g. 'possible' means a non-zero probability, 'likely' means a probability between, say, 0.5 and 0.9). The difficulties with this approach are many, not the least of which are that it produces confusion (e.g. how small does a probability have to be before we call it zero and say something is not possible?) and that no one can establish a consensus as to what the probability ranges are that people use to define uncertainty terms.

At the other extreme is an approach that attempts to avoid the representation problem by treating terms operationally, giving them no explicit meaning, numerical or otherwise. If a hypothesis is labelled 'likely' then it may be followed up, if 'unlikely' it is disregarded, if 'definite' it is acted upon, and so forth. While its foundations are obviously weak, simulations can deliver surprisingly good decision-making performance by comparison with statistical methods, at least in limited situations (e.g. Fox, Barber and Bardhan, 1980). Nevertheless operational representations of uncertainty are unconvincing because they do not address the fact that we seem to, or at least claim to, 'know' something about uncertainty. The appearance of AI and expert systems are stimulating a new debate about uncertainty; AI originally introduced the idea of 'heuristics' in a more explicit sense than that used by Tversky and Kahneman, namely as non-algorithmic decision rules. Do heuristics in the AI sense indicate a new view of uncertainty? Practical developments to date suggest not. Programmers of AI have generally coped with uncertainty merely by modifying explicit but deterministic knowledge representations, like semantic nets and production rules, with numerical coefficients derived from Bayesian concepts, fuzzy logic or other theories. In other words, the nature of uncertainty is still implicitly represented in numbers (Fox, 1985).

However, computational concepts could lead to a major reorientation of ideas about probability methods, not just a new arena in which to use them. An important contribution of AI, seen clearly in expert systems, is that they pursue a novel approach to the design of symbol-manipulating mechanisms. In 'knowledge-based' systems virtually any concept, function or process can be represented explicitly within the computer, not just implicitly within an algorithm or abstractly as numbers (e.g. Fox, 1984).

As in psychology, this fruitful idea has been disregarded in discussions of the representation of uncertainty. Knowledge about uncertainty is not made explicit—qualitative knowledge is simply used in an *ad hoc* combination with some numerical uncertainty calculus. The alternative seems obvious: uncertainty, like any other concept, is a subject that we have knowledge about and which we might articulate.

UNCERTAINTY AS A TYPE OF KNOWLEDGE

As we have seen it is common to represent uncertainty as mathematical and unidimensional probability, and to interpret terms like possible, probable etc., as points or intervals on the unit line. I assert that such interpretations are incompatible with the ordinary use of these terms. Their meanings are not unidimensional but, rather, reflect important logical distinctions about different states of belief.

We can illustrate what is meant by a logical distinction by considering the less contentious subjects of place and time. Place can be represented by means of x, y, z coordinates in Euclidean space but, for much problem-solving, qualitative terms are used. It can be convenient to distinguish important places like here and there, and more complex ones like somewhere, elsewhere and everywhere. Time is normally represented by reference to a continuous scale as well, but we use a complementary qualitative vocabulary which distinguishes concepts like now, sometime, never and relations like before, after, during and so forth. The formal nature of these languages of place and time is unclear. 'Here' is a subjective concept while 'everywhere' is not; 'now' is an instant, while 'never' is an unbounded interval. However, the terms clearly reflect real distinctions which are complementary to scientific, quantitative representations.

Computational studies are producing a greater clarity about how to go

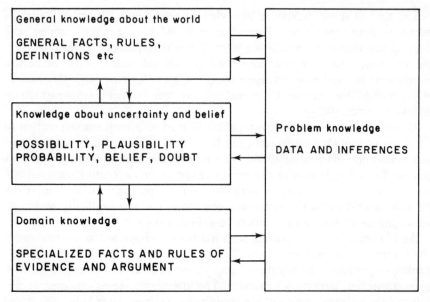

Figure 1.

about representing knowledge, particularly in explicitly representing logical facts and rules. Some knowledge can be thought of as general (e.g. facts and rules about the behaviour of all physical objects and materials); some knowledge is more focused (e.g. the facts and rules describing anatomical structures and disease processes), while some is highly specific, such as the symptoms and signs of a particular patient on a particular day. In this light we can see why uncertainty is a generic concept. Any knowledge whether general, focused or specific can be associated with uncertainty. Uncertainty knowledge is a specialized form of knowledge about how to describe general, focused or specific beliefs yet it straddles all other types (Fox, 1985). Figure 1 illustrates the relationship.

We can make distinctions about uncertainty which emphasize different logical aspects rather than degrees of uncertainty. I shall describe three types here; possibility, plausibility and probability. From these terms a range of other linguistic terms seem to be derivable (Fox, 1985) but we shall only consider these three here. The quantitative meaning of these terms is ambiguous but I believe that their logical thrust is not.

Possibility

Consider some proposition P, which may be any fragment of knowledge—a general rule, a domain fact, an item of data or a current hypothesis. P is said to be possible if no conditions that are necessary for P are violated. P may have no necessary conditions, or we may be ignorant of the state of these conditions, or we may have evidence against P; these circumstances do not affect a statement of possibility.

Here is a fragment of knowledge about possibility and possibilistic terms, expressed as an executable set of rules. The rules are written in the programming language Prolog (Clocksin and Mellish, 1981) with the standard operator precedences modified to improve readability.

P is not possible if not (P is possible).   (1a)

P is not possible if P is exclusive of Q   (1b)
    and Q is certain.

P is not possible if P is impossible.   (1c)

P is impossible if C is a necessary condition for P   (1d)
    and C is not possible.

P is not impossible if not (P is impossible).   (1e)

The concept of possibility turns on the notion of a necessary condition. Such necessary conditions are often subject dependent (e.g. 'cancer should always be assumed to be possible' because there are no necessary conditions by which it can be refuted) or derived by applying general knowledge to subject knowledge (e.g. the generalized rule of inference (1a) which embodies the rule 'anything is possible unless you can prove that it is not').

Plausibility

P is plausible if P is possible and the balance of argument is for P. An 'argument' is indirect. It is assembled by the application of some process of reasoning to a set of givens. The givens might be the axioms of mathematics, the theories of evolution or medicine that are current, or the beliefs a person has about the behaviour of others. In 'it is plausible that the butler did it' the plausibility of the statement is determined by arguments from certain assumptions about motive and opportunity, rather than, say, direct evidence that he was found with a smoking gun or seen running away immediately after the crime (and even these require indirect arguments to interpret them).

This is a subject-independent logic program for plausibility:

P is plausible if A is argument for P and   (2a)
    not (P is exclusive of Q and
        Q is more plausible than P).

P is not plausible if not (P is plausible).   (2b)

P is not plausible if P is implausible.   (2c)

P is implausible if P is exclusive of Q and   (2d)
    Q is more plausible than P.
P is not implausible if not (P is implausible).   (2e)

Recognized forms of argument in science include special case (P is a special case of P'), analogy (P is an analogy of P'), and model-based arguments (P follows from some causal model M). Recognized forms of argument in legal proceedings include motive and opportunity. Recognized forms of argument in human affairs are based on theories of virtue and malice. (To say that we argue something is not of course to assert that all arguments are defensible. Even when wholly logical we may not accept the axioms accepted by someone else.)

Probability

P is probable if P is possible and the balance of evidence is in favour of P. The most universally recognized form of evidence is the presence of some sign taken to be associated with P (e.g. frequentistically).

This is a logic program for probability:

P is probable if E is evidence for P and   (3a)
    not (P is exclusive of Q and
        Q is more probable than P).
P is not probable if not (P is probable).   (3b)
P is not probable if P is improbable.   (3c)
P is improbable if P is exclusive of Q   (3d)
    and Q is more probable than P.
P is not improbable if not (P is improbable).   (3e)

The program requires a criterion for the relation is more probable than in (3a) (analogous to 'is more plausible than' in 2a). Although classical probability methods treat this relationship as one concerned with relative magnitude we could choose any ordering function to determine the truth of the predicate. In the absence of numerical probabilities we could establish that 'P is more probable than not(P)' by accepting observational evidence in preference to circumstantical evidence, or by preferring reliable reports of the evidence in preference to unreliable ones. While numerical functions are best understood, e.g. those which compute and compare likelihood ratios, they are not apparently the only possibility.

Note the fundamental claim that plausibility by indirect argument is different from probability by direct evidence. The forms of plausibilistic reasoning and probabilistic reasoning are different. Bayesians and others have argued that 'subjective probability' subsumes all forms of arguments about belief. On that view the two types of argument both lead simply to a degree of belief in P. This conflation of different methods for generating and assessing beliefs not only violates common intuition, it also ignores the many different ways in which beliefs are developed. These different methods are an important source of flexibility in decision-making and problem-solving.

Readers concerned with some of the more technical aspects of belief, and particularly the fundamental problem of how beliefs are combined or revised in the light of new information, will ask what kind of revision rules are possible with this sort of logical interpretation of uncertainty terms. There is insufficient space to deal with this problem here but the problem is discussed elsewhere (Fox, 1986).

ARGUMENTS IN FAVOUR OF THE KNOWLEDGE APPROACH

I have given one argument, an intuitive one, to support the exploration of knowledge-based interpretations of uncertainty terms. Since these intuitions are controversial I now attempt to give further supportive evidence and arguments. These are historical evidence, linguistic and documentary evidence, and a theoretical argument about why having a variety of uncertainty concepts is advantageous.

Historical evidence

Before about 1660 when the modern Pascalian concept of probability emerged we had no formal methods for making predictions from incomplete or unreliable information. Since then many rival interpretations of uncertainty have appeared and some have disappeared. Although a formidable range of practical probabilistic methods has been established for making predictions under uncertainty, philosophical issues about the true meaning of probability remain (e.g. whether probability is a subjective or objective concept).

Many texts continue to re-examine issues about the nature of uncertainty, and to challenge the narrow interpretation in terms of mathematical probability and even the generality of evidential justifications (e.g. 'probability is a distinctly minor note in the history of scientific argument' Glymour, 1980, p. 66). In his delightful essay on the history of probabilistic ideas, the philosopher Ian Hacking shows clearly that the modern concept of probability was not only not obvious, it is still controversial and old ideas can still recur. He gives an example of the early idea of 'equipossible' hypotheses— hypotheses that satisfy the principle of 'no reason to the contrary' (see 1a above). As Hacking puts it, 'the definition [of equally possible cases] was in full vigour a century after Laplace and is still not dead'.

But though Hacking appears to regard the notion of equipossibility as monstrous, he slips a familiar usage into an extraordinarily telling summary of the current state of the debate: 'I am inviting the reader to imagine . . . that there is a space of *possible* theories about probability that has been rather constant from 1660 to the present . . . perhaps an understanding of our space and its preconditions can liberate us from the cycle of probability theories that has trapped us for so long' (Hacking, 1975, p. 16, my emphasis).

The fact is that possibility is different from probability and people have known it for a long time. History records the row between those who would like to be parsimonious and reduce the number of concepts of uncertainty to a single, manageable numerical idea (the probabilists), and those like the author who defend the importance of developing some common distinctions.

Linguistic and documentary evidence

Why did Hacking make this apparently inconsistent slip in using the term possible? My view is simply that like the rest of us he sometimes needs the notion of possibility to talk about uncertain ideas. Hacking cannot say with confidence that 'there is a space of theories about probability' so he chooses to comment instead that 'it is possible that (there is a space of theories about probability)'. I think that he means by this, roughly, that more than one theory may be worth considering but he cannot or will not attach a number or another description of likelihood to them. This is general. We routinely use a language which lets us use sentences which comment upon 'subordinate' sentences. One way we use this capability is to comment upon our belief in sentences.

To illustrate this further, given the base sentence 'John Smith has cancer' there are many complex comments we might make, such as 'I was told the other day by a man I believe to be reliable that (John Smith has cancer)', or certainty sentences like:

  it is possible that (John Smith has cancer)
  it is plausible that (John Smith has cancer)
  it is probable that (John Smith has cancer)

I claim that these and other linguistic forms are distinct, and that the distinctions are obvious to most native users of English. An implication of this linguistic argument for different aspects of uncertainty is that we should be able to find some evidence of consensus.

One obvious place to look is in a dictionary. I have selected what seem to be relevant parts of definitions of the primary terms from two dictionaries; *Webster's New World Dictionary of the American Language* (*WNWO*) (second edition) and *The Concise Oxford Dictionary* (*COD*).

Possible: 'is used of anything that may exist, occur, be done etc. depending upon circumstances' (*WNWD*) 'that can exist, be done or happen' (*COD*).

Plausible: 'applies to that which at first glance appears to be true, reasonable, valid etc. but which may or may not be so although there is no connotation of deliberate deception [a plausible argument]' (*WNWD*) '(of arguments, statements, etc.) specious, seeming reasonable or probable' (*COD*).

Probable: 'applies to that which appears reasonable on the basis of evidence or logic but is neither certain nor proved' (*WNWD*) 'that may be expected to happen or prove true' (*COD*).

Broadly speaking, I take these definitions to be supportive of the kind of analysis I have proposed. It is of particular note that there is no hint of quantitative interpretations of uncertainty in these definitions. However, while the linguistic evidence is enough to make my thesis plausible there is some residual doubt. In particular although the words 'evidence', 'argument' and 'logic' appear, the sharp distinction drawn between plausibility and probability, which derives from the directness of their support, is not supported by these authorities. Clearly the sharp logical definitions do not give anything like a complete account of common usage. Nevertheless, I claim that the distinctions are assumed by the dictionary definitions even if practical usage is not sharp or consistent.

Rational justification for the distinctions

Since the distinctions between different kinds of uncertainty cannot be unequivocally supported by documentary evidence we require further arguments to support them. I shall argue that the distinctions between types of uncertainty are valuable for problem-solving and decision-making in the practical world.

Applied mathematics deliberately seeks models which are abstractions (simplifications) of the world. Models are valid if features of the problem they are applied to do not violate their assumptions. However, natural and artificial decision-makers like doctors and scientists and programs for understanding language or controlling robots, must routinely encounter uncertain situations. Many of these are novel and therefore the validity of particular assumptions is dubious or unknown.

Artificial intelligence has always been especially concerned with ill-defined problems. It advocates 'weak methods' for problem-solving which embody only weak assumptions: To illustrate, the decision rule that 'claiming a breakthrough in cancer is unwise' influences my organization's public relations policy. This heuristic is hard to formalize or quantify (what is a breakthrough?) but not vacuous. In the present state of the art, formalization of the policy would introduce unrealistic restrictions on its possible meanings.

A place where restrictive assumptions creep into decision-making under uncertainty is in assumptions about quantitative and distributional features of the decision situation. Questions are often raised about conditional independence assumptions in discussions of Bayesian decision-making techniques for example, but more fundamental assumptions about whether an underlying function is even continuous can be doubtful. Often in decision-making one simply has no knowledge of the quantitative properties of the domain.

One field where it is impractical to rely upon the availability of quantitative information is in medical general practice. In the medical specialities, which focus on just a few of the many diseases that can confront us, Bayesian decision-making techniques have often been applied and it has proved valuable to collect statistics carefully (such as the joint frequencies of symptoms and diseases). This has often been shown to lead to more accurate diagnoses. In general practice on the other hand the range of problems is so large that the collection of such statistics is impractical. What is worse, with changes in patterns of disease, changes in medical knowledge and changes in medical policy, the value of such a body of statistics if it existed might well be only temporary.

General practitioners must therefore continue to cope with uncertainty without the benefit of a comprehensive source of quantitative data, so they clearly need methods for dealing with uncertainty which do not require these parameters. It is apparent that general practitioners use such methods all the time. For example, rules like the following are immediately intelligible:

> refer the patient for investigation of a disease if
>> there is evidence the patient has the disease
>> and the disease is a kind of life-threatening condition
>> and the disease is not impossible

This rule depends upon evidence, though is not probabilistic in the mathematical sense. Similarly we could write plausibilistic rules, as when, say, the general practitioner encounters some hitherto unseen symptom or sign. If the symptom can be explained by a causal argument from the known action of a drug leading to certain side-effects through interaction with another existing condition then the physician may decide to change the medication rather than refer the patient for investigation.

I think that this argument about the need to deal with uncertainty without the benefit of numbers extends well beyond medical decision-making. We are all, in a sense, general practitioners.

Another area where weak decision-making methods are surely required is in scientific decision-making and the formation of hypotheses. In scientific research the evidence, the hypotheses and even the interpretation of the problem are constantly changing. It is quite impractical to define a stable decision space and its quantitative parameters. Nevertheless, the working scientist still makes decisions under high levels of uncertainty. Which evidence is reliable? What does it mean? How must I change my model? And so forth. I suggest that as scientists we routinely use weak methods to deal with such problems.

A nice example of the apparent use of a weak method by a scientist is to be found in Anderson (1983). Anderson makes extensive use of large-scale computer simulations in building cognitive theories. The difficulty with simulation techniques is that the form of the computer program is not naturally constrained; it is as easy to build a bad simulation as a good one and one can be tempted to make retrograde changes to a model to accommodate spurious or dubious findings.

Anderson is consequently cautious about the criteria which must be satisfied before he will change his theory. Of course he is not usually in a position to calculate a probability for the correctness of each new component of the theory. However, he claims to use a rule for deciding when to admit a significant change to the model which seems both intelligible and stringent (Anderson, 1983, pp. 42–3):

> the mechanism is admissible if
>> there is a broad range of evidence for the mechanism
>> and existing mechanisms cannot explain phenomena
>> and there is a good argument for the adaptive value of the mechanism

This rule exemplifies the use of a weak method. It shows how a combination of different qualitative forms of argument can provide a clear decision rule even though quantitative parameters are not available. Interestingly, the rule uses all three types of uncertainty distinguished here. The first condition is plainly evidential (probabilistic). The second condition is possibilistic as it deals with the conceivable capabilities (necessary properties) of the existing model. The third clause is plausibilistic because it requires an argument from biological assumptions and theory.

Again, this extends beyond science. Although many decisions in industry, law, policy, government etc., may be cast in a well-defined form, most cannot. Practitioners are routinely faced with new, ill-formed problems which are not immediately amenable to solution by classical techniques. Weak methods which exploit different types of uncertainty offer an approach to describing the decision procedures which are used.

Further arguments for the practical benefits of using logical and not only numerical methods in computer-based decision-making can be found in Fox (1986).

CAVEATS

In closing I should make clear that my arguments in favour of logical analysis of uncertainty concepts and for the use of weak methods should not be taken as arguments against the value of classical numerical methods in decision-making, nor as a denial that quantitative features of problems influence human decision-making. We have seen that probability theory has yielded a formidable array of techniques for making predictions under uncertainty. When these assumptions are certainly, probably or plausibly satisfied one should consider using them. I only point out that there are many decisions where it is unlikely, or just unclear, whether these assumptions are satisfied yet we must still take a decision.

It is also obvious that as we accumulate experience we often build up a sense of the degree to which events are related, as well as knowledge of the fact that they are related. Many experimental data on decision-making suggest that skilled decision-takers can exploit quantitative information, whether this is in real problems like forecasting the weather or in artificial ones like estimating the proportions of black to white balls in an urn. My claim is that in real problems where we can use our general knowledge of physics, physiology, psychology etc., we have more resources to draw upon in coping with uncertainty, and that it is perfectly rational to do so. A reasonable expectation from this is that when we have a great deal of knowledge but little experience relevant to a decision then the knowledge will dominate, while when the reverse is true we can expect the statistics to dominate, however imperfect our ability to use them. It is in these latter circumstances that the analyses of Tversky and Kahneman and others are most helpful.

REFERENCES

Anderson, J. (1983). *The Architecture of Cognition*. Cambridge: Harvard University Press.

Clocksin, W. F., and Mellish, C. S. (1981). *Programming in Prolog*. Berlin: Springer-Verlag.

Fox, J. (1980). Making decisions under the influence of memory. *Psychological Review*, **87**(2), 190–211.

Fox, J. (1984). A short account of knowledge engineering. *The Knowledge Engineering Review*, **1**(1).

Fox, J. (1985). Knowledge, decision making and uncertainty. In W. Gale and D. Pregibon (eds) *Proceedings of Workshop on AI and Statistics*. Bell Laboratories, John Wiley (May).

Fox, J., Barber, D. and Bardhan, K. D. (1980). Alternatives to Bayes: A quantitative comparison with rule-based diagnostic inference. *Methods of Information in Medicine*.

Fox, J. (1986). Three arguments for extending the framework of probability. In *Proceedings of Workshop on AI and Decision Making, AAAI Los Angeles 1985*. Amsterdam: North-Holland.

Glymour, C. (1980). *Theory and Evidence*. Princeton: Princeton University Press.

Hacking, I. (1975). *The Emergence of Probability*. Cambridge: Cambridge University Press.

Newell, A., and Simon, H. A. (1972). *Human Problem Solving*. Englewood Cliffs, NJ: Prentice-Hall.

Tversky, A., and Kahneman, D. (1974). Judgement under uncertainty: Heuristics and biases. *Science*, **185**, 1124–31.

Part 3: Some cognitive models

Modelling Cognition
Edited by P. Morris
© 1987 John Wiley & Sons Ltd.

9

Recognition and recall in MINERVA 2: analysis of the 'recognition-failure' paradigm

DOUGLAS L. HINTZMAN
University of Oregon

MINERVA 2 is a model of human memory that is intended to account for data from both episodic and generic memory tasks using the same system (Hintzman, 1984). Specifically, the model was developed with the aim of explaining memory for specific experiences, as represented by recognition memory and memory for frequency (Hintzman, in preparation), and the acquisition of abstract concepts, as represented by 'schema abstraction' experiments (Hintzman, submitted). In the present study, the model was applied to the 'recognition failure' paradigm (e.g. Tulving and Wiseman, 1975)—a problem that was not considered when the assumptions of the model were first laid out.

There are at least two reasons for extending a simulation model to a task for which it was not originally designed: an obvious one is to provide further tests of the theoretical ideas the model represents. A less obvious reason is that a model that is applicable to a broad set of problems, as is MINERVA 2, can suggest the sorts of processes humans apply to the task and the kinds of variable that may affect their performance. That is, the model can help to provide an analysis of the task. The present article emphasizes both of these goals.

THE MODEL

MINERVA 2 is primarily concerned with long-term or secondary memory (SM), although it also assumes that there is a temporary store or primary memory (PM) that communicates with SM. MINERVA 2 is a multiple-trace model—that is, it assumes that each experienced event, even one that is identical with a previous event, is represented in memory by its own trace. Thus theoretically, SM is viewed as a vast collection of episodic memory traces. However, the effects of contextual features on retrieval are such that in simulating of performance on an experimental task, only traces formed during the experiment need be considered.

For mathematical simplicity, a specific event is represented in MINERVA 2 as a vector of feature loadings having the values: +1, 0 and −1. The array labeled 'probe' at the top of Figure 1 illustrates the representation of an event in the model. There are N features, $j = 1 \ldots N$, ordered from left to right, and every feature is assigned a value in each event. A value of 0 indicates that, for that particular event, the indicated feature is either irrelevant or unknown.

Encoding an event in memory consists of copying the event vector into SM (represented by the large box in Figure 1). Encoding may be imperfect; in the model each individual feature is stored with probability L (the learning rate). If a particular feature is not stored, the value entered into the trace is 0. Typical SM traces of several events are shown in Figure 1.

Retrieval is always produced by a retrieval cue, or 'probe'. A probe is assumed to activate all memory traces in parallel, and all traces are assumed to respond simultaneously, producing a single composite 'echo' that emanates back from SM. What makes this composite response different for each probe is that the contribution of each trace to the echo depends on its similarity to the probe.

The similarity of a given trace, i, to the probe is given by

$$S_i = \sum_{j=1}^{N} P_j T_{i,j} / N_R,$$

where P_j is the value of feature j in the probe, $T_{i,j}$ is the value of feature j in trace i, and N_R is the number of 'relevant' features (i.e. the number of js for which either $P_j \neq 0$ or $t_{i,j} \neq 0$). Here S_i behaves much like a Pearson r, being zero when the probe and trace i are orthogonal and +1 when they are identical. S_i can be negative, and although values approaching −1 are mathematically possible, they are extremely unlikely and have no particular theoretical meaning in the work presented here.

The degree to which a trace is activated is a positively accelerated function of its similarity to the probe. The simulations reported here used the activation function, $A_i = S_i^3$. The nonlinearity of this A_i function allows retrieval to be quite selective: in principle, all SM traces are activated by the probe, but the response of SM as a whole is dominated by those traces that most closely match the probe. (Note that the expression for A_i preserves the sign of S_i, so that a trace can have negative activation.) To illustrate S_i and A_i using the first

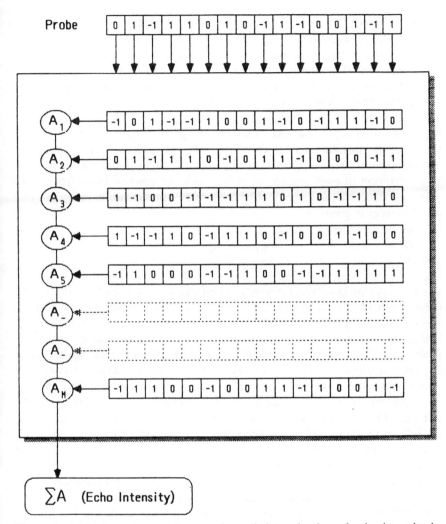

Figure 1. Activation of traces by a probe and determination of echo intensity in MINERVA 2.

two traces in Figure 1', $S_1 = -3/15 = -0.2000$ and $S_2 = 6/11 = 0.5454$; hence $A_1 = -0.0080$ and $A_2 = 0.1623$.

The simultaneous activation of all traces by a probe produces a single echo. The echo has two properties, *intensity* and *content*. The *intensity* of the echo is found by summing the activation levels of all traces:

$$I = \sum_{i=1}^{M} A_i,$$

The more traces there are in SM that match the probe, and the more closely they match it, the greater will be the echo intensity. If there are no SM traces similar to the probe, then the value of I should be near 0. Echo intensity serves as a kind of familiarity signal, and has been used in modelling frequency judgments and recognition memory (Hintzman, 1984, in preparation). Likewise in the present work, recognition memory is based upon echo intensity, I.

The *content* of the echo is the summed content of all SM traces, each weighted by its activation level. One can imagine a two-level network, with the set of M episodic traces at the higher level, passing activation downward through positive and negative links to the set of N features, at the lower level. The activation of each feature is the net result of positive input from some activated traces and negative input from others. The activation of feature j by all SM traces is given by

$$C_j = \sum_{i=1}^{M} A_i T_{i,j}.$$

C_j values can be positive or negative. Their profile across features represents the content of the information retrieved from SM. Determination of echo content is depicted schematically in Figure 2.

Because traces activated by a probe can contain information not in the probe itself, the system is capable of retrieving associated information. As an example of associative recall, assume that the stimulus term (or cue) of a paired associate is encoded in the left half of a trace ($j = 1 \ldots 8$) and the response term (or target) is encoded in the right half ($j = 9 \ldots 16$). If just the left half of the original pair is used as a probe, with $C_9 \ldots C_{16} = 0$, then both the left and right halves of the echo produced by that probe will contain C_j values that are nonzero. Typically, the C_j values for $j = 9 \ldots 16$ will resemble the response-term information in the original pair.

The resemblance between the original and retrieved information is less than perfect, however, since the echo is influenced not only by the strongly activated target trace, but also by other, weakly activated ones. This 'ambiguous-recall problem' can be handled in two ways:

1. A solution that is elegant but wasteful of computer time is to convert the echo into a secondary probe, retrieve the secondary echo and turn it into a probe, and so on for several cycles. Under most conditions, this eventually produces a virtually perfect copy of the target information.
2. A quicker solution is to have all the possible response terms stored somewhere outside SM, correlate the echo with each of them, and declare the one yielding the highest Pearson r to be the one that was retrieved. (Methods 1 and 2 usually, but not always, give the same result.)

The second method was adopted in the simulations reported here.

Probe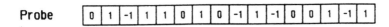

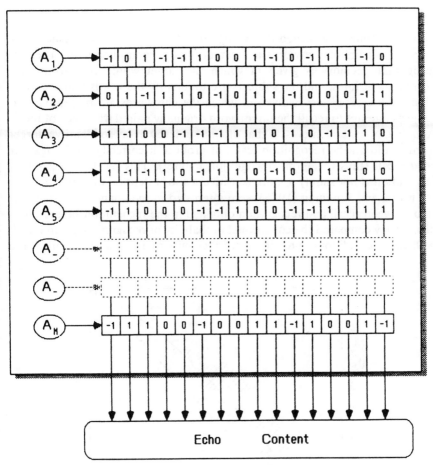

Figure 2. Determination of echo content by activated traces in MINERVA 2.

Simulation with MINERVA 2 uses what is essentially a 'Monte Carlo' procedure. For each simulated subject, event vectors are generated randomly, and the features that are encoded in memory (with probability L) are also determined randomly. Data are produced for a large number of 'subjects', and the data are then averaged as are data from experiments. The appropriateness of the model's behavior can be judged by comparing obtained functions with those reported in the experimental literature.

Since MINERVA 2 can be applied to both recognition (using echo intensity) and cued recall (using echo content), the decision to explore the relation between the two was a natural one.

THE TASK

In what is sometimes called the 'recognition-failure' paradigm, human subjects study pairs of cue words and target words. Some time later, a test of recognition memory is given in which the target words are mixed with distractors or lures, and the subjects are to identify the words that are 'old'. Later still, a recall test is given in which the cue words are presented, and subjects attempt to recall the target word originally paired with each of them. A finding of general interest is that often a subject will fail to identify a target word as old on the recognition test, but produce it correctly on the test for cued recall (thus the term, 'recognition failure'). This result suggests that recognition is not simply a more sensitive test of retention than recall.

Tulving and Wiseman (1975) were interested in the quantitative relationship between recall and recognition obtained in the recognition-failure paradigm. They compared the conditional probability of recognition, given recall, with the unconditional probability of recognition (i.e. that of recalled and

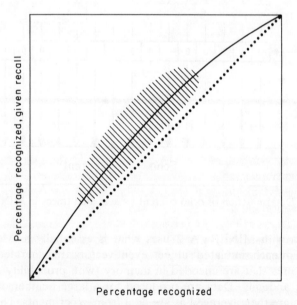

Figure 3. A schematic illustration of the relationship between recognition of recalled targets and recognition of all targets, as presented by Tulving and Wiseman, 1975.

nonrecalled targets combined). If there is a positive correlation between the two measures, then the conditional value should be greater than the unconditional one. Plotting the conditional against the unconditional values obtained in several experiments, Tulving and Wiseman (1975) obtained a scatter of points, most of which fell in in the shaded region of Figure 3—slightly above the diagonal line that would indicate equality (i.e. no correlation between recognition and recall). They fitted the data with a mathematical function shown by the curve in Figure 3. The function does not figure in the present theoretical treatment (but see Flexser and Tulving, 1978).

THE SIMULATIONS

To simulate performance of a single subject in the recognition-failure paradigm, MINERVA 2 was first given a list of cue–target pairs to store in SM. Each pair consisted of 20 randomly generated feature values of $+1$, 0 and -1, each occurring with a probability of 1/3. Ten of the 20 features were reserved for the cue and 10 for the target. Following learning, recall and recognition were tested as follows:

(a) The cue-half of one of the original pairs was used as a probe for cued recall.
(b) The target-half of the content of the resulting echo was correlated with each acceptable target. Recall was scored as correct if the original target yielded the highest r and incorrect otherwise.
(c) The correct original target was used as a recognition probe.
(d) The intensity of the resulting echo, I, was added to a distribution of I values for either recalled or nonrecalled targets, depending on the outcome of step (b).
(e) Steps (a) through (d) were repeated for each of the remaining pairs in the list.

Recognition performance can be determined from the I distributions accumulated by testing a large number of simulated subjects. Figure 4 illustrates how this is done, and how the analysis used here is related to signal detection theory and d'.

The four curves of Figure 4 are smoothed empirical frequency distributions of I values obtained with MINERVA 2. The *New* distribution was obtained by using randomly generated target vectors as probes. The R distribution was obtained by testing with correctly recalled targets, and the NR distribution by testing with targets that were not recalled. The *Old* distribution (representing all of the original targets) is the sum of the R and NR distributions.

As applied to recognition memory, signal detection theory concerns the discrimination between items from the *New* and *Old* distributions. It assumes that the subject sets up a criterion (C) on the intensity scale, and calls items

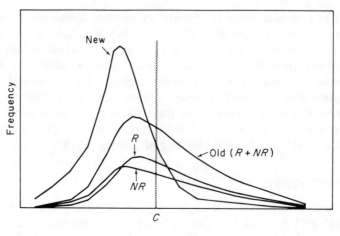

Figure 4. Smoothed echo intensity distributions for new, recalled (R), nonrecalled (NR), and recalled + non-recalled (old, R+NR) targets as generated by MINERVA 2; C is an arbitrary criterion.

giving $I < C$ 'old' and items giving $I > C$ 'new'. An ROC graph plots the percentage area to the right of C under the *Old* distribution (the hit rate) versus the percentage area to the right of C under the *New* distribution (the false alarm rate). An ROC curve can be swept out by plotting on the same graph the points determined by several different values of C. The inferred difference between the means of the two distributions, relative to the variability of the *New* distribution, is called d'.

In the present analyses, by contrast, the area to the right of C under the R distribution is plotted on the ordinate, and the area to the right of C under the *Old* distribution (of which the R distribution is part) is plotted on the abscissa. The *New* distribution plays no role in the recognition-failure analysis. The two measures are both hit rates, which, because they depend crucially on C, may be unrelated to d'. For a given simulation run, once the R and *Old* distributions have been determined, several pairs of hit rates can be obtained empirically, simply by choosing several arbitrary values of C. In most of the data to be reported, three or four representative points will be shown.

The first simulation run used a list length of 16 cue–target pairs, a learning rate of $L = 45$ percent, and 50 simulated subjects (800 observations per data point). The black triangles in panels A and B of Figure 5 show the recognition-failure results. The points fall virtually on the diagonal line that is predicted by the hypothesis that recognition and recall are stochastically independent. This result is surprising, because in MINERVA 2 recognition

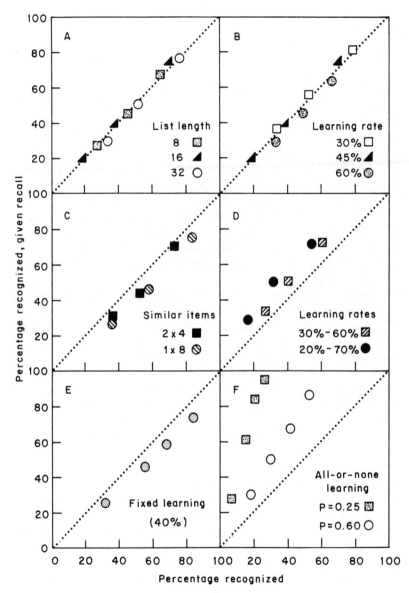

Figure 5. Data from several experiments with MINERVA 2 (for explanation, see text).

and recall are based on the memory trace, which strongly suggests that the points should fall somewhere above the diagonal line.

To learn whether the result was a fluke due to the list length or learning rate that had been used, four more simulations were done. First, the learning rate was held constant at 45 percent and the list length was set at 8 and 32; then the list length was held constant at 16 and the learning rate was set at 30 and 60 percent. Although both manipulations affected the rate of correct recall, neither had an appreciable effect on the apparent independence of recall and recognition (see panels A and B of Figure 5). Correct recall proportions for the conditions in panel A were: LL = 8, 0.54; LL = 16, 0.31; LL = 32, 0.16. Those for panel B were: L = 30 percent, 0.17; L = 45 percent, 0.31; L = 60 percent, 0.54.

Taken at face value, these results might be taken as showing that cued recall and recognition are 'independent' processes in MINERVA 2. Knowing how the model works, however, we can say that although recall and recognition are different tasks—and therefore necessarily involve some processes that are not the same—they are based on the same stored information. Thus, in this case, it would be difficult to know just what the theoretical meaning of 'independence' would be.

The question is worth looking into more deeply, because there is more than one way to generate data that are consistent with the hypothesis of stochastic independence. Because of Simpson's paradox, a positive correlation between recognition and recall induced by certain factors can be neutralized by a negative correlation induced by other factors (Hintzman, 1980). Put another way, there are two ways to obtain a zero or near-zero correlation between two measures. In one case, there are no other variables that are covariates of both measures (true independence). In the other case, there is at least one variable that is correlated in the same direction with both of the measures (inducing a positive correlation) and at least one that is correlated in opposite directions with both of them (inducing a negative correlation). The positive and negative correlations roughly cancel one another, yielding apparent independence.

Let us examine more closely the processes underlying recognition and cued recall in MINERVA 2. Recognition hit rate depends on echo intensity, which depends in part on the degree to which the target probe matches the ten target features in the memory trace. Since learning is probabilistic, the number of original features stored, and therefore available to match the probe, can vary (with L = 45 percent, counts between 3 and 7 will occur about 90 percent of the time). The more such features there are, the higher should be the echo intensity.

Cued recall is more complex. The more *cue* features were stored, the more strongly the cue probe can activate the memory trace, and the more *target* features were stored, the better the C_j values in the echo will match the original target vector. The latter determines the probability of correct recall.

Because both recognition and recall improve as a function of the number of target features stored, this variable should induce a positive correlation between the two measures. The number of cue features stored varies independently of the number of target features stored, so this value can dilute the overall correlation between recall and recognition, but cannot neutralize it. To summarize, the 'goodness of encoding' of target information in the trace should be positively correlated with both recall and recognition, and so other things being equal, the two measures should not be independent (cf. Flexser and Tulving, 1978).

Could there be some other factor, correlated in opposite directions with recall and recognition, that tends to cancel the goodness-of-encoding effect? A likely candidate is intralist similarity. Pair vectors are generated randomly in the model, so the degree to which a target item is similar to others will vary from pair to pair.

Consider the effect of target similarity on recognition memory. In particular, let us focus on the pair A–B. Suppose the list contains another pair, C–B', where B' is similar to B. What effect will B' have on the recognition hit rate for B? Presentation of B as a probe will produce strong activation in the A–B trace, and moderate activation in the C–B' trace. Echo intensity therefore will be greater than it would be if C–B' did not exist. Put differently, the generalization effect known as 'false recognition' should also exist for 'true recognition': similarity of an item to other targets in the list, regardless of whether the item is new or old, should increase the probability of identifying the item as 'old'. Unpublished experiments from my laboratory confirm this prediction of MINERVA 2.

Next consider cued recall. What effect will the existence of C–B' have on the recall of B to A? In the model, the existence of B as an acceptable response increases the likelihood of identifying the target segment of the echo as B' rather than B, and therefore of scoring recall as incorrect. Thus, the effect of intralist similarity should be to decrease the probability of correct cued recall. This prediction has been confirmed by several experiments investigating the effects of response-term similarity on the learning of paired associates (Hall, 1971, pp. 140–6).

To summarize, high intralist similarity should help recognition and hurt recall, while low similarity should hurt recognition and help recall. Thus variation in similarity should induce a negative correlation between recognition and recall. Thus the hypothesis is that the apparent independence shown in panels A and B of Figure 5 is an example of Simpson's paradox: the positive correlation between recall and recognition induced by variation in goodness of encoding was roughly balanced by the negative correlation induced by variation in similarity. (It is important to note that it is not similarity *per se* that produces this effect, but *variation* in similarity. A covariate must vary in order to have an observable effect.)

This hypothesis can be tested by doing experiments with the model. One experiment is to leave variation in goodness of encoding as it was originally, and increase the variation in similarity. If the hypothesis is right, this should increase the strength of the negative correlation, bringing performance below the diagonal line. Accordingly, another simulation was performed. Everything was done as before except that only 8 independent targets were stored (low similarity items). To generate the other 8 targets, two 10-feature target 'prototypes' were used, and 4 target vectors were generated from one prototype and 4 from the other by changing the signs of 2 of the 10 features chosen at random. This produced 2 sets of 4 high-similarity response terms. The data showed a slightly negative correlation, as shown by the points labeled '2 × 4' in panel C of Figure 5. To see whether this outcome could be improved upon, another simulation was run in which the 8 high-similarity targets were generated from a single prototype. These data are labeled '1 × 8' in panel C. As was anticipated, the two simulations show that increasing the variation in similarity among response terms, by increasing the similarities of half of them, produces a negative correlation between recognition and recall.

A second experimental test of the hypothesis is to leave variation in similarity as it was originally and increase variation in goodness of encoding beyond that produced by a single value of L. Two simulations were done. In one, the features in half the pairs in the list were learned with $L = 30$ percent and those in the other half with $L = 60$ percent. In the other, the two rates were $L = 20$ percent and $L = 70$ percent. Data from both simulation runs are shown in panel D of Figure 5. As expected, increases in variability in degree of learning beyond that originally allowed produced an overall positive correlation between recognition and recall.

A third experimental test of the hypothesis that the apparent independence shown in panels A and B resulted from balancing effects of variation in learning and variation in similarity is to leave variation in similarity as it was originally and eliminate all variation in degree of learning. This can be done by having the model store a fixed percentage of features in each trace, instead of applying the learning parameter independently to each feature. Accordingly, another simulation was done that was the same as the original except that exactly four features of every ten feature cue and target were stored. The data, shown in panel E of Figure 5, fall below the diagonal. Thus, when degree of learning is held strictly constant, random variation in similarity among target items induces a negative correlation between recognition and recall.

These experiments with the model demonstrate clearly that the apparent independence seen in panels A and B of Figure 5 reflects, not true independence of recognition and recall, but a balance of the effects of two factors. Variation in goodness of encoding induces a positive correlation between the two dependent variables, and variation in similarity induces a negative correlation. The mixture of the two effects was such that they roughly canceled each other out.

I have applied MINERVA 2 to another problem concerning the recognition-failure paradigm. It has been hypothesized that recognition failure of recallable words occurs because most words have more than one meaning. To test this hypothesis, Muter (1984) compared cued recall and recognition of the names of famous people. The surnames of half of the famous people were common (e.g. James Fenimore *Cooper*), and those of the other half were unique (e.g. Søren *Kierkegaard*), and presumably had only one meaning. As predicted, recognition failure was rare for unique names that could be recalled, but not for common names that could be recalled. Points for the common names fell just above the diagonal of the recognition-failure graph, and those for the unique names fell far above the diagonal.

The single-meaning interpretation of Muter's (1984) unique-name results may be correct, but there is another way to explain his findings. Muter does not say whether he matched the two sets of names for degree of fame, and it seems likely that many of his unique names were known by some of his subjects and not by others (e.g. Søren Kierkegaard, Ivan Turgenev, Arthur Rimbaud). Differences in subjects' knowledge in itself would be expected to produce a positive correlation between recall and recognition. To demonstrate these effects, two additional simulations were run with MINERVA 2. In these simulations, unlike the previous ones, learning was all or none—that is, a given trace was either encoded or not encoded in SM. The probability of storing a trace, P, was introduced as a new learning parameter, and the old parameter L (the percentage of features stored *given* that the item is encoded) was set at 100 percent. One simulation was done with $P = 0.60$ and one with $P = 0.25$. The results are shown in panel F of Figure 5. In both cases, the points are well above the diagonal. The curve for $P = 0.25$ roughly coincides with that obtained by Muter (1984), and the correct recall rates were similar as well: 24 percent for the model and 26 percent in Muter's study. (It might be noted that large deviations from the diagonal are harder to obtain with high than with low recall rates, as is apparent in panel F, because the data plotted on the ordinate are included in those plotted on the abscissa.)

A final point to make about recognition-failure data is that Flexser and Tulving (1978, Figure 2) found no relationship *across experiments* between performance on cued recall and recognition tests. This puzzling finding may reflect the use of the hit rate as the measure of recognition memory, instead of d' or some other measure that corrects for response bias. As is clear from Figure 4, hit rate can vary from near 0 percent (a high C) to near 100 percent (a low C) with no change in d'. By itself, therefore, hit rate is a very unreliable index of recognition memory.

CONCLUSIONS

What can be concluded from these simulations? First, they demonstrate clearly that what at first appeared to be a relationship of simple independence between two dependent variables (panels A and B of Figure 5), was really the reflection of a much more complex situation. The fact that Simpson's paradox can confound interpretation of the behavior of a model as simple as MINERVA 2 reinforces cautions that were made earlier about contingency analyses of memory retrieval (Hintzman, 1980). Stochastic independence (or dependence) in such analyses can be misleading.

Second, the simulations support the theoretical ideas underlying MINERVA 2. The model appears to provide a reasonable account of the relationship between recall and recognition as studied in the recognition-failure paradigm, even though it was developed with other experimental tasks in mind. The common failure to recognize recallable words is completely consistent with the model. The simulations suggest, moreover, that the recognition-failure phenomenon is multiply determined. In any particular experiment, the obtained correlation between recognition and recall will depend on a number of factors, including recall rate (which constrains distance from the diagonal), various factors that influence the variability in goodness of encoding (which tends to push the curve upward), and factors that can have opposite effects on recognition and cued recall (and therefore push the curve downward). Specifically, the simulations identify variation in intralist similarity as a variable that can have opposite effects on the two measures.

Does the model make any new predictions? The curve relating conditional recognition to unconditional recognition should be pushed upward by manipulations that increase variation in goodness of encoding (as Muter (1984) may have unintentionally done with his unique names), and downward by manipulations that increase variation in similarity. In principle, by minimizing variation in goodness of encoding and making similarity highly variable, one should be able to push the curve below the diagonal. However, memorability of items can vary considerably (Rubin, 1985), and there seems to be no way of bringing encoding processes under rigid experimental control. A further possible source of positive correlation, inherent in the recognition-failure paradigm itself, is transfer from the recognition test to the recall test. In practice, therefore, creating an overall negative correlation between recognition and recall through manipulation of similarity may not be possible.

ACKNOWLEDGEMENT

This research was supported by Grant No. BNS-8403258 from the National Science Foundation.

REFERENCES

Flexser, A. J., and Tulving, E. (1978). Retrieval independence in recognition and recall. *Psychological Review*, **85**, 153–71.

Hall, J. F. (1971). *Verbal Learning and Retention*. Philadelphia: J. B. Lippincott.

Hintzman, D. L. (1980). Simpson's paradox and the analysis of memory retrieval. *Psychological Review*, **87**, 398–410.

Hintzman, D. L. (1984). MINERVA 2: A simulation model of human memory. *Behavior Research Methods, Instruments and Computers*, **16**, 96–101.

Hintzman, D. L. (1986). 'Schema abstraction' in a multiple-trace memory model. *Psychological Review*, **93**, 411–428.

Hintzman, D. L. (1986). Judgments of frequency and recognition memory in a multiple-trace memory model. (Tech. Rep. No. 86-11). Eugene, Oregon: University of Oregon Cognitive Science Program.

Muter, P. (1984). Recognition and recall of words with a single meaning. *Journal of Experimental Psychology: Learning, Memory, and Cognition*, **10**, 198–202.

Rubin, D. C. (1985). Memorability as a measure of processing: A unit analysis of prose and list learning. *Journal of Experimental Psychology: General*, **114**, 213–38.

Tulving, E., and Wiseman, S. (1975). Relation between recognition and recognition failure of recallable words. *Bulletin of the Psychonomic Society*, **6**, 79–82.

Modelling Cognition
Edited by P. Morris
© 1987 John Wiley & Sons Ltd.

10

A model of memory organization for interacting goals

NOEL E. SHARKEY
Centre for Cognitive Science, University of Essex, UK

GORDON H. BOWER
Department of Psychology, Standford University, USA

When we hear that our old friend Harry spent yesterday evening rummaging through dustbin (garbage cans) we may be puzzled. He has always worked hard and earned good money. We may try to *explain* his actions by inventing hypothetical contexts. It is possible that Harry just split up with his wife, hit the bottle and became a down and out. However, when we hear that Harry has a new job as a private detective we fell more enlightened. One of the *goals* of a private detective is to find out information about people which is not readily available and one course of action is to search through their dustbin. Thus we are ready to believe that our friend's purpose for garbage rustling was to satisfy some goal which was derived from his role as a detective. This explanation also fits better with our knowledge of Harry's other goals.

This same puzzle also occurs in stories, plays and films where we, the reader or viewer, must often calculate the purpose of a character's actions by interpreting them in the light of some goal. Sometimes it works the other way round. We know the goals of some character and we can make predictions about what actions that character will make in order to satisfy their goals. For instance, if someone is hungry it is reasonable to infer that they have a goal of wanting to eat food soon. It also seems reasonable to predict that that person will probably either eat at home or go to a restaurant. In turn we may use such predicted plans to see the relationship between some action and a goal. The perception of this relationship, we believe, is crucial to 'understanding' the action. Take, for example, the sentence, 'Wilma picked up the yellow pages.'

In isolation from a context, we can probably get the idea that Wilma is a woman and that she lifted some yellow pages (probably the phone book). But we need more of a context in order to understand the utterance. This sentence might be the last in a story about a young girl whose driving ambition was to find the magic book before the evil sorcerer destroyed it with his potion. Of course the potion turned the pages yellow and blotted out the text. In this case the final line of the story is understood as a total frustration of Wilma's driving goal. Alternatively, if we read the sentence pair, 'Wilma was hungry. She picked up the yellow pages', we understand this by imagining *not* that Wilma was going to eat the guide but rather that she picked up the guide to read it which in turn was part of a plan to get information about the location of restaurants where she could go and eat to satisfy her hunger goal. Thus our understanding of 'picking up the yellow pages' is quite different in both of the cases described here. Their meaning varies according to our perception of the actor's goals.

Research on the goals and plans of actors has attracted considerable interest among the AI community (e.g. Fikes, Hart and Nilsson, 1972; Saceroti, 1974; Newell and Simon, 1972). Most of this research has been concentrated on the construction of plans for solving problems. However, Schank and Abelson (1977) were concerned with the way in which goals and plans were used for 'understanding'; particularly in cases where large amounts of world knowledge were necessary, useful and available. They proposed that, in order to make sense of a story, an AI system would need to assume that the behaviour of actors is goal directed. That is, it would need knowledge of human intentionality, of the types of goals people have and of the types of plans people devise in the service of these goals, to understand action sequences that are described in narratives or observed directly. According to Schank and Abelson (1977) and Wilensky (1983), text understanding involves finding the implicit connections between sentences. They call this process explanation-driven understanding. Since stories are about people, explanations usually take on an intentional flavour that can be stated in terms of plans and goals. In their systems, a particular element of behaviour is explained by its role in some hypothesized task network, and permissible classes of explanation mirror permissible structures in that network. For Wilensky, an action is explained by finding it to be an instantiation of a plan that its actor is pursuing; a plan is explained by finding a goal to which it is directed; and a goal is explained by finding the theme which gave rise to the goal, or a plan to which the goal is instrumental.

Wilensky (1983) presents an account of a Plan Applier Mechanism (PAM) which 'understands' simple plan-based episodes by applying knowledge about goals and actions and how they fit in with plans. PAM begins by using the first few lines about an actor in a text to set up expectations about the actor's plan or goal. If the goal is stated, then an action consistent with that goal is expected to follow in the next few lines of text. If no goal is stated PAM assumes that the statement suggests a plan, and a main goal associated with that plan is inferred. If actions or goals mentioned in a text are statements which match some inferred plan, that plan is taken to be the explanation for those actions.

THE GOAL INTEGRATION NETWORK (GIN) MODEL

One problem with AI models is that they tend to be expressed in a way which is *not* readily available to the test methodology of cognitive psychology (Sharkey and Pfeifer, 1984; Sharkey and Brown, 1986). Given that a know-ledge of goals may help in the understanding of other people's actions we want to know what *processes* are operating in the understanding task. One way to conduct research of this type is to translate the AI theory into a notational form which is more fitting for empirical psychological inquiry. Sharkey and Bower (1984) have discussed the relation between goals and plans in terms of a network structure in which a goal is represented as a proposition in memory and is linked to a number of plans that may satisfy it (see also Bower, 1982; Foss and Bower, 1986).

Our model is being developed as the Goal Integration Network (GIN) model. GIN uses a notation in which a set of representational elements are represented as nodes that are linked together to form a network. Processing resources are then allocated by means of a passive parallel spreading acti-vation mechanism. Thus whenever a concept node receives activation from some external source it broadcasts it to all of the neighbouring nodes to which it is linked. The extent to which a node is active reflects its degree of availability in memory. Consequently, if the concept node of a new input is related to the concept node of the previous input, the former concept node will be preactivated and thus any decision about it will be faster. Such models have already been used in a number of different domains such as letter recognition (e.g. McClelland and Rumelhart, 1981), word recognition (e.g. Sharkey and Mitchell, 1985), fact retrieval (e.g. Anderson, 1983), vision (e.g. Feldman and Ballard, 1982), concept learning (Rumelhart and Zipser, 1985), speech production (Dell, 1985), semantic nets (Shastri and Feldman, 1986), word-sense disambiguation (Cottrell and Small, 1983) and parsing (Waltz and Pollock 1985). The advantage of applying the same sort of mechanisms in so many different domains is that modelling tools can be developed and shared to establish a set of domain-independent unifying principles. In addition, converting AI systems into such a principled framework enables us to devise psychological processing predictions that can be tested on humans and can lead to principled refinements of the systems.

However, the prime motivation for developing a parallel process account of goal/plan interaction was so that GIN could be linked with models of knowledge access and application being developed by Sharkey (e.g. the subnode competition model: Sharkey and Mitchell, 1985; the Knowledge Access Network (KAN): Sharkey, 1986a, 1986b; Sharkey and Sharkey, 1986; and the Binary and Continuous Activation System (BACAS): Sharkey, Sutcliffe and Wobcke, 1986). In essence, these models behave as if they had scripts (Schank and Abelson, 1977) as data structures. However, both KAN and BACAS are connection machines. Each has two processing layers: a micro-layer, consisting of many processing elements which represent the system's conceptual knowledge; and a macro-layer consisting of a number of Threshold Knowledge Units (TKUs) which tie bundles of micro-elements together to form patterns corresponding to 'canned' plans. In brief, activation from the external input accumulates on elements in the micro-layer and these broadcast it to the TKUs in the macro-layer. When a TKU reaches a preset threshold, it then feeds the activation back into the micro-layer and activates a pattern of elements relevant to the current input. Thus the models are essentially distributed content addressable memory schemes.

Although both KAN and BACAS use their architecture and processing mechanisms to complete patterns of relevant information, it is solely the bottom-up or external stimulation which determines which knowledge structure or plan the system will settle on. There is no way in either system for internal activation to help 'preselect' likely patterns. In other words, neither system uses knowledge of human intentionality to set up expectations about the likely future actions of known actors. We hope to use GIN to remedy this weakness. However, GIN is still at an early stage of development. The experiments reported here are a first step to give us a broad definition of the model.

Our strategy is first to test the plausibility of the idea that goals and plans are stored in memory as an associative structure. That is, a structure in which the relationship between a goal and the various means of fulfilling that goal (e.g. through plans and actions) is represented as an associative network in memory. To illustrate the point with a simple example, a goal such as seeking a girlfriend will be represented as a single node in the network. This node will have links to associated general plan nodes (e.g. CONSULT PROFES-SIONAL) and these, in turn, to more specific action nodes (e.g. use dating service).

Our starting assumption is that whenever a goal is retrieved from memory the plans associated with fulfilling that goal become more available to other memory processes. This happens because activation spreads from the goal node to its related plan nodes and thence throughout the network to associated actions. These actions should then be ready to be used by a decision process.

We began examining the feasibility of our model by utilizing a well-known empirical property of spreading activation network models, the *fan effect*

(Anderson and Bower, 1973). The notion underlying the fan effect is that the more propositions that are linked to a source node the less activation each proposition will receive from that source (cf. Anderson, 1983). The effect is that the more propositions that are activated from a single source (the greater the fan) the slower will be any decision relating to those propositions. This notion leads to the prediction that the more goals a person is holding active in memory, the slower will be the decision about any action related to those goals.

In more detail, this prediction follows from two processing assumptions. First, activation will be divided approximately equally among the K active goals for a given character; thus a character node with activation A will send activation A/K down each goal link. Second, it is assumed that the time required to check whether a stated action instantiates a candidate action node is shorter the greater the activation on that node. A simplified portion of this model is illustrated in Figure 1.

In Figure 1(b) the character has three goals—so the amount of activation at each of these nodes will be approximately one-third of that in (a), the one-character case. Beneath the goal nodes are common associated plan nodes. There are two plan nodes shown here although obviously different subjects know differing numbers of familiar plans for each goal. But to simplify a large unknown here, we will assume that each goal has a certain average number of known plans associated with it—we have indicated this in Figure 1 by drawing two plans under each goal—but this is just some arbitrary number. The point is that activation divides out again at the plan nodes, but there will still be about one-third of the activation at the plan nodes in (b) than there will be at the plan nodes in (a). The simplest way to view this is that the amount of activation arriving at a plan node is A/P, where A is the total amount of activation available to the memory structure and P is the number

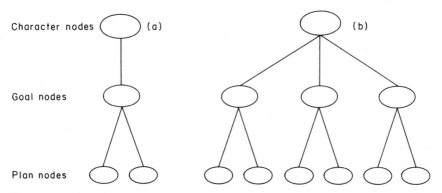

Figure 1. A simplified network structure for (a) an experimental trial where one goal is presented, and (b) one in which three goals are presented.

of plans to be retained in memory. (This is an extremely simple view of the activation mechanism (see Sharkey and Sharkey, 1986), but it suffices for the present level of description.)

It is assumed that the memory decision time is inversely proportional to the amount of activation on an action node. That is, the more activation that arrives at the critical node, the quicker the subject will be able to make a decision and respond. The following equation (derived from Anderson, 1983) captures this portion of the model:

$$RT = k + \frac{1}{p\left(\dfrac{A}{bn}\right)} \tag{1}$$

where RT is the total response time, k is some constant time to read the stimulus and output a response, p is the activation from the probe, A is the total shared activation in the memory set, b is the number of goal branches and n is the number of plans connected to the goals.

Experiment 1

The research reported here is part of a project involving a number of experiments on how readers organize several goals in memory at the same time, and use this goal structure to understand actions in the narrative. For example, as people read a story they might extract and focus on the goals— and even invest them with special processing status. They may then retrieve them when they are needed to explain some action. Furthermore, readers are often required to keep track of several goals of several characters, all at the same time. The tasks we used to test these ideas, in the four experiments described in this chapter, were very similar and so we shall give a general description before going on to the experiments.

The goal/action decision task

Briefly, subjects sat facing a computer screen on which text was to be presented. They were instructed to read and understand goal sentences which would appear one at a time in the centre of the computer screen. Each of these sentences was of the form 'x wanted y', e.g. 'John wanted to learn Spanish.' Each goal stayed on the screen for 3–5 seconds (depending on the experiment) and was followed by a blank 1-second pause before the next presentation. On a given trial subjects would see either one, three or five goals. At the end of a trial there was an audible bleep from the computer and the words 'And so' appeared on the screen for 1 second. This was a prompt for an action sentence of the form 'And so x did z', e.g. 'And so John went to

Spain.' The subject's task was to decide as quickly as possible whether that action satisfied one of the goals they had read in the preceding set. This decision was timed by the computer and used as the dependent measure. After a practice session, each subject saw a large number of such trials half of which were 'yes' responses and half of which were 'no'.

We assume that people have lots of information about cultural plans for achieving common goals and they retrieve and use this information to make their decision. We shall not try to characterize this process here, instead we will simply assume that single-action, single-goal decisions occur at a more or less constant rate when we average across the diverse collection of goals and actions we used in our experiments. Our initial experiment was undertaken to see whether we would get orderly effects as we varied the number of independent goals ascribed to the single character in the narrative vignette. Thus, we presented subjects with sets of one, three or five goals (using the procedure described above), and asked them to decide as quickly as possible whether a probe action that came immediately afterwards satisfied any one of them. An example of the stimulus materials is shown in Example 1.

EXAMPLE 1

GOAL1:   Heather wanted to: overcome her shyness.

GOAL2:   Heather wanted to: live very extravagantly.

GOAL3:   Heather wanted to: have some time on her own.

ACTION: And so Heather took classes in social skills.

Example 1 illustrates three independent goals and a 'True' action that satisfies goal 1.

The mean decision times collected in Experiment 1 are shown in Figure 2.

Notice how the decision times increase with the number of goals. The one-goal condition gave shorter decision times than the three-goal condition which gave shorter times than the five-goal condition. In addition, we fitted equation (1) to the data in Figure 2 and found an almost perfect fit. This is illustrated in Figure 3. However, since three parameters were estimated to fit each curve, the closeness of the fit is not important. What is important is that the theory predicts a curve which is the same general shape as the data. There is thus a clear relationship between our results and the basic fan effect (Anderson and Bower, 1973). None the less, there is a clear distinction between the tasks used. In the Anderson and Bower studies, the positive probes were identical matches with the memory set items; but in our study, the probes *do not* directly match any of the items in the goal memory set. Rather they are related as a plan of action to satisfy one of the goals. This means that our subjects cannot find a direct match between the probe and any

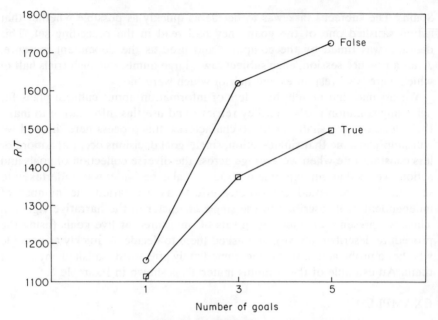

Figure 2. Mean *RT* in milliseconds for Experiment 1.

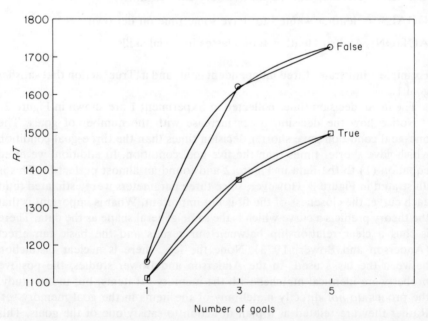

Figure 3. Fit of the model to the mean *RT* in milliseconds for Experiment 1.

item in their memory set. Instead they must retrieve the plans associated with the goals in their memory set and then match these against the probe action. In a sense, subjects must discover and report whether or not there is a fairly direct connection between a goal in the memory set and the action in the memory probe.

Experiment 2

Once we had demonstrated the basic fan effect for goals, we wanted to investigate how decisions are made from goal sets in which the goals were related to one another. According to Wilensky (1983) goals may be related in several ways. For example, the goals may conflict with one another, be independent or help one another. We have investigated some of these. The work that we shall concentrate on in this chapter concerns how goals may be related to each other through a helping relation, via a common plan or action. For example, suppose we wanted to buy a comb, some aspirin and some orange juice. Rather than leave the house on three separate occasions we would formulate a plan to buy all of the items at the same shop. Wilensky called this type of positive goal relationship 'goal-overlap'.

In Experiment 2 we compared decisions for sets of three overlapping goals (goals which share a common plan), with sets containing three independent goals and sets containing a single goal as in the preceding experiment. One set of goal-overlap materials is illustrated in example 2.

EXAMPLE 2

GOAL1:   Brian wanted: to be of service to the community.

GOAL2:   Brian wanted: to drive a big shiny truck.

GOAL3:   Brian wanted: to wear a uniform.

ACTION: And so Brian decided to become a fireman.

Example 2 illustrates three goals that overlap on the 'true' action of becoming a fireman. For the one-goal condition, one of the goals was selected to go along with the action. For the three-independent-goal condition one goal was again selected from the appropriate set plus two goals from other sets.

As before, we expected the three-independent-goal condition to take a longer time to verify than the one-goal condition. But what do we expect for the goal-overlap condition? One possibility is that the slower decision times observed earlier with larger memory sets reflect merely the size of the memory load. If this is the case, then in Experiment 2 we would expect the decision time for three overlapping goals to be slower than the decision time for a single goal since the subject must hold in memory the three overlapping goals, the same as with three independent goals. Another possibility is that the three overlapping goals will lead to true decisions that are as fast as the one-goal condition. Our reasoning for this hypothesis was that in the goal-overlap condition the total activation divides equally among the three goals (see Figure 4). However, for overlapping goals the activation from the three goals reconverges on a common action node. This reconvergence causes the overlapping plan to have approximately the same amount of activation as it would in the presence of a single goal. This can be seen from our modification of equation (1) shown in equation (2)

$$RT = k + \frac{1}{p\left(\dfrac{A}{bn}\right)} \qquad (2)$$

From this reasoning we expected no response time difference between the one-goal and the goal-overlap conditions but both conditions should produce faster responses than the three-independent-goal condition. The mean reading times for this experiment are shown in Figure 5.

The results accorded with our predictions. When the goals shared a common plan the fan effect was completely wiped out. Clearly, the goal-overlap case is as fast as the one-goal case but not faster. Three-independent-goals, on the other hand, produced significantly slower decision times than the other two conditions combined. Thus, something like the reconvergence of split activation is a plausible account of our data.

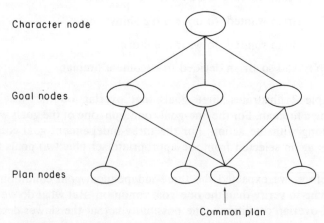

Figure 4. One character node is illustrated with connections to three goals. These goals are shown with links to a common plan.

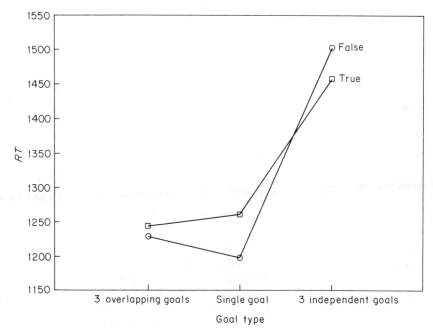

Figure 5. Mean *RT* in milliseconds for Experiment 2.

Experiment 3

One aspect of the results from Experiment 2 that puzzled us was the data for the false responses. Our subjects' decisions that an action *did not* satisfy any one of three overlapping goals were as fast as their decisions that it did not satisfy one simple goal. This is strange. There seems little reason to propose, a priori, how this could happen. In terms of the activation model, we felt that the speed of rejecting a probe action in the goal-overlap condition may have reflected a subject strategy rather than some automatic property of the network model. For example, subjects may have been responding on the basis of the most active plan node. In our model, this would be the common plan node, and if the probe did not match, they would indicate 'False'. In Experiment 2, such a strategy would have produced correct responses nearly all of the time in the goal-overlap condition. To test this analysis, in Experiment 3 we again presented sets of overlapping goals. But we made things considerably more difficult for subjects this time. On 33 per cent of the True trials the action probe related to only one of three overlapping goals and on 33 per cent it related to all three of the overlapping goals. On the final 33 per cent, the true action was related to one independent goal. A sample of the materials and conditions is illustrated in Example 3.

EXAMPLE 3

GOAL1: Ellen wanted: to do something intellectually challenging.

GOAL2: Ellen wanted: to have an interesting profession.

GOAL3: Ellen wanted: to help the sick and the elderly.

ACTION-TYPE1: And so Ellen played chess with some friends. (1/3 related)

ACTION-TYPE2: And so Ellen trained to become a doctor. (3/3 related)

Example 3 illustrates a set of three overlapping goals along with two alternative actions. ACTION-TYPE1 satisfies only one of the goals (GOAL1), whereas ACTION-TYPE2 is a common plan for all three. The one-goal condition chosen from this set would be GOAL1.

For this experiment, we predicted that 'False' decisions for the three overlapping goals should be materially slower than the same decisions for in the one-goal condition because subjects could no longer rely on the strategy of only checking the common plan for the three overlapping goals. This is because, as previously mentioned, on 50 per cent of the true overlapping goal trials the action would not be part of the common plan. It would only satisfy

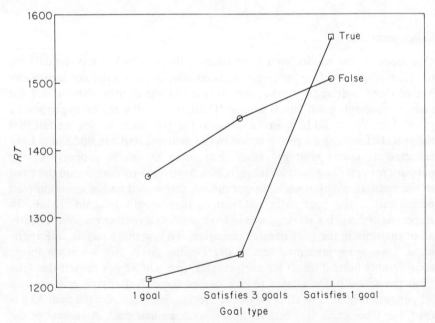

Figure 6. Mean *RT* in milliseconds for Experiment 3.

one of the goals. Thus the subject should have to check all the goals thoroughly before deciding that a probe is false. The decision means are shown in Figure 6.

The results came out more or less as we predicted. The condition in which only one goal from a three-goal set was satisfied (ACTION-TYPE1) was very slow (approximately equal to the three-independent-goals in the previous experiment). The probe representing a common plan (ACTION-TYPE2), as before, was as fast as the one-goal condition, and, as we had expected, the decision times on the False trials were greatly increased by the presence of the overlapping True condition where only one goal was satisfied. This suggests, as predicted, that subjects in Experiment 2 were using a strategy of checking the probe against the most active plan node and deciding false if it did not match.

Experiment 4

Of course it is a rare story that has only a single character. Rather, the reader typically has to keep track of several characters and monitor several goals for each of them. In experiment 4, we tried to create a task similar to that which story-readers have when they monitor the goals of two characters at the same time. On every trial we introduced two new characters, and assigned goals to them. To simplify the study, we used the sets of three overlapping goals from the previous experiment, except that now we assigned one goal to character no. 1 and two goals to character no. 2. Some of the materials are illustrated in Example 4.

EXAMPLE 4

GOAL 1: Margaret wanted to improve her diet.

GOAL 2: Lucy wanted to cut down her cholesterol intake.

GOAL 3: Lucy wanted to bring an end to killing animals.

Common Action: And so Margaret decided to eat vegetarian food.

Common Action: And so Lucy decided to eat vegetarian food.

Distinctive Action (D1): And so Margaret decided to eat less salt.

Distinctive Action (D2): And so Lucy gave money for wildlife conservation.

Crossover False: And so Lucy decided to eat less salt.

Crossover False: And so Margaret gave money for wildlife conservation.

Remote False: And so Margaret bought hersent a nice postcard.

Remote False: And so Lucy bought herself a nice postcard.

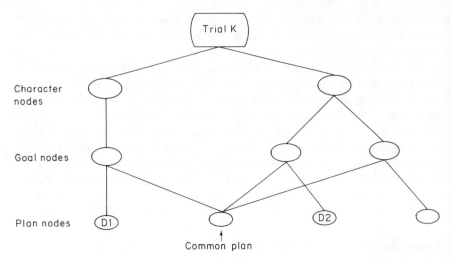

Figure 7. The theoretical associative structure for a goal set in Experiment 4. See text for explanation.

Figure 7 illustrates the theoretical associative structure on which we based our predictions.

The GIN model predicts that subjects should be fast to agree that a distinctive action D1 satisfies Character no. 1's single goal. They should also be fast to verify that character no. 1 can satisfy a goal by performing the common action. Furthermore, because of the convergence of activation, the subject should rapidly verify that character no. 2 can satisfy a single goal by performing the common action. However, subjects should be much slower to verify that distinctive action D2 satisfies one of the goals of character no. 2, because compared to action D1, D2 suffers from a two-to-one fan effect.

The results for the decisions on the True trials are shown in Figure 8.

We expected the lower three means (Figure 8) to be the same, and indeed they do not differ significantly from one another. But we expected and found all three of these means to be much smaller than the mean for the time to verify the distinctive action for the two-goal character.

Another interesting result came from considering the False decisions. Returning now to the theoretical diagram, we made up two kinds of False conjectures (Figure 7). One type contained actions that were simply unrelated to any goal stated for that trial. We called these Remote Falses, which the subject should reject quickly. The second type of False item described a character performing an inappropriate action that was irrelevant to the goals of the character, but one that would have been appropriate for the goals of the other character presented on that trial. We called these Crossover Falses; we tested both kinds of Crossovers, where character no. 1 performed distinctive

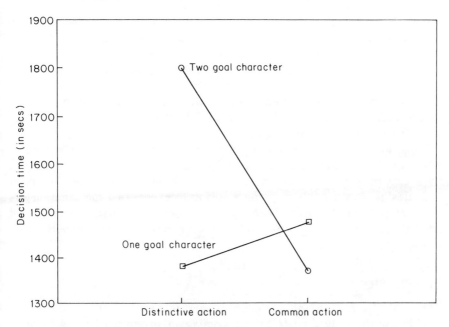

Figure 8. Mean decision times for True decisions in Experiment 4.

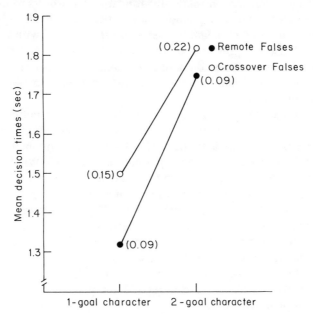

Figure 9. The mean false decision times for Experiment 4. The error proportions are shown in parenthesis.

action D2, or where character no. 2 performed distinctive action D1. The Crossover Falses of either type should be much slower than the Remote Falses, because activation from the top trial-node spreads to and retrieves the probed plan; and this forces the subject to check whether that plan fits a goal assigned to the probed actor. In the memory-search literature, this verification check of 'spurious intersections' is well known to slow down the times to reject related Falses. The plausibility of this analysis is upheld by the results for Falses, which are shown Figure 9.

Thus, we may conclude that our model of plan verification is plausible; it has suggested several experiments, and its predictions have been upheld in those experiments. Although we have conducted these experiments with brief vignettes as materials, there is some reason to expect that the same factors that retard comprehension here will generalize to larger segments of naturalistic narratives. However, that is a conjecture that awaits experimental testing.

CONCLUSIONS

The results from our four experiments suggest that we can think of the reader tracking a character's goals as the *keeping in memory* of an associative structure surrounding that character, to which the character's actions will be related. Furthermore, we can relate this fundamental process of understanding an action to the familiar phenomenon called the fan effect, which, for independent goals, shows a familiar set-size effect. Thus, with slight modifications, models that apply to the fan-effect experiments will also apply to our experiments and with predictions that seem to work out correctly. This means that our model can be extended with reference to the psychology literature on memory.

However, our model goes beyond the simple notion of fan effects. We have demonstrated, in the last three of our experiments, how fan effects can be disrupted by presenting goals to the subjects which they automatically organize in a way predetermined by the experimental materials. What is more, we were able to predict in advance, from our model, the time relationship of the decisions. Our explanation of these effects entails the assumption that people have *prewired* structures in memory corresponding to goals and plans. When we present our experimental materials, subjects bind the character variable to the appropriate goal proposition in their network. The structure is then kept active until needed to understand an action.

We have illustrated the ways in which we think that the network is wired. GIN allocates special architecture to related goals such as those that overlap on a common plan. This notion ties in with the research in AI (e.g. Schank and Abelson, 1977; Wilensky, 1983). However, it is presented here with a more principled processing mechanism. Clearly, a considerable amount of experimentation still remains to be carried out on goal relationships in memory. We have made a start on this with a number of studies on conflicting goals which we hope to report in the near future.

More importantly, we have now begun to conduct experiments to investigate whether or not canned plans are informationally encapsulated with respect to goals. That is, do different goals link to individual elements of a plan or does a goal link involve activation of *complete* plans? As we said earlier, we wish to build the GIN model on top of the KAN or BACAS models. The current experiments tell us that this is possible, but the *encapsulation* experiments will tell us how to do it.

REFERENCES

Anderson, J. R. (1983). *The Architecture of Cognition*. Cambridge, Mass.: Harvard University Press.

Anderson, J. R., and Bower, G. H. (1973). *Human Associative Memory*. Washington, DC: Holt, Rinehart and Winston.

Bower, G. H. (1982). Plans and goals in understanding episodes. In A. Flammer and W. Kintsch (eds) *Discourse Processing*. New York: North-Holland.

Cottrell, G. W., and Small, S. L. (1983). A connectionist scheme for modelling word sense disambiguation. *Cognition and Brain Theory*, 6, 89–120.

Dell, G. S. (1985). Positive feedback in hierarchical connectionist models: Applications to language production. *Cognitive Science*, 9, 3–23.

Feldman, J. A., and Ballard, D. H. (1982). Connectionist models and their properties. *Cognitive Science*, 6, 205–54.

Fikes, R. E., Hart, R. E. and Nilsson, N. J. (1972). Learning and executing generalized robot plans. *Artificial Intelligence*, 3, 251–88.

Foss, C. L., and Bower, G. H. (1986). Understanding actions in relation to goals. In N. E. Sharkey (ed.) *Advances in Cognitive Science*, Vol. 1. Chichester: Ellis Horwood.

McClelland, J. L., and Rumelhart, D. E. (1981). An interactive model of context effects in letter perception: Part I. An account of basic findings. *Psychological Review*, 88, 375–407.

Newell, A., and Simon, H. A. (1972). *Human Problem Solving*. Englewood Cliffs: Prentice Hall.

Rumelhart, D. E., and Zipser, (1985). Feature discovery by competitive learning. *Cognitive Science*, 9, 75–112.

Saceroti, E. D. (1974). Planning in a hierarchy of abstraction spaces. *Artificial Intelligence*, 5, 115–35.

Schank, R. C., & Abelson, R. P. (1977). *Scripts, Plan, Goals and Understanding*. New Jersey: Lawrence Erlbaum.

Sharkey, N. E. (1986a). A model of knowledge-based expectations in text comprehension. In J. Galambos, J. Black and R. P. Abelson (eds). *Knowledge Structures*. Hillsdale, NJ: Lawrence Erlbaum.

Sharkey, N. E. (1986b). Language understanding by parallel pattern completion. In *Proceedings of the European Joint Conference on Artificial Intelligence*, Brighton.

Sharkey, N. E., and Bower, G. H. (1984). The integration of goals and actions in text understanding. *Proceedings of the Cognitive Science Society*, 6.

Sharkey, N. E., and Brown, G. D. A. (1986). Why artificial intelligence needs an empirical foundation. In M. Yazdani (ed.) *Artificial Intelligence: Principles and Applications*. Chichester: Ellis Horwood.

Sharkey, N. E., and Mitchell, D. C. (1985). Word recognition in a functional context: The Use of scripts in reading. *Journal of Memory and Language*, **24**, 253–70.

Sharkey, N. E., and Pfeifer, R. (1984). Uncomfortable bedfellows: Cognitive psychology and artificial intelligence. In M. Yazdani and A. Narayanan (eds) *The Implications of Artificial Intelligence*. Chichester: Ellis Horwood.

Sharkey, N. E., and Sharkey, A. J. C. (1986). KAN: A knowledge access network model. In R. Reilly (ed.) *Communication Failure in Dialogue*. Elsevier: North-Holland.

Sharkey, N. E., Sutcliffe, R. F. E. and Wobcke, W. (1986). Mixing binary and continuous connection schemes for knowledge access. *Proceedings of AAAI Conference*, Philadelphia.

Shastri, L., and Feldman, J. A. (1986). Neural nets, routines, and semantic networks. In N. E. Sharkey (ed.) *Advances in Cognitive Science*, Vol. 1. Chichester: Ellis Horwood.

Waltz, D. and Pollock, J. B. (1985). Massively parallel parsing: A strongly interactive model of natural language interpretation. *Cognitive Science*, **9**, 51–7.

Wilensky, R. (1983). *Planning and Understanding: A Computational Approach to Human Reasoning*. Mass.: Addison-Wesley.

Modelling Cognition
Edited by P. Morris
© 1987 John Wiley & Sons Ltd.

11

Why to speak, what to say and how to say it: modelling language production in discourse

GEORGE HOUGHTON and STEPHEN ISARD
*Laboratory of Experimental Psychology, School of Biological Sciences,
University of Sussex, Falmer, Brighton BN1 9QG*

1. INTRODUCTION

This chapter describes a computational model of the processes of language production in a two-person dialogue. (A more complete account appears in Houghton, 1986.) The model involves two actors in a simple world, who produce dialogue in the course of attempting to achieve simple practical goals within that world. The world (an elaboration of that used in Power, 1974) consists of two spaces, IN and OUT, separated by four DOORS of different colours. These doors may be OPEN or CLOSED and in addition each door has a BOLT which may be UP or DOWN. The world also contains a number of BLOCKS of different sizes, shapes and colours which can be picked up and carried around. The goals that the actors attempt to achieve involve changing the positions of objects in the world (including themselves). In the course of building and executing plans to achieve these goals the actors may find that they need each other's help. As in Power's program, it is at these points that conversation arises between them. The important differences between this model and Power's grow out of the fact that this model generates its own utterances (section 3), where Power's printed out prestored strings. In making explicit the sort of information needed to construct utterances, we were also led to establish more principled relationships between the basic planning mechanism and the management of dialogues, somewhat along the lines suggested in Power (1979), and between the syntactic form of an utterance and its conversational role (cf. section 2).

Here is an example of a dialogue produced by the program. The situation before the dialogue begins is that Fred is out and Doris is in and Fred has the goal of getting in. Fred believes, mistakenly, that one of the doors is unbolted. He knows how to get doors to move but is unfortunately unable to perform the necessary action. He does not know how to get bolts to change their position. (Such handicaps, as well as the initial positions and goals, are specified by the user of the program at the beginning of each run.) The utterances of the actors have been transcribed into conventional English spelling. The model actually spells its words phonetically to facilitate input into a speech synthesizer.

Fred—Doris.
Doris—Yes.
Fred—I want to be in.
Doris—I see.
Fred—Could you push the yellow door?
Doris—No, because the bolt isn't up.
Fred—Is there a bolt that is up?
Doris—No.
Fred—How do you get a bolt to move?
Doris—You get to be in, then you slide it.
Fred—Could you slide the green bolt?
Doris—OK.
Fred—Push the door.
Doris—OK.
(At this point, with the door open, Fred moves through it and his goal is achieved.)

An outline of the model

There are a number of issues which any reasonably comprehensive model of human discourse production must address. These issues can be grouped around the following sorts of questions:

1. *Why do we speak at all?* That is, what role does language play in the context of global non-linguistic behaviour? In what way is it adaptive or advantageous to be able to communicate?
2. *How do we know what kind of message is appropriate to our needs?* How do we choose an utterance type suitable to the current state of the conversation? How are utterance types related to our purposes for speaking in the first place?
3. *How do we encode our communicative intentions?* What are the formal resources provided by a language and how are the various communicative demands of the language user mapped on to these formal options?

As we move from questions of type 1 to type 3 we move from the general domain of purposeful human behaviour down to the specifically linguistic domain. The model is organized to reflect this hierarchy in the organization of behaviour.

At level 1, the actors have a general planning capability which includes conversation in their repertoire of ways of getting things done. At this level 'asking Fred' has the same sort of status as 'going and looking' or 'giving a push' as possible tactics for finding out whether a door is unlocked.

At level 2 there is a knowledge of how 'dialogue games' work. If you are going to start an exchange for the purpose of getting some information, you often (but not always) start with a question. You then expect a response which in some way bears on your question, although it may not actually be a direct answer.

Finally, at level 3, comes the construction of individual utterances. A particular intended message must be converted into a syntactically well-formed utterance which conveys that message in the current conversational context.

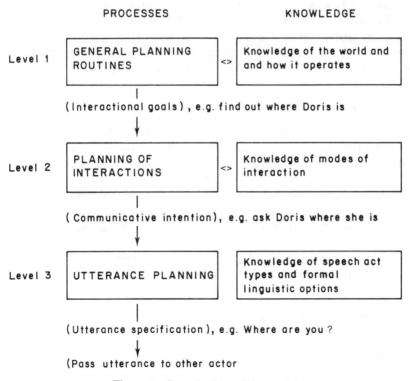

Figure 1. Organization of the model.

The overall organization of the model is diagrammed in Figure 1. In the boxes on the left (under the heading 'PROCESSES') are the types of planning activity involved at each level. In the boxes on the right are the kinds of knowledge to which the associated processes have access. Between the process modules there are labels indicating the kind of information which is passed from one level to the next.

The planning component of the model uses a standard depth-first, backward-chaining algorithm and has no claim to interest or originality in its own right. It was developed in order to provide a setting for the components at the other two levels, whose description occupies the remainder of the chapter.

2. THE ORGANIZATION OF DISCOURSE

This section discusses level 2 of the model as shown in Figure 1. Activity at this level takes place in the context of interactional goals which have been formulated at the level above—for example, to get someone to open a door for you. The work done here is to determine appropriate sorts of communication for initiating and carrying on a conversation intended to achieve a given goal. For instance, 'address a request to Fred' might be a good way to start. The actual formulation of the request takes place at the next level down and is covered in section 3. Before describing how the model works, we first discuss the motivation for including this particular level of organization.

Turn-taking

The fields of ethnomethodology and discourse analysis (cf. e.g. Sacks, Schegloff and Jefferson, 1974; Goffman, 1981; Stubbs, 1983) have devoted considerable attention to the structure of dialogues. In particular, they have coined terms such as 'adjacency-pair' (Sacks, Schegloff and Jefferson, 1974), 'exchange structure' (Stubbs, 1983) or 'game' (Power, 1974) for sequences of utterances such as a question and its answer or a greeting and its acknowledgement, which cohere as larger units. The exchange seems to be the appropriate level at which to locate at least part of the significance, as opposed to literal meaning, of an utterance in context.

Consider the following two brief exchanges:

Example 1
S1. Hey mac, how come all the bars're shut?
S2. It's three fifteen.

Example 2
S1. It's three fifteen, Dave.
S2. Thanks.

The two examples display the same individual act of telling the time serving different roles. Offering it in reply to S1's question in Example 1, S2 not only supplies information, but also signals his understanding of the situation and his agreement to take part. If S1 then accepts the reply as answering his question, the goal of the exchange is achieved and the episode is successfully ended.

In Example 2, the same utterance opens an interaction. Closing in this case requires some signal of acceptance or rejection of the information.

Component parts of an exchange need not be contiguous, for example:

Example 3
S1. Where does Kate keep her tool box?
S2. Why d'you ask?
S1. I've got a puncture and need to get my back wheel off.
S2. I see. She keeps it under the stairs there.

In Example 3, S2 asks a clarificatory question before answering the question which initiated the dialogue. The last contribution of S2 contains two sentences. The first closes off the embedded exchange, and the second answers the question asked by S1.

The general form of these exchanges may be illustrated as follows:

INITIATOR: OPENING EXPRESSION
      (Defines type and purpose of the interaction)
ADDRESSEE: RESPONSE
      (Requires recognition of type of interaction and
      formulation of appropriate response)
INITIATOR: POSSIBLE CLOSING EXPRESSION
      (The initiator monitors for 'uptake' of the
      interaction by the addressee, and assesses any
      response made against the goal of the inter-
      action. May utter a closing expression (e.g. 'Thank
      you') on the successful completion or abandon-
      ment of the intial goal)

The task of the ADDRESSEE in this scheme is to recognize the kind of interaction which the INITIATOR wishes to establish. The particular nature of the interaction undertaken is defined by the speaker's immediate and *intentionally apparent* goal in initiating the interaction. The addressee, having interpreted the initiator's intention, is obliged, on pain of being rude or uncooperative, to choose a response within the conventions of the interaction type.

This imposition of an obligation to respond once one has been engaged explains the well-known proliferation of politeness formulae in opening expressions, particularly addressed to strangers, even when doing them a favour, as in Example 4.

Example 4
S1. Excuse me sir, I think you may have just dropped your wallet.
S2. Really? Gosh, thank you very much!

In other situations, such as at a shop or stall, the situation and roles of the participants are sufficiently well understood to begin with to obviate the need for explicit negotiation of the interaction:

Example 5 (at the newspaper stand)
S1. *The Guardian*, please.
S2. (exchanges newspaper for money)

Thus we may suppose that individuals are able to recognize interaction types and have means for initiating them. Psychologically, being involved in an interaction may be seen as the sharing by individuals of an 'interaction frame' in which each participant takes on a particular role and allots the complementary role to their interlocutor. The interaction is successfully established when both participants have activated the same interaction frame and have allotted themselves and the other the appropriate roles defined within it. (We might want to add that each also believes that the other believes them to be involved in the interaction in the appropriate role. For a discussion of 'mutual intention' in co-operative action see Power, 1982.) Recognition appears to be essentially automatic; once the initial utterance has received superficial decoding, it is impossible not to try to infer the purpose of the utterance and hence what sort of interaction one is engaged in. By this stage, simply doing nothing, that is, doing what you would have done anyway if you had not been addressed, becomes significant, in that it now signals a refusal to co-operate.

Interactions and speech acts

Speech-act theory within the philosophy of language, as descended from the seminal work of Austin (1962), concerns itself largely with the individual utterance as a unit of communication and says little about the larger episode in which an utterance may occur. This may be partly because the topic began with Austin's (1962, p. 5) analysis of explicit performatives such as:

1. I name this ship the *Queen Elizabeth*.
2. I give and bequeath my watch to my brother.

which do not occur embedded in a longer exchange.

Searle (1969) offers an analysis of a variety of speech acts which are distinguished by the content of a number of 'preparatory', 'sincerity' and 'essential' conditions for their performance. Questions, for instance, have the following conditions:

1. *Preparatory:*
   (i) the speaker does not know the answer.
   (ii) it is not obvious to both speaker and addressee that the latter will provide the information needed if the speaker does not ask.
2. *Sincerity:* the speaker wants the information.
3. *Essential:* counts as an attempt to elicit the information from the addressee.

In such an analysis, the two utterances of 'It's three fifteen' given in Examples 1 and 2 above would both be treated as assertions (which indeed they are) and would therefore both be given the same preparatory, sincerity and essential conditions. The differing *roles* of the two utterances in the exchange do not form part of the analysis.

The relationship between individual speech acts and the larger conversational units in which they are embedded is not one that has been much addressed by speech-act theorists. An exception is Wunderlich (1980, pp. 293–5), who makes the following remarks concerning the relation of speech acts to conversational 'moves' and conventional interaction types:

> No speech act is performed in isolation. Moreover no speech acts follow each other in arbitrary sequence . . . for instance, a question is something that calls for an answer, a proposal something that calls for consideration, an apology something that calls for an acknowledgement. . . . The notion of move is used to characterize the function of a speech act for the ongoing [*sic*] of the discourse. One may distinguish between initiating, reacting and continuing moves. . . . Some speech acts, in particular questions or requests, have a tendency to function as initiating moves. . . . Whether an assertion is called an answer, or a confirmation or something else, depends solely on its position in the speech act sequence. . . . A speech act pattern is a conventionalized ordered sequence of speech acts. The positions of this sequence have to be filled in by speech acts of a certain kind. . . . If one speaker starts with a speech acts belonging to a certain pattern then it is expected that the respective addressee, too, should stick to this pattern, even if he interrupts it by a counter-question or alike [*sic*].

The proposal here is thus the fairly obvious one that exchanges should be considered as conventional sequences of speech acts. Wunderlich (1980) also notes that 'for several reasons, in speech-act analyses linguists and philosophers tend to over-emphasize the class of *initiating* speech acts' (emphasis added). It is possible then that the familiar 'conditions on speech acts', since they seem to concern opening moves, ought to be considered, at least in part, as conditions on interaction types, and that speech acts such as questions are conventional opening moves for 'getting information' interactions. We can explore some consequences of this possibility with respect to the conditions on questions given above.

We noted earlier that interactions are characterized by the apparent goal of the initiator. In the speech-act framework, the goal of questioning seems to be expressed in the sincerity condition. If we state the condition as a goal instead, then the first part of the preparatory condition—that we do not already know the answer—is presupposed. The second part should really be subsumed under a more general principle of rational action—do not make efforts to achieve things which are going to happen anyway—rather than stated as a peculiar feature of asking questions. The essential condition corresponds to a general relationship between conventional interaction types and their goals, namely that initiating an interaction counts as an attempt to achieve the goal. So, assuming that preparatory rules need not be stated separately, we might postulate a 'getting information' exchange type, which

(a) is a way of achieving the goal of finding something out;
(b) requires an addressee who might have the information; and
(c) whose initiation counts as an attempt to elicit information from the addressee.

A speaker who has decided on such an interaction, with an appropriate addressee to hand, then needs to perform some linguistic act which will convey his purpose. The conventions of English make a syntactically interrogative sentence a standard choice. On the other hand, the speaker might say 'I wonder if you could tell me . . .', making what is, literally, an assertion about his own state of mind. Such an 'indirect' speech act (cf. Searle, 1975; Davison, 1975) employs a form (in this case the declarative) which is not in itself indicative of the speaker's intended goal. However, in certain contexts, for instance when approaching a stranger, such expressions *conventionally* signal politeness and a reluctance to intrude and can be construed fairly clearly as openings to getting information. This simply means that people brought up in a society such as ours know more than one way of initiating a particular type of interaction, and that the choice of strategy is partly determined by the social relations holding between the participants.

The rest of this section describes how the computer model formalizes some of the ideas just discussed.

Interaction frames

In the model, the actors' knowledge of the conventional form and function of interactions is stored in what we shall call interaction frames (IFs). The actors currently have access to four IFs, corresponding to different interactional goals.

Interaction Frames

Name	Function
1. MAKE_KNOWN	Impart information
2. FIND_OUT	Obtain information
3. GET_DONE	Get a favour done
4. GET_ATTENTION	Call someone

Interaction frames specify:

1. The type of goal the interaction is to be used for (for instance, having someone tell you something);
2. tests for preconditions to attempting the interaction (for instance, that the addressee is not already known to be incapable of supplying the desired information);
3. Procedures for carrying out the non-verbal activities that the interaction might require of either initiator or addressee (for instance, searching your memory for information);
4. The type of reply expected of the addressee.

An actor's level one planner considers initiating an exchange in two sorts of cases. The first is when a goal arises which explicitly involves the other actor, for instance that the other actor should know a particular fact, or that they should push a particular door. The other case is when an actor has tried and failed to establish some fact through the use of its own resources.

Initiating an interaction

The first step in trying to satisfy a goal through conversation is to select an IF which is meant to achieve goals of the appropriate sort. The preconditions of the interaction are then tested and any failure is reported back to the planner so that it can try another tack.

If the preconditions hold, there is a check on whether the other actor has already been engaged in conversation. If not, then a conventional introduction takes place. This consists of an attention-getting game followed by the actor's announcement of their main goal (a making-known game).

The actor then assigns themselves the role of initiator and the other the role of addressee in the chosen sort of interaction and sets about preparing their opening utterance. Behind every utterance that the model produces is a formal object called a message structure, which corresponds approximately to the intuitive idea of a communicative intent. More precisely, a complete message structure specifies:

1. A speaker;
2. An addressee;

3. The role of the utterance within an interaction (initial, response, closing);
4. Overt illocutionary force;
5. Semantic content;
6. The syntactic structure of the utterance;
7. What things are mentioned in the utterance (topics—this information is consulted during the construction of subsequent utterances, for deciding issues such as whether an object can be referred to with a pronoun).

A speaker who wants to prepare the initial utterance of an exchange sets up a new message structure, fills in items 1, 2 and 3 in the obvious way, and puts the intended goal of the interaction in item 5. Items 4, 6 and 7 are left blank initially, to be filled in by the language-generation mechanism of the next section. The language-generation routines are then invoked to fill in the rest of the structure, in particular item 6, the actual English utterance which encodes the message. It is important to point out that we have been concentrating on building a model of language generation, rather than comprehension, and that at this stage in the development of our model, it is the complete message structure, rather than just the English encoding, which is passed to the addressee. Comprehension is thus effectively bypassed for the moment, because the addressee has immediate access to all of the information in the structure, instead of having to reconstruct it from the English utterance.

Responding to an utterance

An actor that receives a message first checks to see whether there is an incomplete interaction in progress. If not, then the current message is taken to be the start of a new interaction. In this case, the actor accesses the IF appropriate to the goal of the interaction (which is explicitly given in the message structure). At this point, the two actors are in accord as to which game they are playing, and what their respective roles are. The addressee then runs the procedure which the IF associates with the addressee role, using the current message as input to the procedure. For instance, if the goal of the IF is to get something done, then the recipient will attempt what is required, as specified by the content of the message. If the goal is to get information, then the recipient will attempt to compute the information requested by the message content.

Once whatever action is necessary has been attempted, the content of a reply is computed, based on the outcome of the action and the form of reply given in the IF. A message structure containing the reply is then sent off to be filled in by the language-generation module, and eventually passed back to the initiator of the exchange.

The original actor now finds itself in the middle of an incomplete interaction, of which it is the initiator. It compares the incoming message against the reply type defined by the IF. If the utterance is not as expected then the actor should assume an interruption has occurred, and start a new game with itself as recipient. At the end of the nested game, the actor could hope to get a reply to its original utterance. At the moment, however, no interrupting games occur and so all replies are as expected.

The initiating actor looks up and runs its procedure in the IF for dealing with replies. If the reply is the answer to a question, for instance, the procedure will update the actor's knowledge of the world according to the information contained in the reply. The actor can then carry on with its building and executing of plans from the point where it first considered the possibility of communicating.

3. THE PRODUCTION OF UTTERANCES

This section discusses the level of the model at which representations of communicative intent are mapped on to utterance tokens. We first describe the formalism used for representing linguistic knowledge, then outline the knowledge available to our system and how it is used in constructing an utterance.

Making linguistic choices

The problem of language production, as with all purposeful action, is that of selecting, from a repertoire of behavioural possibilities, those actions likely to achieve a particular goal in a manner that is both efficient and consonant with situational constraints. The peculiar aspect of linguistic action is that it is almost entirely conventional—that is to say, the means available bear no natural, physical or common-sense relationship to the goals they might achieve. A person placed in an entirely novel linguistic environment has no chance of guessing or calculating the constructions of the language he is faced with. He may reasonably suppose that the language has ways of referring and of asking questions, but he will have no idea what these ways are. The conventions of a particular language, as well as being largely arbitrary and unpredictable, are often irregular and communicatively somewhat redundant. Thus in explaining linguistic behaviour, we have to pay attention, not only to the communicative demands of the speaker, but also to the conventional demands of the language—what it requires you to say, what it may let you omit.

Halliday (1970, p. 141) writes:

> Why is language as it is? The nature of language is closely related to the demands we make on it, the functions it has to serve ... [however,] a] purely extrinsic account of linguistic functions, one which is not based on an analysis of linguistic

structure, will not answer the question; we cannot explain language simply by listing its uses. . . . At the same time, an account of linguistic structure that pays no attention to the demands we make of language is lacking in perspicacity, since it offers no principles for explaining why the structure of language is organised in one way rather than in another.

The systemic linguistic theory that Halliday expounds provides a formalism for representing the interconnected sets of choices that lie behind the production of a well-formed utterance in a given language. The set of choices we are concerned with here does not define what the correct forms in the language are. Rather, it specifies what the speaker must consider, what information must be taken into account, in order to be able to produce a linguistically acceptable construction, given a communicative intention and a situational and discourse context. In English, for instance, a speaker must always decide whether to make a noun phrase definite or indefinite ('the door' vs. 'a door'). A speaker of Latin is not always forced to make such a choice.

To describe interdependencies between choices in the language as a whole, systemic theory uses networks of choices which feed into each other. (Individual choice points in the network are referred to as systems, hence the name systemic grammar.) The usefulness of this construct for a computational model of language production was first exploited by Davey in his PROTEUS system, which plays noughts and crosses and then produces a monologue describing the game it has played. (This model was produced in 1974, and is published as Davey (1978). Winograd (1972) employed a syntax derived from the work of Halliday, but Winograd concentrated on analysis rather than generation, and the notion of systems of choices, though described in his thesis, played no crucial role in the working of his program.) As well as networks of choices, Davey used Halliday's form of syntactic rules, particularly as developed in a version by Hudson (published as Hudson, 1981). However, the use of a systemic network to represent what structural choices are available does not commit one to any particular sort of syntactic formalism, and we describe below the alternative we have chosen.

System networks may be postulated for various sorts of linguistic objects. A example system offering a choice between two types of clause is shown in Figure 2.

Each time we make a choice, we determine a *feature* (in this case INDICATIVE or IMPERATIVE) to be possessed by the structure (in this case a clause) that we are specifying. The choice of a particular feature at a given

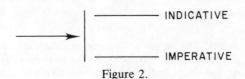

Figure 2.

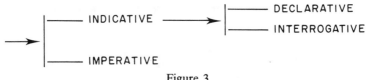

Figure 3.

point in the network also determines what further choices will need to be made. Thus the system of Figure 2 might occur as part of a larger network classifying clause types (Figure 3). Figure 3 says that a sentence can only be classified DECLARATIVE or INTERROGATIVE if it is already INDICA-TIVE (and if it is INDICATIVE, it *must* be either DECLARATIVE or INTERROGATIVE).

Eventually we reach a point where there are no more choices to be made, and we are left with a list of features which constitute a record of the path we have followed through the network.

Note that systems as described so far merely encode a set of available options. They do not in themselves contain any information about how one goes about deciding which option to take in any particular case. Clearly, a program which uses a system network to generate utterances must associate with each system a test for deciding which branch to take in a given set of circumstances.

Our set of tests is large (one for each node in each network) and we shall not describe it in detail. To give a general idea of what information the tests draw on, however, the clause-level decisions of Figure 3 are made by consulting the illocutionary force slot of the message structure, which has itself been filled in by traversing an illocutionary force network that looks up the type of the current interaction and the status of the current utterance as initial or reply.

The most elaborate tests in this model occur in the noun-phrase network, which needs to know such facts as whether the object the noun phrase is meant to describe has been mentioned recently (that is, whether it is listed as a topic in a message structure) and whether other objects of the same type (i.e. other doors, if it is a door) have been mentioned.

Realization rules

Once a set of features has been chosen, the next job is to build a syntactic structure. The rules which do this are called *realization rules* in the termin-ology of systemic grammar. A simple rule might run along the lines of:

IF: the clause features contain DECLARATIVE
THEN: the clause consists of NP VP

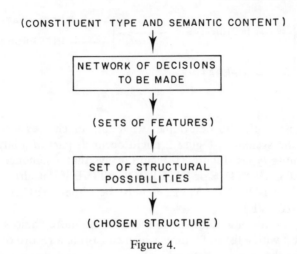

Figure 4.

i.e. declarative sentences consist of a noun phrase followed by a verb phrase. The internal structure of the phrases might then be derived from similar rules which respond to features at the phrase level (which would be derived by traversing an appropriate phrase-level system network).

Figure 4 diagrams the process for a single level. The 'chosen structure' at the end might then set off the whole process again at a lower level, until eventually a string of words is produced. (In Davey's (1978) program there is an intermediate level between the output of the system networks and the derivation of constituent structure called the *function set*.) A pen and paper system that generates utterances in this sort of way is given in Fawcett (1981).

Our program contains networks for phrasal constituents (sentences, noun phrases, verb phrases, prepositional phrases etc.), as well as the network mentioned above for overt illocutionary force, and an 'information status' network which is traversed whenever a noun phrase is to be constructed. The information status network derives features such as NEW, GIVEN and INFERRABLE (cp. Prince, 1981) which are used in the noun phrase network proper, primarily to decide when pronouns and definite reference can be used. For instance, if just one door has been recently mentioned, the bolt attached to that door becomes INFERRABLE, which licenses reference to it as 'the bolt', even when the bolt itself has not been previously mentioned, as in Doris's third utterance of the example dialogue at the beginning of the chapter.

Linguistic forms

Finally we reach the level of the model which decides upon actual English words, and the order in which they are to occur. The program's knowledge at this level is of three different sorts: syntactic, morphological and lexical.

The grammar

Our syntactic component is based on work done in the Generalized Phrase Structure Grammar (GPSG) framework (Gazdar and Pullum, 1982; Gazdar *et al.*, 1985). In particular, it

(a) is context-free;
(b) makes use of complex symbols;
(c) separates immediate dominance from linear precedence;
(d) associates semantic rules with syntactic rules.

Some comment on items (b) and (c) may be useful.

Item (b). A syntactic category symbol in the grammar consists of two parts—a part of speech symbol (e.g. noun, verb, NP, PP) and a possibly empty set of *features*. Features are used for specifying subtypes of the main syntactic category represented by the part of speech symbol, so that S[INV] represents an inverted sentence, and NP[PRO] a pronominalized noun phrase. Features are also consulted by the morphological component to determine the final forms taken by words. Thus, the feature NEG attached to a verb of the appropriate type will cause the negative 'n't' to be attached to the end of the verb. Some examples of the features in use are:

Feature type	Possible values
case	[NOMINATIVE ACCUSATIVE]
number	[SINGULAR PLURAL]
person	[FIRST SECOND THIRD]
polarity	[POSITIVE NEGATIVE]
sform (sentence form)	[DECLARATIVE IMPERATIVE INV WH COMP]
pptype (prepositional phrase type)	[BY OF TO THROUGH FOR]

Item (c). In standard phrase structure grammars, a rule of the form

$$S \rightarrow NP \ VP$$

says both that a sentence can consist of a noun phrase and a verb phrase (immediate dominance), and that the noun phrase precedes the verb phrase (linear precedence). In GPSG, the two facts are stated separately. For instance, one expansion of the noun phrase category might say that a noun phrase can consist of a noun and a determiner, while another might specify a noun, a determiner and a relative clause. The requisite order, to the extent that it is fixed, is expressed by a linear precedence rule. This allows word-order generalizations to be expressed directly and once only—e.g. in noun phrases, any determiner precedes the head noun. Further discussion of the use of this device may be found in Gazdar and Pullum (1981, 1982).

Expansions

The basic job of the syntactic component is to convert the output of a systemic network, representing a set of linguistic decisions, into a structure which realizes those decisions, so that, for instance, a WH (e.g. WHy, WHere, WHen) interrogative sentence will expand differently from a declarative, passive one. The solution adopted here is to associate features directly with the kinds of expansions that they represent.

An *expansion* specifies that a syntactic constituent with a particular part of speech symbol and a particular set of features attached must have certain subconstituents. For example, a sentence with features DECLARATIVE and ACTIVE must contain a noun phrase and a verb phrase. The expansion can also mention further features, which, if they appear, indicate the presence of further constituents. For example, if the sentence has the feature ADJUNC-TIVE as well as DECLARATIVE and ACTIVE, then it also has an adverbial conjunct as well as the basic noun phrase and verb phrase. Associated with each such decomposition of a syntactic category into constituents is a semantic rule, mentioned in (d) above, which indicates how the semantic content of the larger unit is to be distributed among its parts. For example, if a sentence is to be expanded as a noun phrase and a verb phrase, and the semantic content of the sentence predicates an action of an actor, the verb phrase subconstituent will be given the task of describing the action, and the noun phrase the actor. The assignment of a semantic content to a word-level constituent leads to a search of the lexicon for a word whose meaning matches the given semantic content.

Expansions are grouped together into packages for the purpose of linear precedence rules, which are stated as applying to all of the expansions in a package.

The lexicon

The lexicon contains all the words the actors need for carrying out their interactions, except for regularly inflected forms, such as 'pushed', 'isn't', 'holding', which are produced by morphological processes from stems con-tained in the lexicon and bound morphemes from the bound morpheme dictionary. The lexicon is subdivided into sections corresponding in the main to the syntactic class of the items in the section. There are currently thirteen subsections in all. The major ones are the following nine:

1. Nouns—e.g. bolt, door. Includes proper names 'Fred' and 'Doris'.
2. Adjectives—e.g. green, big, open.

3. Verbs—e.g. want, push, move. Includes modals, 'could', 'can' etc., and auxiliary 'do'.
4. Pronouns—e.g. I, me, you, one.
5. Determiners—e.g. the, a.
6. Prepositions—e.g. by, to, over, through.
7. Complementizer—e.g. that.
8. WH-adverbials—e.g. why, how.
9. Adjuncts—e.g. if, when, because.

Content words (here just nouns, verbs and adjectives) have associated with them a semantic content, which is an expression in the predicate calculus-like language in which the level 1 planning mechanism works. Function words (determiners, pronouns, etc.) are associated with sets of syntactic features in place of a semantic content, so that the pronoun 'it' is inserted into an utterance on the basis of its being a [DEFINITE THIRD SINGULAR NEUTER] pronoun, not because it has a semantic content especially suited to represent its referent. (The judgement that a pronoun, as opposed to a noun phrase containing content words, will adequately convey the referent in the present context, will have been made while traversing the noun-phrase system network.)

Morphology

The model contains a bound morpheme dictionary representing items such as 'n't', 'ing' and plural 's'. These are looked up when a regularly inflected word possesses an associated feature, such as NEG or PLURAL.

Producing an utterance

The input to the linguistic component is a message as described in section 2 and the output an annotated tree structure with phonological words on the leaves. The flow of control is top-down and depth-first (left to right) using a recursive algorithm which stacks constituents being built until the one at the bottom of the stack (corresponding to the symbol at the top of the tree) is complete. We note in passing that all types of constituent are produced by the same algorithm. There are rules and systems specific to each phrasal type, but there are no procedural 'VP specialists' hidden away.

Utterance construction begins with the input of a message from an actor's interaction planning system to its 'language faculty'. Before anything interesting is done, the message is examined to see if it is a 'simple move'. Simple moves are such things as answering 'yes' or calling someone by name. These utterances simply bypass the linguistic system altogether since they have no grammatical structure.

If the message is not 'simple' then the FORCE network is activated to select the speech-act type to be used. The choice is largely dictated by the interaction being played and the role of the utterance in it, as discussed earlier. The result is placed in the appropriate slot in the message structure.

Assuming the message contains a propositional element of some kind, we begin construction of a sentence with an essentially empty tree structure that contains nothing but a top 'S' node. The S system network is now activated, resulting in the generation of a set of features.

In the manner described in the discussion of the grammar, these features are used to select an expansion, and the semantic content of the whole sentence is divided appropriately among the meaning-bearing subconstituents. Empty tree structures representing the subconstituents are attached below the S node in the order prescribed by the relevant linear precedence rule.

We now enter a loop where we continually treat the left-most unexpanded node of the tree in the manner just described for the S node—first traversing the relevant system network, then choosing an expansion—until a complete tree structure has been formed with words at all the leaves.

4. CONCLUSION

The program we have described embodies a fully worked out account of how a non-linguistic goal might give rise to a particular form of words under appropriate circumstances. It performs principled computations based on explicitly represented knowledge at all levels. There are no strings of words stored away to pop out at opportune moments. In fact, the capabilities of each level of the program are greater than what is required by the overall task. We hope to exploit at least part of this spare capacity in extending the program to speak its dialogues aloud. The problem of greatest interest here is the generation of appropriate intonation contours to suit the point of the utterances. We believe that the knowledge encoded at the message level is adequate for determining what contour to use, and that the syntactic mechanism will enable us to align the contour correctly with the words that are produced.

ACKNOWLEDGEMENT

Steve Draper offered helpful comments on a draft of the chapter.

REFERENCES

Austin, J. L. (1962). *How to Do Things with Words*. Oxford: OUP.
Davey, A. (1978). *Discourse Production: A Computer Model of some Aspects of a Speaker*. Edinburgh: Edinburgh University Press.
Davison, A. (1975). *Indirect speech acts and what to do with them*. In P. Cole and J. L. Morgan (eds) *Syntax and Semantics*, Vol. 3: *Speech Acts*. London: Academic Press.

Fawcett, R. (1981). Generating a sentence in systemic functional grammar. In M. A. K. Halliday and J. R. Martin, (eds) *Readings in Systemic Linguistics*.

Gazdar, G., and Pullum, G. (1981). Subcategorization, constituent order and the notion 'Head'. In M. Moortgat, H. v. D. Hulst, and T. Hoekstra (eds) *The Scope of Lexical Rules*. Dordrecht: Foris.

Gazdar, G., and Pullum, G. K. (1982). *Generalized Phrase Structure Grammar: A Theoretical Synopsis*. IULC Publications (August).

Gazdar, G., Klein, E., Pullum, G. K. and Sag, I. (1985). *Generalised Phrase Structure Grammar*. Oxford: Basil Blackwell.

Goffman, E. (1981). Replies and responses. In E. Goffman, *Forms of Talk*. Oxford: Basil Blackwell.

Halliday, M. A. K. (1970). Language structure and language function. In J. Lyons (ed) *New Horizonz in Linguistics*. Harmondsworth, Middlesex: Penguin.

Houghton, G. (1986). The production of language in dialogue. Thesis submitted for the degree of D.Phil., University of Sussex.

Hudson, R. A. (1981). Systemic generative grammar. In M. A. K. Halliday and J. R. Martin (eds) *Readings in Systemic Linguistics*.

Power, R. (1974). A computer model of conversation. Unpublished Ph.D. Thesis, University of Edinburgh.

Power, R. (1979). The organization of purposeful dialogues. *Linguistics*, 17.

Power, R. (1982). *Mutual Intention*. University of Padua Institue of Psychology Report 64.

Prince, E. F. (1981). Toward a taxonomy of given-new information. In P. Cole (ed.) *Radical Pragmatics*. London: Academic Press.

Sacks, H., Schegloff, E. and Jefferson, G. (1974). A simplest systematics for the organisation of turn-taking for conversation. *Language*, **50**, 696–735.

Searle, J. R. (1969). *Speech Acts: An Essay in the Philosophy of Language*. London: CUP.

Searle, J. R. (1975). Indirect speech acts. In P. Cole and J. L. Morgan (eds) *Syntax and Semantics*, Vol. 3: *Speech Acts*. London: Academic Press.

Stubbs, M. (1983). *Discourse Analysis: The Sociolinguistic Nature of Natural Language*. Oxford: Basil Blackwell.

Winograd, T. (1972). *Understanding Natural Language*. New York: Academic Press.

Wunderlich, D. (1980). Methodological remarks on speech act theory. In J. R. Searle, F. Kiefer and M. Bierwisch (eds) *Speech Act Theory and Pragmatics*. Dordrecht: D. Reidel.

12

Modelling the recognition of faces and words

ANDREW W. ELLIS, ANDREW W. YOUNG and DENNIS C. HAY
Face Recognition Unit, Department of Psychology, University of Lancaster

INTRODUCTION

In the third of his 1984 BBC Reith Lectures, entitled *Minds, Brains and Science*, John Searle issued the following invitation:

> Consider face recognition. We all recognize the faces of our friends, relatives and acquaintances quite effortlessly; and indeed we now have evidence that certain portions of the brain are specialized for face recognition. How does it work? Well, suppose we were going to design a computer that could recognize faces as we do. It would carry out quite a computational task, involving a lot of calculating of geometrical and topographical features. But is that any evidence that the way we do it involves calculating and computing? Notice that when we step in wet sand and make a footprint, neither our feet nor the sand does any computing. But if we were going to design a program that would calculate the topology of a footprint from information about differential pressures on the sand, it would be a fairly complex computational task. The fact that a computational simulation of a natural phenomenon involves complex information processing does not show that the phenomenon itself involves such processing. And it may be that facial recognition is as simple and as automatic as making footprints in the sand (Searle, 1984, p. 52).

In this chapter we shall review the attempts made by ourselves and others to understand and model some of the cognitive processes involved in recognizing familiar faces. The data we address will come from everyday experiences, including difficulties and errors in face recognition, as well as from laboratory experiments. We shall not analyse here the data from neuro-psychological case studies though we believe that cognitive models of face recognition should explain and be modifiable by such data (see Hay and

Young, 1982; Bruce and Young, 1986). We shall argue that successful face recognition, which includes knowing who the seen person is and what their name is, requires the co-operation of several independent but intercommunicating subcomponents or modules, and that recognition difficulties arise through temporary failure of a component or connection.

We also wish to explore some of the similarities and differences between face recognition and word recognition. The differences are fairly easy to see, but we believe that an exploration of the similarities can help elucidate both modes of recognition (for example, the phenomenon of *resemblance* is of obvious importance in face recognition but has been relatively little studied in the domain of word recognition, yet we believe that it is an important phenomenon in both domains).

FACE RECOGNITION UNITS?

Let us begin with Searle's proposition that face recognition 'is as simple and as automatic as making footprints in the sand'. Most of us leave footprints in the sand from time to time, but rarely face prints. Probably the closest things to face prints are life- or death-masks made by pressing one's face into plaster of Paris. But in what sense, if any, can we say that plaster of Paris 'recognizes' a face pressed into it? The answer, we would suggest, is in no sense whatsoever. Plaster of Paris registers an impression of a face, but *recognition* involves more than simple registration. Recognition involves the realization that a stimulus (in this case a face) *has been seen before*. Unfamiliar faces can be registered or perceived, but only familiar ones can be recognized.

The face shown in Figure 1 belongs to someone who is well known in a particular walk of life. Readers will all be capable of registering the face, but it will only be recognized by a subset of readers. What, in Searle's terms, 'happens quite effortlessly' inside the head of a reader who recognizes Geoffrey Boycott that does not happen inside the head of someone unlucky enough not to know the face of that master cricketer? The answer proposed by cognitive psychologists from Plato to H. Ellis (1987) is that recognition occurs when a stimulus makes contact with a representation of itself which was laid down in the brain of the perceiver when the stimulus was previously encountered.

This idea is perhaps most familiar in the area of word recognition. It is over 20 years since Triesman (1964) and Morton (1964) suggested that each word with which a listener or reader is familiar has a separate stored description ('logogen') which must be triggered in order for the word to be recognized on a specific encounter (see Morton, 1964, 1969, 1979a, b). Cognitive theories of word recognition may differ in their particulars (Henderson, 1982; Mitchell, 1982), but the concept of stored representations is common to them all and has been incorporated into a number of influential computer simulations of word recognition (e.g. Klatt, 1979; McClelland and Rumelhart, 1981).

Figure 1. An individual well known in a particular walk of life (cricket) but unfamiliar to many people (photo supplied by the Press Association).

It took rather longer for the concept to be applied to face recognition, but Hay and Young (1982) proposed the existence of 'face recognition units' for familiar faces, a notion which has since been developed by Bruce (1983), H. Ellis (1987) and Bruce and Young (1986). Learning to recognize the face of a new acquaintance involves creating a new face recognition unit (henceforth FRU), and recognizing that person on subsequent occasions involves activating the appropriate FRU. Once an FRU is activated it provides access to information that you have stored about that person—their occupation, likes and dislikes, where they live and so on. This person information, which we might loosely label 'semantic', in turn provides access to the individual's name which is thought, for reasons we shall discuss later, to be retrieved from a separate phonological memory store.

Do FRUs have thresholds?

In developing the concept of FRUs, Hay and Young (1982) took over from Morton's logogens the notion that each recognition unit has a *threshold*. An

FRU's threshold determines the amount of stimulus information that must accrue before it 'fires' and the person is recognized. When a face is seen, processes of visual analysis (called 'representational processes' in Hay and Young, 1982) create a description of it. To the extent that the newly created description matches that stored in the FRU, the level of activation in the FRU increases, but the face is only 'recognized' as that of the person encapsulated in the FRU once the FRU's threshold is exceeded.

Threshold models of this sort can account for several of the different experiences which can accompany the perception of a face. Some of these are included under the headings below.

Correct identification

Here the FRU is appropriately fired by its 'proper' face and that person is correctly identified. This would include the correct recognition of Geoffrey Boycott as himself, or your sister as herself.

Correct rejection

Here a new face fails to activate any FRU to threshold level so the face is correctly classified as unfamiliar. This is the response appropriately given to the majority of faces you see in town when you are out shopping.

False positive identification

Here you mistakenly identify one person as someone else who is familiar to you. In a diary study by Young, Hay and Ellis (1985) of 922 naturally occurring recognition errors made by 22 people over a 7-week period such misidentifications constituted the largest single category of reported errors (34 per cent of errors). Eighty-seven per cent of these involved the mis-identification of a complete stranger as someone familiar. False positive misidentifications tended to occur under poor viewing conditions—the person often being glimpsed briefly or seen at a distance—and were usually corrected within a matter of seconds.

False positive errors are normally based on physical similarity. The stranger looks *like* the person he or she is mistaken for. It would seem reasonable to argue that when such errors are based on misidentification of the person's face what happens is that the visual description of the stranger shares sufficient features in common with the stored description of a familiar person in an FRU that the FRU 'misfires' and leads you to believe that you have actually seen the familiar person.

The remaining 13 per cent of misidentifications in the Young, Hay and Ellis (1985) study involved the misidentification of one familiar person as another familiar person. Typically this involves the misidentification of someone encountered infrequently as someone encountered frequently (e.g misidentifying a casual acquaintance as a close friend). This again is compatible with a common threshold assumption, namely that each firing of a recognition unit results in a slight but permanent lowering of that unit's threshold. The FRUs for frequently encountered faces will come to have low thresholds which may be exceeded by stimulus input from a less familiar but physically similar face before activation in that person's FRU exceeds its own threshold. Errors therefore will tend to take the form of less familiar stimuli being mistaken for more familiar ones.

Failure to recognize a familiar person

If, when you look at a person you know, that person's FRU does not become strongly activated, then you may fail to recognize him or her. Some 12 per cent of the errors reported by the Young, Hay and Ellis (1985) diarists were failures to recognize a familiar person.

There may be a number of potential causes of failure to recognize a familiar person (McWeeny, 1985) but the most obvious, and the one easiest to explain in terms of FRUs, is change of appearance. If someone you know has shaved off a heavy beard, trimmed previously flowing locks, lost a lot of weight or aged considerably since you last saw them, then the stimulus pattern they present may no longer overlap sufficiently with that stored in the FRU to cause that recognition unit to become strongly activated. A poor view of the person—another common cause of recognition failure—can be given a similar explanation.

A somewhat different cause of recognition failure occurs when you fail to recognize someone you pass because you are preoccupied with other matters, or day-dreaming (McWeeny, 1985). Assuming that these errors also spring from failures of FRU activation, we might propose that navigating your way along the street, while simultaneously thinking about something else, constitutes a type of 'dual-task' or 'selective-attention' situation. It has been suggested that in such circumstances stimulus input may be attenuated or dulled (Triesman, 1964; Broadbent, 1971); such attenuation of input might underlie those recognition failures due to preoccupation or similar.

All of the above experiences induced by faces can be explained on a threshold model, along with certain others that we shall discuss later. There are, however, other types of experience which we believe a threshold model cannot cope with, and which force a modification of the concept of an FRU. One of the most striking of these is the phenomenon of *resemblance*.

RESEMBLANCES

A cognitive neuropsychologist acquaintance of ours once remarked that since turning 40 every second person he saw reminded him of someone else. To prove the point he gestured towards a tall, gaunt, haunted-looking man with brushed-back hair who was passing by. 'Look,' he said, 'there goes Wittgenstein.' Now one would not mistake that man for Wittgenstein in a false positive misidentification, but the resemblance was obvious once it was pointed out.

Threshold models are designed for saying 'That is X' or 'That is not X': it seems to us that they cannot readily account for the common experience of thinking, 'That looks quite like X though I know full well it isn't.' Resemblances lurk midway between 'Yes' and 'No', as do experiences reported by our diarists like not knowing whether a seen person is X or not. One way to encompass feelings of *resemblance* (or what Schank, 1982, calls 'perceptual reminding') within threshold models would be to have two thresholds—a low threshold which, once exceeded, signalled 'This looks like X' and a higher threshold which once exceeded, signalled 'This *is* X' (cf. Baron, 1981). Our own preference, however, is to dispense entirely with thresholds and allow FRUs to give a *continually graded* output rather than the all-or-nothing output of units governed by thresholds. This would make FRUs more like the recognition nodes in activation models of word recognition such as that proposed by McClelland and Rumelhart (1981). Figure 2 illustrates the

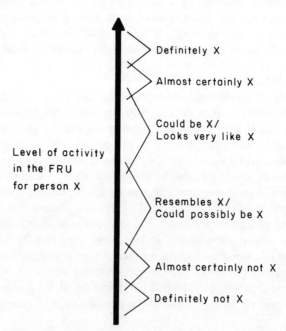

Figure 2. Possible experiential states accompanying different levels of activation with a face recognition unit.

different experiential states that might accompany different levels of activation in an RFU.

A small experiment

In the diary study of Young, Hay and Ellis (1985), incidents based on resemblance formed their own category, with subcategories that will be discussed later. In almost all of these natural incidents the faces which induced the feeling of resemblance (the 'source faces') were themselves unfamiliar. It is apparently unusual for one familiar person to spontaneously remind you of another familiar person. When dealing with diary corpora it is, however, hard to exclude explanations based on sampling artefacts. Perhaps the majority of people our diarists saw were unfamiliar and that is why such people induce most feelings of resemblance. To assess this possibility we conducted a small experiment in which subjects were shown a mixture of famous and unfamiliar faces and were asked to indicate how many people they could think of who *looked like* the face in front of them. For this experiment, 30 faces of very well-known public figures (politicians, TV personalities, sportsmen and women, etc.) were chosen. Thirty pictures of the faces of unfamiliar people obtained from the archives of a provincial newspaper were then selected. These were matched to the familiars on sex, approximate age, presence or absence of beards, moustaches, jewellery, etc.

The subjects, who were all students at Lancaster University (5 males, 10 females) were tested either singly or in pairs. The experimental session began with 10 practice faces (5 familiar, 5 unfamiliar) followed by the 60 experimental faces which were shown in a fixed, random order. Each face was displayed as a slide on a screen while the subjects studied it. After 5 seconds each subject had to write down a number, which was the number of people he or she could think of who looked like the target face. It was emphasized that these could be public figures or individuals known personally to the subject in his or her private life. After the face had been removed and the number of resemblances written down, the subject was given sufficient time: (a) to indicate if the face on the screen had been a familiar one and, if so, who it was (the name or a brief description was accepted); (b) to write brief notes on who each of the resemblances were; and (c) to rate on a scale from 1 = very slight resemblance to 7 = very strong resemblance, how closely each likeness resembled the target face.

Despite our having selected 30 of the most well-known public figures as our familiar faces, there were 33 instances of complete failure to recognize the face of a public figure (7.3 per cent). There were no false positive recognitions of unfamiliar faces as familiar. In all, the familiar, recognized faces yielded a total of 174 resemblances at a mean of 11.6 per subject (standard deviation = 8.96), or 0.39 per famous face recognized. In contrast, the unfamiliar faces yielded a total of 289 resemblances at a mean of 19.3 per subject (standard deviation = 6.63), or 0.64 per face. Thirteen of the 15 subjects generated more resemblances to unfamiliar than famous faces. The difference between the number of resemblances per famous, recognized face and the number per unfamiliar face was significant ($t = 5.17$, d.f. = 13, $p < 0.01$). Although unfamiliar faces yielded more resemblances than famous ones, the rated degree of resemblance of likenesses to targets did not differ (mean for famous faces = 3.63, mean for unfamiliar faces = 3.60).

The effect, then, seems genuine. Both the diary study and the above small experiment show that resemblances are more easily noticed in unfamiliar faces. Why should this be? We have argued that resemblances may in part be explicable in terms of intermediate levels of activation in FRUs. Our task, then, becomes one of explaining why unfamiliar faces cause intermediate activity in more FRUs than do familiar faces or, alternatively, why intermediate levels of activity are easier to detect when generated by an unfamiliar face than by a familiar one. The second type of explanation is effectively couched in signal detection terms. In addition to any intermediate levels of activation caused by resemblance, a familiar face will cause strong activation in one FRU, its own. Just as the presence of the sun in the sky by day renders the stars undetectable, so the presence of one bright FRU may make it harder to detect the presence of others glowing dully.

A different explanation of the effect could flow from the possibility mentioned above that familiar faces may somehow prevent as many other FRUs from ever achieving a sufficient level of activation for a resemblance to be noticed. This could happen if FRUs, in addition to receiving activation from visual analysis systems, also actively *inhibit* one another. McClelland and Rumelhart (1981) incorporated inhibition between word recognition units in their computer simulation. As the activation level in one of their units (nodes) increases, so the power of its inhibitory influence upon other units increases. This has the effect of damping down unwanted noise in the system, and means that the final output of the word level when presented with a familiar word for which a recognition unit exists is not multiple signals of varying strengths from multiple units, but one unit signalling strongly and the rest hardly at all.

Translated into our proposed FRU system, this would mean that a familiar face will activate its FRU strongly and that the activated unit will inhibit other FRUs which might otherwise have been activated by the degree of overlap between their stored specifications and those of the presented face. An unfamiliar stimulus face, in contrast, will not cause strong activation in any one unit, and the intermediate levels it induces in those units sharing a degree of resemblance may be insufficient to allow any one unit to inhibit the others. Hence unfamiliar faces will cause more units to achieve intermediate levels of activation than will familiar faces, and the unfamiliar faces will generate more feelings of resemblance.

The concept of inter-unit inhibition is not entirely unproblematic. Is it really the case, for example, that when we learn a new face or word we not only establish a new recognition unit for it but also grow inhibitory links from that unit to all others in the system? Introducing inhibitory mechanisms does, however, have the advantage of allowing the recognition system to take the decision as to who a face is rather than deferring that decision to a later system. If the face recognition system gave multiple graded responses to all faces, then the decision as to who a particular face is would need to be taken at a later stage. But, if the most strongly activated FRU is allowed to inhibit the others, only one signal will remain after an initial settling-down period and a decision, right or wrong, will have been taken.

It is perhaps worth interjecting at this point our belief that the concepts being employed here can be translated without too much difficulty into the language of 'parallel distributed processing' (e.g. McClelland and Rumelhart, 1985). To achieve this we would need to make two principal assumptions. The first is that each of the cognitive subsystems that we postulate should probably be represented by a *separate* processing network. We would thus see the mind and brain as an aggregation of networks, each functioning as a semi-independent 'module'. Secondly, each 'recognition unit' would be represented as a pattern of activity or interconnections which has been established previously over the array of elementary processing units which comprises a particular network. The 'level of activity' in a recognition unit would be represented as the degree of overlap between the current state of the network and a previously established state.

While the majority of resemblance experiences can, we believe, be accounted for in terms of partial activation of FRUs, there may be a few exceptions. Suppose our acquaintance had not seen someone who merely looked like Wittgenstein, but had seen someone who apparently was Wittgenstein. If he was a firm believer in ghosts, then he might have concluded that this was indeed Wittgenstein's spectral projection, but he would otherwise be more likely to decide that this was someone who was the philosopher's double. His knowledge that Wittgenstein is dead would lead him to deny the evidence of his senses. Some of the errors described in the Young, Hay and Ellis (1985) diary study stemmed from this sort of refusal to recognize. To account for them we must claim that even though an FRU has been activated and person information accessed, other knowledge can sometimes intervene and cause the individual to conclude in a very deliberate, rational way that resemblance rather than identity is involved. But such considerations lead us beyond the FRUs.

BEYOND THE FRUs

A particularly striking and potentially embarrassing recognition failure occurs when you see a face that you know to be familiar but you are temporarily unable to 'place' the person. At worst, he or she approaches you jovially and engages in conversation, clearly recognizing you, while you search desperately to try to think where you have met this person before.

In terms of cognitive modelling such 'familiarity only' errors, plenty of which were recorded in the Young, Hay and Ellis (1985) diary study, seem to be pointing to a separation of FRUs from the long-term memory store in which person information is held. In 'familiarity only' errors the FRU has been activated (because the face is acknowledged to be familiar), but the relevant person information is temporarily inaccessible. The fact that one can have familiarity without person information suggests that these two aspects of the response to a familiar face emanate from two separate and dissociable cognitive subsystems. Feelings of familiarity arise, we believe, from the output of the FRUs, while person information is retrieved from a more general long-term memory store.

People report feelings of familiarity without person information, but never report looking at a face and thinking 'I know he works in the local foodstore though his face doesn't look at all familiar.' We shall take the non-occurrence of this logically possible experiential state as evidence that person information is accessed after and via the system which gives rise to feelings of familiarity rather than, say, in parallel to it.

We can apply the same logic to another pair of possible recognition difficulties, one of which occurs commonly and the other not at all. The one that occurs commonly is when you see someone, recognize them as familiar, know who they are in the sense of where you know them from etc., but you are temporarily unable to recall their name. The difficulty everyone seems to have with names makes them ideal material for studies of tip-of-the-tongue states (Yarmey, 1973; Reason and Lucas, 1984) or memory-search strategies (Williams and Hollan, 1981; Read and Bruce, 1982). The error that does not occur is where you recognize someone as familiar, know that their name is, say, Geoffrey Boycott, but you cannot retrieve the appropriate person information (the fact that he is a cricketer). We take the occurrence of the first error type and non-occurrence of the second as supportive of our claim that people's names are retrieved after and via person information from a separate cognitive subsystem or store (arguably the same speech output lexicon from which the rest of one's speech production vocabulary is retrieved).

Interestingly, both of the positive error types noted above have resemblance analogues. Respondents in the Young, Hay and Ellis (1985) diary study reported incidents where they had seen an unfamiliar person, knew that the unfamiliar person resembled (but was not) a familiar acquaintance, yet could not remember who that acquaintance was. Alternatively, they might know who the familiar person they were being reminded of was, yet be unable to recall his or her name. In the former case an intermediate level of activation in an FRU is generating a feeling of resemblance but the relevant person information is temporarily inaccessible. In the latter case the person information has been assessed but the name eludes retrieval.

Some further experimental data

To summarize so far, we have argued that seeing a familiar face calls into operation at least three separate, functionally distinct cognitive subsystems in a linear order. The first subsystem declares the face to be familiar, the second provides person information, and the third supplies the name. Chronometric studies of the latencies of different types of response to familiar faces support this proposed sequence. Experiments by Young, McWeeny, Hay and Ellis (1986) and Young, McWeeny, Ellis and Hay (1986) have consistently found familiarity decisions (Is this face familiar?) to be faster than semantic decisions (e.g. Is it a politician?), with naming latencies slowest of all. This is, of course, the pattern one would predict given the linearly arranged stages of the model.

Readers may feel unhappy with our separation of names from other person information. Why should a name be any different from the other things we know about a person? We would first note that in tip-of-the-tongue states people may have apparent access to full semantic information about a concept (an object or person) yet be temporarily unable to recall the concept's verbal label (Reason and Lucas, 1984). Similarly in 'anomic' aphasia patients may know all there is to know about, say, an object depicted in a drawing, yet be unable to name it (Kay and Ellis, in press).

Our experiments have found marked differences in the ease with which person information and names can be learned. In one such experiment (McWeeny *et al.*, in press) subjects were shown sixteen unfamiliar faces, one at a time. For each face they were given the person's (invented) occupation and surname. The subjects then went back through the faces trying to provide the name and occupation for each. Where they failed, the omitted information was supplied by the experimenter. This continued until the subject went twice through the set without a mistake.

A feature of the design is that half the occupations used were 'ambiguous' in that they can also occur as surnames (e.g. baker or carpenter). The remaining occupations were unambiguous (e.g. architect or solicitor). Similarly, half the surnames were ambiguous (e.g. Cook, Porter) and half were unambiguous (e.g. Knowles, Rothwell). If an ambiguous term occurred as an occupation for a given subject it did not also occur as a surname, and none of the occupation–name pairings contained more than one ambiguous term.

Subjects required an average of 7.38 runs through the set of 16 faces before reaching the criterion of two successive correct runs. Of interest is the number of individual trials in which the subject was able to provide the name but not the occupation, or the occupation but not the name. These results are shown

Table 1   Mean number of trials in the study of McWeeny *et al.* (in press) where subjects were able to give the occupation only or the name only to faces being learned (see text for details)

	Occupation only recalled		Name only recalled	
	Unrecalled name ambiguous	Unrecalled name unambiguous	Unrecalled occupation ambiguous	Unrecalled occupation unambiguous
Mean	13.44	10.69	0.76	0.88
S.D.	6.99	4.60	1.53	1.36

in Table 1 where it can be seen that occupations were very much easier to learn than names. There was no significant difference between ambiguous and unambiguous occupations or between ambiguous and unambiguous names. What is important to note, however, is that the ambiguous occupations and names were, in fact, identical verbal labels. Thus it is much easier to learn and remember that someone *is* a cook, carpenter, baker or porter than to learn and remember that he or she is called Cook, Carpenter, Baker or Porter. This effect may be attributable to a differential ease and efficiency with which information can be registered in and/or retrieved from the person information store as compared with the phonological name store.

COMPARING FACE AND WORD RECOGNITION

We have argued so far that theoretical concepts developed to explain word recognition (particularly visual word recognition) can be profitably adapted to the creation of models of face recognition. On reflection this should not perhaps surprise us. Although cognitive psychologists have been late to discover face recognition, the skill is much older than visual word recognition. In fact, reading is so recent a development, and until this century so restricted in its extent, that there can exist no biological predisposition to develop visual word-recognition processes. It would not be surprising, therefore, if the brain, faced with the requirement to create a visual word recognition capability, were to adapt principles of operation from other modes of visual processing such as face or object recognition.

Stimulus categories

We can begin a comparison of face and word recognition by noting similarities between the *stimulus categories* that can be identified. A familiar face is like a familiar word—both being known stimulus configurations identified by individual nodes in the perceivers' recognition systems, and both having meanings and names (phonological forms). An unfamiliar face, like an unfamiliar word, is just an existing configuration for which a perceiver has no recognition unit. If the unfamiliar face is that of a person you have read about or know from the radio, or if the unfamiliar written word is one you have heard in use and corresponds to a concept you already possess, then the relevant semantics/ person information may already be present. All that is required then is to form a new access route via new recognition units. Alternatively, the person or word may be totally new, in which case the perceiver must create a new recognition unit *and* a new semantic entry to match.

Cognitive psychologists have utilized extensively the 'lexical decision' paradigm in which subjects must decide as quickly as possible whether or not a letter string forms a familiar word. Now because one person's unfamiliar word is another's familiar word, the cognitive psychologist usually contrasts real words with invented non-words. These are normally 'legal' non-words in the sense that they are letter strings which could be words but happen not to be (e.g. SLEN; FLABERTY). H. Ellis (1987) has objected to the parallel drawn by Bruce (1983) between the lexical decision task and tasks in which familiar faces have to be discriminated from unfamiliar ones. Ellis argues that 'whereas non-words are more or less meaningless, not to say strange and unexperienced outside the very circumscribed context of looking at non-words written in an unknown language, unfamiliar faces are commonly encountered and are anything but meaningless' (Ellis, 1987).

Although we do not commonly encounter genuine non-words, any but the most highly literate individual often encounters words in the course of reading which he or she has not met in print before. These real but unfamiliar words are the true equivalents of unfamiliar faces—configurations for which recognition units could exist but happen not to. Because an experimenter cannot control which words a subject will or will not have encountered before entering the laboratory, it is convenient to invent legal non-words rather than use real if uncommon words, but this should be no more objectionable than if one could use a sophisticated visual display system to create lifelike unfamiliar faces for use in an 'Is this face familiar?' task (cf. Haig, 1984). The facial equivalent of the illegal non-word (e.g. CHKURHT) is presumably something like the rearranged faces employed by Hay (1981) and Young, Hay and McWeeny (1985).

Response categories

Not only are the stimulus types in some ways equivalent, but many of the responses to which words and faces can give rise (including experiential states) are equivalent too. A list of such comparisons is shown in Table 2. Some of these are straightforward and (we hope) unobjectionable. Correct recognition of familiar items as 'old', and correct classification of unfamiliar

Table 2   Equivalences between responses to faces and words

Faces	Words
Correct recognition	Correct recognition
Correct rejection of a novel face as unfamiliar	Correct rejection of a novel word (or invented non-word) as unfamiliar
False positive misidentification of an unfamiliar face as familiar	False positive misidentification of an unfamiliar word or invented non-word as familiar
False positive misidentification of one familiar face as another	False positive misidentification of one familiar word as another
Failure to recognize a familiar face	Failure to recognize a familiar word
Resemblance from an unfamiliar face	Resemblance from an unfamiliar word or non-word
Resemblance from a familiar face	Resemblance from a familiar word
Feeling of familiarity only	See text
Inability to remember name	See text

items as novel, are the primary goals of both word and face recognition. The false positive misidentification of one person as another has its counterpart in reading errors where one word is misidentified as another (Vernon, 1929; Weber, 1968; Cowie, 1985) or where a reader fails to spot a misprint (non-word) and reads it as a word (Pillsbury, 1897; Downey, 1918; Cohen, 1980; Monk and Hulme, 1983). In both cases, visual similarity between the misread item and the word it is mistaken for is crucial.

Words do not change their appearance in the way that people sometimes can, so there is perhaps less likelihood of failing to recognize a familiar word than of failing to recognize a familiar person. Nevertheless, lexical decision experiments always generate a proportion of trials on which a subject rejects a letter string which is, in fact, a word. In our experience this happens most often when the word is a fairly uncommon one like DAIS or POMADE. Sometimes the subject will realize soon after pressing the 'No' button that the letter string is in fact a word, but by then it is too late.

Coltheart (1978) argued that rejecting a 'legal' stimulus (e.g. a letter string which could be a word) as unfamiliar can never be a positive decision, only a negative one. All you can say is that you fail to recognize the stimulus as familiar. According to Coltheart, in a speeded response task this involves waiting a given time after stimulus presentation, then pressing the 'No' button if recognition has not occurred. Arguably, word recognition units for uncommon words like DAIS or POMADE start at very low resting levels of activation and may accumulate activation more slowly than units for more common words. The unit may have failed to emerge from the background noise before the criterion time is up, so the word is incorrectly rejected, though it may emerge shortly afterwards, causing the subject to realize that the response given was wrong.

Do readers ever gaze at a word thinking 'I know I've seen that word before but I can't think what it means' in the same way that you can sometimes gaze at a face and think 'I know I've seen that face before but I can't think who it is'? It may occur, but it seems to us that feelings of familiarity only are more readily elicited by faces than by words. One possible reason for this difference may be that while faces are only perceived in one modality (vision), words are effectively perceived in two (vision and hearing). We shall present evidence shortly which supports the view that familiar names access their pronunciations by a route independent from, and probably faster than, the route that accesses their meanings. Thus in addition to trying to access person information visually from the printed word, readers can, if they choose, convert the word rapidly into an internal sound-form which can direct an independent search for person information.

Sound-forms corresponding to written names can also be derived by applying low-level spelling–sound correspondences. The first time you encounter a name in print—say *Gorbachev*—you can 'sound it out' piecemeal fashion to generate a sound-form which you may then recognize as a name you have heard before though you have not previously encountered it in print.

The opportunity written words provide for deriving their sound forms by use of spelling–sound correspondences may also be one reason why the inability to recall someone's name may not have a common counterpart in the inability to recall a written word's spoken form. In English this could only happen for 'irregular' words like YACHT or LEOPARD which defy pronunciation by low-level spelling–sound correspondences. Do normal readers ever know the meaning of such words though they cannot recall their pronunciations? The 'anomic' aphasic patient EST, whose inability to recall object names despite full awareness of their meanings and uses is reported in Kay and Ellis (in press), showed something like this phenomenon in his reading (Kay and Patterson, 1985). He could reliably access word meanings from print, but was often only able to guess at their pronunciations by applying spelling–sound correspondences. When the written words were irregular this resulted in responses like *SIEGE* 'a seeg . . . a seeg . . . everybody . . . seeg . . . you're all there . . . everybody there . . . a seeg and you don't want anybody else to come in' or GAUGE 'something about a railway . . . godge'.

Resemblance phenomena in visual word recognition

We argued earlier that feelings of resemblance induced by faces arise because a seen face, which may be either familiar or unfamiliar, causes an intermediate level of activation in an established FRU by virtue of overlap between the appearance of the stimulus face and the 'trigger features' of the FRU. In our experience, words do not induce quite the same spontaneous acknowledgement of resemblance as faces do, and word–word (or non-word–word) resemblance has been little discussed in the word-recognition literature. But with a little digging it is possible to unearth several results and observations which suggest that resemblance functions for words as well as for faces.

First, the 'wordlikeness' effects for non-words. Coltheart *et al.* (1977) showed that non-words which resemble real words, being capable of transformation into one or more words by single letter changes, are rejected more slowly in lexical decision tasks than non-words which require more letter changes to create a real word. Arguably this is because a wordlike non-word causes considerable activity in the recognition units (logogens) for the real words it resembles, so that the decision that no unit is going to become strongly activated (i.e. that the letter string is a non-word) is delayed. The same word-level activity can explain the finding that subjects are faster to affirm that a wordlike non-word contains a prespecified letter than a non-wordlike non-word. Rumelhart and McClelland (1982) who reported this finding also showed that unpronounceable letter strings which resemble several real words (e.g. SLNT) share the same wordlikeness advantage as conventional pronounceable non-words (e.g. SINT).

Glushko (1979) argued that non-words are pronounced by *analogy* with familiar real words rather than by the application of non-lexical grapheme–phoneme conversion rules. He showed that non-words like *nade* which resemble a set of real words which all have consistent pronunciations (e.g. *fade, made, wade*) are read aloud faster than non-words like *mave* which resemble a set of real words which have differing and inconsistent pronunciations (*have* vs. *gave*). Some theoriests have tried to argue that all pronunciation of non-words and unfamiliar words is lexically mediated (e.g. Henderson, 1982), whereas others wish to maintain separate lexical and non-lexical routes while building into their models ways by which the non-lexical route could be subject to lexical bias (see Kay, 1985). However analogy is finally agreed to exert its influence, it remains true, as Henderson (1982, p. 140) observed, that 'the concept of "resemblance" is crucial to the analogy formulation'.

In the 'picture–word interference' paradigm subjects are shown a picture (typically a line drawing of an object) over which is printed a word or non-word whose relationship to the picture name can be systematically varied. Subjects can be invited to perform various tasks on either the picture or the word/non-word, giving the experimenter the opportunity to examine patterns of facilitation or interference between the two simultaneously visible stimuli (see Lupker, 1985, for a review). We shall discuss various findings shortly when we report extensions of the paradigm to face–name interference, but of more immediate interest here are reports of graphemic similarity (resemblance) effects.

Relative to a picture-only condition, superimposing a picture's own label facilitates naming of the picture, possibly because name retrieval is now being prompted from two sources instead of just one. Superimposing an unrelated label slows picture naming, arguably because of the interference it generates at the name retrieval stage (Lupker, 1985). A semantically unrelated label which shares letters in common with the picture name (e.g. BOOT on the picture of a foot) interferes considerably less than a visually dissimilar label (Lupker, 1982; Underwood and Briggs, 1984; Rayner and Springer, 1986). What may be happening here is that the resemblance of BOOT to FOOT partially activates the visual input logogen for foot. That partial activation helps speed up the accessing of the semantics of FOOT which is already being directed by the picture, and so is a facilitatory influence. Set against that, however, are the inhibitory effects arising from simultaneous activation of the semantics and/or phonology of BOOT. The net result is interference, but less that from a visually dissimilar label (e.g. BALL), all of whose influences are inhibitory.

Turning from the laboratory to everyday life, some jokes and puns depend on appreciating the resemblance between two words or between a non-word and a word. An example is:

Question: 'What's sweet and yellow and swings through trees?'
Answer: 'Tarzipan.'

That particular joke depends for its effect on the reader or listener detecting the resemblance of 'Tarzipan' to both 'Tarzan' and 'marzipan'. The second resemblance is particularly interesting because the fact that listeners can access 'marzipan' from 'tarzipan' must be problematic for models of auditory word recognition such as the 'cohort model' of Marslen-Wilson (1984) which place great emphasis on word onsets. Similarly:

Question: 'What's got sandwiches, a chocolate biscuit and an apple in it, and
swings around in the belfry?'
Answer: 'The lunchpack of Notre Dame.'

The independence of face and word recognition

While we are keen to explore similarities between face recognition and word recognition, there are also differences which must be acknowledged and explained. The first point to note is that logogens and FRUs are almost certainly housed in separate, independent modules rather than clustering together in one common recognition system. The best evidence here is neuropsychological. On the one hand, patients have been reported who, as a result of brain injury, have an impaired ability to recognize once-familiar words as visual forms. These patients are commonly referred to as 'surface dyslexics' (Ellis, 1984; Patterson, Marshall and Coltheart, 1985). Their symptoms imply loss of, or loss of acces to, visual word recognition units (logogens), yet they can be quite unimpaired in their recognition of faces or other visual objects. Conversely, 'prosopagnosic' patients who, following brain injury, may be unable to recognize once-familiar faces may have no difficulty in reading (Hecaen, 1981). Such a 'double dissociation' between word recognition and face recognition implies functionally (and anatomically) separate recognition systems for the two classes of stimulus. We know of no compelling evidence, however, to suggest that there are separate stores for semantics or names accessed from faces or names, so those remain single systems in our model.

There is, in contrast, good evidence that words have forms of direct access to phonology that faces do not enjoy. If you have never seen the name KINNOCK or NIXON written down before, the chances are you will still be able to pronounce (name) it correctly. (NB. We assume for the purposes of this chapter that written names are processed just like any other form of written word.) Skilled readers of alphabetic orthographies like English possess procedures for sublexical spelling–sound conversion which enable them to assemble plausible candidate pronunciations for unfamiliar words (Ellis, 1984). These procedures can be retained in 'surface' dyslexic patients who have impaired direct visual word recognition but can be impaired in 'phonological' dyslexics whose visual word recognition is relatively intact (Funnell, 1983; Coltheart, 1986). This has led to the suggestion that sublexical spelling–sound conversion forms a quite separate system from whole-word recognition, though this issue remains contentious (see Kay, 1985, for a review).

Regardless of the outcome of that particular dispute, it remains the case that English contains many words of varying degrees of irregularity which resist the application of spelling–sound conversion procedures. A fair number of names fall into this category: there is an element of snobbery attached to knowing that BEAUCHAMP is pronounced 'Beecham' or that CHOL-MONDELEY is pronounced 'Chumley', and anyone not having previous experience with such names is unlikely to arrive at the correct pronunciation by sublexical assembly. Irregular names must be retrieved as wholes, and in fact it is quite probable that the pronunciations of even regularly spelled names are retrieved as wholes once they become familiar.

Further experimental data

Cattell (1886) reported that objects are recognized faster than words, while words are named faster than objects. More recently, Potter and Faulconer (1975) found that subjects could classify pictures as belonging to a category such as 'furniture' faster than they could classify the corresponding words, whereas object labels were named faster than pictures. Warren and Morton

Table 3 Mean vocal reaction times (in milliseconds) for correct classification (politician vs. TV personality) or naming of celebrities' faces and names (from Young, McWeeny, Ellis and Hay, 1986, Experiment 4)

	Classification	Naming
Faces	692	853
Names	749	548

(1982) interpreted this result as compatible with a model in which object names can only be retrieved via their semantic representations (hence for objects semantic decision time is faster than naming time), while for words there are separate and independent routes for accessing meaning and pronunciations, with the latter being faster than the former. A similar model was advocated by Nelson, Reed and McEvoy (1977).

Young, McWeeny, Ellis and Hay (1986) found that faces behave similarly to objects in such tasks, with person names behaving like object names. Subjects classified faces on familiarity or occupation faster than written names, while names were named faster than faces. Put another way, faces were categorized faster than they were named, but written names were named faster than they could be categorized (see Table 3). These results are compatible with a model which holds that the name of a person whose face is seen is accessed by first accessing the semantic information you have about that person. In contrast, the semantics and pronunciations belonging to a written name are accessed simultaneously and in parallel.

Young, Ellis, Flude, McWeeny and Hay (1986) further explored the parallel between objects and their names on the one hand, and faces and names on the other, using a face–name interference paradigm. This is similar to the picture–word interference paradigm mentioned earlier except that instead of object labels superimposed on pictures Young *et al.* used names printed alongside photographs of faces. The relationships of the face and name was systematically varied (see Figure 3). In the first experiments carried out by Young *et al.* (1986), four different tasks were employed. In Experiment 1, subjects were asked to name the face while ignoring the written name, or to name the written name while ignoring the face. In Experiment 2, subjects performed a semantic classification on the face (e.g. politician or entertainer?) with instructions to ignore the name, or classified the name while ignoring the face.

In the two classification tasks, the classification of names was subject to interference from faces while the classification of faces was relatively free from interference from accompanying names. This pattern was reversed in the

Figure 3. Stimuli of the sort used in face–name interference experiments.

naming tasks: written names interfered with face naming but faces did not interfere with name naming. The same finding for the naming conditions was obtained by Young, Flude, Ellis and Hay (1986).

Young and his co-workers went on to explore how interference is modified by different relationships between faces and names, but we shall limit ourselves to the main interaction between stimuli and tasks represented in Table 4. This summarizes the results of Young *et al.*'s (1986) first experiments (but see also Young, Hay and Ellis, 1986). Once again the interaction is the same as has been found for pictures and words (Lupker, 1985).

It might be noticed that for both classification and naming, the type of stimulus which is immune to interference is the one which is responded to faster (Smith and Magee, 1980). Faces are classified faster than names and are less subject to interference, while names are named faster than faces, and for this task it is the names that are immune to interference. Work on picture–word interference suggests, however, that relative speeds do not explain the interaction. Glaser and Dungelhoff (1984) and Rayner and Springer (1986) staggered the presentation onsets of the picture and the word. They showed that the pattern of which stimulus is interference-prone and which interference-free remains the same even when the stimulus which is processed more slowly is presented first and so given time to exert any interference it might be capable of.

McLeod and Posner (1984) used data from dual-task performance (where subjects attempt to carry out two tasks simultaneously) to argue that some routes through the cognitive system from input to output are 'privileged'; that is, not subject to interference from elsewhere in the system. They identified the auditory–vocal repetition pathway involved in repeating or shadowing speech as one such 'privileged loop'.

The mechanisms involved in pronouncing familiar words aloud also appear interference-free and so should qualify for privileged status on McLeod and Posner's criteria. The other interference-free route we have identified is the route to person information from faces. This is not a through-route, so the term 'loop' does not seem appropriate, and it might be preferable to talk of

Table 4   Patterns of interference in face–name interference

		Semantic classification	Naming
	Face	Not subject to interference	Interfered with by names
Stimulus being operated upon	Name	Interfered with by faces	Not subject to interference

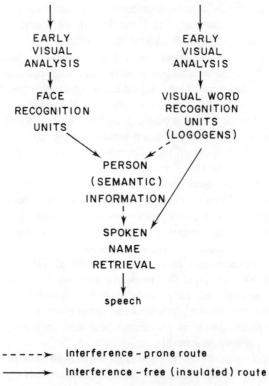

Figure 4. A possible functional architecture for the
recognition of familiar faces and words.

routes as *insulated* rather than privileged. Figure 4 summarizes the functional
architecture which we believe characterizes the processes of face and word
(name) recognition, and indicates which routes we consider to be insulated
and which subject to interference. The conventional reminder that such
models only tell half the story—the other half having to do with the internal
workings of the components and the nature of their intercommunications—is
in order. We also acknowledge that the distinction between insulated and
interference-prone routes does little more than redescribe the data, albeit in a
more concise way which draws together and integrates data from several
different experiments. It remains to be explained how interference occurs
when it does occur, and how some routes manage to be interference-free.

'CONTEXT' EFFECTS IN FACE RECOGNITION

It has been known for a long time that the process of recognizing a word can
be made faster and more accurate ('primed') if the word is immediately

preceded by another that is similar in meaning (Pillsbury, 1897; O'Neill, 1953; Engler and Freeman, 1956; Meyer and Schvaneveldt, 1971). Bruce (1983) and Bruce and Valentine (1986) have reported similar effects for face recognition. Thus subjects are faster to decide that the face of Art Garfunkel is familiar if it is preceded by Paul Simon than if it is preceded by the face of an unrelated individual such as Stan Laurel. Although people talk of 'Simon and Garfunkel' rather than 'Garfunkel and Simon', Bruce and Valentine (1986) showed that the magnitude of the priming effect is independent of the order in which the two faces occur.

The question can then be asked: Is this priming effect semantic or associative, arising from the fact that members of the pair tend to be seen together? John Lennon and Paul McCartney are both pop stars; so are Mick Jagger and Keith Richard. But would Keith Richard prime Paul McCartney by virtue of their common semantic category membership, or will he only prime the pop stars with whom he is closely associated?

Bruce's (1983; Bruce and Valentine, 1986) experiments do not help us answer this particular question because all their semantically related pairs are also associatively related (Paul Newman and Robert Redford; Stan Laurel and Oliver Hardy; Richard Burton and Elizabeth Taylor, etc.). The issue has, however, been addressed in the area of object recognition. Several studies have shown priming between pairs of object pictures, but typically these have been both associatively and semantically related (e.g. Sperber *et al.*, 1979; Huttenlocher and Kubicek, 1983). Lupker (1985), however, summarizes several of his own experiments which failed to find priming between objects which come from the same semantic category but are not associated.

It seems to us reasonable that priming of object or face recognition should be based on association rather than category membership. Priming of this sort is surely a kind of *anticipation* (though we do not mean to imply that it is consciously mediated). Priming is the cognitive system using its current perceptual experiences to prepare itself for what it is likely to encounter next. Suppose you meet a friend while out shopping. The friend is a cognitive psychologist, but also a keen cricketer and a talented operatic tenor. Upon recognizing your friend do you really want to prime FRUs for other individuals who share a common category (George Miller? Geoffrey Boycott? Placido Domingo?)? Such priming would serve no purpose whatsoever, because the fact of having just met your friend in town makes it no more likely that the next face you see will be that of George Miller, Geoffrey Boycott or Placido Domingo.

If the face of your friend is to prime anyone, then it should prime other people you commonly see your friend with—his wife, children, friends, neighbours or close colleagues. That priming is associative, not semantic.

Another question which has exercised students of word recognition and which can be extended to face recognition is, *where* does associative priming exert its influence? Does priming aid the *perception* of a face, for example, or post-perceptual processes such as the activation of relevant person information? Bruce and Valentine (1986) found an interaction between semantic priming and stimulus quality: identification of blurred faces benefited significantly more from priming than did identification of clear faces. Similar results have been obtained for word recognition (e.g. Meyer, Schvaneveldt and Ruddy, 1975; Becker and Killion, 1977; Sperber *et al.*, 1979). Following the logic of Sternberg (1969) these results have been interpreted as indicating that priming affects a perceptual stage which is also affected by stimulus degradation. Bruce and Valentine (1986) suggest that priming may occur at the level of FRUs. Thus, seeing Paul Newman would cause partial activation in the FRU for Robert Redford so that less external visual input would be needed to maximally activate the FRU for Robert Redford.

When we turn to the diary study of Young, Hay and Ellis (1985), however, a somewhat different picture of context effects emerges. The type of recognition error that seems most affected by context is not the total failure to recognize a person but the isolated feeling that the person is familiar without the relevant person information being available. Meeting a familiar person out of their normal setting can induce 'familiarity only' feelings which diarists commonly report having resolved by mentally searching through alternative possible contexts in which the person might be known until the right one is hit upon and the person recognized properly.

These observations suggest that general context or setting partially activates person information for individuals one is used to meeting in that setting, making the person information more available when a familiar face is seen. This is a different sort of context from person-to-person priming, and operates at a different cognitive locus. This proposal parallels that of Seidenberg *et al.* (1984) who argued that associative or semantic priming from one word to the next facilitates word recognition through effects at the recognition unit (logogen) level, whereas wider sentence context effects facilitate the post-lexical activation and integration of word meanings. More generally, our suggestions parallel Memon and Bruce's (1985) view that there are a number of distinct context effects which need to be teased apart.

CODA

I was walking along the street in Lancaster when I saw in front of me a tallish man in his early twenties. He had a distinctive face and gait, and I knew he reminded me of someone. At the same time I knew he wasn't that someone.

After five seconds or so it 'clicked' (partially) and I realized that he was reminding me of a British comedian. I could picture the comedian's face and could remember some of the programmes I had seen him in, but for a time I could not remember his name. The surname came first—Atkinson—and I knew that his Christian name began with 'R'. I 'blocked' for a while on Richard before the correct name, Rowan, came to mind. The young man had reminded me of Rowan Atkinson. The whole incident lasted perhaps one and a half minutes.

This incident happened to one of us (A.E.). It was a particularly dramatic error in its combination of 'familiarity only based on resemblance' followed by 'inability to remember name', but we have plenty of examples of each component type in the records of our diaries. We would like to think that the sort of cognitive models of person recognition that we and others are currently building will allow us to account for such everyday experiences, as well as accounting for data from laboratory experiments (and neuro-psychological case studies).

Contrary to Searle, we do *not* always 'recognize the faces of our friends, relatives and acquaintances quite effortlessly'; sometimes considerable effort is involved. Face recognition is nothing like 'as simple and as automatic as making footprints in the sand': it is a complex skill which draws upon a number of separate and distinct cognitive subsystems. We *can* understand it, but we shall only do so if we do not shrink from embracing the empirical and theoretical techniques of cognitive modelling.

ACKNOWLEDGEMENTS

The research was supported by the Economic and Social Research Council and the University of Lancaster Social Science Research Committee. We should like to thank Kate McWeeny and Brenda Flude for their contributions to the projects from which the ideas expressed here arose, and Vicki Bruce for comments and discussion.

REFERENCES

Baron, R. J. (1981). Mechanisms of human facial recognition. *International Journal of Man–Machine Studies*, **15**, 137–78.

Becker, C. A., and Killion, T. H. (1977). Interaction of visual and cognitive effects in word recognition. *Journal of Experimental Psychology: Human Perception and Performance*, **3**, 389–401.

Broadbent, D. E. (1971). *Decision and Stress*. London: Academic Press.

Bruce, V. (1983). Recognizing faces. *Philosophical Transactions of the Royal Society of London*, **B302**, 423–36.

Bruce, V., and Valentine, T. (1986). Semantic priming of familiar faces. *Quarterly Journal of Experimental Psychology*, **38A**, 125–50.

Bruce, V., and Young, A. W. (1986). Understanding face recognition. *British Journal of Psychology*, **77**, 305–27.

Cattell, J. McK. (1886). The time it takes to see and name objects. *Mind*, **11**, 63–5.

Cohen, G. (1980). Reading and searching for spelling errors. In U. Frith (ed.) *Cognitive Processes in Spelling*. London: Academic Press.

Coltheart, M. (1978). Lexical access in simple reading tasks. In G. Underwood (ed.) *Strategies of Information Processing*. London: Academic Press.

Coltheart, M. (1986). Cognitive neuropsychology. In M. Posner and O. S. M. Marin (eds) *Attention and Performance*, Vol. XI. Hillsdale, NJ: Lawrence Erlbaum Associates.

Coltheart, M., Davelaar, E., Jonasson, J. T. and Besner, D. (1977). Access to the internal lexicon. In S. Dornic (ed.) *Attention and Performance VI*. Hillsdale, NJ: Lawrence Erlbaum Associates.

Cowie, R. (1985). Reading errors as clues to the nature of reading. In A. W. Ellis (ed.) *Progress in the Psychology of Language*, Vol. 1. London: Lawrence Erlbaum Associates.

Downey, J. (1918). The proof reader's illusion and general intelligence. *Journal of Philosophy, Psychology and Scientific Methods*, 15, 44–7.

Ellis, A. W. (1984). *Reading, Writing and Dyslexia: A Cognitive Analysis*. London: Lawrence Erlbaum Associates.

Ellis, H. D. (1987). Processes underlying face recognition. In R. Bruyer (ed.) *The Neuropsychology of Face Perception and Facial Expression*. New Jersey: Lawrence Erlbaum Associates.

Engler, J., and Freeman, J. T. (1956). Perceptual behaviour as related to factors of associative and drive strength. *Journal of Experimental Psychology*, 51, 399–404.

Funnell, E. (1983). Phonological processes in reading: New evidence from acquired dyslexia. *British Journal of Psychology*, 74, 159–180.

Glaser, W. R., and Dungelhoff, F. J. (1984). The time course of picture–word interference. *Journal of Experimental Psychology: Human Perception and Performance*, 10, 640–54.

Glushko, R. J. (1979). The organization and activation of orthographic knowledge in reading aloud. *Journal of Experimental Psychology: Human Perception and Performance*, 5, 674–91.

Haig, N. D. (1984). The effect of feature displacement on face recognition. *Perception*, 13, 505–12.

Hay, D. C. (1981). Asymmetries in facial recognition: Evidence for a perceptual component. *Quarterly Journal of Experimental Psychology*, 33A, 267–74.

Hay, D. C., and Young, A. W. (1982). The human face. In A. W. Ellis (ed.) *Normality and Pathology in Cognitive Functions*. London: Academic Press.

Hecaen, H. (1981). The neuropsychology of face recognition. In G. Davies, H. Ellis and J. Shepherd (eds) *Perceiving and Remembering Faces*. London: Academic Press.

Henderson, L. (1982). *Orthography and Word Recognition in Reading*. London: Academic Press.

Huttenlocher, J., and Kubicek, L. F. (1983). The source of relatedness effects on naming latency. *Journal of Experimental Psychology: Learning, Memory and Cognition*, 9, 486–96.

Kay, J. (1985). Mechanisms of oral reading: A critical appraisal of cognitive models. In A. W. Ellis (ed.) *Progress in the Psychology of Language*, Vol. 2. London: Lawrence Erlbaum Associates.

Kay, J., and Ellis, A. W. (in press). A cognitive neuropsychological case study of anomia: Implications for psychological models of word retrieval. *Brain*.

Kay, J., and Patterson, K. E. (1985). Routes to meaning in surface dyslexia. In K. E. Patterson, J. C. Marshall and M. Coltheart (eds) *Surface Dyslexia: Neuropsychological and Cognitive Analyses of Phonological Reading*. London: Lawrence Erlbaum Associates.

Klatt, D. H. (1979). Speech perception: a model of acoustic–phonetic analysis and lexical access. *Journal of Phonetics*, **7**, 279–312.

Lupker, S. J. (1982). The role of phonetic and orthographic similarity in picture–word interference. *Canadian Journal of Psychology*, **36**, 349–67.

Lupker, S. J. (1985). Relatedness effects in word and picture naming: Parallels, differences and structural implications. In A. W. Ellis (ed.) *Progress in the Psychology of Language*, Vol. 1. London: Lawrence Erlbaum Associates.

McClelland, J. L., and Rumelhart, D. E. (1981). An interactive activation model of context effects in letter perception: Part 1. An account of basic findings. *Psychological Review*, **88**, 375–407.

McClelland, J. L., and Rumelhart, D. E. (1985). Distributed memory and the representation of general and specific information. *Journal of Experimental Psychology: General*, **114**, 159–88.

McLeod, P., and Posner, M. I. (1984). Privileged loops from percept to act. In H. Bouma and D. G. Bouwhuis (eds) *Attention and Performance*, Vol. 10. London: Lawrence Erlbaum Associates.

McWeeny, K. H. (1985). Face processing: An investigation of everyday problems in learning and recognising faces and names. Unpublished M.Phil. thesis, University of Lancaster.

McWeeny, K. H., Young, A. W., Hay, D. C. and Ellis, A. W. (in press). Putting names to faces. *British Journal of Psychology*.

Mandler, G. (1980). Recognizing: The judgement of previous occurrence. *Psychological Review*, **87**, 252–71.

Marslen-Wilson, W. (1984). Function and process in spoken word recognition—A tutorial review. In H. Bouma and D. G. Bouwhuis (eds) *Attention and Performance*, Vol. X: *Control of Language Process*. London: Lawrence Erlbaum Associates.

Memon, A., and Bruce, V. (1985). Context effects in episodic studies of verbal and facial memory. *Current Psychological Research and Reviews*, **4**, 349–69.

Meyer, D. E., and Schvaneveldt, R. W. (1971). Facilitation in recognizing pairs of words: Evidence of a dependence between retrieval operations. *Journal of Experimental Psychology*, **90**, 227–34.

Meyer, D. E., Schvaneveldt, R. W. and Ruddy, M. G. (1975). Loci of contextual effects in visual word recognition. In P. M. A. Rabbit and S. Dornic (eds) *Attention and Performance*, Vol. V. London: Academic Press.

Mitchell, D. C. (1982). *The Process of Reading*. Chichester: John Wiley.

Monk, A. F., and Hulme, C. (1983). Errors in proofreading: Evidence for the use of word shape in word recognition. *Memory and Cognition*, **11**, 16–23.

Morton, J. (1964). A preliminary functional model for language behaviour. *International Audiology*, **3**, 216–25. (Reprinted in R. C. Oldfield and J. C. Marshall (eds) *Language*. London: Penguin Books, 1968.)

Morton, J. (1969). Interaction of information in word recognition. *Psychological Review*, **76**, 165–78.

Morton, J. (1979a). Word recognition. In J. Morton and J. C. Marshall (eds) *Psycholinguistics Series*, Vol. 2. London: Elek Science, and Cambridge, Mass.: MIT Press.

Morton, J. (1979b). Facilitation in word recognition: Experiments causing change in the logogen model. In P. A. Kolers, M. Wrolstad and H. Bouma (eds) *Processing of Visible Language*, Vol. 1. New York: Plenum.

Nelson, D. L., Reed, V. S. and McEvoy, C. L. (1977). Learning to order pictures and words: A model of sensory and semantic encoding. *Journal of Experimental Psychology: Human Learning and Memory*, **3**, 485–97.

O'Neill, W. M. (1953). The effect of verbal association on tachistoscopic recognition. *Australian Journal of Psychology*, 5, 42–5.

Patterson, K. E., Marshall, J. C. and Coltheart, M. (eds) (1985). *Surface Dyslexia: Neuropsychological and Cognitive Analyses of Phonological Reading*. London: Lawrence Erlbaum Associates.

Pillsbury, W. B. (1897). A study in apperception. *American Journal of Psychology*, 8, 315–93.

Potter, M. C., and Faulconer, B. A. (1975). Time to understand pictures and words. *Nature (London)*, 253, 437–38.

Rayner, K., and Springer, C. J. (1986). Graphemic and semantic similarity effects in the picture–word interference task. *British Journal of Psychology*, 77, 207–22.

Read, J. O., and Bruce, D. (1982). Longitudinal tracking of difficult memory retrievals. *Cognitive Psychology*, 14, 280–300.

Reason, J., and Lucas, D. (1984). Using cognitive diaries to investigate naturally occurring memory blocks. In J. E. Harris and P. E. Morris (eds) *Everyday Memory, Actions and Absent-mindedness*. London: Academic Press.

Rumelhart, D. E., and McClelland, J. L. (1982). An interactive activation model of context effects in letter perception: Part 2. The contextual enhancement effect and some tests and extensions of the model. *Psychological Review*, 89, 60–94.

Schank, R. C. (1982). *Dynamic Memory: A Theory of Learning in Computers and People*. Cambridge: Cambridge University Press.

Searle, J. (1984). *Minds, Brains and Science: The 1984 Reith Lectures*. London: British Broadcasting Corporation.

Seidenberg, M. S., Waters, G. S., Sanders, M. and Langer, P. (1984). Pre- and postlexical loci of contextual effects on word recognition. *Memory and Cognition*, 12, 315–28.

Smith, M. C., and Magee, L. E. (1980). Tracing the time course of picture–word processing. *Journal of Experimental Psychology: General*, 109, 373–92.

Sperber, R. D., McCauley, C., Ragain, R. and Weil, C. M. (1979). Semantic priming effects on picture and word processing. *Memory and Cognition*, 7, 339–45.

Sternberg, S. (1969). The discovery of processing stages: Extensions of Donders' method. *Acta Psychologica*, 30, 276–315.

Triesman, A. M. (1964). Verbal cues, language, and meaning in selective attention. *American Journal of Psychology*, 77, 206–19.

Underwood, G., and Briggs, P. (1984). The development of word recognition processes. *British Journal of Psychology*, 75, 243–56.

Vernon, M. D. (1929). *The Errors Made in Reading*. Medical Research Council Special Report Series, No. 130. London: HMSO.

Warren, C., and Morton, J. (1982). The effects of priming on picture recognition. *British Journal of Psychology*, 73, 117–30.

Weber, R.-M. (1968). The study of oral reading errors: A survey of the literature. *Reading Research Quarterly*, 4, 96–119.

Williams, M. D., and Hollan, J. D. (1981). The process of retrieval from very long-term memory. *Cognitive Science*, 5, 87–119.

Yarmey, A. D. (1973). I recognize your face but I can't remember your name: further evidence on the tip-of-the-tongue phenomenon. *Memory and Cognition*, 3, 289–90.

Young, A. W., Hay, D. C. and Ellis, A. W. (1985). The faces that launched a thousand slips: everyday difficulties and errors in recognising people. *British Journal of Psychology*, 76, 495–523.

Young, A. W., Hay, D. C. and McWeeny, K. H. (1985). Right cerebral hemisphere superiority for constructing facial representations. *Neuropsychologia*, 23, 195–202.

Young, A. W., Ellis, A. W., Flude, B. M., McWeeny, K. H. and Hay, D. C. (1986). Face-name interference. *Journal of Experimental Psychology: Human Perception and Performance*, **12**, 466–75.

Young, A. W., Flude, B. M., Ellis, A. W. and Hay, D. C. (in press). Interference with face naming. *Acta Psychologica*.

Young, A. W., Hay, D. C. and Ellis, A. W. (1986). Getting semantic information from familiar faces. In H. D. Ellis, M. A. Jeeves, F. Newcombe and A. W. Young (eds) *Aspects of Face Processing*. NATO ARW series. The Hague: Martinus Nijhoff.

Young, A. W., McWeeny, K. H., Ellis, A. W. and Hay, D. C. (1986). Naming and categorising faces and written names. *Quarterly Journal of Experimental Psychology*, **38A**, 297–318.

Young, A. W., McWeeny, K. H., Hay, D. C. and Ellis, A. W. (1986). Access to identity-specific semantic codes from familiar faces. *Quarterly Journal of Experimental Psychology*, **38A**, 271–95.

Author Index

Abelson, R., 146, *164*, 187, 188, *197*, 232, 234, 246, *247*
Alwood, 162, *163*
Anderson, J. R., 94, 95, 96, 98, 102, 103, 112, 118, 120, *131*, *132*, *133*, 135, 137, 138, 143, 146, 162, *163*, *165*, 201, 211, *212*, 233, 235, 237, *247*
Austin, J. L., 254, *266*

Baddeley, A. D., 182, *184*
Ballard, D. H., 233, *247*
Ballstaedt, S., 143, *164*
Barclay, J. R., 188, *196*
Barber, D., 202, *212*
Bardhan, K. D., 202, *212*
Baron, R. J., 274, *293*
Bartlett, F. C., 189, *196*
Becker, C. A., 292, *293*
Becker, J., 18, *19*
Bennett, G. K., 86, *90*
Berg, C. A., 57, *90*
Bilodeau, I. McD., 108, 132
Black, J. B., 188, *196*
Bloom, B. S., 94, *132*
Bonar, J., 103, *133*
Bovair, S., *164*
Bower, G. H., 188, *196*, 233, 235, 237, *247*
Boycott, G., 270–272, 278
Boyle, C. F., 112, *132*
Braine, M. D. S., 9, *20*
Bransford, J. D., 143, *164*, 188, 193, *196*
Brewer, W. F., 188, 189, 193, 194, *196*, *197*
Briggs, P., 285, *296*
Broadbent, D. E., 174, 182, 183, *184*, 273, *293*
Brooks, R. E., 118, *132*

Brown, G. D. A., 233, *247*
Brown, J. S., 93, 94, 99, *132*, 187, 190, *197*
Bruce, D., 278, *296*
Bruce, V., 270, 271, 278, 281, 291, *293*, 295
Burton, A. M., 17, *19*
Burton, R. R., 94, *132*

Carbonell, J. R., 93, *132*
Card, S., 142, *164*
Cattell, J. McK., 286, *293*
Cattell, R. B., 57, *90*
Charney, D., 143, 144, 145, 156, 161, *164*, 165
Chi, M. T. H., 18, *19*
Chiesi, H. L., 143, *164*
Clancey, W. J., 95, *132*
Clement, J., 191, *197*
Clocksin, W. F., 205, *212*
Cohen, G., 282, *293*
Cohen, V. B., 83, *132*
Collins, A., 190, *197*
Collins, H. M., 18, *20*
Coltheart, M., 282, 284, 285, 286, *294*
Cottrell, G. W., 233, *247*
Craik, F. I. M., 143, *164*
Cowie, R., 282, *294*

Darwin, C., 63
Davey, A., 260, 262, *266*
Davidson, J. E., 63, 64, 66, 71, 73, 84, *90*, *91*
Davison, A., 256, *266*
De Jong, G., 23, 29, 40, *56*
de Kleer, J., 94, *132*, 187, 190, *197*
Dell, G. S., 233, 247
Dixon, P., 157, *164*

299

Dooling, 188
Downey, R., 282, *294*
Draper, R. C., 18, *20*
Dumais, S. T., 138, *165*
Duncan, J., 178–81, *184*
Dungelhoff, F. J., 289, *294*
Dupree, D. A., 194, *196*

Efstathiou, J., 12, *20*
Egeth, H. E., 177, *184*
Ehrlich, K., 103, *133*, 188, *197*
Ekstrom, R. B., 65, *90*
Ellis, A. W., 272, 273, 275, 277, 278,
    279, 281, 283, 285, 286, 287, 289,
    292, *294*, *296*, *297*
Ellis, H. D., 271, 279, 281, *294*
Engler, J., 191, *294*

Farrell, R., 95, 103, 104, 118, 120, *132*,
    146, *163*
Faulconer, B. A., 286, *296*
Fawcett, R., 262, *267*
Feldman, J. A., 233, *247*, *248*
Fikes, R. E., 232, *247*
Fitts, P. M., 137, *164*
Fleming, A., 63
Flexser, A. J., 221, 227, *229*
Flude, B., 287, 289, *297*
Foss, C. L., 233, *247*
Fox, J., 13, *20*, 202, 203, 204, 211, *212*
Franks, J. J., 189, *196*
Freeman, J. T., 291, *294*
French, J. W., 65, *90*
Funnell, E., 286, *294*

Garbart, H., 184
Gazdar, G., 263, 264, *267*
Gelade, G., 171, 177, *185*
Gentner, D., 7, *20*, 144, *164*, 187, 190,
    197
Gilson, C., 146, *164*
Glaser, E. M., 86, *91*
Glaser, R., 18, *19*
Glaser, W. R., 289, *294*
Glushko, R. J., 284, *294*
Glymour, C., 207, *212*
Goffman, E., 252, *267*
Goldin, S. E., 84, *133*
Goodman, 75, *90*
Gordon, 188
Graesser, 188
Green, R. H., 18, *20*

Hacking, I., 207–8, *212*
Haig, N. D., 281, *294*
Hall, J. F., 225, *229*
Halliday, M. A. K., 259–260, *267*
Hart, R. E., 232, *247*
Hay, D. C., 269, 270, 272, 273, 275, 277,
    278, 279, 281, 287, 289, 292, *294*,
    296, *297*
Hayes, J. R., 135, 138, *164*
Hecaen, H., 286, *294*
Henderson, L., 270, 284, *294*
Hintzman, D. L., 215, 218, 224, 228, *229*
Hitch, G. J., 182, *184*
Hobbs, J., 144, *164*
Hoffer, A., 111, *132*
Hollan, J. D., 190, *197*, 278, *296*
Hom, J. L., 57, *90*
Houghton, G., 249, *267*
Hudson, R. A., 260, *267*
Hulme, C., 282, *295*
Huttenlocher, J., 291, *294*

Jefferson, G., 252, *267*
Jeffries, R., 96, 107, *132*
Jevons, W. S., 9, *20*
Johnson, M. K., 193, *196*
Johnson-Laird, P. N., 5, 7, 10, 12, 13, *20*,
    187, 188, 191, 192, *197*
Jurgensen, R. C., 100, *132*

Kahneman, D., 12, *20*, 201, 202, *212*
Kaufman, A. S., 57, *90*
Kaufman, N. L., 57, *90*
Kay, J., 279, 283, 284, 286, *294*
Kekulé, 64
Kieras, D., 135, 138, 139, *164*
Killion, T. H., 292, *293*
Kintsch, W., 187, 191, 193, *197*
Klatt, D. H., 270, *295*
Klein, E., *267*
Kohler, W., 62, *90*
Kolodner, J. L., 22, 25, *56*
Kubicek, L. F., 291, *294*
Kuhn, 14

Lakatos, 14
Larkin, J. H., 17, *20*
Lebowitz, M., 22, *56*
LeFevre, J., 138, 157, *164*
Lewis, M., 108, *132*
Lichtenstein, E. H., 194, *197*
Lieberman, K., 182, *184*

Lucas, D., 278, *296*
Lupker, S. J., 284, 285, 289, 291, *295*

Magee, L. E., 289, *296*
Maier, N. R. F., 62, *90*
Mamdani, A., 12, *20*
Mandl, H., 143, 146, *164*
Marr, D. B., 71, *90*
Marshall, J. C., 285, *296*
Marslen-Wilson, W., 285, *296*
McClelland, J. L., 233, *247*, 270, 274, 276, 277, 284, *296*
McEvoy, C. L., 287, *295*
McGuire, W. J., 163, *164*
McKendree, J., 98, 107, 109, 111, *132*
McLeod, P., 289, *295*
McWeeny, K. H., 273, 279, 280, 281, *295*
Mellish, C. S., 205, *212*
Memon, A., 292, *295*
Merrill, M., 145, *165*
Meyer, D. E., 291, *295*
Michalski, R. S., 15, *20*
Minsky, M., 187, 188, *197*
Mischel, W., 62, *90*
Mitchell, D. C., 233, 234, *247*, 270, *295*
Monk, A. F., 282, *295*
Moran, T., 142, *164*
Morgan, K., 143, 144, 146, 161, *165*
Morton, J., 270, 271, 286, 287, *295*
Muter, P., 227, 228, *229*

Nakamura, G. V., 188, 189, 193, *197*
Neisser, U., 4, *20*
Nelson, D. L., 287, *295*
Neves, D. M., 110, *132*
Newell, A., 99, *132*, 138, 142, *164*, *165*, 232, *247*
Nickerson, R. S., 171, *184*
Nisbett, R. E., 15, *20*
Nilsson, N. J., 232, *247*
Nitsch, K. E., 145, *165*
Norman, D. A., 190, *197*

Oldbrechts-Tyteca, L., 146, *165*
O'Neill, W. M., 291, *296*
O'Shea, T., 99, *133*

Pang, D., 12, *20*
Pani, J. R., 189, *197*
Papert, S., 93, *133*
Parleins, D., 62, *90*

Patterson, K. E., 283, 285, *296*
Perelman, C., 145, *165*
Perrig, W., 193, *197*
Pfeifer, R., 232, *248*
Piaget, J., 58, *90*
Pillsbury, W. B., 282, 291, *296*
Pirolli, P., 95, 103, 104, 106, 118, *132*, *133*
Plato, 271
Pollock, J. B., 233, *248*
Polson, 135, 138, *164*
Popper, K., 14–15
Posner, M. I., 289, *295*
Potter, M. C., 286, *296*
Power, R., 249, 252, 254, *267*
Prince, E. F., 262, *267*
Pullum, G., 263, 264, *267*

Raaheim, K., 57, 58, *90*
Rabbitt, P. M. A., 175, 176, *184*
Ratcliff, R., 174, *185*
Rayner, K., 285, 289, *296*
Read, J. O., 278, *296*
Reason, J., 278, *296*
Reder, L. M., 143, 144, 156, 161, 162, *163*, *165*
Reed, V. S., 287, *296*
Rees, E., 18, *19*
Reiser, B. J., 107, 109, *132*
Rich, C., 104, *133*
Rodgers, B., 175, *185*
Rosenbloom, P. S., 138, *164*, *165*
Ross, B. H., 105, *133*, 147, 162, *165*
Rubin, D. C., 228, *229*
Ruddy, M. G., 292, *295*
Rumelhart, D. E., 187, 188, *197*, 233, *247*, 270, 276, 277, 284, *296*

Saceroti, E. D., 232, *247*
Sacks, H., 252, *267*
Sag, I., *267*
Sauers, R., 95, 103, 118, 120, 132, 146, *163*
Sawyer, 188
Schank, R. C., 14, 21, 22, 27, 29, 32, 33, 35, *56*, 187, 188, *197*, 232, 246, *247*, 274, *296*
Schegloff, E., 252, *267*
Schneider, W., 138, *165*, 171, *185*
Schnotz, W., 143, 146, *164*
Schoenfeld, A., 146, *165*
Schvaneveldt, R. W., 291, *295*

Searle, J., 254, 256, 267, 269, 293, *296*
Seashore, H. G., 86, 90
Seidenberg, M. S., 292, *296*
Sharkey, A. J. C., 234, 236, *248*
Sharkey, N. E., 233, 234, 236, *247*, *248*
Shastri, L., 233, *248*
Sheil, B. A., 103, *133*
Shneiderman, B., 103, *133*
Shriffrin, R. M., 138, *165*, 171, *185*
Shrobe, H., 104, *133*
Siklossy, 104, *133*
Simon, H. A., 12, *20*, 99, *132*, 135, 138, *164*, 165, 183, *185*, 201, *212*, 232, *247*
Skinner, B. F., 108, *133*
Sleeman, D., 93, 94, 99, *133*
Small, 233
Smith, M. C., 289, *296*
Smyth, M., 10
Snow, R. E., 57, *90*
Soloway, E., 103, 104, *133*
Sommers, F., *20*
Sperber, D., 13, *20*, 291, *296*
Spilich, G. J., 143, *164*
Springer, C. J., 285, 289, *296*
Sternberg, R. J., 57, 58, 59, 63, 64, 66, 71, 73, 74, 81, 84, 89, 90, *91*
Sternberg, S., 171, *185*, 292, *296*
Stevens, A., 94, *133*, 187, 190, *197*
Stevens, A. L., 7, *20*
Stubb, M., 252, *267*
Sulin, R. A., 188, *197*
Sutcliffe, R. F. E., 234, *248*

Taylor, R., 93, *133*
Tennyson, R., 145, *165*
Tergan, S., 143, 146, *164*
Tetewsky, S. J., 81, *91*
Thagard, P., 15, 16, *20*
Thomson, P. M., 105, *133*
Thurstone, L. L., 86, *91*
Thurstone, T. G., 86, *91*
Townsend, J. T., 174, *185*

Treisman, A. M., 171, 177, *185*, 220, 273, *296*
Treyens, J. C., 188, 194, *197*
Tulving, E., 105, *133*, 143, *164*, 215, 220–221, 227, 229
Turner, T. J., 188, 196
Tversky, A., 12, *20*, 201, 202, *212*

Underwood, G., 285, *296*

Valentine, T., 291, *293*
van Dijk, T. A., 187, 191, *197*
Van Lehn, K., 99, *133*
Vance, C., 23, 30
Vemon, M. D., 282, *296*
Virzi, R. A., *184*
Voss, J. F., 143, *164*

Waltz, D., 233, *248*
Warren, C., 286, *296*
Wason, P. C., 5, *20*
Watson, G., 86, *91*
Weber, R. M., 282, *296*
Weinstein, C. E., 143, *165*
Wertheimer, M., 62, *91*
Wesman, A. G., 86, *90*
Wiksrom, 162
Wilensky, R., 239, 246, *248*
Williams, M. D., 190, *197*, 278, *296*
Wilson, D., 13, *20*
Winograd, T., 14, 260, *267*
Wiseman, S., 215, 220–221, 229
Wobcke, W., 234, *248*
Wolley, F., 145, *165*
Wunderlich, D., 255, *267*

Yarmey, A. D., 278, *296*
Young, A. W., 270, 271, 272, 273, 275, 277, 278, 279, 281, 287, 289, 292, *293*, *296*, *297*

Zipser, 233, *247*

Subject Index

Abstract memory, 183
Abstract rules, diversity of, 141
Abstract understanding, promotion of, 106
Abstract working memory, 182
Accommodation, 58
Acquisition of information, effect of elaborations on, 143
Acquisition of procedures, influence of verbal instruction on, 138
Acorn Atom, 171
ACT, mechanism for knowledge compilation, 105
ACT simulations, 106
ACT* theory, xii, 93, 94, 95–98, 99, 107–109, 110, 137
Action sequences, understanding of, 232
Adjustment and anchoring, 201
Algorithm, 146
    depth-first backward-chaining, 252
Algorithm design, 118, 120, 123
Algorithm-design mode, 121
Alphabetic orthographies, 286
Alvey Directorate, 3
Analogy, 144, 145
    drawback, 149
    role in skill learning, 148
Anomic aphasia, 279
Aristotelian syllogisms, 7
Articulatory loop, 182, 184
Artificial Intelligence (AI), 15, 25, 199, 203, 209, 246
    literature, 19
    research approaches, 4, 15
    understanding programs, 31
Artificial Intelligence techniques, 93, 94
Assimilation, 58
Associative network, 234

Associative recall, 218
'Atmosphere' effects, 9
Attention-getting game, 257
Automatic/control processes distinction, 174
Availability, 201

Basic, 17
Bayesian decision-making techniques, 209
Behaviour, hierarchy in organization of, 251
Belief, 14
Benzene ring discovery, 64
Binary and Continuous Activation Systems (BACAS), 234, 247
Bottom-up routine, 40

Category effect, 178
CDR-recursion plan, 104, 120
'Central executive', 182
Code generation, model for, 119
Cognition, architecture of, 201–202
Cognitive abilities test, number series subtests of, 73
Cognitive intelligence, 4, 12, 13, 14, 16
Cognitive modelling, weaknesses, xiv
    new power of, xii
Cognitive models, coping with novelty, 57
Cognitive principles in design of LISP tutor, 130
Cognitive processes, higher, 4
Cognitive psychologists, 3, 5, 280
Cognitive psychology, xi, xii
    journals, 17

Cognitive science, xi, xii, 6, 94
  journals, 17
Cognitive skill acquisition, 138
  tripartite model of, 138–143
Cognitive structures, 58
Cohort model, 285
Componential subtheory of intelligence,
  60–61
Command editing, 149–150
  increasing the salience of alternative
    procedures, 159
  learning to integrate a collection of
    operations, 154
  learning to judge when one procedure
    is better than another, 160
Command editing procedure, motivation
  of use, 150
Component skills, 136
Composition, 97–98
Comprehension of language, 9
Computational model of language
  production, xiv, 249
Computational modelling, 170
Computational models, 6
Computer models, importance of, xi
Computer operating system, 139
Computer programmers, 38
Computer programming, for creativity,
  xii
Computer simulations of word
  recognition, 270
Computer text-editor, 139, 162
Computer tutoring, xii, 94, 98, 130
Computers in education, role of, 93
Concept projection, model of, 78–80
Concept projection task, 74–78
Conceptual Dependency Theory, 35
Conceptual elaborations, 156, 157
Conceptual system, novel, 74
Conflict-resolution principle, 113
Content-free processes, 17
Contextual subtheory of intelligence,
  60–61
Control processes, see Automatic/control
  processes
Convergent-discriminant validation, 67
Conversational units, 255
Creative machines, 55
Creativity, 21, 55
Curiosity, programmed, 33
CYRUS, 22–31, 49, 51
Cyrus Vance, 30

Data bases, management of, 6
Debugging, cognitive model for, 108
Debugging of programs, 108
Decision-making, xiii, 199, 200
  qualitative bases for, 13
Declarative knowledge, 137, 140
Declarative memory, 95
Diary study, 292
Differential Aptitude Test, 86
Dimensions, generic, 189
  specific, 189
Discourse, organization of, 252
Discourse analysis, 252
Domain knowledge, 95
Domain-specific productions, 105
DOS operating system, 148
Dynamic memory, 22, 25
  structures of, 27, 32
Dyslexics, phonological, 286
  surface, 285–286

Encoding, 216
Economic and Social Research Council,
  xii, 17
EMACS, 139
Encoding problems, 68
Episodic memory traces, 216
Episodic model, 192, 193, 194–196
Episodic model passages, 195–196
Error states, diagnosis and correction of,
  108
Errors, immediate feedback on, 107–109
Ethnomethodology, 252
Euler circles, 10
Examples, functionality, 149
  motivation, 149
  role of learning how to execute
    procedures, 154–158
  selecting procedures, 158
  situational, 159, 161–162
Exemplification, 144
  as aid to learning, 145
Exemplification mapping, 146
Expectation based top-down processing,
  see Top-down processing
Expectation failures, 27, 31, 32, 53
Expectations, 41, 52
Expected utility models, 11
Expected utility theory, 12
Experiential subtheory of intelligence,
  60–61
Expert knowledge, 'elicitation' of, 18

Expert system shells, 18
Expert systems, 5, 12, 15, 17–19, 94, 180
  decision-making, 199
  development of, 5
'Expertise', 16
  development of, 19
Experts, 15, 137, 142
  tacit knowledge in, 18
Explanation patterns, 35–39
Explanations, 35–37
  construction of, 28, 33
  in depth, 34
  hypothetical, 38
  problem of, 27, 28–29
  verification of, 33
External uncertainty, 12

Face and word recognition, comparison
  of, 280
Face and word recognition, independence
  of, 285
Face-name interference, 289
Face recognition, 269–293
  context effects in, 290–293
  familiarity and, 278
  models of, xiv, 269
Face recognition errors, 272
Face recognition units, 270–278,
  283–285, 291–292
  trigger features of, 284
Fact learning, 136, 140
Fan effect, 234–235, 237, 246
Fan effect for goals, 239, 240
Features search, 173
Fortran, 17
Forward and backward deductions,
  112–113
Frames, 187, 188
French Kit for Reference Tests of
  Cognitive Factors, 65
FRUMP, 23, 29, 40, 43, 50
Functionality of procedures, 139

Generalized Phase Structure Grammar
  (GPSG), 263
Geometry, teaching of, xii
Generic knowledge structures, 189, 192
Generic memory, 188
Geometry tutor, design principles, 117
Geometry tutors, 93, 95, 99–103,
  111–118
Geometry, problem proof, 100

Gestalt psychologists, 62
Gifted subjects, 66–71, 72–73
Goal, specific matches, 53
Goal/action decision task, 236
Goal based triggers, 51
Goal decomposition, 120
Goal Integration Network (GIN) Model,
  xiv, 233–247, 244, 246
Goal structure, 93, 98
  communication of, 99
Goals, xiv, 25, 29, 37, 43, 231, 232, 237,
  249
  interactional, 252
  making salient, 161
  overlapping, 239, 240, 241, 242
  set of, 43
  tracking of characters, 246
Goals in memory, organization of several,
  236
'Goodness of encoding' of target
  information, 225, 226
Grain size adjustment, 109–110
Grammars, xiv

Henmon Nelson Test, 10, 65
Heuristic searches, 17
Heuristics, 19, 200–201, 202
Hierarchical structures of programming
  activity, 123
High-school geometry text, 112
Higher cognitive processes, see Cognitive
  processes, higher
Human discourse production, model of,
  250
Human engineering, 111, 113–116
Human intentionality, 191
Hypothesis-driven system, 43

Ideal student model, 113
Illocutionary force network, 261
Indexing, problem of, 27, 28–29
Individual speech acts, 255
Induction rules, 15
Inductive reasoning ability, 80
Inference engine, 5
Information processing theory of insight,
  71
Information status network, 262
Information technology (IT), 3, 13, 17
In-mapping, 9
Insight, model of, 61–71
  nothing-special view of, 62–63

Insight (contd)
    special-process view of, 62
    tests of model, 64–71
Insight of selective combination, 63,
    65–71
Insight of selective comparison, 64,
    65–71
Insight of selective encoding, 63, 65–71
Insight tasks, 62
Institute of Scientific Information (ISI)
    data base, 17
Intellectual development, continuity in,
    57
Intelligence, 57–61
    general, 73
Intelligent computer assisted instructed,
    (ICAI), 93
Intelligent information processing, 60–61
    knowledge-acquisition components,
        60–61
    metacomponents, 60–61
    performance components, 60–61
Intelligent tutoring, 94, 95
    principles for, xii
Intelligent tutoring paradigm, 93
Interaction, initiating an, 257–258
Interaction frames, xiv, 254, 256–257
Intermediates, 137
Internal uncertainty, 12
Intersection, 104
Inter-unit inhibition, 276–277
IPP, 22–34, 39, 41–43, 44, 50–51
Iraqi Embassy example, 26, 32–37,
    39–41

Justification of actions, 33
    of events, 32

Knowledge, focused, 204
    general, 204
    specific, 204
Knowledge Access Network (KAN), 234,
    247
Knowledge based systems, 203
Knowledge bases, 5, 18
Knowledge compilation, 96–98
Knowledge data base, 51
Knowledge domains, representing
    complex, 187
Knowledge engineering, 18

Knowledge structure, global, 193
    specific, 192
Knowledge structures, static, 21, 27

Learning to generate instances of a rule,
    155
Learning processes, understanding of,
    135
Lexical decision experiments, 282
Lexicons, xiv, 264
Linguistic choices, 259
Linguistic forms, 262
Linguistic knowledge, representing, 259
Linguistic models, 13
Linguistic theory, 13, 260
LISP, teaching of, xii, 95, 109
LISP code, 120
LISP errors, 108
LISP functions, 98, 109, 129, 141, 146
LISP programming, 97, 103–104, 110,
    118
LISP programs, misconceptions and slips
    in writing of, 124
LISP texts on problems, 104
LISP tutor, interaction with, 120–131
LISP tutors, 83, 99, 111, 118–131, 129
Logic, 7–11
    classical, 8, 10
Logogen, 270, 271, 285
Long-term memory, 97, 215

Machine inference, 9
Machine intelligence, 16
Mappings, general-to-specific, 146
    specific-to-specific, 146
Mathematical models, 200
Memory decision time, 236
Memory images, 189
Memory-search, 176
Memory-search literature, 246
Memory-search model, 177
Memory-search strategies, 278
Mental model, 139, 187, 188–189, 191,
    192
Mental models, xiii
Mental models, causal, 187, 190–191,
    192
Mental representation, 100
MINERVA 2, xiii, 215–228
'Monte Carlo' procedure, 219
'Moonbeams', 6, 17–19
MOPs, 27, 32

Morphology, 265
Multi-modality character of learning
    situation, 106

Natural language understanding, 94
Neuropsychological case studies, 269
New procedures, learning how to
    execute, 139–142
Newspaper-reading programs, 40
Nonentrenched relationship, 74, 79
'Nonentrenched' tasks, 57
Nonentrenchment, models of, 81–89
Non-gifted subjects, 66–71, 72–73
Normal subjects, see Non-gifted subjects
Novel concepts, learning of, 139
Novelty, 57–89
    coping with, xii, 57
    in acting on comprehension, 58–59, 61
    in task comprehension, 58–59, 61,
        73–80
    responses to, 74
    selectivity in coping, 71–73
    situational, 59
Novices, 124, 137

Occupation and surname, memory for,
    279
'Old lamps', 6

Parallel distributed processing, 277
Parallel model for the memory-search
    data, 175
Parallel processing, 173
Parsing, integration with memory, 26
Pascal, 17
Pedagogy, standard, 103, 110
Personality traits, 62
Philosophers, 6
Philosophy of Science, 14–15
    Baconian, 15
Physics expertise, 17
Picture-word interference paradigm, 284
Plan Applier Mechanism (PAM),
    232–233
Plans, xiv, 25, 37–38, 232
Plausible, dictionary definitions, 208
Plausibility, 205–206
POPLOG, 8
Possibility, 204–205
Possible, dictionary definitions, 208
Pragmatics, 13
Priming effect, 291–292

Private human tutor, 93, 94, 109, 130
Private tutor, 109, 111
Probability, 206–207
    classical theories, 206
    judged, 12
Probability models, 200
Probability theories, 11, 15
Probability theory, common, 13
Probable, dictionary definition, 209
Problem-solving, 69
    by analogy, 64
    complex, 108
    instruction in, 105–106
Problem-solving heuristic, 138
Procedural learning, 96–97
Procedural memory, 95
Proceduralization, 97
Procedures, motivation for use of, 142
    rules for selecting between, 142
Production rules, 113
Production systems, 96, 137
    models, 93, 98
Programmed learning devices, 19
Programming languages, high level, 5
Project Aristotle, 9, 10
Projection task, 75–78
PROLOG, 8
Pronunciations by analogy, 284
Proof graph, 113
Prosopagnosic patients, 286
PROTEUS system, 260
Puzzle books, 10

Q-T rules, see Question transformation
    rules
Question answering module, 30
Question transformation process, 30–31
Question transformation rules, 49–55
Questioning, 21
    relationship with understanding, 21
Questions, background, 40
    basic operating, 35–37, 43
    failure, 35–37
    journalist level, 41, 43
    levels, 44–47
    program generation of, 43
    specific, 35–37
    types of, 43–47

Real world testing of research ideas, 3
Realization rules, 261–262
Recall, cued, 224, 225, 227

Recognition, cued, 224
  names of famous people, 227
Recognition decision, 171
Recognition error, 292
'Recognition failure' paradigm, xiii, 215,
  220, 227, 228
Recognition memory, 220
Recognition of familiar person, failure,
  273
Recursive functions, learning to program,
  103, 130
Reminding, 25, 27–28, 33, 38, 162
Representativeness, 201
Research funds, application for, 19
Resemblance, 270, 293
Resemblance phenomena in visual word
  recognition, 283
Resemblances, 273–277
Resemblances in unfamiliar faces, 276
Retrieval, 159, 216
Retrieval of object names, 287
Retrieval routes, multiple elaborations
  provided by, 144
Right problem, 124–129
Risk generalizations, 15

SAM, 43
Schema passages, instantiated, 194–195
Schemas, xiii, 187, 188, 189–191, 192
  causal, 192
  global, 192, 195
  instantiated, 192, 193, 194–196
  local, 193
Scripts, 25, 187, 188
Search, self-terminating, 173
  variable parallel, exhaustive, 173
Secondary memory (SM), see Long-term
  memory
Selection task, 87
Selective encoding, 63, 65–71
Selective encoding experiment, 68
Self-terminating parallel comparison,
  model of, 178
Semantics, 13
Semiconductor crystal growing, 18
Serial but self-terminating chain of
  comparisons, 173
Serial exhaustive chain of comparisons,
  173
Serial self-terminating search, 176
Several characters, keeping track of, 243

'Shells', for cognition, 5
  for reasoning, 14
Short-term memory, 182
Signal detection theory, 221
Simpson's paradox, 224, 225, 228
Sinclair QL, 171
Situational examples, 146
Situation models, 187, 191–192
Skill, execution component, 136, 142
  retrieval of best procedure for, 143
Skill learning, xiii, 136
  cognitive mechanisms of, 137
  three components of, 143–147
Spatial 'scratch-pad', 182
Speech act framework, 256
Speech act theory, 254
Speech synthesizer, 250
Spelling-sound correspondences, 283
Spreading activation, 233
  model, 241
Spurious intersections, verification check
  of, 246
SRA Primary Mental Abilities, adult
  level, 86
Statistical inference, 13
'Steak and Haircut' story, 27
'Strategic-logical', 10
Structural analogue hypothesis, 189
Student as production set, 98–99
Subdirectories, 151–153
Sublexical spelling-sound conversion
  forms, 286
Syntactic elaborations, 156, 157
Syntax, 13
Systems, problem of being too powerful,
  170

Target information, 225
Target similarity on recognition memory,
  225
Target skill, successive approximations,
  110
Task novelty, 58
Temporary memory, 181
Text comprehension, 191
Text editing system, study of experienced
  users of, 142
Text editor command, 105
Text understanding, 232
Theory development, inadequacies in, 26
Threshold Knowledge Units (TKUs), 234

Tip-of-the-tongue states, 278, 279
Top-down code generation, 120
Top-down processing, 26, 103
TOPs, 27, 29
Torrance creativity test, 66
Triarchic theory of human intelligence, 59–61, 89
TRIG, *see* Triggers
Triggers, types of, 47–55
Tutor planning mode, 29
Tweaking remindings, 37–39
Two-person dialogue, 249

Uncertainty, as knowledge type, 203–207
  coping with, 200, 202
  different kinds of, 209
  knowledge-based interpretation of, 200, 207
  model of, 200–203
  nature of, 57, 207
  operational representation of, 202
Understander's hypotheses, 53
Understanding, program, 33, 40
  question-driven, 41
  system, 25
Understanding cycle, the, 39–41

Understanding system, creative and analytical, 44
Unusualness, 51
US–Soviet relations, analogy, 6
User interface, 5
Utterance, producing an, 265–266, 259
  responding to, 258–259

Venn diagrams, 10
Verbal analogies test, 12–13
Verbal theories, replacement by small-scale computational models, 169
Visual analysis systems, 276
Visual and memory search, 171
Visual search, 176

Wondering, 55
Word recognition, cognitive theories of, 270
  models of auditory, 285
Word recognition units, 282
'Wordlikeness' effects for non-words, 284
Working memory, 97, 98
Working memory load, 93
Working memory load minimization, 107